BRICKMAKING
& BRICK BUILDING
IN THE MIDLANDS
(1437-1780)

BRICKMAKING & BRICK BUILDING
IN THE MIDLANDS
(1437-1780)

MIKE KINGMAN

BREWIN BOOKS

BREWIN BOOKS
19 Enfield Ind. Estate,
Redditch,
Worcestershire,
B97 6BY
www.brewinbooks.com

First published by Brewin Books 2023

© Michael Kingman 2023

The author has asserted his rights in accordance with the Copyright, Designs and Patents Act 1988 to be identified as the author of this work.

All rights reserved. No part of this publication may be reproduced, stored in a retrieval system, or transmitted in any form or by any means, electronic, mechanical, photocopying, recording or otherwise, without the prior permission in writing of the publisher and the copyright owners, or as expressly permitted by law, or under terms agreed with the appropriate reprographics rights organisation. Enquiries concerning reproduction outside the terms stated here should be sent to the publishers at the UK address printed on this page.

The publisher makes no representation, express or implied, with regard to the accuracy of the information contained in this book and cannot accept any legal responsibility for any errors or omissions that may be made.

A CIP catalogue record for this book is available from the British Library.

ISBN: 978-1-85858-758-5

Printed and bound in Great Britain
by 4edge Ltd.

CONTENTS

	List of Tables	vi
	List of Illustrations	vii
	Abbreviations	viii
1	Introduction	1
2	Early Brick Building in Midland England	5
3	The Technology of Brickmaking	22
4	Brick Production 1437-1780	47
5	The Fuels Employed in Brick Production	83
6	Timber and Brick as Building Materials	105
7	The Transport of Brick	131
8	Fire as a Factor in the Adoption of Brick	145
9	Why Did People Build in Brick 1660-1780?	162
10	The Cost of Brick Building	188
11	Municipal Support for Brickmaking and Brick Building	209
12	Brick Building 1540-1660	232
13	Brick Building 1660-1780	240
14	The Industrial and Horticultural Use of Brick	271
15	Conclusion	293
	Select Bibliography	295

LIST OF TABLES

Table 1: Kiln Size	31
Table 2: Brick Production on the Edge Estate, Sherbourne, 1785	33
Table 3: Brick Production on the Shugborough Estate, 1701	36
Table 4: The Range of Bricks Produced	65
Table 5: The Price of Estate Produced Bricks	69
Table 6: The Price of Non-Estate Produced Bricks	71
Table 7: The Estimated Output of British Coalfields, 1560s-c.1700	92
Table 8: The Price of Constructional Timbers, 1690	123
Table 9: The Costs of the Carriage of Brick in the Midlands, 1560-1780	133
Table 10: Lichfield Houses with Inventory Evidence of Chimneys, 1641-1680	158
Table 11: Stratford-upon-Avon Houses with Inventory Evidence of Heated Upstairs Rooms/Chimneys, 1626-1699	159
Table 12: Constituent Costs of Selected Brick Buildings	194
Table 13: Midland Evidence for Building Wage Rates	206
Table 14: House Names Suggesting the Use of Brick	247
Table 15: Midland Turnpike Trusts before 1780	269

LIST OF ILLUSTRATIONS

Figures

Figure 1: Sources of Building Materials for Yoxall Court House, 1683-1685 — 140

Photographs

Plate 1: St John's Almshouses, 1495, Lichfield	I
Plate 2: Lichfield Close, 'Court of an Ancient Brick House at Lichfield', J. Buckler (1807)	I
Plate 3: Diaper work, c.1500, Abbot Penny's Wall, Leicester Abbey	II
Plate 4: Bridge Chapel House, Derbyshire	II
Plate 5: Dual Hearth and Room Divider, 1675, Middleton Hall, Warwickshire	III
Plate 6: 'Brick Cottage', Wreake Valley style, 1686, Syston, Leicestershire	IV
Plate 7: Friar Gate, Derby, built following the Improvement Act of 1768	IV
Plate 8: Pear Tree Farm, Yoxall, brickwork of c.1700, c.1740 and c.1780 fronting a medieval house	V
Plate 9: Church Street, Ashbourne. 17th century/18th century houses in 'one of the finest streets in Derbyshire', Pevsner	V
Plate 10: False front, Bridge Farm, Yoxall, Staffordshire	VI
Plate 11: Bradgate House, 16th century ruin, Bradgate Park, Leicestershire	VI
Plate 12: Hawkstone Hall, 1701-20, Salop	VII
Plate 13: Hodsock Priory gatehouse, Nottinghamshire	VII
Plate 14: Great Bolas Church, nave and tower rebuilt 1726-29, Salop	VIII

ABBREVIATIONS

BLAC: Birmingham Library Archives and Collections.
BBSI: British Brick Society Information.
CA: Cheshire Archives.
DAJ: Derbyshire Archaeological Journal.
DRO: Derbyshire Record Office.
NA: Nottinghamshire Archives.
NBR: *Nottingham Borough Records*, ed. Stevenson, W.H., Vol. II, 1399-1485, Vol. III, 1485-1547. Vol. V, 1625-1702, ed. Guildford, E.L., Vol. VI, 1702-1760, ed. Foreman, T. Vol. VII, 1760-1800, ed. Gray, D., and Walker, V.W., (1882-1900).
RBL: *Records of the Borough of Leicester*, ed. Bateson, M., Vol. III, Cambridge, (1903).
ROLLR: Record Office of Leicestershire, Leicester and Rutland.
SA: Shropshire Archives.
SBT: Shakespeare Birthplace Trust.
SHC: Staffordshire Historical Collection.
SRO: Staffordshire Record Office, documents previously held at Lichfield Record Office are now held at Stafford with document references SRO L …
TBR: Tamworth Borough Records.
TBAS: Transactions of the Birmingham Archaeological Society, later TBWAS Transactions of the Birmingham and Warwickshire Archaeological Society.
TLAHS: Transactions of the Leicestershire Archaeological and Historical Society, initially the Leicestershire Architectural and Archaeological Society, from 1915 The Leicestershire Archaeological Society.
TSalopAHS: Transactions of The Shropshire Archaeological and Historical Society, formerly the Shropshire Archaeological and Natural History Society of 1877 and later the Shropshire Archaeological Society until 1987.
TSAHS: Transactions of the Staffordshire Archaeological and Historical Society, formerly Transactions of the South Staffordshire Archaeological

and Historical Society, previously Transactions of Lichfield Archaeological and Historical Society.
TTS: Transactions of the Thoroton Society.
WA: Wedgwood Archives.
WRO: Warwickshire Record Office.
WSL: William Salt Library.

Chapter 1

INTRODUCTION

'Brick ... the safest, the cheapest the most commodious of all materials'.
Daniel Defoe[1]

BRICK IS so familiar in our modern landscape that it is difficult to imagine a time when it was a rare feature of Midland England. By the nineteenth century the use of brick was almost universal in the area and familiarity has bred indifference if not contempt. As early as 1790 John Throsby described the stone-built Trent Bridge at Nottingham as 'disfigured with brick and the ordinariest materials; from being repaired at a variety of periods'.[2] W.G. Hoskins in his 1951 study of *Midland England* described the 'Etruria Marl' which 'gives the famous Staffordshire blue bricks, and contributes its own small share to the peculiar ugliness in the Pottery towns' and in Leicester 'red-brick is irredeemably commonplace and nothing will now hide its meanness'.[3] More critically, Alec Clifton-Taylor has written that 'brick is by far and away the commonest building material in Leicestershire … it affords very little pleasure … one's heart bleeds for the people who have to contemplate such ugliness'.[4] In these unsympathetic comments the quality of the landscape was determined by brick buildings.

---

1 Defoe, D., *A Tour through England and Wales,* (1724-27), **1**, London: Everyman, (1927), 349.
2 Thoroton, R., *Thoroton's History of Nottinghamshire,* **2**: *Republished With Large Additions by John Throsby,* ed. John Throsby, Nottingham, (1790), 128.
3 Hoskins, W.G., *Chilterns to Black Country,* London: Collins, (1951), 20.
4 Clifton-Taylor, A., 'Building Materials,' in Pevsner, N., rev. Williamson, E., *The Buildings of England, Leicestershire and Rutland,* Penguin, (1984), 57.

It is easy to overlook the early importance of brick as a locally distinctive material because few authors have emphasised the colour of early brick building and how dramatic an impact this could be. Even today, descending Lady Elizabeth's Hill in south Warwickshire and seeing below the beautiful red brick building of Compton Wynyates creates a vivid impression. (Initially built in two main phases between 1493 and 1528, local tradition based on Leland's *Itinerary* suggests that the brick was originally used at Fulbrook Castle, although traces of brick kilns were exposed in early twentieth century drainage work.[5]) The house stands in the Cotswold Fringe of the county and is surrounded everywhere by villages whose main building material is Jurassic limestone. In a landscape of creams, ironstones and seasonal agricultural hues, the brick red house must have been, and still is, a striking statement. Similarly, for the travellers after 1495 approaching Lichfield from the south, the first significant building they observed as they reached the city walls was the bright red of the St John's Almshouses. With their tall chimneys and brilliant colour, they must have been an obvious focus in a cityscape of dull timber buildings, soot encrusted stone churches and industrial workshops. Just as the almshouses marked the entrance to the city, the brick-built Milley's Hospital of 1503 made a colourful feature opposite the entrance to the Cathedral precinct. Nearly three centuries later Lord Torrington in 1789 noticed the dramatic impact of brick in the Nottinghamshire landscape, 'At Grantham they leave of the Stone and build with a flaming red brick of which Newark is built and looks like a new town'.[6]

This study is concerned with the explanations for the adoption and diffusion of brick in Midland England between 1437 and 1780. It provides a reasoned explanation for the pattern and volume of brick building and examines such factors as the technology of brickmaking, the price of bricks, building costs, the availability of other building materials, the impact of fire, urban culture, and the social value attached to brick. It also emphasises that any explanation for the adoption of brick must include the capricious tastes and irrational purchasing preferences of people. Nowhere is this more emphasised than at Canons Ashby house in Northamptonshire. This manor house, built

---

5   Leland, J., *Itinerary of John Leland in or about the years 1535-1543,* **2**, ed. Toulmin Smith, L., London, (1965), 28.

6   Byng, Sir J., *Torrington Diaries,* **3**, ed. Bruyn Andrews, C., London: Eyre & Spotiswood, (1934), 136.

from the local dark brown Jurassic ironstone, in a landscape in which this stone predominated, had a new brick frontage in 1551. The brick is of many colours, is misshapen, badly laid and in contrast to the stone is remarkably ugly. What pressures were experienced by the Dryden family which persuaded them to replace stone with brick?[7] John Newman provided a neat summary of those features, 'When all the external factors are weighed, political, cultural, economic, climatic, the truism remains that buildings are erected by people for people'.[8] This study is not only a consideration of the material composition of buildings, but also of the choices and decisions of the builders within a cultural landscape.

The initial date of 1437 is that of the earliest surviving brick building in the region, Prior Overton's tower at Repton. The terminal date of 1780 was chosen to exclude the possible effects of a mature canal network on the commercial and industrial market for brick in a period when large-scale production was required to meet the vast demands of an increasingly industrial environment. Nationally by 1785, duty was paid on 358.8 million bricks and by 1793 this total had risen to 908.9 million.[9] This study considers a pre-industrial period when bricks, many produced on-site and in relatively small quantities, were an expensive and heavy material of considerable prestige.

Any definition based on spatially definable boundaries will be contentious, but for this study Midland England is defined as the pre-1974 historic counties of Derbyshire, Leicestershire, Nottinghamshire, Shropshire, Staffordshire and Warwickshire, a combination which is near to William Marshall's definition in 1790 of the 'Midland District'.[10] This classification is arbitrary as these counties are not a formally geographically or economically integrated region. They possess a variety of landscapes, building stones, soils, vegetation patterns and forms of settlement. Defoe, for example, described the north-west of Derbyshire as 'the most desolate, wild and abandoned country in all England'.[11] In general they are landlocked, less open to the commercial

---

7   The same pressures of fashion led to the rendering of the brick in 1710 and to the removal of the plaster in the late nineteenth century.
8   Newman, J., 'A "Polite" View of Vernacular Architecture', *Vernacular Architecture*, **15**, (1984), 11.
9   Mitchell, R.B., *British Historical Statistics,* Cambridge: CUP, (1988), 235.
10 Marshall W., *The Rural Economy of the Midland Counties,* **1**, Dublin, (1793), 2.
11 Defoe, 17.

influences of London and share an overlapping community of interest and people. In the context of making brick, most enjoy the common features of accessible red Triassic clays, early working coalfields which provided coal to fire the brick kilns and the fireclays which were so valuable in producing bricks for the lining of other furnaces and kilns. They were also counties which before 1780 had limited cross-regional river transport. The Trent was only navigable downstream from Burton-on-Trent after 1700, but travel was hindered by the shallows between Burton and Shardlow and the huge meanders at West Burton and Bole were a constant impediment until 1793 and 1797 respectively. Downstream there were 67 shallows and 12 fords between Wilden Ferry and Gainsborough over which barges could not carry a cargo greater than ten tons. The Lower Avon was only navigable from Stratford-on-Avon after 1672. The cities of Leicester and Nottingham opposed improvements to the Derwent, so it was not made navigable from Derby to Derwent Mouth until 1721. The lack of large-scale transport was one of the most important factors in restricting the early extensive production and wholesale adoption of brick.

Chapter 2

EARLY BRICK BUILDING IN MIDLAND ENGLAND

THE LONG-ESTABLISHED story of the early use of brick in England is familiar and has previously been accepted with little disagreement. Conventionally bricks were first made during the Roman period and were reused in later Saxon and medieval buildings, particularly in churches. This introductory date has been modified by recent research at the Roman city of Silchester where an earlier pre-Conquest brick-built building, which may have been a bathhouse, has been identified. This Iron Age structure clearly influenced by the Roman baths in Gaul may well be the earliest brick building in Britain.[12] After Roman brickmaking, historians consider the earliest bricks made in England are those discovered in the Essex parish church of Bradwell-juxta-Coggeshall where new research using the recently developed luminescence technique has dated the brick to 1038+/-60.[13]

Very few early brickworks have been excavated but documentary evidence survives of their existence, mainly in eastern England where twenty-eight medieval brickworks have been recorded in existence between 1400 and 1450. The majority were in towns and their actual sites have been identified at Boston,

---

12   *The Times*, 11/9/2019.
13   Baili, I.K., Blain, S., Graves, C.P., Gurling, T. and Semple, S., 'Uses and recycling of brick in medieval English buildings: insights from the application of luminescence dating and new avenues for further research'. *Archaeological Journal*, **167**, **1**, (2010), 165-196. St Martin of Tours, Chipping Ongar, is dated 1040+/- 30, but may be of imported brick.

Caister, Hull and Beverley.[14] There may be a connection between this eastern distribution and the immigration of skilled craftsmen from Germany and the Low Countries where brick was more widely used. At Repton, Pevsner described Prior Overton's Tower as in 'a style more Hanseatic than English'.[15] At Kirby Muxloe castle, Leics, in 1482-83, 'Anthony Docheman' (Yzebronde) was employed as a bricklayer and some of the other bricklayers were also foreign or Flemings who had initially settled in East Anglia, ('Docheman' was a catch-all adjective for a northern European, a brickmaker named Baldwin Docheman was recorded at Tattershall Castle in the 1430s.[16]) In total, between 1480 and 1483 a minimum of 1,350,000 bricks were laid with the Flemings probably responsible for the sophisticated brickwork of diapers and arrow loops. The bricks themselves were made locally, (claims have been made for the significance of 'Brickmans Hill' 6 km to the South-East, but the earliest reference to that place name is 1281).[17]

The traditional hypothesis of the importation of bricks as ballast in ships returning from the Low Countries was regarded with some scepticism for heavy bricks banging together in the hold of a ship would hardly be fit for use. Robin Lucas has called this the 'economic nonsense of giving over valuable cargo space to low-value, high-bulk goods'.[18] Despite this pragmatic common sense, there are a steady flow of references to the importation of brick from the Low Countries. As early as 1428-30 the Southampton Port Book recorded the import of 'bakstone', i.e. baked stone, from Antwerp and Middleburg. It also recorded the import of brick from Hythe in Kent.[19] The continental bricks cost the large sum of 4s 5d per 1,000 while the Kentish bricks were a penny cheaper. In the late seventeenth century brick was imported in considerable quantities

---

14   Smith, T.P., 'The Medieval Brickmaking Industry in England, 1400-1450', *British Archaeological Reports.* British Series, **138**, (1985), 128.

15   Pevsner, N., rev. Williamson, E., *The Buildings of England, Derbyshire,* (New Haven and London: Yale UP, (1978), 307.

16   Hamilton Thompson, A., 'The Building Accounts of Kirby Muxloe Castle 1480-1484', *TLAHS,* **11**, (1915-16), 208. The employment of 'Flemings' or Germans in the fifteenth century to make or lay bricks was not uncommon, see Lloyd, N. *A History of English Brickwork*, London: Montgomery, H.G., (1925), reprinted ACC Collectors Club, (2003), 14.

17   Squires, A., 'A Provisional List of Woodlands in Medieval Leicestershire (excluding Rutland) 1200-1530'. *TLAHS,* **69**, (1995), 93.

18   Lucas, R., 'The Brick Trade in Colonial America', *Georgian Group Journal,* **7**, (1997), 147. Smith, T.P., 'Bricks, Tiles and Ballast: A Sceptical View', *BBSI.* **85**, (October, 2001), 5-9.

19   Studer, P., ed. 'The Port Books of Southampton 1427-1430', *Southampton Record Society,* **15**, (1913), 76, 99.

via the Lincolnshire ports. William Massingberd, the builder of Gunby Hall, in 1692 recorded the landing of his bricks at Hull and their transhipment by boat to Salfleet.[20] The memory of the Dutch connection was preserved in the recommendation that 'Holland bricks' and 'Holland earth' should be used for the paving of horse stables.[21] Neve, in his *The City and Country Purchaser's and Builder's Dictionary* of 1726, recommended for paving a 'brick brought out of Flanders … that is neater and stronger than common or Clay bricks'.[22] In 1635 Sir Richard Leveson sent a local cobbler to Burton-on-Trent with a letter 'to stay a dutch masons journey',[23] and in 1668 a passport was requested from the Duke of York, for 'a vessel of Rotterdam, laden with bricks and other materials for the King's house at Plymouth'.[24] As late as 1763-64 the account book for the River Weaver recorded the carriage of 'Flanders brick'.[25]

The export of bricks was mainly to the Caribbean, an area with few building materials. For example, in 1660 a naval frigate 'there to be ballasted with bricks' was sent to Jamaica 'to complete the fortifications'.[26] In 1743 Vice-Admiral Vernon reported that the Hospital in Jamaica was in need of English bricks, 'the *Phoenix, Priscilla* and *Shirley* are carrying 91 thousand bricks and seek to send more'.[27] For the initial British settlement of Australia, the 'First Fleet' included 5,000 bricks, wooden moulds and a convict bricklayer.

The usual explanations for brick production are often derived from a geographically or geologically determinist view. From this perspective brick was produced by default because alternative resources were not locally available. The distribution of early buildings was explained by the absence of good building stone with brick adopted as a cheaper substitute. In his study of Leicestershire brick, Alan McWhirr has written that 'the extent to which brick was used as a

---

20   Kingman, M.J., 'Brick in the Massingberd Papers', *BBSI,* **149,** (2022).
21   Worsley, G., *The British Stable,* Yale UP, (2004), 44. Whether these were imported is uncertain, but no reference to their manufacture in England is recorded.
22   Neve, R., *The City and County Purchaser's and Builder's Dictionary,* 2nd ed. London, (1726), 135.
23   SRO, D593R/1/2.
24   *CSPD, Charles II, 1668-69,* ed. Green, M.A.E., London: HMSO, (1894), 132. Hamilton Thompson, 208.
25   Willan, T.S., *Navigation of the River Weaver in the Eighteenth Century,* Manchester: Chetham Society, (1951), 210.
26   *CSPD, Colonial, America and West Indies: November 1660,* ed. Sainsbury, W.M. London: HMSO, (1860), **1,** *1574-1660,* 490-492.
27   National Archives, Admiralty Records, ADM/122/25.

building material … depended to a very great extent on the availability of other building materials and therefore the local geology'.[28] David Hey, in the detailed *Oxford Companion to Family and Local History,* suggests that brick became a 'prestigious building material … where no local building stone was available', and that in the seventeenth century, 'yeomen and husbandmen in districts devoid of suitable stone rebuilt their timber-framed houses in brick'. In Worcestershire it was suggested that the county 'is not outstandingly rich in building stone … For the rest, an abundance of clays and marls … together with plenty of timber, results in a great range of warm red brick and timber combination in buildings'.[29] Such an argument is not totally convincing, as equally famous for brick and timber buildings was the adjacent Arden Warwickshire, but here there were at least five formations of easily worked sandstone, for the Halesowen, Keele, Kenilworth, Bromsgrove and Arden Sandstones were readily quarried.[30]

Jane Wight in her *Brick Building in England* acknowledges the cultural, 'even sociological background' to her study but begins her account with a determinist explanation, 'Brick was revived in England in the Later Middle Ages, largely to fill a lack in nature in the prosperous, relatively highly-populated Eastern Counties, where good stone was absent'.[31] Such strongly determinist conclusions require qualification. There may be a degree of truth in the assertion that bricks were used in areas with poor building stones, but in eastern England there were hundreds of churches, castles and monastic buildings built of either imported or local stone.

Norfolk is commonly viewed as a county without stone and with many early brick buildings. Carrstone, the only freestone in the county and quarried at Castle Rising, was used extensively at the Roman settlement and fort at Brancaster. Yet there is also a wide range of other building stones including Leziate quartzite, Red Chalk, Chalk, Flint and cemented Pleistocene sands and gravels.[32] In Hunt's *Mineral Statistics* of 1858, four 'Building stone quarries' were recorded in Norfolk and whilst this is a small number it is as many as those individually recorded for Bedfordshire, Berkshire, Buckinghamshire,

---

28   McWhirr, A., 'Brickmaking in Leicestershire before 1710'. *TLAHS,* **71**, (1997), 38.
29   Miller, T., 'Geology', in Pevsner, N., *The Buildings of England, Worcestershire,* Penguin, (1968), 49.
30   English Heritage, *A Building Stone Atlas of Warwickshire,* (2011), 7-8.
31   Wight J., *Brick Building in England from the Middle Ages to 1550,* London: John Baker, (1972), 17.
32   Allen, J.R.L., Norfolk's Native Building Stone, *Norfolk Historic Buildings Group,* Newsletter, **11**, (2006), 8.

Essex and Huntingdonshire. The number of 'Brick pits' at 111 was second only to those situated in Staffordshire/Worcestershire.[33]

The absence of stone may be too simplistic an explanation for the use of brick. Henry VIII, the richest and most powerful man in England, who could presumably have built palaces and houses in stone had he so chosen, built or rebuilt six palaces in brick. In 1520 for the pavilion at the 'Field of the Cloth of Gold' in France, where Henry sought to impress the French king, Francis I, he imported English bricks and bricklayers. Brick was selected not because of the absence of stone or timber, but because of the prestige attached to it. The wealthy Duke of Bedford, the brother of Henry V, built Fulbrooke Castle in brick only a few miles north of the stone resources of the Cotswold escarpment. Recently David Kennett has studied the income of patrons of early brick houses in England. Based mainly on the Tax Returns of 1436, he concluded that in the fifteenth century the men who built in brick were precisely those who could have afforded to build in stone:

> *Brick houses were built only by the very richest men. The lead in choosing brick as the visible building material for a new house came from the king. The first builder of a great brick house was King Henry V at Richmond Palace, where construction was continued by his son, King Henry VI. The builders have strong social connections: as members of the king's court and between themselves. The builders could also build in stone, especially their burial places, but the known benefactions of the very richest men who built in brick are themselves brick-built. The houses they built were large and far above the average size of the contemporary house. The houses reflect their status as members of "the power elite".*[34]

The chronological and spatial pattern of early brick buildings reveals a steady movement from east to west over time. By the fifteenth century significant brick buildings were erected in Oxfordshire, as at Stonor House (1416-1417) and beyond the Lincolnshire Wolds, for example at Tattershall Castle (1432-48) which required 7,000,000 bricks. Once brick had spread to the West Midlands, the pattern of its diffusion was more erratic and much looser. Possibly

---

33 Hunt, R., *Mineral Statistics of the United Kingdom of Great Britain and Ireland for the Year 1858,* British Geological Survey, (1860), 127.
34 Kennett, D., 'Early Brick Houses in England: Patrons and Incomes', *BBSI*, **98**, (2005), 11-12.

the earliest bricks in the Midlands were the few recorded in the excavation of Hulton Abbey, whose context and irregularity suggested that they were fired in the thirteenth or fourteenth century. The bricks were probably fired in a tile kiln.[35] Brick was employed most skilfully in Prior Overton's Tower, Repton, on the boundary of Derbyshire and Staffordshire, in 1437,[36] and in Leicestershire in the mid-fifteenth century at Groby Hall and at Bradgate House (c.1490-1520). In the adjacent county of Warwickshire, after Fulbrook Castle (possibly of the 1430s), brick spread rapidly. Early brick buildings were erected at Compton Wynyates between 1493 and 1528 and by the parvenu Spencers at Wormleighton in c.1512. In the north of the county, brick was employed at Weston Hall in the 1490s, Pooley Hall c.1509 and Sheldon Manor House. Within one generation of these Midland buildings, it had swept westward to Bachegraig, Vale of Clwyd, (1567) and Plas Clough near Denbigh, (1567-9).[37] It may be significant that both were built by Sir Richard Clough, the Antwerp agent of Sir Thomas Gresham and a man familiar with the brick buildings of the Low Countries and who may have employed Flemish builders.[38] (The banqueting hall at Bentley Hall, Walsall, shown in Robert Plot's engraving, is very similar to that at Bachegraig – possibly Flemish builders were also employed here.) Such an increasingly disparate pattern is a reminder that the choice of material was a personal decision. The selection of brick reflects an essentially radical view of the function and appearance of a house or a previous experience of brick in London, at the royal court or in the Low Countries. Thus in 1614 Richard Daniel, a London mercer, retired to his hometown of Truro to build the first traceable brick house in Cornwall[39] and in Lancashire, Carr House

---

35   Klemperer, D. and Boothroyd, N., 'Excavations at Hulton Abbey, Staffordshire, 1987-1994'. *Society of Medieval Archaeology Monographs,* **21**, (2004), 86-87.

36   Pevsner, *Derbyshire,* 307. Its internal decoration is like that of Ewelme (Oxfordshire) of a comparable date. Wight, 247.

37   Davies, J., *The Making of Wales,* Stroud: Alan Sutton, (1996), 77.

38   Kennett D., 'Caister Castle, Norfolk and the transport of brick and other building materials in the Middle Ages', in Bork, R. and Kann, A., eds. *The Art, Science and Technology of Medieval Travel,* Routledge, (2008), 60-63. Gresham in 1567-71 was building the Royal Exchange, probably from Flemish bricks. In building Bach-y-Craig, Clough may have had the assistance of Hendrik van Passe of Antwerp.

39   Pevsner, N. rev. Radcliffe, E., *The Buildings of England, Cornwall,* London: Penguin, (1970), 83. Pevsner dates the brickwork at Ince Castle to 1630. It may be even earlier, there is a date cartouche over the door for 1540. Leland in 1539 recorded 'a right fair house of bryke' at Stevenstone. *Itinerary,* 173.

bears an inscription dated 1613 recording its building by Thomas Stones of London, haberdasher, and Andrewe Stones of Amsterdam, merchant.[40]

In central England brick was adopted slowly and hesitantly. Before 1530 there were only five or six brick buildings in each of Leicestershire, Nottinghamshire, Shropshire and Warwickshire and even fewer in Derbyshire.

Derbyshire: Repton Priory, Prior Overton's Tower, (1437), at No.10 Cornhill, Allestree, the Derby city planners have listed 'a modest brick cottage' of the early sixteenth century. Derby prison of 1531 was built of brick and stone, (demolished 1756). Fifteenth century brickwork survives at Barton Blount Hall gatehouse and in its north and west walls. Barbara Hutton, in the *Derby Housing Record*, has recorded five examples of fifteenth century brick walling, all of which also contained timber.[41]

Leicestershire: Groby Old Hall, (mid-late fifteenth century brick walls). A few bricks have been recovered from Bagworth fortified house and may date from the 1470s.[42] The two south towers of Ashby de la Zouch castle have been dated to 1474. Kirby Muxloe Castle, (1481-84), Bradgate House, (c.1490-1520) and Knaptoft Hall, (1525-30). Brick was used on a decorated precinct wall at Leicester Abbey (c.1500). It was built by Abbot John Penny and includes his initials and over 40 different patterns created by dark headers. In 1929 the Leicester Archaeological Society reported on 'the removal of the old wall of Greyfriars convent … It has been wisely provided that the bricks shall be reserved for the repair of bishop (sic) Penny's wall, in Abbey Lane, which was built about the same time as the friars' wall'.[43] On the site of the Greyfriars friary in 2012, archaeologists, looking for the body of Richard III, noted that 'stains of brick dust found on masonry fragments suggest the east end of the church may have been built in brick.' If this was the case, this places it amongst the earliest medieval brick-built buildings in the city.[44]

---

40 English Heritage Building ID: 184266.

41 Hutton, B., 'Derby Buildings Record', *Derbyshire Miscellany,* **16 pt3**, (2002), 79-92.

42 Emery, A., *Greater Medieval Houses of England and Wales, 1300-1500, **2**,* Cambridge: CUP, (2000), 218.

43 *Leicestershire Archaeological Society*, Annual Report, (1929), X. A photograph of the wall can be seen at the online site 'Picryl history Leicester'.

44 Morris, M., *The Greyfriars Project: The Search for the Last Known Resting Place of King Richard III*, (2013), 13. The friary was poorly endowed, in 1538 at the Dissolution its net revenue was only £1 2s. Was the east end of the church rebuilt in brick because it was cheaper?

Nottinghamshire: Hodsock Priory gatehouse, (c.1500), Holme Pierrepont Hall, (c.1509), Scrooby Palace, (early sixteenth century), Kneesall, Old Hall Farm, (c.1525) originally a hunting lodge,[45] Lenton Priory, where after its dissolution a survey of 1554 described the Prior's Lodging as 'all of fayre bricke',[46] Aspley Hall contained a medieval brick tower described in the same rental, it was probably a hunting lodge of the Priory. The gatehouse of Hill's Farm, Rampton, (early sixteenth century). The earliest reference to brick production is 1482-3 at Mapperley,[47] in that year the Nottingham Council purchased bricks for repairs to the Crown Inn, possibly for its chimney.[48]

Shropshire: At Tong Castle, John Leland recorded that 'Sir Henry Vernon a late daies made the castel new al of brike', Vernon died in 1515 which would suggest a terminal date for the rebuilding. Pepper Hill, larger than Tong Castle, was built by Sir John Talbot, probably in 1519. A brick dovecote? at Willey Old Hall is listed as 'early 16th century'.[49] A 'College' at Bridgnorth which provided rooms for chantry priests was described as brick when it was burnt down in July, 1646. The date of erection is not known but it was certainly in existence in the 1490s.[50] Belswardine Hall dates to the 1540s. (T. Mugridge, a consultant brickmaker to English Heritage and the National Trust, has claimed dates of 1428-9 for an internal wall at Wattlesborough Castle, 1434-5 for a chimney stack at Stourton Castle (Staffs) and 1485-90 for a kitchen extension at Rock Farm, St Martins, Oswestry.) These claims are not supported by documentary evidence, although a wall at the farm, revealed in the BBC 2 programme 'Restoration Home', would certainly appear to be pre-Reformation.

Warwickshire: Fulbrook Castle (probably built by the Duke of Bedford, d.1435), Hugh Clopton's house at Stratford-on-Avon, (c.1483, later Shakespeare's New Place and demolished in 1759), Weston Hall, Weston under Wetherley, (1490s), Compton Wynyates (c.1500 and c.1520), Pooley Hall, (c.1509), Wormleighton Hall, (c.1512) and Sheldon Hall, (early sixteenth century).

---

45   Summers, N., 'Old Hall Farm, Kneesall', *TTS,* **76***,* (1972), 17-25.
46   Barnes, F.A., 'Lenton Priory after the Dissolution, Its Buildings and Fair Grounds', *TTS,* **91**, (1987), 82.
47   Bishop, M., Badderley, V. and Mordan, J., *An Archaeological Resource Assessment of Post-Medieval Nottinghamshire 1500-1750,* Nottinghamshire County Council, (n.d.) 4.
48   *NBR,* **II**, 391.
49   *VCH, Salop,* **10**, (1998), 450-455.
50   Clark-Maxwell, W.G., 'The Chantries of St Leonards Church Bridgnorth', *TSalopAHS,* **41 pt2** (1922), 234.

Staffordshire: There were at least 15 and possibly as many as 19 brick buildings. These were in: Lichfield Cathedral Close; 4 or 5 Prebendal houses, Library, Choristers' House, Chantry Chapel, Vicars Choral house, Canons' House?[51] Lichfield: St John's Hospital, the Grammar School, Milley's Hospital. Pillaton Hall. Rolleston-on-Dove, the Grammar School. Hamstall Ridware Hall, pre-1518? Enville Hall. Aldridge, 'The Red House'? Winshill, Burton-on-Trent, 'The Brick House'? A few bricks were recorded in an archaeological excavation at Hulton Abbey, Stoke-on-Trent with a suggested date of the thirteenth or fourteenth century.

The uncertainty in the total is the result of optimistic attributions for which the evidence is uncertain. For example the term 'Red House', which was commonly used in the seventeenth and eighteenth centuries to indicate a brick house, appears in a will of 1541 in Aldridge, a later important brick producing centre, and the phrase 'Brick House' appears in an inventory of 1556 at Winshill in Burton-on-Trent.[52] A date of pre-1518 has been suggested for Hamstall Ridware Hall on the basis of an indistinct pattern of headers on the east wall of the tower which, with the eye of faith and some imagination, may be of an eagle. The eagle was the Cotton family's coat of arms, they sold the estate in 1518. (A similar claim is made for indistinct diaper work at Groby Hall which may represent the arms of the Ferrers family and thus dates the house to before 1445.) Even allowing for a degree of exaggeration and the possibility that these houses could have been built after 1530, the central question remains, why in Staffordshire, amongst the poorest of the Midland counties, should there be such a relatively large number of brick buildings?

Recent research into the patrons of fifteenth century brick building has emphasised their wealth and prestige. Wight has noted that 'one coherent and identifiable group of fifteenth century people who stimulated the fashions for brick were the bishops'.[53] The brick buildings of members of the episcopacy, such as Bishops Waynflete, Rotherham, Morton, Alcock and Fisher are well known and the buildings they promoted in Yorkshire, Cambridge University and in the South have been fully described. What the concentration of buildings in Staffordshire suggests, is that this episcopal network also encompassed the

---

51 Houses for canonical residence were conferred by the bishop, others by the Dean and Chapter.
52 Gould, J.T., 'Settlement and Farming in the Parish of Aldridge', *TSSHAS*, **XX**, (1979-80) 51. SRO, L B/C/11, William Hampe, 1556.
53 Wight, 137.

less well-known Bishops of Lichfield and Coventry who, with their senior diocesan clergy, promoted brick buildings in the county, an area generally less well investigated by architectural historians. The Bishopric of Lichfield and Coventry was often an initial stage within a chain of promotion whereby royal officials and administrators were rewarded with the see, and then with greater responsibilities moved to the richer dioceses, such as Durham or Lincoln. Many of the Lichfield bishops were members of an episcopal network, in that they were friends, colleagues, family members and close associates of the brick building bishops and, as royal administrators, were familiar with royal palaces, the buildings of central government and of the major aristocratic families.

At Lichfield there were two important promoters of brick building. Bishop John Hales, (1459-90), was Keeper of the Privy Seal in 1470-71 a post in which he was both preceded and succeeded by Thomas Rotherham, one of the most important brick-building bishops.[54] He was a friend of Thomas Lord Stanley, and brought to the cathedral wealthy scholars and diocesan administrators, such as Thomas Milley and Dean Heywood. Bishop William Smith (1493-96) was educated in the household of James Stanley, Earl of Derby. Stanley's stepmother was Lady Margaret Beaufort, the founder of St John's and Christ's Colleges, Cambridge, whose building in brick was organised by Bishop Fisher. More importantly she was the mother of Henry VII. Smith was ordained as bishop by Bishop Morton, later Archbishop of Canterbury and the builder in brick of Croydon Palace, the Bishop's Palace, Hatfield and Wisbech Castle.[55] Smith, the founder of Brasenose College, was extremely wealthy and an important royal official as Lord President of the Council of Wales and the Marches of which the Stanleys were also leading members.[56] When Bishop Hales died in December 1490, Smith was given custody of the temporalities of the see in the following March 'with liberty to apply its revenues to his own use without rendering account to the crown'.[57] He was not officially appointed to the see until early 1493. Rarely in attendance at Lichfield, (Latimer described him as an 'unpreaching prelate'), he nevertheless financed the impressive St

---

54 Kennett, D., 'Thomas Rotherham, a Fifteenth-Century Bishop and Builder in Brick: a preliminary note', *BBSI,* **112**, (2010), 6-17.
55 Morton had been Archdeacon of Chester in 1485 – at that time a Lichfield appointment.
56 Beresford, W., *Diocesan Histories, Lichfield,* SPCK, (1883), 175. Beresford states that, as Lord President, Smith was allowed £20 *per week* for the table, for himself and the Council.
57 *DNB,* **53**, 135.

John's Hospital and a grammar school near to the Hospital which was probably built of brick, for when purchased by local citizens in 1577 it was described as 'a tenement or brick-house'.[58] A successor, Bishop Blythe (1503-31), whose mother was the sister of Thomas Rotherham, was a royal emissary to Hungary and Lord President of the Council of the Marches and may also have built in brick. John Leland reported that 'the chorists have a goodly house lately buildyd by Bysshope Blithe'.[59] It was demolished in 1756.

The Council of the Marches was based in Ludlow and was served by Lichfield cathedral clergy. It may not be entirely coincidental that the MP for Ludlow in 1491-2, at a time when Bishop Alcock was President of the Council, was Richard Littleton, the builder of Pillaton Hall, the earliest brick-built secular building in Staffordshire.[60] The earliest brick building in Ludlow is late sixteenth century and housed the Secretary to the Council. In Shropshire Tong Castle was rebuilt in brick by Sir Henry Vernon, the Guardian and Treasurer to Arthur, the eldest son of Henry VII, who lived at Ludlow Castle and in 1499 was made Prince of Wales with Sir Henry as Chief Counsellor.

Evidence of early brick buildings in Lichfield Close is limited as none of the buildings survive in their entirety and any consistent building records, if they ever existed, have been lost. One of the problems in identifying the brick of the Close is the impact of the Civil War. The Close was besieged three times; twice in 1643 and once in 1646, with devastating results. A survey of the houses in the Close in 1649 described some as 'much ruined', 'out of repair' and 'spoyled'. It described the 'house of Mr Jofray late Canon Resident situate at the corner of the Close South side of being greatly ruined broken and torn with Granadoes' (artillery shell). This was probably a brick house.

Much of the evidence for brick-building is derived from early nineteenth-century historians who were writing before some of the buildings were radically altered. In 1806 Thomas Harwood wrote that, Halse (Hales) had 'erected several good brick buildings in the Close', more precisely, 'In the south-west part of the Close are three prebendal houses, enjoyed by the fifth, the first, and the sixth residential. These houses were built for the residence of the canons, by Bishop Hales and were probably some of the earliest brick buildings in

---

58 Laithwaite, P., *A Short History of Lichfield Grammar School,* Lichfield, (1925), 25.
59 Leland, 102.
60 Pillaton Hall was built between 1495 and 1502, either in anticipation of Richard Littleton's marriage to a wealthy heiress, Alice Winnesbury, or following the death of her father in 1502.

the kingdom. In each of them was a spacious hall, in which they lived in a collegiate manner'.[61] A Lichfield brickmaker, Robert Bird, is recorded in 1466 and may have provided the bricks.[62] The location of these three prebendal buildings was derived from Henry Wharton's *Anglia Sacra* of 1691.[63]

In summary Wharton wrote that Hales built splendid brick buildings, '*splendidas aedes latericias*', near to the pool to the west and that Canon Henry Ediall built in brick nearby and next to Canon Thomas Milley. George Strangeways, Professor of Theology, built similar 'houses' in the eastern part of the Close, '*qui similes posuit ad orientalum partem Clausi.*' His house was not therefore one of the three brick prebendal houses in the south-west of the Close. This would suggest at least four brick houses were allocated to prebends. There may have been more, for in his description of Thomas Milley as a 'great benefactor', Harwood states that 'he built at his own expense *some* (my italics) handsome brick buildings'. This comment was echoed by John Leland who reported that 'The prebendaries houses in the close buildyd by dyvers men be very fair'.[64]

The prebendal houses were large and sophisticated, a painting by Buckler in 1806 of Milley's house, entitled *Court of an Ancient Brick House at Lichfield* shows a two-storeyed building with a range of mullioned Perpendicular windows.[65] It was substantially remodelled in 1814. The house of Ediall, the executor of the will of Archbishop Morton, also painted by Buckler, was a substantial three-storeyed house with heated upstairs rooms. The brickwork was decorated with dark headers representing a cross and St Peter's keys on the west chimney stack and St Laurence's gridiron on the south wall.[66] It was extensively rebuilt in 1812 although some early brickwork still survives on the north face. The third prebendal brick house mentioned by Wharton was demolished in 1800 to make room for Newton's College.[67] Strangeway's house

---

61 Harwood, T., *The History and Antiquities of the Church and City of Lichfield*, London, (1806), 298. His comments on 'the earliest brick buildings' are interesting evidence of the lack of understanding of the chronology of brick building.

62 SRO, L, D. 30/XVIII, f. 23v.

63 Wharton, H., *Anglia Sacra, sive Collectio historiarum, partim antiquitus, partim recenter scriptarum, de archiepiscopis & episcopis Angliæ.* (A collection of the lives of English archbishops and bishops), (1691), 454-455.

64 Leland, **2**, 102.

65 WSL, SV-V.157b.

66 WSL, SV-V.157a.

67 *VCH, Staffs.* **14**, (1990), 59.

may have been the one occupied by Bishop Hackett in 1660 before the building of a new palace, in which case it was extremely large for after restoration it was described as having thirty-five rooms. In 1667 Henry Greswold built a 'prebendall house in the close at Lichfield … from ye very foundation at about £300 charge to me besides the materials of ye ruins … *the brick building onely not being ruined I left for stabling*' (my italics). An earlier brick building was therefore incorporated in the later prebendal house.[68]

One of the problems for the historian is in explaining why, in this poor diocese, there should be so many expensive and fashionable brick buildings. According to the *Valor Ecclesiasticus* of 1537, Lichfield was the poorest of the secular cathedrals with a common fund of only £436 10s 3½d.[69] Modestly endowed, its estates, although the second largest in Staffordshire after the Duchy of Lancaster, were only valued at £683 in 1537.[70] The answer in part is that so many of the clergy were also royal officials with other sources of income or had considerable personal wealth. Dean Heywood, for example, paid for frescoes in the cathedral, the glazing of the chapter house, St Blaise Chapel, new bells, an organ and a brick library. In 1468 he supported the building of a brew-house and bakehouse for the chantry priests and in 1471 he financed the rebuilding of the common houses of the Vicars Choral. For the Chapter he gave land at King's Bromley and Alrewas worth 51s 5¾d.[71] Harwood in 1806 recorded having seen 'An Indenture by which the said Peter Burrell and the Vicars do bind themselves in lieu of *a great sum of gold* (my italics) given them by that good Dean Heywood to the new-erecting of their common houses in the Close'. Heywood also gave Burrell, the Subchanter, 'fifty acres of arable, eighteen of, meadow and sixty of pasture'.[72] In 1485 he gave the Vicars and the Subchanter two pastures and two acres of arable to finance two 'great waxen tapers'.[73] In 1481 'Two monstrances', used for keeping relics, were given by Heywood and in 1490 he donated £40 towards the building of a brick library, '*ex parte boreali*

---

68   WRO, CR1291/246/1-15.
69   *VCH, Staffs*, **3**, (1970), 155.
70   Rowney, I., 'Change and Decay: The Bishopric of Lichfield and Coventry, 1350-1550', *Staffordshire Studies, essays presented to Denis Stuart*, ed. Morgan, P, Keele UP. (1987), 40.
71   *VCH, Staffs*, **3**, 161.
72   Harwood, 282.
73   SRO, L D30/10/1/4.

in cimeterio', (in the northern part of the Cemetery).[74] In 1493 Canon Yotton gave 100 marks to complete the library.[75] Donations by the canons to the 'Bag of Whalley', the common fund of the canons, hint at their wealth. In June 1504, Thomas Milley gave the huge sum of £200 10s.[76] Dean Denton was described as 'a great benefactor to this church and to Windsor, of which he was a canon, and expended on the chantry priests there £489 7s and indeed was very generous to all places where he had any relation'.[77] Denton was Chancellor to Princess Mary, royal negotiator in Ireland and President of the Council in Wales. George Strangeways, Archdeacon of Coventry, was presumably wealthy for as royal chaplain to Henry VII he gave the king a wonderful 'Book of Hours' which had previously belonged to Rene of Anjou, the nominal King of Naples.

It was at Lichfield that John Leland offered a more pragmatic explanation for building in brick and contributed to the belief that brick houses were built because timber was in short supply. Although that relationship is not specifically stated, in the context of a description of William Smith's almshouses, he noted in his *Itinerary*:

> *Whereas of auncient tyme all the quartars of the contrye about Lichefild were as forest and wild ground, and naturally somewhat bareyne, now the grownd about it by tyme and culture waxithe metely good and the woods be in many places so cut downe that no token is that evar any were there. Whereapon in hominum memoria wood is waxid dere in respect of the old price at Lichefeld.*[78]

Episcopal financial records demonstrate increased sales of wood, particularly in the second half of the fifteenth century under Bishop Hales. It was Leland who in the 1530s originated the practice of describing Roman bricks as 'Briton Brykes'. This practice was followed by other antiquaries like William Camden but it was not until the seventeenth century that their origins were properly discussed.[79]

---

74 Cox, J.C., *Catalogue of the Muniments and Manuscript Books Pertaining to the Dean and Chapter of Lichfield*, (1881-83), 90-91.
75 Beresford, 173.
76 Harwood, 258.
77 Browne, Willis. *A survey of the Cathedrals of York, Durham, Chester etc*, (1742), 399.
78 Leland, **2**, 103.
79 Harris, O., 'John Leland and the Briton Brykes', *The Antiquaries Journal*, **87**, (2007), 346-356.

In the wider Midland region, senior clergy financed important brick buildings. Prior Overton's tower at Repton has already been mentioned. Later patrons included Richard Sherbourne, Bishop of Chichester. In his birthplace of Rolleston-on-Dove, Sherbourne paid for the erection of a brick grammar school. Built about 1520, it was mostly burnt down in 1630 but one original wall survives. Sherbourne was one of the most important of Henry VIII's officials as he was the ambassador who negotiated Henry's marriage to Catherine of Aragon. A red brick wing of the Bishop's Palace at Chichester and a brick tower at Cakeham, Sussex, testify to his enthusiasm for brick building. On a much grander scale John Vesey, alias Harman, appointed Bishop of Exeter in 1519, diverted considerable funds into the economic regeneration of his birthplace, Sutton Coldfield. There he restored the marketplace, built a grammar school, several stone houses and erected a large brick mansion at Moor Hall. Vesey had strong connections with the diocese of Lichfield – he had been Vicar of St Michael's Coventry, Archdeacon of Chester (then a Lichfield appointment), Chancellor of Lichfield and Lord President of the Marches of Wales.

Other non-Lichfield clergy also encouraged building in brick. In Nottinghamshire, Scrooby Palace, a substantial timber-framed house of 39 rooms built for the Archbishop of York, was given a brick front between 1501 and 1507, perhaps on the occasion of the visit of Margaret Tudor, the daughter of Henry VII in 1503. Hodsock Priory, which has a brick gatehouse of c.1500, despite its name was never an ecclesiastical building and was so named in the nineteenth century. At Leicester the abbot John Penny rebuilt part of the abbey wall in brick c.1500. Leland noted, 'This Peny made the new bricke work in Leicester Abbay, and much of the bricke waulles'. Amongst its intricate diaper patterns are included the initials *jp*. Significantly all but one of the decorations are on the outside of the wall – they were built to impress visitors and travellers rather than the monks and monastic staff. Recent research has suggested that the east end of the Greyfriars church was rebuilt in brick. It must date from before its dissolution in 1538.

The above evidence confirms the significance of ecclesiastical patronage in promoting and encouraging the use of brick, but more importantly provides evidence of the mechanism by which taste and style were diffused from southern and eastern elites to the Midlands. Personal wealth was obviously a prerequisite, but brick building also required an awareness of fashion gained by familial, administrative and personal contact. Those factors can also be identified in the secular buildings of the period, where Leicestershire provides the most dramatic evidence of the political prestige perceived to be attached to brick mansions. In the fifteenth century the Grey and Hastings families were aristocratic rivals within the county. Their intense hostility was reflected in the building of prestigious manor houses in the newly fashionable brick, a material intended to reflect their wealth and proximity to the Crown. Lord Hastings, Lord Chamberlain and a close associate of Edward IV, in 1474 sought permission to fortify four manor houses in Leicestershire. Little work was begun at Bagworth or Thornton, but at Ashby de la Zouch new brick walls and towers enclosed a grandiose stone tower. More spectacularly at Kirby Muxloe, where building began in 1480, an extravagant fortified brick house, 'the most imposing and least useful of all fifteenth-century castles', still stands uncompleted following the execution of Hastings by Richard III in 1484.[80] (The financial records show that within three days of the execution the freemasons, bricklayers and carpenters stopped work.) Thomas Grey, (1461-1501) a stepson of Edward IV, initially built brick additions to the ruined castle at Groby. Their precise date is difficult to determine but probably lies somewhere in the third quarter of the fifteenth century. Grey, politically more astute, who had fled to the Low Countries with Henry Tudor, confirmed the supremacy of his family with the building of Bradgate House in c.1500, perhaps begun at the time of his promotion as Marquis of Dorset. Minor branches of the Grey family continued the tradition of early brick building at Enville Hall, a new red brick house with turrets and crow-stepped gables beside a deer park erected in the 1530s and a smaller manor house at Sheldon.

Before 1530 the use of brick in these grand buildings was an indication of the prestige attached to it. Brick was a material for fine architecture, but it was also a clear expression of wealth, rank and power, for example Hugh Clopton, at Stratford-on-Avon, was High Sheriff and later Lord Mayor of London. Those at the royal court, or those who aspired to be, built in brick to demonstrate their ready acceptance of the values and standards of the monarchy and the leading ecclesiastical authorities. The provincial gentry were often men in close contact with the Crown and sought to demonstrate their wealth and status by introducing brick to the area, for example, Sir Edward Belknap of Weston

---

80   Carpenter, C., *Locality and Polity: A Study of Warwickshire Landed Society, 1401-1499*, Cambridge: CUP, (2009), 201.

Hall had fought for Henry VII at both Stoke Field and Blackheath and under Henry VIII was 'Master of the Ordnance,' 'Surveyor of the King's Prerogative' and responsible for the 'bankett house' at the Field of the Cloth of Gold.[81] Sir Thomas Cockayne of Pooley Hall fought with Henry VIII at Tournai in 1513, Sir William Pierrepont of Holme Pierrepont also fought at Tournai after which he was made 'knight banneret' and accompanied him to the Field of the Cloth of Gold. Earlier in 1503 he had been appointed 'Knight of the Sword' by Prince Henry. Sir William Compton of Compton Wynyates accompanied the king to Tournai and previously was a ward of Henry VII and page to Prince Henry. He was such a close personal friend that in 1527 he was given the unusual permission to wear his hat in the king's presence (this 'hat trick' was also held by John Forester of Old Hall, Wellington). The court connections were maintained when his son, Peter, became a ward of Cardinal Wolsey, the initial owner of the brick Hampton Court Palace. The brick gatehouse at Hodsock Priory was built by Sir John Clifton in 1541 probably in anticipation of a visit by Henry VIII. Sir John Hussey of Kneesall, Comptroller of the Household and Chief Butler of England was initially an MP and a judge. In 1529 he entered the House of Lords and was sufficiently close to the King to be selected to carry the canopy at the christening of Princess Elizabeth and become Chamberlain to Princess Mary to whom his wife was an attendant. Anthony Emery has written that housing 'should be seen in a context in which conspicuous expenditure, lavish furnishings and display, and large numbers of staff, household and retinue were evidence of a man's standing'.[82] Before 1530 brick building in the Midlands was the preserve of the wealthy and well-connected, its diffusion beyond this social elite was a slow and tentative process. Even in London and as late as 1557 the Venetian ambassador reported that 'They have lately commenced building with bricks, most especially "i milordi," but at great cost'.[83]

---

81 Belknap's proximity to the Crown was demonstrated in 1550 when, 'in consideration of the services of the said Belknappe to Henry VII. At the battle of Blakeheathe he was freed from any penalties arising from inclosure'. Calendar of Patent Rolls, 1549-1551, **III**, London, (1925), 428, (82) Emery, 216, (83) 20th June 1557. *CSP, 'Relating to English Affairs in the Archives of Venice'*, ed. Rawton Brown, **6**, London: (1887).

82 Emery, 216.

83 *CSP, 'Relating to English Affairs in the Archives of Venice'*, ed. Rawton Brown, **6**, 1555-1558, 'Appendix: Miscellaneous 1557', London: HMSO, (1887), 1658-1673.

Chapter 3

THE TECHNOLOGY OF BRICKMAKING

RECENT RESEARCH into vernacular architecture and early polite architecture has devoted relatively little attention to the manufacturing process of brick. Malcolm Airs, for example, in his authoritative book *The Tudor & Jacobean Country House: A Building History* defines the 'early part of the sixteenth century … as … the first great age of English brickwork', but devotes only three pages to a summary of its manufacture.[84] This chapter examines the technological potential of pre-industrial brick making, the range of physical and human resources which supported it, the scale of the industry and those structural elements which either hindered or encouraged its growth.

One explanation for this scarcity of analysis and description lies in the lack of archaeological evidence derived from ground surveys and excavation. The clamp was a temporary structure and although kilns of this period have been excavated locally at Atherstone in Warwickshire and Flintham Hall in Nottinghamshire, they are rare evidence of structures in which constant heating and cooling eventually destroyed their integrity and left little evidence to be recovered.[85]

---

84   Airs, M., *The Tudor & Jacobean Country House: A Building History,* Sutton, (1993), 114-7.
85   Scott, K., and Mory, A., 'Brickmaking in North Warwickshire', *TBWAS,* **89**, (1979), 138-143. They describe a brick kiln excavated at Atherstone, Warwickshire. This 'Scotch' kiln, built about 1753, had walls about 3 feet thick and measured approximately 22 feet x 17 feet. It was fired by coal with a capacity of approximately 40,000 bricks. An excavation of a late seventeenth or early eighteenth-century kiln at Flintham Hall, Nottinghamshire revealed a rectangular kiln measuring approximately 17 feet x 14 feet 4 inches with walls approximately 15 inches thick. A height of between 11½ and 14½ feet was suggested. Alvey, R.C., 'A Post-Medieval Brick Kiln at Flintham Hall, Nottinghamshire', *TTS,* **86**, (1982), 118-123.

Documentary source material is not abundant. David Whitehead, in his study of brickmaking in the West Midlands, writes of 'the men who made these bricks … make fleeting appearances in the institutional and private records of the Tudor and Stuart era'.[86] But there is sufficient evidence, although not consistently available for every decade, to trace from the 1480s onwards the methods of production, the technology employed, the costs of raw materials, the costs of transport and a degree of continuity in families and generations of brickmakers.

Handicaps to Brickmaking

Brick productivity was hindered by a variety of factors. Governed by the seasons, firing was legally confined to the months between 1st March and 29th September, as late as 1763 at Lockington Hall the accounts include 'for Burning the Last Kiln' on 20th September.[87] Poor weather in the summer months therefore did not allow for an opportunity to catch up on lost production. As an essentially outdoor activity, inclement weather could cause serious delays. As the Strelley agent noted in 1698, 'the Great Lord of Heaven and Earth hath reserved such a power in his hand that he can and doth att his pleasure send a colde winterly season in the midest of the Spring'.[88]

At the Trentham Estate in 1701 the steward wrote to Sir John Leveson Gower that 'He (Mr Englesfield, the mason) had intended to have seen what a Brickmaker had done but ye weather has been such they could not work'.[89] At Attingham in 1722 the steward reported that it had been 'so wet a summer that no bricks have been made at Weston Common'.[90] A report to Lord Harley at Welbeck on April 14th, 1717, noted that 'the weather begins to be good and we will begin to make brick as soon as we can get some straw, but nobody thrasheth wheat yet'.[91] (Straw was used in the kiln for firing, to keep apart courses of bricks and for wiping and drying green bricks. In 1664 the brickmaking accounts for Coughton Court included '15 thrave of straw

---

86   Whitehead, D., 'Brick and Tile making in the Woodlands of the West Midlands in the 16th and 17th centuries', *Vernacular Architecture,* **12**, (1981), 42-47.

87   ROLLR, DE1536/134.

88   NA, DD/E/117/1 c.1695-1763.

89   SRO, D868/9/55.

90   SA, 112/1/2420.

91   NA, DD4P63/61. The report continues, 'I have thought of burning some roots in to Charcoal …' The purpose of this is not certain as 'all the brick is Carried from the Clamp', so the straw and charcoal were not required for the actual firing of the brick.

for the Bricke-worke', and in 1665 14 thrave 'for the Clamp'.[92] In 1719 the brickmaking accounts of Humphrey Greswold included the purchase of 110 thraves of straw).[93] At Hawkstone in March 1726 the steward reported that 'the workmen … are only hindered from work by want of lime which cannot be got until the roads are better which he expects will not be until the middle of next month. This will give time to finish them by next Hay harvest and sooner they will not be wanted'.[94] In 1744 the steward at Okeover Hall reported on a 'shortage of stones and bricks'.[95] Such shortages were not uncommon, an agreement to build Newark Town Hall in 1774 required the two bricklayers to 'erect Brick Work by 1st October, in Case they shall not receive any Hindrance from the Want of Bricks, Lime or Sand'.[96]

The manufacture of bricks was a slow process and most effectively carried out near the site where they were required, thus enabling the builder or estate steward both to supervise the process and to reduce transport costs. For a small number of urban buildings, the most economical method of brickmaking was to extract the clay from immediately below the proposed structure and fire it on site. This also had the incidental advantage of providing a vault or cellar. The accounts for The Mass House, in Wolverhampton, in 1728, include, 'To deduct out for Clay being taken from which was in the Vaults at 4d per Thousand comes to 36,000', (i.e. sufficient clay for 36,000 brick).[97]

Custom and practice produced a seasonal pattern in which the clay was dug in autumn and allowed to weather during the winter months, although John Stephens of Downton Hall, near Ludlow, wrote in 1810, 'I find to make your Brick and Tile the Clay should be Dug a year before used'.[98] More usually it was allowed to stand for five or six months and in the spring it was tempered, that is, spread out, sprinkled with water and trodden, or turned with spades, into a pliable mass of even consistency. Some, but not all, pebbles were extracted to prevent the cracking or splitting of the clay during firing. On some estates aristocratic owners of the holes from which the clay had

---

92   Moore, N. J., 'The Supply of Bricks to Coughton Court, Warwickshire in 1663-65', *BBSI*, **69**, (1996), 12.
93   WRO, CR1291/292.
94   SA, 112/1/2733.
95   DRO, D231M/E113.
96   NA, DDT/134/7.
97   SRO, D 590/634.
98   SA, 6683/3/27.

been extracted could exploit them as garden ponds or water features. In 1711 William Anson noted in his journal, 'Monday April 6th 1711 wee put 19 or 20 doz of Good Carpe into the papermill poole out of Mr Whitbys pitts & then I put 6 spawnes & 6 moltes into my brick holes'.[99] At Malvern Hall, the Greswold brickmaking accounts of 1718 included 'taken out of ye Uper Brickhill Pit 60 Brace of Carpe'.[100]

The bricks were then moulded and dried under rough shelters and finally fired in either clamps or updraught kilns. Until the nineteenth century moulding was done by hand. For stock bricks the moulder working at a table sanded his or her wooden mould and threw into it with some force a lump of clay. The sand acted as a releasing agent, prevented adhesion of the clay and aided its removal from the mould. Silica, when added to pure clay in the form of sand, prevented cracking, shrinking and warping and is frequently mentioned in Midland brickmaking accounts. As early as 1615 on Sir William Herricke's estate at Beaumanor, the steward reported that 'the brickmaker had already made seven thousand bricks and needed a great deal of sand'.[101] In 'slop-moulding', used to produce place bricks, there was no stockboard and the mould and top of the brick were wetted and the water was used instead of sand to stop the clay sticking to the mould. The disadvantage of slop moulded brick was the need for it to be dried for a longer period before firing. An Act of 1730 allowed that 'Stock-Bricks and Place-Bricks may be burnt in one and the same place, so as the Stock-Bricks be set in one distinct Parcel and not intermixed with Place-Bricks'.[102]

The moulder continued by slicing the surplus from the top of the mould with a 'strike', stick or similar implement. Thomas Wilsford in *Architectonice: The Art of Building* (London, 1659) estimated that a man and a team of 6 helpers could make 6,000 bricks in just five hours.[103] Stephen Primatt in 1667 wrote, 'about 9,000 is accounted a reasonable day's work'.[104] Nathaniel Lloyd suggested 2,000 bricks could be made in an extended summer's day and,

---

99   SRO, D615 P(A) /1/12.
100 WRO, CR1291/292.
101 Bodleian Library, MS.Eng.hist./c.482/fol.91.
102 Shaw, J., *The Practical Justice of the Peace and Parish and Ward Officer*, 'In the Savoy', **2**, (1756), 263.
103 Wilson, R., and Mackley, A., *Creating Paradise, The Building of the English Country House 1660-1880*, London: Hambledon Continuum, (2000), 387.
104 Primatt, S., *The City and Country Purchaser and Builder*, London: Speed (1667), 130.

perhaps more realistically, Houghton in 1683 suggested that 'a man without help will make a thousand (bricks) in a day', although he does record for a wager of £10 the production in one day of 22,000 bricks.[105] There is very little documentary evidence of the pace of moulding, but the building accounts for Ingestre Hall in 1724 suggest that brickmaking and moulding were separate occupations and that less than 1,000 bricks were moulded per day.[106] There is no evidence in the Midlands of the mechanisation of any stage in the process of brickmaking, this did not occur until the middle of the nineteenth century with the invention of the wire cutting machine in 1841 and the first extruding machine in 1875.[107]

The Pug Mill
The pug mill was a vertical tank with horizontal interior blades driven from a vertical central shaft by horse, mule or later by a steam engine and certainly was in use in the nineteenth century. The purpose of the mill was to turn and mix the weathered clay to produce a finer material and therefore a better brick. The origin and use of the pug mill within the British brickmaking industry has been the subject of some debate. The consensus is that the pug mill probably was used in the pottery industry during the eighteenth century but, until the end of the century, references to it within the brick industry are uncertain and ambiguous.

In almost all cases where documentary evidence survives of the mixing of clay, it is to the traditional method of turning over-wintered clay by treading by foot or turning by spade; for example in an agreement of 1689 the Coventry brickmaker, Rowland Heathly, was required to 'Digg and turne over twice before the first day of March next ensuing Soe much Clay … as will make Forty Thousand of Brick'.[108] There is however one early and so far unique reference to the mechanical preparation of clay.[109] Charles Wood, (1702-1774), of Low mill, Egremont, Cumberland, was an ironmaster visiting

---

105 Houghton, J., ed. Bradley. R., *A Collection of Letters for the Improvement of Husbandry and Trade*, published as 'A Catalogue of all sorts of Earths, the Art of Draining, of Brewing, of all sorts of Husbandry London., (1726/7), 4, 397. The actual letters were written in 1681-4.
106 SRO, D240/E/F/1/2.
107 Hudson, K., *Building Materials*, London: Longman, (1972), 52.
108 SBPT, DR10/1476.
109 Hyde, C.K., 'The Iron Industry of the West Midlands in 1754: Observations from the travel account of Charles Wood', *West Midland Studies*, **6**, (1973), 39-40.

the Worcestershire Stour and Severn valleys to collect evidence of different methods of ironworking.[110] In 1754 he recorded in his diary:

> *Saturday September 7, At Stourbridge … He (Mr. Bowyer) went with us to view their Clay, the best of which is in solid hard lumps, is picked clean from all veins of any other matter. It goes to Glass house pots & is ground and sifted fine. The smaller sort, which is not picked, is ground by a Stone and made into Brick. This Clay lyes 20 yards under the Surface. Observation – Low Mill clay, if clean picked, seems to be much better for use in bricks than theirs, but not as good as that separated for Glass house pots. The Lowmill method of grinding their clay & preparing it, is in my opinion much better & more expeditious than theirs. The best picked Clay would make excellent Brick, but it is too dear for that use.*

The key phrase is, 'ground by a stone and made into Brick', the word 'picked' is derived from handpicked and means that pebbles, stones, soil and similar materials were removed by hand. Possibly as the clay was 'not picked' the grindstone was sufficiently powerful that such denser materials were crushed and able to be fired. 1754 is too early for the use of a rotary steam engine so, by implication, the source of power must have been a horse, mule or some form of water powered mill. Whether grinding by a stone, possibly like a cider press or a corn mill, allows the machine to be called a pug mill is uncertain. Dobson in his *A Rudimentary Treatise on the Manufacture of Bricks and Tiles* of 1850 made a clear distinction between rollers and the pug mill, noting that the pug mill was used where brick earth was of milder quality.[111] Wood particularly emphasizes that brick clay is in 'solid hard lumps'. The grinding of the brick clay seems to be an extension of the preparation of refined and high-quality clay for crucibles for the Stourbridge glass industry. Of further interest, but unfortunately not developed, are the references to the 'Lowmill method of grinding their clay' and this 'best picked clay would make excellent

---

[110] According to the article, Wood's diary, on microfilm, was held by Flynn M.W. of the University of Edinburgh. The same reference is given in. Rees, D.M., *Mines, Mills and Foundries*, (1967), National Museum of Wales. Wood and a friend, Gabriel Griffiths, visited four blast furnaces, 11 forges and two slitting mills.

[111] Dobson, E., *A Rudimentary Treatise on the Manufacture of Bricks and Tiles*, (**Pt 1**, London: Crosby Lockwood, 1850), 24-26.

brick', Wood here implies that the costs of picking would prevent its use for brickmaking. The potentially high labour costs may be the explanation for the poor quality of so much of early brick and the presence of surface pebbles and consequent star-burst disfigurements on the surface of fired bricks.[112] Whether the grinding of the clay significantly improved the quality and hardness of the brick is unclear and the date of the introduction of this process is also not known, but as early as 1718 the Coalbrookdale ironworks purchased 'Sturbridge bricks'.[113] These bricks were probably made from fireclay and were consequently more fire resistant.

The Clamp

The clamp was the traditional method of production of the itinerant brickmaker. The word was derived from the Middle Dutch word *klamp* meaning a 'heap'. Often built near the building under construction, its size varied with the number of bricks required. One of the few brick clamps to have been excavated in this country is a fourteenth-century coal-fired example from Boston. This measured at its maximum 23' x 15'.[114] The clamp was constructed by putting a foundation layer of burnt bricks on a level piece of ground to provide insulation from rising damp and then spreading a layer of wood or coal over it. The 'green' bricks were stacked above it, burnt bricks were laid over the top and the stack was sealed with clay and set on fire which was then allowed to burn itself out. The clamp was favoured by brickmakers when bricks were required for a single project because it was less labour intensive and cheaper to construct and burn than the kiln. The major drawback of this form of production was the inability to control the firing process. Clamps attained maximum heat almost immediately, but the heat was not distributed evenly to all areas of the structure. Consequently clamp-fired material included a greater percentage of over and under-fired bricks. The soft and under-fired 'semel' bricks were either used for 'casing' interior walls or expensively re-fired.[115] The temperatures achieved are difficult to discover but archaeological investigation

---

112 Kingman, M., A Mid-Eighteenth-Century Brick Clay Mill? *BBSI*, **124**, (2013).

113 SA, 6001/329, 4 31; 6001/330, 37.

114 Mayes, P., 'A Medieval Tile Kiln at Boston, Lincolnshire', *Journal of the British Archaeological Association*, 3rd series, **28**, (1985), 86-106. The clamp was probably used to manufacture bricks for the tile kiln.

115 Barley, M., *The English Farmhouse and Cottage*, London: Routledge (1976), 207.

of the slag in a clamp at Anstey, Leics, suggested working temperatures of 800°C-1,000°C.[116] An experimental firing of a wood-fuelled brick clamp produced bricks of an uneven condition from the heart of a clamp where temperatures of over 1,600°C were reached.[117] The estate accounts of the Dowager Countess of Mountrath at Walsall include three rare references to the 'watering of brick' to cool it down, 'Aug 28 (1774) Paid a Man for watering brick many times when the Bricks were just drawn from the Kiln and too hot to use 3s 10d'.[118]

Determining the use of semi-permanent kilns or temporary clamps is often complicated by the use of the term 'clamp' for both methods of production.[119] In an inventory of 1658, Michael Biddulph, the extremely wealthy owner of houses at Lichfield and Elmhurst, possessed a 'brickclampe' worth £6 13s 4d. Such a sum would suggest that this was a permanent kiln rather than a temporary clamp.[120] At Aqualate an agreement of 1677/8 referred to 100,000 bricks 'to be delivered at the kilns or clamps' as though the two terms were synonymous. At Sherbourne the detailed brickmaking accounts of the Edge Estate include 'Total costs of all clamps and Kilnes £94 3s 7¼d', with no distinction made between them.[121]

In her study of *Building Capitalism*, Linda Clarke has London evidence of clamps making individual firings of between 60,000 and 100,000 bricks over a period of between two and six weeks.[122] Angerstein in his travel notebook of 1753 describes a clamp sited between Hounslow and London as 'a pile of green bricks was built 15 feet high, 44 feet wide and 180 feet long … covered with clay to preserve the heat'.[123] No structure of this size or capacity has been

---

116 *Archaeology in Leicestershire and Rutland, 1994. TLAHS,* **86**, (1994), 97-99.
117 Mugridge, T., 'Broseley Clay Weekend, June 2001, Results of Clamp Firing', *BBSI,* **86**, (2001), 6.
118 SRO, D1287/G/6.
119 Smith, *Medieval Brickmaking,* 39-57.
120 Vaisey, D.G., ed., 'Probate Inventories of Lichfield and District', *SHC,* (1969) 105-112. At Hamstall Ridware Hall, Thomas Leigh's inventory of 1662 includes, 'Item a clamp of brick there at £5 0 0'. LRO, B/C/11.Campbell. J.W.P. and Sant, A., 'The Manufacture and Dating of English Brickwork 1600-1720', *Archaeological Journal,* **159** (2002) 182, state that 'no doubt many entries … for kilns simply mean clamps. It is unclear whether the reverse is true; that the term clamp is used for kiln'. The Staffordshire evidence would suggest that clamp is used as a term for a kiln.
121 NA, DD/E/92/3/1.
122 Clarke, L., *Building Capitalism,* London: Routledge, (1992), 138.
123 Angerstein, R.R., ed. Borg, T., *Illustrated Travel Diary,* 1753-1755. Science Museum, (2001), 19.

documented in the Midlands. George Vernon started building Sudbury Hall in 1661, by 1690 1,377,000 bricks had been fired in his park and nearby, but each firing produced only 16,000 to 20,000 bricks.[124]

The precise component costs of brickmaking are rarely revealed, but the Ingestre Cash Book for 1724 includes:

eating and drinking	*1s 0d*
Carriage of Stack of Coles	*4s 6d per stack*
Casting Clay	*6d per 1,000*
finding out ye clay (1 day)	*1s 0d*
Moulding	*2s 6d per 1,000*
burning the brick	*10s 0d per clamp*

This would suggest a total price for a clamp of 11,000 bricks of approximately £3 or 5s 5d per 1,000 for a product which was sold commercially at prices between 8 and 10s per 1,000.[125]

The Kiln

Updraught kilns allowed higher and more uniform temperatures to be obtained than in the clamp. By the second half of the seventeenth century the usual updraught kiln was of the 'intermittent' type known as a 'Scotch' kiln. It was a large chamber, open at the top or with a temporary wooden roof and with a series of fire holes along each side opposite one another. After loading with raw bricks, a layer of old bricks was then spread over the top, the ends of the kiln were bricked up, roughly plastered with clay and fires were lit in the fire holes. The dried bricks were stacked inside in such a way that the hot gases could surge up between them. Under this method of manufacture, the shade and condition of the brick varied a great deal, those nearest the fire being the darkest and most over-fired.

These kilns were 'intermittent' in that they worked to a cycle of fill-fire-cool-empty. Subject to intense heat, almost none have survived above ground but two kilns excavated at Flintham Hall and Atherstone give some indication of their size. The Atherstone 'Scotch' kiln was 3 feet thick and measured 22

---

124 Barley, M., *Houses and History*, London: Faber & Faber, (1986) 182.
125 SRO, D240/E/F/1/2.

feet by 17 feet, the Flintham kiln was 15 inches thick and measured 17 feet by 14 feet 4 inches. The capacity of these kilns is difficult to estimate for no evidence of their height survives. At Kirby Muxloe a 'Newe Kylne' was built in 1482 and the accounts record that there was 'payd for Brennyg (burning) of the same kilne by the space of a wyke to the number of Breke 100,000'. This number seems exceptionally high and unique in the Midlands as Dobson, in 1851, estimated that an average size kiln of 15 feet by 20 feet could hold up to 40,000 bricks. The kilns at Flintham and Atherstone presumably had maximum capacities of between 20,000 and 40,000. Loads considerably less than this however seem to have been more typical. Documentary evidence of the number of bricks produced per firing is scarce and not always accurate for it may not include spoiled or broken brick but average kiln size would seem to be between 11-15,000 per firing with 8-10 firings per season.

Table 1: Kiln Size

Date	Number of Bricks per firing	Estate Owner	Notes
1482	100,000	Lord Hastings, Kirby Muxloe	The 'Newe Kylne' bricks fired in a 'wyke'
1690	18,000	Lady Wilbraham, Weston Park	Required 9 stacks of coal
1698	11,590	Sir William Anson, Shugborough	'The first kill full'
1701	Average 12,200 goods per burning	Sir William Anson	9 firings
1716	2 'killn of bricks' 10,700, bricks, 1,560 quarries	Humphrey Greswold, Solihull	2nd kiln, 12,600
1720		Hill Estate, Attingham	Steward hoped to burn 150,000 'in the summer', about 8-10,000 per firing
1724	13,900 'drawn from the kiln'	Fielding Estate Newnham Paddox	

1727-8	8 'burnings' for 164, 567, average 20,568 per kiln	Giffard Estate, Chillington	For the 'Mass House', Wolverhampton
1731-1750	13,000 per firing	Bridgeman Estate, Castle Bromwich	
1737-1754	11 firings per season	Paget estate, Beaudesert	
1751	10,350 'Building Brick', 2,470 'dressed'	Hatton Vicarage	'The fifth Kiln of Brick made for him'
1766	15,536	Earl Ferrers Staunton Estate	Fired on 14th June, next firing on 22nd June, 15,970

Detailed records of kiln production and costs are rare, the Edge Estate records of 1785 at Sherbourne describe 'clamp' production, but their detail suggests that they are kiln accounts for it would not have been economic to build a clamp every 11 days. The 'clamp' cost £1 1s to build and was in operation from May 28th to November 18th, 1785, during which period there were 11 burnings, i.e. one every 16 days. The greatest concentration was in May, June and July when there were six burnings in 65 days, i.e. one every 11 days. Under each date are usually three numbers, thus for May 28th the document reads 21,000/700/58, for June 27th it reads 1,600/600/25. They may refer to different types of brick or tiles produced. Within each week's tally is the number of bricks loaded and in one year 117,700 were loaded. The cost of the bricks was 7s 6d per 1,000, with 3d per 1,000 for loading and 1s for unloading each consignment of coals, the clay cost £6 5s with repairs and unlisted wages. The newly instituted Brick Tax, at 2s 6d per 1,000, cost £24 16s 9½d, paid in three instalments which suggests a total production of about 200,000 brick equivalents including specialist bricks, tiles and quarries. The total cost with tax was £94 3s 7¼d. The labour force seems to have been composed of the brickmaker and 'boy' and presumably other estate workers were paid for loading bricks and unloading coal. Of importance is the relatively small number of bricks produced on one estate in one year, 117,000 bricks were only sufficient for three small houses. The figures suggest that, at least on the

Edge Estate, the kiln was relatively inefficient and required repair after each firing and a complete rebuild after four firings. Such repairs were not expensive but consumed time in a legally restricted production year.

Table 2: Brick Production on the Edge Estate, Sherbourne, 1785

	Amount Loaded	Loads of Coals	Repairs etc.
28/5	10,700	2	
14/6	15,000	4	Mending Clay and Holes, 1s 6d
27/6	15,500	2	" " " "
11/7	15,000	2	" " " "
17/7	17,000	2	New Clamping
27/7	16,500	2	Mending Clay and Holes 1s 6d
17/8	15,000	2	" " " "
7/9	2,000	2	" " " "
4/10	6,000	2	" " " "
14/11	5,000	2	Repairing the Clamp 3 days 6s
18/11		2	Clamping and Daubing 5s

The cost of building a brick kiln varied with the quantity of building materials readily available. On aristocratic or gentry estates where timber, clay and labour were more easily available, the costs could be low. For example five detailed agreements with four different brickmakers for the burning of 1,150,000 bricks by Lord Gower in 1720-21 included the provision of materials and 12s per 'Oven'. In 1760 an agreement for 1,000,000 bricks between Harry Lankford 'gentleman' and William Fearnihough 'brickmaker' allowed the brickmaker 30 shillings towards the cost of the 'Oven'.[126] The level of investment was erratic, in 1728 Thomas Birch of Wolverhampton paid £1 4s 10d for his kiln and a

---

126 SRO, D3359/12/1/187.

further £9 12s 8d for 169 man-days for 'sinking and leveling the ground'. At Sherbourne 'building a new oven' cost 10s 6d, whilst on the Penbury Estate in 1773 the cost was only 8s 6d and in 1786 at the Ecton copper mine the kiln cost 19s.[127] The security of these figures is difficult to guarantee, at Lapley Hall in 1667 'building one of ye killne houses' cost £4.[128] For the building of 'a New Brick Kiln' at Kelham Hall in 1726 the cost was £31 18s 1d, this price included £6 2s 9d for 'leveling the Brickyard' and £1 15s for 'Beer'.[129] The time taken to build a kiln varied with its size, in 1482 at Kirby Muxloe three men were employed for '8 wikes'.[130]

The explanation for the discrepancies in expenditure may in part be the cost of preparing the ground, with some sites being traditionally used and therefore requiring no initial preparation. In 1706 a contract between Thomas Allen, Rector of Stoke-on-Trent, and John Edwards of Little Fenton, brickmaker, required Edwards to 'make and burn at his charge 50 or 60 thousand of Bricks of Statutable fire in the same place where he made the last year and upon the same terms'.[131]

Some kilns may have been cheaper because they were built with unfired bricks whose only cost was that of moulding. An early seventeenth century kiln excavated in Chester was built in this manner.[132] There is a possibility that kilns could be demolished and re-erected. In 1641 Henry, Earl of Holland, Chief Justice and Justice-in-Eyre of the Royal Forests on this side (of the) Trent, wrote to the officers and ministers of his Majesty's Forest of Windsor, 'I have thought fit to license and authorise Thomas Dodsley to continue the making of bricks in a brick-kiln lately removed by him from the place where formerly it was, and to maintain the same without let or hindrance'.[133]

The term 'brickyard' as a centre of concentrated production was rarely used, for most non-estate brickmakers were also farmers with the greater part of their wealth invested in stock and farming equipment. At Kirby Muxloe over one million bricks were fired at the 'Breke hous' or the 'Breeke place'. The

---

127 Porter, L., *Ecton Copper Mines under the Dukes of Devonshire 1760-1790*, Ashbourne: Landmark, (2004) 196.
128 SRO, L B/V/6. Within Lapley glebe terrier.
129 46 NA, DP70/1.
130 Hamilton Thompson, 307.
131 SRO, D(W)1742/46.
132 Ward S., '17th Century Kiln'. *BBSI*, **42**, (May 1987), 19.
133 *CSPD, Charles 1*, 1640, February, 1641, ccclxxxiv, 109.

earliest reference to 'brickyard' is in 1617 in the inventory of John Corbett of Anslow. Corbett had an estate estimated at £15 of which 'bricks and tiles' were valued at only 7s 8d. Other early references include one in 1697 on the Strutt Estate at Derby, a brickyard at Market Harborough in 1699, at Bordesley in 1750, at Allesley in 1757, at Nottingham in 1764, at Southwell in 1771 and a 'brickyard' in Shrewsbury in 1777. At Newton Solney, in Derbyshire, Newton Hill Farm was previously Brickyard Farm with adjacent fields named Brickkiln Close, Brick-Kiln Howgh (valley) and Brickyard Howgh.[134]

Although little physical sign of kilns persists, evidence of their existence often survives in the form of place names and field names, amongst the earliest are Brick Close at Rothley in 1567 and Brick Kiln Close at Long Eaton in 1608. In South Derbyshire five adjacent villages, Catton, Foremark, Newton Solney, Stanton-By-Bridge and Swarkestone each had a Brick Kiln Close. In the eighteenth century there are many dozens of similar placenames which may represent short-term exploitation of local clay deposits as at Brick Kiln Farm leased from the Greswold Estate in 1747[135] and Brick Kiln Field at Smisby.

The Manufacture of Tiles
In theory the production of roofing tiles required special attention. Tiles were a more refined product; they had to be very compact to prevent moisture and frost from permeating them and causing them to crumble. It has been suggested that the clay had to be finer, stiffer and tempered more carefully because a greater surface area was exposed to the weather. Houghton's treatise stated that 'Tiles are made of Earth much better than Bricks, inclining to that which Potters use'.[136] An early reference to a 'tyle kilne' was recorded at Pinwall Grange on the estates of the dissolved Merevale Abbey, although these could be floor tiles.[137]

Generally contemporary records rarely reflect a clear distinction between tile or brick production.[138] Where both were produced it would seem to be evidence of the existence of a more permanent kiln. At Knowle in 1696 the

---

134 Fraser, W., *Field Names in South Derbyshire,* Norman Alderd, (1947), 101.
135 WRO, CR 1291/102, 174.
136 Houghton, 2.
137 Courtney, P., 'The Monastic Granges of Leicestershire', *TLHAS,* **56**, (1980-81), 37.
138 *Patent Roll 1549-1551,* 433.

churchwardens recorded the purchase of 'Tiles from the Brick Kiln'.[139] At Stretton, in 1730, on the Congreve Estate, Isaac Stock signed a receipt 'for thirty odd thousand of brick and twenty odd thousand of tyles made by me'.[140] At Trentham, the accounts of 1737-46, in which the manufacture of brick, lime and tile is often mentioned, frequently refer to a 'brick kiln' and a 'lime kiln', but never to a tile kiln.[141] William Anson's records below indicate that, at least on his estate, roofing tiles, floor tiles, gutters, crests and three different varieties of brick were all fired in the same kiln at the same time. The table also records a short period of production of only five months with an apparent maximum capacity of 15,000 brick priced at 8s 4d per 1,000.[142]

Table 3: Brick Production on the Shugborough Estate, 1701

When burnt	L Brick	N Brick	S Brick	Quarry	Tyles	Ridge	Gutter	Leach Kill	Wages £ s d
June 7	5,900	5,800			300			12,000	2 8 0
June 11	11,050	1,200	250		2,500			15,000	3 0 0
June 28	10,350	450		1,000	3,000			14,800	2 19 8
July 9	10,950	(Kiln Brick 194)		386	1,540			12,800	2 11 0
July 30	9,650			198	3,100		218	13,250	3 2 6
Aug 26	11,450				1,900			13,450 (sic)	2 13 7
Sept 11	11,800	1,000		540	1,500	68		13,900	2 15 6
Oct 27	13,000	Price	at	xp	per	c		13,000	2 12 0
		7,450	1,250	2,040		68		108,200	22 7 3
						Digging	in	May	3 5 0
									25 12 0

The significance of the capital letters L N and S is unclear, they may represent 'Long', 'Nogging' and 'Smooth', but it is highly unlikely that thousands of long bricks would have been made. They may denote 'Large, Normal and Small?'

---

139 Downing, T., *Records of Knowle,* Privately Printed, (1914), 277.
140 SRO, D1057/J/2/9.
141 SRO, D593/F/3/2/11-20.
142 SRO, D615P (A)/1/7.

On very large estates where there was sufficient demand it may have been more economical to establish a specialist tile kiln. At Welbeck Abbey in the 1720s and 1730s a tile kiln was let intermittently at £16 pa.[143] On the Greswold's Solihull estate there are specific references in 1719 to the building of the 'Brickill', the 'Brick Hovill', the 'tyle house' and a 'Tyle Hovill'. The 'Tyle kill' required 8,400 bricks and over £16 was spent building the 'Tyle Hovill', the total bill for all the above was the considerable sum of £45 3s 7d.[144] Although there is no evidence that different clays were employed, the clay required for each product may have been altered by the amount of sand mixed with it. Not all tiles were of clay, in stone areas of the Midlands thinly bedded slate was used, for example in Shropshire Harnage stone was frequently employed.

The frequent references to 'crests' as well as 'tiles' highlight an essential difference in form, the crest or ridge tile crucially holds down the top course of flat tiles. In most of the calmer southern and eastern areas a light clay ridge, usually in a 'hog's back' shape created by bending a flat slab of clay over a former, will suffice. Tilers preferred this shape because of its closeness to the tiles. In other windier and wetter areas a heavy and long ridge tile was frequently employed. These 'saddle-back' ridge tiles were initially made from stone but by the mid eighteenth century were of clay burnt blue or brindled and measured approximately 14 inches by 14 inches or larger. A small rib was formed on one end and a cap at the other which enabled the ridges to lap over each other. They proved heavy enough to withstand wind and water even without mortar bedding. Low pitched roofs behind the fashionable parapet were a problem for tilers for clay ridges could not be successfully laid on hips and ridges at low pitches of 30° and even lower. Heavy sheet lead fixed onto a timber roll served as an alternative and gave rise to the imitative design of 'roll-top' ridge tiles.[145]

In Table 3 the kiln is listed as 'Kill', this was not an uncommon corruption but has for some landscape historians led to confusion with 'Hill'. The 'brick hill' was a feature of many aristocratic estates and has survived as a common

---

143 NA, DDP5/1/1.
144 WRO, CR299/536.
145 Emerton. G., 'Ridge Tiles in North Staffordshire', *BBS North Midlands Bulletin*, **3**, (1975), 6-11.

field and place name.¹⁴⁶ Amongst the earliest references is that of 1599 at Pipewell, Nottinghamshire. In Shropshire there are initial references in 1649 at Morton Corbett and in 1698 at Upton Cressett two of the earliest brick buildings in that county. In Derbyshire the Hopton Estate sold 'Brickhill Peece' in 1718. The Littleton accounts for 1753 include mention of the 'building (of) 2 Brickhills in the Park', and as they were erected in November they probably reflect the storage of a summer surplus of bricks. Their cost, £5 5s 1d, is an indication of the size of these structures.¹⁴⁷ To protect the bricks from the frost they may have been covered as in the Welbeck Abbey accounts of 1727 there is a rare reference to 'Tho Whale at Carburton for four hundred of Ling (heather) for covering the Brick & Tile 0 18s 0d'.¹⁴⁸

The purpose of the 'brick hill' was only rarely as a site for resale but was used mainly for the storage of brick for estate repairs. As the estate steward at Attingham wrote in 1725, 'For this purpose the brick earth in Joseph's upper pool lies ready dug – they may as well make brick and tile of it as not, for a stock should be kept ready to mend neighbouring farms'.¹⁴⁹ It may have been more than just a store of bricks but also the site of the kiln and associated buildings. The brick accounts of William Anson at Shugborough include references to the carriage of coal to the 'Brickhill', implying that this was the site of the kiln.¹⁵⁰ On the Earl of Chesterfield's sequestrated estate in 1650 a 'brickhill leas' was listed at Cubley, later this is described as 'brickkiln leas'.¹⁵¹ In 1756 the Littleton Estate accounts included a payment for 'Repairing Brickhill'.¹⁵² At Meerbrook where, in 1750, there was a non-estate built kiln, bricks and coal were stored at the 'brickeiel'.¹⁵³ John Field has suggested that 'the *Brickhill* names may well be from an earlier *Brick-kil(n)* form of the place

---

146   SRO, D260/M/E/425/7 includes a 1709 reference to 'Brick Hill Piece' at Walsall and SRO, D3361/2/1 lists 'Brick Hill Leasow' at Baswich where the church was rebuilt in brick in 1742.
147   SRO, D(W)260/M/E/116, 32.
148   NA, DDP5/1/.
149   SA, 112/1/1733.
150   SRO, D615/P(A)/1/5.
151   Cox, C.J., 'Documents Relative to the Sequestration of the Estates of Philip Earl of Chesterfield', *DAJ*, **11**, (1889), 108.
152   SRO, D 260/M/E/116.
153   SRO, D 1028/2/1, '1 loade of Coales to thies brickeiel'.

name.¹⁵⁴ However, according to Eilert Ekwall an earlier meaning of the name is the 'top or summit' of a hill and it may be that by building the kiln on a hill a better draught could be obtained.¹⁵⁵ In this sense 'brickhill' was a term for a brickyard or 'brickbank', which was a word used at the Anson Estate at Shugborough in 1704.¹⁵⁶

The actual storage and layout of the bricks has not been previously described. Charles Trubshaw was a member of an important family of civil engineers, architects and builders. In the 1750s he kept a building notebook of contracts, designs, wages and of the purchase of materials. Within the notebook is an intriguing entry entitled *'Bricks at ye Kiln'*.¹⁵⁷

Pitches
8⅓ 100 in a Row 14,070 25 72 in a Row 30,600 15 70 in a Row 17,850
(Total) 62 220
Note ye Pitches are 17 deep

The author's initial assumption was that these figures were a description of the loading of a brick kiln with the bricks in piles of 17, but with reconsideration the second entry of 30,600 would seem far too large for one kilnful and the phrase 'at ye brick kiln' would suggest a geographical location rather than a listing of content. A possible interpretation is that these figures represent a very rare description of the method by which bricks were stacked in a 'brickhill'. Thus, the first entry describes a cuboid measuring 8⅓ feet by 17 feet by 100 bricks giving a total of 14,110, (14,070 in the document), the second entry gives a cuboid of 30,600, whilst the third entry gives a total of 17,850. The use of the word 'pitches' as a description of a pile of bricks would seem to be unique and is possibly of local dialect as the *Oxford English Dictionary* contains no appropriate reference in its nine pages of definitions.

---

154 Field, J., *English Field Names, A Dictionary*, Newton Abbot: David & Charles, (1972), 29.
155 Ekwall, E., *The Concise Oxford Dictionary of English Place-Names*, 4th ed. Oxford: OUP (1960), 64. A survey of five nineteenth-century Scotch kilns at Fordingbridge Brick works, Sandalheath, Hampshire, showed four of them were built into slightly rising ground. Hammond, 'Brick Kilns', 174.
156 SRO, D615 P(A)/1/8.
157 Kingman, M., 'The Building Notebook of Charles Trubshaw of Colwich, Staffordshire, 1753-56', *BBSI* **111**, (November, 2009), 17-20.

The Hovel

Often included in contracts for brick and tile was the provision of a '*hovel*' for the brickmaker.[158] It was a semi-permanent building which was easily erected. In 1763 on the Staunton Harold Estate Thos. Richards was paid £2 2s 4d 'for taking Down and putting up the Brickhovel'. The documentary evidence suggests that it had two different uses. It was probably used as a brick-moulding shed where the shelter provided by the hovels was important. In the summer of 1725 Francis Chambre, the steward at the Hawkstone Estate of Richard Hill reported, 'the brick and tile is not yet made, nor could it possibly be because of the bad weather, without the charge of Hovels to work under'.[159] It may also have been employed for storing damp and unfired bricks and tiles for as long as three or four weeks or until the green bricks were sufficiently dried to be fired. This was an important process; clay had to be dried before firing to allow for economical firing with reduced cracking, shrinkage and waste.

The contract previously mentioned between Thomas Allen and John Edwards included the requirement that 'also that the sd Tho Allen shall build in the Brom furlong a hovill 12 foot wide & 18 foot long for the said John Edwards to dry tiles in'.[160] Houghton describes how the process of manufacture was continued, 'then comes a little boy about twelve or sixteen years old and takes away three of these bricks and pallats and lays them upon a hackstead, a raised place where they were covered in straw' for a period later defined as 'for 3 weeks or a month'.[161] Evidence for the existence of such a raised area in Midland hovels is rare, but the Giffard accounts of 1728/9 do include reference to the brickmaker being paid 'for wheeling the clay down to the Corhack'.[162]

William Anson's 'Brickman' accounts of 1699 also reveal the making of a 'Hovell' at a cost of 14s and the purchase of 36 sheaves of 'Heath' (heather)

---

158 SRO, D(W)260/M/E/116, p, 324. The word 'hovel' was not exclusive to brickmaking and possessed a general meaning as a poor-quality shed or temporary building. At Yoxall in 1612 the curate's house included a 'hovill with 3 beefe', SRO, L, B/V/6 Y1. In the same village in 1712 part of a hovel and a shed on the waste land were rented for one penny, SRO, L, D/15/1/4/6. Near Rushall there was a 'hovel' attached to a furnace, SRO, D260/M/T/1/78. There was a 'pot hovel' in Briery Ridding, SRO, D3272/1/8/2/1-2 and references to a 'carthovel' and 'Waggon hovel Close' in Warwickshire. WRO, CR1368 4/39 and CR8/36.
159 SA, 112/1/2717.
160 SRO, D(W)1742/46.
161 Houghton ii, vi, 186, 396.
162 SRO, D593/634.

and straw 'to thatch it'. At Malvern Hall 60 thraves of straw were required to thatch the 'Tyle Hovill'. At Teddesley Hall in 1753 the 'Brick Hovel' was thatched with '300 bundles of Heath to secure the Bricks'.[163] On the Paget Estate at Beaudesert several hovels were erected during a period of intense building in the 1570s and 1580s. In 1578 under the heading of 'The charges of the Brycke wall', the Bailiff, William Warde, recorded the payment of 2s 'for the makynge of the hovell'.[164] Undated but probably in 1581, Warde noted a payment of viiis 'to Lipkyne for setting up other hovells'.[165] The size of the hovel is rarely given but at Malvern Hall, Solihull, the Greswold steward recorded, 'To John Coal for setting up Tyle Hovill at Thickbroms which was a Leven Bays at 11s 5d a bay £6 1s 0d', later that year he was paid £2 10s for thatching the hovel at 5s per bay, these figures would suggest a building at least 100 feet long.[166] This may have been unusually large for a rare Staffordshire reference from Newcastle-under-Lyme in 1712 describes the new hovel as '30 feet long'.[167]

Clay and Brick Earth

In 1987 Ian Smalley attempted to produce 'a more rigorous definition for the term "brickearth" and to show that the distribution of a geologically distinct loessic brickearth had a significant influence on the location of early brick buildings in the southern and eastern parts of England'.[168] Smalley emphasised that the major deposits of loessic brickearths were in the Middle and Lower Thames Valley. Similarly in eastern England Smalley's explanation for early brick buildings is the presence of isolated deposits of loess. T.P. Smith has posed the question 'Why did the wealthy men of State and Church not build in brick outside eastern England?'[169] Smalley's answer was 'that the brickearth used by medieval brickmakers is not found in exploitable deposits outside

---

163   SRO, D(W)260/M/E/116, 32.
164   SRO, D(W)1734/3/4/106.
165   SRO, D(W)1734/3/3/270. In 1728, Peter Giffard 'Paid Anthony Spicer for felling a parcel of Alder Poles for building the Brick Hovell' and 'Joseph … for 140 Broome Kidds for thatching ye said Hovell'. SRO, D590/634.
166   WRO, CR299/536.
167   Newcastle-under-Lyme, Corporation Order Book, Vol. 1669-1712, 159.
168   Smalley I., 'The Nature of "Brickearth" and the Location of Early Brick Buildings in Britain', *BBSI*, **41**, (February, 1987), 4-11.
169   Smith, *Medieval Brickmaking*, 6.

eastern England'. Smalley further developed this argument by suggesting that it was 'nineteenth and twentieth century technology which gave us access to the Keuper Marls (Mercian Mudstones) of the English Midlands'.

In 1988 R. and P. Firman responded to Smalley's article.[170] Their interpretation of the location of early brick buildings is radically different from that of Professor Smalley. They concluded that most early bricks were made from 'fine grained sticky … muds and clays … We maintain that the overwhelming weight of evidence indicates that loessic brickearth was rarely used prior to 1440 and was an uncommon, localised source material for at least a hundred years after that date'. They suggest that a wide range of materials were employed including glacial tills (boulder clay) silts, muds and alluvial clays, the deposits actually used '… are not restricted to eastern England … Factors other than the distribution of suitable raw materials must, therefore, also have controlled the distribution of the brick industry'. The importance of their conclusions is that although they allow that a good correlation exists between the paucity of freestone and the distribution of brick, 'exceptions do occur where *the whim of the builder or his client*, (my italics) or both, demanded brick'. Their explanation for that 'whim' is, in their phrase, one of 'Keeping up with the Jones's', i.e. there was a social dimension alongside one of material availability.

In the Midlands there were two sources of material, fluvial deposits and a range of clays, without fabric analysis the original material is difficult to identify. There are no documentary sources for the early use of river muds but it may not be a coincidence that the very early Prior's Tower at Repton stands within yards of the River Dove and that the initial building at Beaudesert did not use bricks from the well-resourced Cannock Chase but from Brereton on the River Trent. An unusual court case in 1653 at Coventry required the defendant to drain the moat around his premises. The mud from the moat required 3,000 cartloads and was valued at the huge sum of £50. No specific reference is made but it is possible the mud was for making bricks.[171] Different types of clay could be fired in the same kiln, Firman in his study of the bricks at Wollaton Hall identified bricks 'characterised by a possible tally or identification mark apparently inscribed with a stick along the upper face'. He

---

170 Firman, R., and P., 'Loessic Brickearth and the Location of Early Pre-Reform Buildings in England – An Alternative Interpretation,' *BBSI*, **47**, (1989), 4-14.
171 Coventry RO, PA/101/23.

suggested that possibly they were inscribed so that when the kiln was opened they could be distinguished from bricks made with another clay.[172]

All clays have a common geological source but their deposition and manner of working are diverse and a variety were employed. In Nottinghamshire during the sixteenth century Boulder Clay was fired and later in Shropshire the Silurian Wenlock Shales were used. In Leicestershire and Rutland the heavy clays of the Lower Lias were not widely used for bricks as they contained calcareous fossils that broke down in the kilns to create carbon dioxide bubbles with deleterious effects. In Leicester City the Mercia Mudstones underlie the eastern parts of Leicester and were quarried from the gently rising hillsides east of the Soar Valley. From the seventeenth century the Mercian Mudstone was the most common clay employed in all the counties. These red and earthenware clays contain a relatively high iron content with greater plasticity and lower firing temperature and resulted in red or yellow colouring after firing. The red clays of the East Shropshire coalfield were particularly suitable for brick manufacture. The brick makers in Nottingham and its immediate vicinity used the clay from the strata of red marl overlying the red sandstone on which the town is built, and which in its turn rests on the coal measures. The marl abounds with loose and thin layers of skerry, or impure limestone, and in many places contains veins of gypsum that were extensively worked for the manufacture of plaster of Paris. Some clay had to be washed to remove dispersed gypsum that was liable to form bubbles in the bricks and hence reduce resistance to weathering.

In North Staffordshire 'Red Earth Farm' may have been the site of a kiln which provided bricks for 10 Church St. the most prestigious brick house in the stone town of Leek.[173] The Carboniferous deposits of the Midland coal measures such as those of the Etruria Formation and the fireclays were regularly used at a time much earlier than has previously been suggested. Robert Plot noted in 1686, 'on a bank by the wayside betwixt Newcastle and Keele where there was a peculiar sort of brick-earth which becomes blue when heated, those bricks only which were placed furthest from the fire having any redness in them'.[174] This was the Etruria Marl which subsequently formed the source of the famous dense and impermeable Staffordshire Blue Brick. Brickmaking clays were readily available

---

172 Firman, R., 'Notes on Wollaton Hall Bricks', in Marshall, P., *Wollaton Hall, An Archaeological Survey,* Nottingham: Nottingham Civic Society, (1996), 114.

173 SJ, 972592.

174 Plot, R., *Natural History of Staffordshire* (1686), reprinted Manchester: Morten, E.J. (1973), 120.

over the region but variations in their physical properties, colour, hardness and mineral content made some deposits better than others. Some clays were unsuitable for brickmaking because they were too calcareous and fusible. The skill of the local brickmaker lay in his awareness of the differences for not all these deposits produced bricks similar in colour or other characteristics. For the rebuilding of a house at Holdgate, Salop, in 1730 it was noted that 'the clay is not very good for brickmaking but there is some 1 mile away which is suitable'.[175] On the line of the Chesterfield Canal the directors hoped to fire 3 million bricks from their own kilns, from 1774 they were compelled to seek supplies from private brickmakers for 'Bricks cannot be completed by reason of the poverty and bad quality of the Clay'.[176] In Birmingham it was recorded that 'the local clay does not readily make bricks suitable for cutting … and the gauged work was confined to arches and radiated lintels of windows'.[177] However Birmingham had other advantages, as the Swedish visitor Svedenstierna noted in 1802, 'a kind ohf clay is found, especially at the end of town, which is already mixed by nature with the proportion of sand necessary for good bricks and no further effort is needed beyond digging out the clay'.[178]

The amount of clay required is difficult to determine, R.W. Brunskill has estimated that '3 cu yds of clay was considered to be sufficient to make 1,000 bricks while one acre of clay 2 feet thick could supply clay for 1,000,000 bricks'.[179] Gerbier in 1663 estimated that 'six foot in length, three foot in breadth, and three foot in depth, which makes one thousand of Bricks'.[180] John Houghton in 1684 estimated that '1 yard deep 2 yards square will make 1,000 bricks'.[181] Contemporary records rarely list the clay obtained other than in 'yards'

---

175 Quoted in Barley, M., *The Buildings of the Countryside, 1500-1750,* Cambridge: CUP, (1990) 84. Rice, M.A., *Abbots Bromley*, Wilding and Son, (1939), 211. Miss Rice recorded an interview with a retired nineteenth-century brickmaker. He emphasised that Abbots Bromley bricks were made from loam and those from nearby Hoar Cross were based on marl. For him the loam produced harder and superior bricks.
176 Richardson, C., ed. *Minutes of the Chesterfield Canal Company, 1771-80,* Derbyshire Record Society, (1996), 77.
177 Ball, J.L., 'Eighteenth-Century Houses in Birmingham', *The Architectural Review*, (1907), 176. Quoted in Walker, B., 'Some Eighteenth-Century Birmingham Houses', *TBAS*, **LVI** (1932), 17.
178 Svedenstierna, E.T., trans. Dallow, E.L., *Svedenstierna's Tour of Great Britain, 1802-3*, Newton Abbot: David and Charles, (1973), 120.
179 Brunskill, R.W., *Brick Building in Britain,* London: Weidenfield & Nicholson (1997), 22.
180 Gerbier, B., *Council and Advise to all Builders,* London: Thomas Mabb, (1663), 55.
181 Houghton, 394.

with little indication of the depth which was dug. Frustratingly typical are the detailed accounts of Richard Hoe, village brickmaker of Hose, Leicestershire. In 1800 there were '692 yards of Clay getting', in 1801 '600 Yardes Clay getting' and in 1802 484 yards of clay were dug. Respectively in those years 185,050, 137,000 and 171,433 bricks and several thousands of tiles were sold.[182]

The exact relationship between 'yards' of clay and bricks is difficult to determine for as many as 15-20% of bricks fired could be wasted or broken.[183] As late as 1839 an Act which tidied up a range of brick duties automatically allowed for 10% of all bricks which were fired to be subsequently damaged. The number of bricks which could be fired was important to those estate owners who leased their lands in expectation of royalty payments. In 1809 a valuation of the Gough Estate, Edgbaston, produced these valuable estimates:

29 bricks per Yard of Clay, Calculation 1,460 bricks in one sq yard depth of mine 1½ yards is 690 Bricks under each surface yard. One acre contains 4,840 sq yards multiply by 600 allowing 90 for waste there is 2,904,000 Bricks made from each acre which supposing the mine rents at 1/6d per thousand amounts to £217 10s per acre.

Gough also added that '1½ bricks make 1 quarry', i.e. clay for one quarry tile will make 1½ bricks.[184] These very optimistic calculations, nearly three times greater than those of R.W. Brunskill, have one weakness in that they do not include the time period in which nearly three million bricks could be produced. The proposed income from 250,000 bricks p.a. would only be earned over nearly 12 years.

The Colour of Brick

In 1994 R.J. Firmin reported on the complex chemistry of clays and brickearths and isolated nine factors which influenced the colours of early bricks. In historic bricks almost all varied hues were due to the presence of iron. Most bricks were some shade of red or pink but could vary according to the state of the

---

182 Kingman, M., 'An Unusual Collection of Leicestershire Brickmaking Accounts, 1776-1809', *BBSI*, **131**, (2015), 6-17.
183 Lucas, R., 'The Tax on bricks and Tiles 1784-1850: its Application to the Country at large, and in particular the County of Norfolk', *Construction History Society*, **13**, (1997).
184 BLAC, MS2126/vol/532.

iron, for example in the Leicestershire and Nottinghamshire Wolds a strong iron content produced bright red bricks, in the north of Nottinghamshire the bricks are browner. In Staffordshire to the north and west of Stone, the bricks are of dark purple-brown, the colour of old copper.[185] An interesting example of their use is at Fradswell where the west tower of the church was built in 1764 of purple brick. In South Staffordshire some buildings were built in a predominantly brown brick, for example, the parsonage at Himley of c.1700. In Bridgnorth brown bricks were used at 10 Northgate. In the area around Newcastle-under-Lyme plum-coloured bricks are found as at Ye Olde House, Madeley, which was refaced about 1700. The presence of manganese dioxide had the effect of producing browns and blacks in otherwise red brick. The reaction of dolomite with iron in the form of haematite produced yellow or paler colours. In Leicestershire yellow and red chequer work is common in the villages around Barksby and Hungarton.

Other key factors included the position of the bricks in the kiln, dark headers could be over-burnt samples, although whether this was deliberate or accidental is not known. In the early kilns or clamps fired by heathland vegetation, heather or gorse gave off potash fumes which glazed the ends of some bricks. In wood fuelled kilns the same effect was created by vaporised soot. These vitrified or 'flared' bricks were used to form patterns in diaper or chequer work and are mainly associated with the sixteenth and early seventeenth centuries, as at Quenby Hall of 1621. But as late as 1670 the huge Sudbury Hall was built in a traditional conservative style with walls patterned with headers and in Leicestershire Twycross House, Twycross, has a front of red and blue bricks dated 1703 with a similarly late frontage at 19 Lichfield Street, Tamworth. At 33 Brook Street, Wymeswold, is a late example of diaper work in an early eighteenth-century house. Jonathan Foyle has suggested that such diaper work was a fashion which originated in Venice and was brought to London by Mediterranean trading contacts from the fourteenth century and was used initially in grand houses and palaces before becoming a decorative feature of smaller houses.[186]

---

185   Clifton-Taylor, A., ed. Simmons, J., *The Pattern of English Building,* 4th ed, London: Faber and Faber, (1987), 232.

186   Foyle, J., Some examples of external colouration on English brick buildings, c.1500-1650. *Bulletin du Centre de recherche du château de Versailles,* (2007), Para. 18.

Chapter 4

BRICK PRODUCTION 1437-1780

*'Don't be afraid! We won't make an author of you, while there's
an honest trade to be learnt, or brick making to turn to.'*
Oliver Twist

The Brickmaker

IN TERMS of the available evidence for the adoption of brick, one approach is the impressionistic picture created by references to brick kilns and to individual brickmakers. It is difficult to generalise about the number and economic status of Midland brickmakers over a lengthy period. Between 1500 and 1660 relatively few brickmakers can be individually identified, many were itinerant and left little or no record of their origins, income or standing in the community. The earliest reference may possibly be that contained within a Rental of 1398 of the chantries of St Leonard's church at Bridgnorth which lists 'De' Henrico Brykman' alongside other occupational names such as 'Jacobo Hatman' and 'Matheo Sherman'.[187] Another early named Midland brickmaker is Robert Bird of Lichfield mentioned in 1466. At Kirby Muxloe castle in 1481-83 John Ellis and his foreman John Faux were employed at the building.[188] An early reference in Staffordshire to itinerant brickmakers is contained within the will of 1544 of John Spenser of Uttoxeter, 'Mr. Blount oweth me for bordyng hys brekemakers 20s'.[189]

---

187 Maxwell Clark, 234.
188 Hamilton Thompson, 196.
189 Woolley, P., *Seven Studies in the Economic and Social History of Uttoxeter and its Adjacent Rural Parishes, 1530-1830*, (1995), 40. These men were probably working on Blount Hall.

The expertise of East Anglian brickmakers occasionally surfaces, in 1601 Sir Charles Cavendish of Bolsover Castle sent a servant named Edmund 'into norfolk for the brickmen'.[190] Tracing details of their employment and scale of manufacture is a difficult task. Sir John Leveson employed a brickmaker named Cempe for one season in 1614 on his Lilleshall Estate but there are no further references to him.[191] More detailed information is available from 1575 when 'Marston of Lychfyeld' and 'Braddock of Brerreton' were identified as suppliers to Sir William Paget at Beaudesert. Braddock was obviously a permanent brickmaker for in 1590 a parcel of land for 'making bricks and tile' was demised to him for 21 years.[192] The Marston name reappears in a petition to the Staffordshire Quarter Sessions of 1589:

> … *your Orator John Tomkys late of Bylston in the county of Staffs gentleman and Edward Marston of Yardley in County of Wigorn Brickmaker.*
>
> … *that whereas the persones & inhabitants dwelling and resident in & about the townes p(ar)ishes and hamlettes of Bylston Wolverhampton Willnall Wednesbury Wednessfielde and other townes and places thereabout in the County of Staffs aforesaide are enforsed for theyr p(ro)vision of bricke & tyle to sende to sundrye remote places in the County of Worcester some distant from them to theyre both greate charge & trouble yt would more please you the premisses considered to grant licence to the sayde Edward Marston to build & erect one cottege in a pasture called Gorstye Croft lying to a place called Gosterne in Wolverhampton aforesayde being p(ar)cell of the land & inheretance of the said John Tomkys for the habitacon of the sayde Edward the one and others for the better provision theareby heareafter of brick & tyle to be by hym & others made for the sayde township.*[193]

The importance of the above petition lies in the suggestion that there was a demand for brick in Wolverhampton and its hinterland and that demand was not met by local production.[194] The petition may, of course, exaggerate

---

190   NA, DD3P 14.19.
191   SRO, D868/1/65.
192   WRO, CR162/249.
193   SRO, QSR/21, Michaelmas, 1589.
194   But there was brick production in or near Walsall as early as 1589. SRO, D 260/M/F/1/5, 3d.

the situation for there were several large brick houses such as Wednesbury 'Old House', Willington Hall and John Leveson's 'Great Hall' built in the area described by the petitioners. North and east of Wolverhampton the land is covered in clay and clayey/sandy drift material which could be used for brick making, but was underlain by the stiff carboniferous clays of the Middle Coal Measures. Was it technologically difficult to fire these local clays? Where brick was provided it apparently came from the traditional brick and tile producing areas of North Worcestershire, possibly from Yardley or Kings Norton. The additional transport costs must therefore have been a deterrent to its increased use. Either Tomkys or Edward Marston, a member of a traditional brickmaking family, had seen the opportunity and in partnership were attempting to meet a perceived demand. Unfortunately, there is no recorded response from the Quarter Sessions. Whitehead describes the parish of Yardley as 'one of the earliest continuous centres of brick and tile making in the West Midlands', and argues that by 'the late 16th century the industry was in a flourishing state'.[195] Amongst the yeoman/tilemakers of that parish was William Mars(t)on.

The evidence of debts and of those listed as executors in probate inventories suggests a network of bricklayers and brick and tilemakers throughout North Worcestershire. In Worcester a family of brickmakers called Marson were later called Marston and 'it is tempting to see a relationship between the Worcester and Yardley branches of the Marston family'.[196] It has been suggested that in this predominantly pastoral area the emphasis on stock-rearing allowed and encouraged alternative part-time employment.

Surviving buildings, 'lost' brick buildings and placenames indicate that there were a number of brickmakers in the region. In 1568 a letter to Shrewsbury Corporation from the Council of the Marches ordered the:

> *pressing of four brickmakers and two tilers to be set forward for Ireland, whither the Lord Deputy of Ireland and the Lord President of the Marches are going, who require them for the setting forward of certain works.*[197]

---

195 Whitehead, 42.
196 Whitehead, 42.
197 The Corporation of Shrewsbury: Miscellaneous papers, The Manuscripts of Shrewsbury and Coventry Corporations [etc.]: Fourth report, Appendix: Part **X** (1899), 45-65. In 1610-11 The Privy Council demanded detailed information on the 'great plantation of Ulster' and recorded the numbers of brickmakers employed.

Most are anonymous and unrecorded, and their social standing can only be guessed. There were specialised brickmakers who travelled some distance for employment but generally they tended to be local men who could be called upon during the short periods of the year when their services were required. Inventory evidence reveals men who were titled 'brickmaker' but whose income was mainly derived from farming. Small scale agriculture was a common safety net against hard times for most craftsmen. In his inventory of 1614, the 'brickmaker' Francis Corbett of Anslow had farm stock worth £10 16s from a total of £16. In 1617 John Corbett had bricks and tiles valued at 7s 8d and implements in the house and brickyard valued at 4s 3d. in a total inventory of £15.[198] Henry Greene of Nuneaton the owner of a tile house, who died in 1637, left £28 15s, of which 'trade goods' presumably tiles and bricks were valued at £2 6s 8d and his ten sheep at £2 10s.[199]

Without the corroborative evidence from probate inventories or similar documentation tracing early brickmakers is difficult. They do however make fleeting appearances in the building accounts of large aristocratic or gentry estates. At Coughton Court between 1663 and 1666 seven brickmakers were paid of whom five are named.[200] One, Edward Vize, rented a kiln from Sir Richard Throckmorton in 1685 and supplied bricks to Studley Church in 1688.[201] At Eccleshall four brickmakers or 'brick burners' were recorded during the 1690s at the time of the rebuilding of the Bishop's Palace.[202] At Berkeswell the parish registers recorded the burials of three brickmakers between 1698 and 1706.[203] At Burton-on-Trent, on the Paget Estate, from 1701 to 1770, there were at least four kilns rented by brickmakers.[204]

In other areas there is a surprising lack of activity. Adams et al. have analysed 320 inventories dated between 1564 and 1791 in Cannock, an area of predominantly yeomen/part-time colliers. In this industrially expanding area of

---

198 SRO, L B/C/1, Francis Corbett, 21st September 1614, John Corbett, 26th November, 1617.
199 Gooder, E.A., 'Clayworking in the Nuneaton Area', in Mayes P., and Scott K., 'Pottery Kilns at Chilvers Coton, Nuneaton,' *Society for Medieval Archaeology,* Monograph series **10**, (1984), 13.
200 Moore, 'Coughton', 12-14.
201 'Spernall', *VCH Warks,* **3** *(1945),* 172-174.
202 Spufford, M., *Poverty Portrayed and Gregory King and the parish of Eccleshall,* Keele UP, (1995), 90, 111, 122, 135.
203 *VCH, Warks.* **4**, 27.
204 SRO, D603/K/17/76.

good brick clays and attainable coal deposits there are only two references to the possession of bricks.[205] In Smethwick, a similar industrial settlement, adjacent to Birmingham, there are no references to brickmakers or bricks in any of the surviving inventories from 1647 to 1747.[206] In Chesterfield in the early period of 1520-1603 within 230 inventories there is not a single reference to bricks.[207]

There were exceptions to the picture of small-scale rural producers. In Stratford-upon-Avon in 1567/8 bricks were provided for the Corporation's properties from four sources including Alderman Adrian Quiney, Richard Hall and Ralph Cawdry, all of whom were members of the Corporation. A fourth supplier, Henry Russell, was a Serjeant at the Mace. Such men, particularly Quiney, were highly regarded. It might be argued that they were nominal purchasers on behalf of the Corporation. Quiney, for example, was also responsible for draperies and groceries. He later also provided tiles, gutters and crests (1575/6) but Hall was paid for 'makeing the botomes of ii ovens' in 1575/6 and for mason's work on a chimney in 1580/1.[208]

The Guild

It may be inappropriate to define brickmaking as an industry for generally it lacked structure and organisation, wage rates and prices were individually agreed and most brick making was a traditional, small scale and part-time occupation within an agricultural context. Exceptions to this were in Coventry, Ludlow and Shrewsbury where, uniquely for the Midlands, there were municipal guilds. Brickmaking and bricklaying were relatively late crafts of lower status and in Ludlow and Coventry were incorporated within other guilds, at Ludlow within The Society of Hammermen and in Coventry within the Pinners, Tilers and Coopers. Only in Shrewsbury was there a guild of Carpenters, Brickmakers, Bricklayers, Tylers and Plasters. There, as late

---

205 Adams, D.P., et al. *Probate Inventories of Cannock, 1562-1791*, (nd. c.1975). In 1699 Thomas Green of Little Wyrley possessed 6,000 bricks valued at £2 2s and in 1702 William Henney of Hatherto owned 'one parshall of brick and like 13s 4d'.

206 Bodfish, M., ed. *Probate Inventories of Smethwick Residents, 1647-1747.* Smethwick Local History Soc. (1992). One bricklayer is mentioned, Abraham Powell died with goods worth £57 9s 9d. The majority of his income was earned as an innkeeper.

207 Bestall, D.M., and Fowkes, J.V., 'Chesterfield Wills & Inventories, 1520-1603'. *Derbyshire Record Society,* (1977).

208 Dugdale Society, *Minutes and Accounts of the Corporation of Stratford-upon-Avon and Other Records, 1553-1620.* **II**, *1566-1577*, 8, 104, 106. **III**, *1577-1586*, 79.

as 1780, an important case before the Lord Chief Justice confirmed that brickmaking was restricted to guild members.[209] The status of the companies can be measured by their relative position in the Corpus Christi processions or their financial contributions to the borough. In 1596 in Ludlow the 'Smeeths' (Smiths or Hammermen) were listed fourth of the 11 guilds in a financial assessment. How far the companies with monopoly control of apprenticeship entrance affected prices and production is difficult to ascertain but certainly in Ludlow brickmakers, even if using their own land, required Corporation permission to erect kilns. Women could be guild members usually as inheritors of their husband's business, but they could also be independent members – in 1796 in Coventry, Thomas Burdett was apprenticed to a husband-and-wife team John and Rebecca Cheshire.[210]

In Nottingham the burgesses were men of some status for the membership included most of the local aristocracy and gentry, although for these men the positions were merely honorary. The burgesses had the freedom of the borough and the right to elect Councilmen and Aldermen, although no brickmakers seem to have risen to these exalted positions. Between 1702 and 1760, 38 men listed as 'brickmakers' were enrolled as burgesses all of whom must have served an apprenticeship of seven years as this was a prerequisite for membership strictly enforced by the Council.[211] Several times in this period the title of 'burgess' was removed from men who had illegally claimed to have served a full apprenticeship. Of the 38 brickmakers 26 were recorded as 'Burgess Born', i.e. their fathers were also burgesses, suggesting that brickmaking was very much a family business. This view is supported by the constant repetition of family names. In the list there are six members of the James family, three of the Oakland family, three of the Tomlin family and four of the Elliot family. Thomas Elliott had provided 600 brick for the Council in 1688 and was fined 5s the following year for 'A Brick kilne upon the plaines'.[212] Of the 58 bricklayers 27 were 'Burgess Born' and again must have served a full apprenticeship. Nottingham obviously had an extensive and trained workforce which may well explain the dominance of brick. In 1697 the Earl of Nottingham employed bricklayers

---

209   SA, 177/1/6, 177/1/7.
210   Hoffman T., *The Rise and Decline of Guilds with particular reference to the Guilds of Tylers and Bricklayers in Great Britain and Ireland*, (2007), 25.
211   *NBR*, **VI**, 310-356.
212   *NBR*, **V**, 356.

from London and Reading, but two Nottingham brickmakers were hired to burn bricks for his great mansion at Burley.[213]

In other towns brick building may have been hindered by the restrictive practices of the Guilds and the civic Corporations. Leicester provides an example of a community which only slowly adopted brick, and which was hostile to 'foreigners' bringing new trades to the City. Nobody other than freemen could practise a trade and the cost of this status was the considerable sum of £20, an amount raised to £30 in 1746. This increase provoked a considerable reaction and following the loss of an expensive court case, in which Leicester sought to maintain the old traditions, all restrictions on freemen were ended.

Apprenticeships

It is revealing that before 1780 there are very few examples of boys or girls apprenticed to brickmaking. The Apprenticeship Books held by the Commissioners of Stamps contain the tax paid on thousands of apprenticeships, but between 1710 and 1810 only four brickmaking apprenticeships were recorded for the whole of Staffordshire.[214] In the small village of Gnosall 178 apprenticeship bonds survive from the period 1691-1816, yet not one person was apprenticed to brickmaking despite a flourishing local trade.[215]

An apprenticeship charity established by German Pole of Radbourne Hall, Derbyshire, provided the premiums for one apprentice per year from six local villages. Between 1685 and 1753, 285 boys and girls were supported, the most common occupations were tailors (55) and cordwainers (42), 41 different trades were listed in which only one brickmaker and two bricklayers were registered.[216] The Warwickshire records for indentures registered at London between 1710-1760 include only 26 references to brickmaking and allied trades.[217] Arguments *e silentio* often require caution and Joan Lane has noted that 'There were some quarter of a million apprenticeships entered in the years 1710-1762 but there

---

213 Hahakkuk, Sir J., 'Daniel Finch, 2nd Earl of Nottingham: His House and Estate', *Rutland Record*, **10**, (1990), 350.

214 Ex. info. Diane Shenton who has compiled an index to all Staffordshire entries. dshenton@btopenworld.com.

215 Cuttack, S.A., ed., 'The Gnosall Records, 1679-1837', *SHC*, (1936). 157 children were apprenticed to 'Husbandry' or 'Housewifery'.

216 Briggs, W.G., 'Records of an Apprenticeship Charity, 1685-1753', *DAJ*, **74**, (1954), 50-52.

217 Lacock, M., 'The Development of the Building Trades in the West Midlands', *Construction History*, **8**, (1992), 9.

is evidence of considerable under-registration'.[218] She states that indenture and apprentice registers were not always well maintained particularly when the children were pauper apprentices and 'It is apparent that certain unhealthy trades, such as hat making or brickmaking were highly pauperised'.[219] In Lichfield printed apprenticeship forms were specifically produced for 'a poor child' and one surviving example is for brickmaking with the child serving to the age of 24.[220] In Warwickshire, between 1700 and 1834, 93% of all apprentices to brickmaking were pauper apprentices.[221] Jack Simmons in his study of Leicester notes that 'Apprentices connected with brick making do not figure often in records – less than forty names appear before 1770'.[222] By comparison with other Midland counties this was a relatively strong formal commitment to the trade. In London, according to *The Information of Parents, and Instruction of Youth in their choice of business*, of 1747, 'The Brick-Maker's Business is by some not reckoned a very reputable Employment … It is a very laborious Business, *and though they take no apprentices* (my italics) … The best Hands make good wages … in dry Weather'.[223] The apprentice generally paid to learn his or her trade which was acquired by imitation of the master. Most apprentices were boys but in Warwickshire in 1755 a girl, Sarah Saunders, paid an apprentice premium of £7 to master bricklayer in Solihull.[224] The usual indenture premium was between £4 and £10 but a rare survival of an apprentice subsidy was the annual payment of £20 from 'Mr. Lloyd's money', left, by his bequest, to the Bailiffs and Burgesses of the Borough of Bridgnorth, 'for the benefit of young tradesmen'. In 1756 it was paid to 2 brickmakers and one mason.[225]

The Status of Brickmakers

Because it was a seasonal occupation and employment was not consistently available, the status of the brickmaker varied considerably perhaps depending

---

218 Lane, J., *Apprenticeship in England, 1600-1914*. London: UCL Press, (1996), 4.
219 Lane, 86.
220 Personal possession of the author.
221 Lane, 83.
222 Simmons, J., *Leicester Past and Present*, **1**, London; Eyre Methuen, (1974), 100.
223 Campbell, R., *The London Tradesman, being a compendious view of all the Trades, Professions and Arts … Calculated for the Information of Parents, and Instruction of Youth in their choice of business*, (1747), 169.
224 Hoffman, 24.
225 SA BB/C/7/7/1/25.

on the alternative employment. How did employers regard the brickmaker? Brickmaking was a new trade in the occupational structure of the country. Were its practitioners perceived as skilled craftsmen or day labourers with a basic proficiency? Late seventeenth century England was a highly stratified society with marked inequalities of wealth, status and power. Contemporary writers describe a society obsessed with social status. For brickmakers this could be reflected in the way in which they were addressed or recorded. Possibly at the lowest level were the frequent references to 'The Brickman' where the man was defined by his occupation and not even by a Christian or surname. As early as 1469 'the Brickmen' were recorded at Chester. Slightly more highly regarded was the use of a Christian name which allowed for individual recognition, in the 1580s the Paget Estate paid cash to 'Harald the brickmaker'. Within the Midland brick accounts are occasional references to the title 'Mr'. As early as 1589 the Persehowse Memorandum Book recorded, 'imprimis to Mr Skevington for xix thousand of brycke after viis i p the thousand'.[226] Is this evidence of brickmakers trying to improve themselves and seeking higher social regard? Philip Stubbes, in a contemporary diatribe, for example railed against the presumption of people lower on the social scale:

> *that now adayes euery Butcher, Shooemaker, Tailer, Cobler, Husband-man, and others; yea, euery Tinker, pedler, and swinherd, euery Artificer and other, gregarii ordinis, of the vileft forte of Men that be, muft be called by the vain name of 'Maifters' at euery woorde.*[227]

The Giffard family of Chillington Hall in 1720 kept 'The account of Bricks Carried to Long Birch', which was a large manor house owned by the family, the entries include:

> *From Mr Clemson's Kiln at Tetnall by Mr Thomas Dods 7,600 at 6s per 1,000*
> *Mr Pitts Carryed 4,800*
> *John Reynolds Carryed 5,900*
> *From Mr Hall's Kiln at Tetnall*
> *From Brewood Kiln which is Mr George Sansoms*
> *From Mr Charles Fowler Esq his kiln at Penford*

---

226 SRO, D 260/M/F/1/5, 3d.
227 Stubbes, P., *'Anatomy of Abuses,'* (1583), 122.

Was the designation 'Mr' a mark of courtesy or were the kilns possessed by farmers or local gentry and worked by others whose identity was subsumed under the ownership of the kiln? Certainly, Charles Fowler was an important landowner who lived at Penford Hall. Is this the explanation for the title being omitted for John Reynolds? On the other hand, there are subsequent references to Thomas Dods and Pitts carrying bricks and being paid as conventional carriers.[228]

Small-scale brick producers often lacked the capital and a consistent market to support anything other than modest enterprises, for example, at Hoe, near Melton Mowbray, Richard Hose between 1781 and 1809 on average fired about 175,000 bricks per year, enough for four or five houses.[229] The larger scale brickmakers with greater resources could generate wealth and accompanying social approval. In the poll book for the 1761 election at Tamworth five brickmakers are listed, three of these are members of the Patrick family who worked 'Patrick's Brickiln Close' in Wilnecote.

In the extensive correspondence concerning the 1766 general election, Lord Townshend described in graphic detail how, by pressure on relatives, debtors, neighbours, by the offer of posts in the army and the Church for sons or relatives of voters and by the purchase of houses to which voting rights were attached, he hoped to secure the seat for his nominee. He noted that, 'Thos Patrick desires some land as soon as it can be spared and witness John Bakers promise to Vote for me', this is signed Thos Patrick. Later in a list of voter intentions it was suggested that 'Joseph Patrick will not promise til he sees how he likes the land he took last Spring'.[230] Here are brickmakers, apparently totally independent of a major aristocrat, negotiating with him almost as equals. In 1750 Thomas Munn, uniquely named as the 'The Gentleman Brick-maker', was executed for smuggling and robbing the *Yarmouth Mail*.

For the entrepreneurial brickmaker the increased demand for bricks provided a stimulus for greater capital investment. The inventory of Richard Harrison of Babworth in 1742 included kilns at Askham, Eaton Moor, Forest and Worksop. His total stock included 106,000 bricks and 7,500 tiles with one kiln valued at £1 10s and the others, with their hovels, at over £3 each. Included in the valuation are references to the presence of 'deals', i.e., building timbers which

---

228   SRO, D590/633/1.
229   Kingman, 'Leicestershire Brickmaking Accounts', 6-16.
230   SRO, D187/2/8/132.

suggests that Harrison was also a builder. Of significance is that the inventory was appraised in January and thus provides a rare example of bricks being held in stock in anticipation of demand. In a total valuation of £102 3s 6d the bricks, tiles, kilns and deals were calculated at £71 13s. i.e., 70% of his assessed wealth.

The example above reflects the more obvious change in status and individual wealth after 1660. The small-scale independent producer is still common for example in a contract in 1689 when Rowland Heathly of Coventry was contracted to produce 40,000 bricks for Humphrey Parrott of Bell Hall, Belbroughton, using the Bell Hall clay.[231] Increasingly however the urban brickmaker expanded his wealth and extended his trade by investment in property and by building for himself.

As early as 1651 John Patten, a Nottingham brickmaker, bequeathed in his will three houses, one of which became a small almshouse.[232] Robert Walker of Mickleover, near Derby, in 1663 left 'land', a house with 'Roomes' and £62 15s in cash. Earlier in 1656 an indenture had described him as a 'yeoman' and referred to 'his houses' as he bought land for £40.[233] Gilbert Oakes of Derby in 1667 left personal possessions worth £66 0s 2d but his will refers to a 'Cottage house or tenement' let to a joiner, a 'Messuage, Burgage or Tenement which I lately bought and builded', a further house and 14½ acres of arable land. Humphrey Deakyn of Tamworth in 1663 left an estate valued at only £5 15s 3d but his will included a 'messuage or tenement lately purchased'. The will of Richard Garnett of Nuneaton in 1690 included a 'lately purchased house (in the Abbey) and own house'. The second most valuable possession of the 'mason' Richard Shepherd of Hartshorne, South Derbyshire, in 1673 was 'The reversion of the leases of the Brickhouse £10 00 00'. In 1684, Thomas Tyder of Shrewsbury had an 'old house' and a 'new building'. His estate was valued at £48 2s 6d of which in his 'Brickyard,' burnt and unburnt bricks, tiles, crests and gutters at £10 13s 6d formed 22% of his total estate. In 1694 John Guest of Birmingham had an estate valued at only £5 yet his will included 'my houses' and the 'house on new street'. One of the wealthiest brickmakers was Godfrey Hazelhurst, the lengthy inventory of this South Normanton coal owner in 1689 valued his possessions at £1,228 10s 6d and included a 'Brick Kill'.[234]

---

231 SBPT, DR10/1476.
232 Orange, J., *History and Antiquities of Nottingham,* Nottingham, (1840), 586.
233 DRO, 5549/6/13/2.
234 SRO, B/C/5/1692/33.

In the Consistory Court of Lichfield between 1650 and 1700 are listed the wills of 18 men who saw themselves, or were seen by others, as brickmakers. Analysis of the diocesan evidence reveals that 12 men inhabited towns or cities, with four in Derby and six in North Warwickshire. These were not the only brickmakers, there were many others who did not leave a will or were not so described, perhaps because it was a seasonal occupation and they saw themselves as mainly involved in another trade or occupation. For example the 1689 inventory of Thomas Owen of Bordesley describes him as both 'brickmaker' and 'yeoman'. He possessed a huge house and an estate worth £257 13s 7d.

Before 1660 brickmaking was predominantly a rural occupation based on aristocratic or gentry estates. Christopher Chalklin suggests that as late as 1750-1820 more than half of all new buildings were erected in the countryside and before 1750 the proportion must have been much greater.[235] A new demand was, however, that created by the fashion for brick-built houses, or the refronting in brick of timber-framed houses, in towns and cities. For brickmakers this was a new market and for many it provided opportunities not just as providers of bricks but to actively participate in the wholesale development of new urban landscapes.

In the larger towns and cities bricklayers and brickmakers often had sufficient capital or could borrow sufficient capital to lease building plots and develop them. For example, Samuel Avery, a bricklayer, leased a plot on the newly opened Colmore Estate in Birmingham in 1747 and built four houses on half the land and leased the rest to a carpenter and joiner. In Lichfield the Orton (Alton) family provide an excellent example of the brickmaker/property developer. In 1679 John Orton fulfilled the traditional role of the brickmaker in supplying bricks for the rebuilding of Lichfield Grammar School. In 1733 the Town Council recorded the enterprise of his son, James, who:

hath at his own costs and charges erected and built a house and three or four bayes of building upon the piece of land in Wade Street upon which Land where the said house now stands a barne formerly stood … lately burnt down.[236]

---

235 Chalklin, C.W., *The Provincial Towns of Georgian England, a study of the building process 1740-1820,* London: Edward Arnold, (1974), xi.

236 SRO, LD77/9/39.

From 1758 there survives a mortgage assignment between 'Richard Orton brickmaker and Nicholas Deakin, gent.[237] Deakin was an important city official having been Lord Mayor in 1734, Chamberlain in 1737 and Sheriff in 1739. This was an interesting relationship which seems to have been based on Deakin lending money to finance Orton's property developments. In 1754 it was noted that, 'and whereas the said Richard Orton often hath occasion to Borrow Money of the said Nicholas Deakin in order to enable him the said Richard Orton to negotiate his affairs and business'. The guarantee for the loan was 'those two little houses or tenements adjoining together and Situate, standing & being in Wade Street … which said premises were heretofore purchased by the said Richard Orton and Mary his wife of and from Theophilus Levett Gentleman'.[238] This would suggest that Orton now had three houses in Wade Street purchased with funds provided by Deakin. A similar partnership was recorded in Nottingham where in 1706 John Cole, gentleman, and Joseph Baker, carpenter, agreed to rebuild 'with brick a substantial tenement' at The Fox and Crown on Bridlesmith Gate.[239]

The Role of Women in Brickmaking

Maurice Barley has suggested that 'women no doubt helped particularly with tempering and as general labourers … Skill was required primarily by the moulders and those who built and loaded kilns'.[240] 'In the building trades of northern England 'women appear as general labourers, carrying sand and water and other low-grade tasks'.[241] On the Littleton Estate at Teddesley, 'Roger's wife' was paid 4s 6d for 'unloading bricks',[242] and on the Walsall demesne of the Dowager Countess of Mountrath in 1766 the steward 'Paid a Woman for Carrying Water to and Watering Brick at Woodward's house 6d'.[243] Similarly at the building of Etruria in 1770, two women were paid 6d per day for 'Watering Brick'. The Ingestre Estate cash book of 1724 however contains very rare references to the employment of women, there Mary Hackett moulded 18,000 bricks between 4th June and 29th

---

237   SRO, LD78/8/8.
238   SRO, LD77/8/8.
239   NA, M12922.
240   Barley, M.W., 'Rural Building in England' in Thirsk, J., ed. *The Agrarian History of England and Wales, V 1640-1750*. Cambridge: CUP, (1984), 597.
241   Woodward, D., *Men at Work. Labourers and building craftsmen in the towns of northern England, 1450-1750*, CUP, (1995), 85.
242   SRO, LD260/M/E/116, 60.
243   SRO, D1287/G/6.

July 1724. She was paid at the same rate as the male moulders, i.e., 2s 6d per 1,000.[244] Such a level of payments was high for both men and women, Neve noted that 'in the country, their usual Price is 6d per 1,000 for the Molder'.[245] Slightly later in 1803 Svedenstierna recorded that in Birmingham brick moulding was the work of 'only invalids, women and girls'. One girl asserted that with another girl and a boy to wheel the bricks to the kiln they could mould 3,000 per day.[246]

References to women brickmakers as owners or renters of kilns are uncommon but by no means unknown. In July 1694, Edward James of Penkridge paid 'gooddey (widow) Bealoe for 20,700 of brick at £10 7s' and on December 1st he paid 'widow Bealoe for 5,500 brick'.[247] As a widow she may have inherited her husband's kiln. Woodward found in several northern towns, between 1450 and 1750, that a 'small number of women attempted to continue the building enterprises of their late husbands, at times with great success'.[248] In Lord Paget's Burton accounts there is a reference for 1703-4 to a kiln held by a man called Henshaw. The following year it was rented by 'Widow Henshaw'.[249] On the Chetwynd Estate the steward's accounts for 1736 include 'John Lockett senr for Coals used at Goody Machin's Brick Kiln fetcht by Ric Brown and John Layton £1 17s'.[250]

A few women equally may have inherited transport resources. In Nottingham in 1688 'Mistris Jackson' carried brick and tile.[251] At Stratford-on-Avon in 1701 Joshua Smith paid Sarah Wilmore for the carriage of 'Bricks and Tiles'.[252] At Welbeck Abbey in 1727 the accounts recorded 'To the Widow Hancock for the carriage of Sand & Tile £1 5 6'.[253] The voluminous building accounts for Hatton vicarage, 1751-55, include a rare reference to a woman blacksmith or at least owner of a smithy, with Sarah Shakespeare paid for ironwork.[254]

---

244 SRO, D240/E/F/1/2.
245 Neve, 44.
246 Svedenstierna, 87.
247 SRO, D1798/HM/27/2. At Stonor Park, Oxon, in 1758 bricks were supplied by Catherine Shurfield 'kiln woman', Steane, J., *Oxfordshire,* Vintage, (1996), 159.
248 Woodward, 85.
249 SRO, D603/F/1/ 5, see p. 303.
250 SRO, D1789/HM/Chetwynd, 105.
251 *NBR*, **V**, 348.
252 SBPT, BRU5/3/134d.
253 NA, DDP5/1/1.
254 WRO, CR3134/17/44, 85.

The Size of Bricks

The dating of bricks and brick buildings is highly contentious, bricks were valuable and frequently reused, so often the date of brick manufacture is not necessarily that of the building. For example, when their house was abandoned the Okeover family ordered in 1744 'A Valuation of all the materials in Wimeswold Hall house belonging to Leeke Okeover Esq'. It included 'all the bricks in the wall of the house, allowing for window vacancies, is about 80,000 which I value at 8s per 1,000. The purchaser to take them as they are … £32'.[255] At Elford in 1758 after the demolition of the late sixteenth-century 'Brick House' 34,000 bricks and 6,800 tiles were redistributed amongst the estate tenants.[256] The pocketbooks of William Anson of Shugborough for 1708 and 1710 both contain references to the sale of 'old bricks' at a price identical to that of newly burnt bricks.[257]

Attempts have been made to produce a typology of bricks of the pre-industrial period based on their size and other characteristics.[258] Generally the later the period, the thicker the brick, for example the few very early bricks from excavations at Hulton Abbey, are dated to the thirteenth or fourteenth centuries and have an average thickness of 1¾ inches with a range of 1⅜ inches to 2³⁄₁₆ inches.[259] Such sizes are not a guarantee of date for there are many much later bricks of similar sizes. That the Hulton bricks can be considered early is owing to the imprint of grass on which they were laid to dry which was an early practice, and of fired glaze and lead which suggests that they were burnt in a floor tile kiln. As bricks were almost always priced by the thousand it was in the brickmaker's interest to make bricks as small as possible. (A very rare example of the purchase by weight was the acquisition in 1769 of 16 cwt of bricks from William Hillard for the Ecton copper

---

255 DRO, 231M/E391.

256 BLAC, MS3878/633.

257 SRO, D615 P(A) /1/12.

258 Harley, L.S., 'A typology of brick with numerical coding of brick characteristics', *Journal of the British Archaeological Association*, **38**, (1974), 63-87. Harley also suggested that bricks could be classified by their colour. Variations in the clay or earth and in the firing process make this proposal difficult to apply. For a more recent attempt to date bricks scientifically see Antrobus, A., 'Luminescence Dating of Brick Chimneys', *Vernacular Architecture*, **35**, (2004), 21-31. Luminescence dating is an archaeological technique based on the emission of light from crystalline mineral inclusions such as quartz. The technique may possibly enable the dating of brickwork which is hard to date stylistically.

259 Klemperer and Boothroyd, 86-7, 101.

mine).²⁶⁰ Conversely, after the imposition of a tax on bricks in 1784 brickmakers benefited from making the bricks as large as was conveniently possible. 'Wilkes Gobs' are well known as an attempt by a Measham brickmaker to evade duty by firing bricks which weighed 16-17lbs and were double the size of conventional bricks. In 1794 an officer of the Commissioners of Excise at Nottingham reported to the Treasury 'that the brick-makers are making unusually large bricks to partially evade the new tax'.²⁶¹ How the bricklayers handled these is not recorded.

Parliament in 1571 decreed that the size of a brick within 15 miles of London should be 9 inches x 4½ inches x 2¼ inches and in 1622 James I issued directions 'for the good and true making of bricks, the size to be 9 inches by 4⅜ inches and 2¼ inches in thickness, and to be sold at not more than 8s. the 1,000, at the kiln'.²⁶² In 1725 the brick size was determined to be not less than 9 inches x 4¼ inches x 2½ inches.²⁶³ The size and quality of the bricks was to be enforced by 'Searchers of Brick and Tile' selected by the Quarter Sessions. Primarily this legislation was aimed at the London brickmakers who were notorious for the poor quality of their product, with brick earth bulked out with 'sea coal ashes' and where some bricklayers overcame the problem of cheaper and rough-shaped bricks by pointing, which did not always follow the lines of mortar between the bricks and thus made the bricks look symmetrical and so more expensive. The 'searchers' focused on an area within 15 miles of London which explains their appointment in the counties of Surrey (1727), Essex (1727) and Kent (1742) but not their creation in Gloucestershire (1727).²⁶⁴ In 1776 an Act laid down minimum sizes for burnt brick as 8½ inches long, 2½ inches thick and 4 inches wide. At this late date this was the only Act applicable to the whole of England. Before this date the size of provincial bricks was determined by custom, tradition and the requirements of the purchaser, for example, a Nottinghamshire contract of 1749 excessively required 'all to be well burnt and full 10 inches long when burnt, five broad and 2½ inches thick'.²⁶⁵

---

260   Porter, L., *Ecton Copper Mines under the Dukes of Devonshire 1760-1790*. Landmark Publishing, (2004), 108.
261   Treasury in-Letters, T1/740/185.
262   CSPD, Jas I, (1619-23), 459.
263   11 Geo1, cap 35.
264   Gloucestershire Archives, Q/SO/5, Surrey History Centre, QS2/6/1730Xmas/22, 1724-34. Giles Jacob, *A New Law Dictionary* of 1729 lists all the penalties for non-adherence to the statuary requirements for the composition and price of bricks.
265   Barley, *The English Farmhouse and Cottage*, Sutton Publishing, (1987), 207.

It has been suggested that fifteenth-century bricks were often only 2 inches deep or less, late sixteenth-century bricks could be 2¼ inches deep and bricks of the late seventeenth and early eighteenth centuries were often 2½ inches thick.[266] There are however many exceptions to these generalisations. Lloyd in his standard work on English brickwork found many variations in sizes and concluded that 'close scrutiny leads to the conclusion that care was not exercised in the making of moulds and that probably half an inch or even more was a common variation in any of the dimensions'.[267] In a lengthy and formal agreement of 1720 between Lord Gower and a brickmaker, Jonathin Latkin, the difficulties of uniform size were acknowledged. 'He shall & will make all the said Brickes of such size & dimension that the same shall be at least nine inches long four inches & an half broad & two & an half thick when the same are burned … *or as near to the said size as possibly may be & the nature of the Clay will admit*' (my italics).[268] The Teddesley Hall accounts of the Littleton family include a reference to the blacksmith being paid for 'planing Brick Moulds'.[269] For the would-be purchaser the size of the mould was crucial. At Coughton Court in 1664 Sir Francis Throckmorton 'gave to him (the brickmaker) more on condition his Mould should be in size tenn Inches and a half in length and five Inches and a quarter in depth: 00 06s 00'. At Knowle in 1673 the churchwardens provided the tile moulds and sent a parishioner with 'ye quarry molds to ye brick kiln'.[270] In 1684 William Leybourne wrote in his *The Builders Guide*, 'The drying and burning will abate something in the thickness, but little in the breadth, and in the length inconsiderable'.[271] The great variety of brick sizes is confirmed by analysis of the brick measurements taken from the brick used in the construction and the last firing of the eighteenth century kiln at Flintham Hall, Notts, where the bricks ranged in length from 7½ inches to 9⅞ inches with an average of 8½ inches, in width they measured from 4 inches to 5 inches and in thickness from 1½ inches to 2⅝ inches.[272] Some were thus even thinner than bricks attributed to the medieval period. At Anstey, Leicestershire,

---

266 Lloyd, 11.
267 Ibid., 11-12.
268 SRO, D593/N/2/2/3/17.
269 SRO, D260/M/E/116, 258.
270 Downing, 238.
271 Leybourne, W., *The Builders Guide*, (London: 1684), 130.
272 Alvey, 121.

an excavated clamp was dated to the seventeenth or eighteenth centuries by its field context, but the archaeologist concluded that 'the dimensions of those retained (bricks) from the Anstey clamps fall within a range from 13th century to late 18th century'. Parson Roades, in 1676, having observed the sorry state of Blithfield Rectory and considering rebuilding commented 'we had no Brick mad at that time within les than 2 miles and these very small and dear'.[273]

The Range of Bricks Produced
In the Tudor period not only were standard bricks produced but also many in extravagant and elaborate shapes. Prominent were the spiral twisted chimney stacks as at Hampton Court with its 241 chimneys (of which none of the originals survive but follow the decorative tradition of the initial work). Midland examples are rare and usually plainer but one detached chimney survives at Colton, with other examples of the star-shaped section typical of the late sixteenth century at Packwood House, Baddesley Clinton, Pitchford Hall, Benthall Hall and the Old House, Shrewsbury. 'Rubbing brick' was low fired brick earth burnt so that no external 'fireskin' was present and the brick could be more easily cut, filed, carved and rubbed. Such skills were preferred to the use of a mould from which it could be difficult to extract complex shapes.[274] This brick was expensive, for the restoration of Coughton Court between 1663-65 thousands of bricks were made locally but the 'Rubbing Bricke' was brought from Worcester about 18 miles distant at a cost of 3s per horse load.[275] In the Midlands an alternative approach was to saw off all six sides so the original faces were removed. The brick could be rubbed to a smooth surface and precise dimensions by the use of a stone or another harder brick.

Moulded or shaped bricks were expensive and tended to be restricted to the wealthier landowners. In the late seventeenth and eighteenth centuries, determined in part by fashion, style and social pressures, brick became the building material of choice for the 'Middling Classes'. The response of the brickmakers was to produce more sophisticated and fashionable bricks, to make not just 'common' bricks but better-quality products which could be

---

273 SRO, D1386/2/1/5.
274 Lynch, G., and Pavia, S., 'The Characteristics and Properties of Rubbing Bricks used for Gauged Brickwork,' *Journal of Architectural Conservation,* **9**, No. 1, (March 2003), 7-22.
275 Moore, *Coughton,* 14.

incorporated into modish housing. Particularly popular was the use of 'front' bricks, a harder and more polished brick used mainly for the street or road frontage of the house and the use of 'arched' brick for window decoration. For timber-framed houses and cottages brick 'nogging' replaced plaster and mud infill. John Harris in volume two of his *Lexicon Technicum, or a Universal Dictionary of Arts and Science* listed 15 different types of brick although two originated in ancient Greece.[276] In the Midlands the following names of bricks have been recorded:

Table 4: The Range of Bricks Produced

Name	Date	Price (per 1,000)	Notes
Semel	1660	2s 6d	'semel stuff', inventory value
Rubbin*	1665		Rubbing
Nottin	1669		Nogging brick?
Well burnt	1677		Aqualate Estate
Arched-Bricks	1686		As described by Plot
Flooring	1688	15s	Thomas Astbury, Swynnerton
Nogging	1688		Thomas Astbury
Broad	1692	10s	Thomas Astbury
Front	1696		Warwick, following the Great Fire
Hard Burnt	1696	15s	Warwick "
Paving	1696		Warwick "
Somwell	1696	14s	Semel? Although this is a high price for an inferior brick
Smooth	1701		Anson Estate
Long*	1704	250s	Only 2 purchased
Great**	1708		Building at Whitmore

---

276 Harris, J., *Lexicon Technicum, or a Universal Dictionary of Arts and Science*, **2**, 2nd ed. (1723). No pagination.

Skew***	1720	6s	Gower estate
Strong	1727		Hints, Staffs
Hollow	1727	40s	'for laying a drain at Humpstone's in a cellar and at several gates', Cheshire
Kiln	1720	166s 8d	Giffard Estate, Only 18 purchased
Fire	1720		Giffard Estate
Paving	1720	20s	Shrewsbury Town Hall
Furnace	1728	125s	Giffard Estate, Only 8 purchased
Long Arch	1728	85s	Giffard estate
Building	1731	12s	Lichfield
Dresst	1733	18s 4d	Dressed, Gough Estate
Howsing	1739	7s	On the same a/c as below and therefore
Building Brick	1739	10s	of inferior quality
Long	1749	166s	308 purchased
Kinge Brik****	1750		Meerbrook kiln
Floor brick	1750		Meerbrook kiln
Windar	1755	165s	Window? or Windsor (high class facing brick) Endorsed 'for long bricks'
Turf	1755	85s	One dozen only
Cumpass	1758		Curved, used in wells, etc
Pillar	1758		For a feeding shed and a pigsty. As below…
Round	1758	30s	Teddesley Estate
Arched	1760	11s 6d	Lankford Estate
Smooth	1761	15s	Tamworth, as 'front' bricks
Windsor*****	1764		Hard furnace brick

Gutter	1769	83s	24 purchased
Sand	1770	39s	160 purchased
Comand (common?)	1770	14s	Beesthorpe Hall
Waster	1770	13s	Beesthorpe Hall
Square fire	1772		Wirksworth
Keyed fire	1772		Wirksworth
Best hard	1775	12s	Ludlow
Soughing	1786		Coal mine drainage, Notts

* Long brick. It has been suggested that they that they were used to reinforce the corners of a building. In discussion with two conservation builders, they had both met them within seventeenth century houses as reinforcements of a hearth running from its back to its front. Usually, small quantities were purchased at 2d-3d. each, e.g. at Perry Hall in 1749 only 28 were bought. Within a Nottingham malt kiln John Houghton described in 1682 the use of 'very long bricks' whose length was 22 inches and thickness 2 inches 'these being heated retain heat a long time which causes a less expence of fuel than is usual in our best kills'. Robert Plot in 1677 had earlier noted this use in Oxfordshire where, 'they make a sort of brick 22 inches long and above 6 inches broad', which some call *Lath-bricks* by reason they are put in the place of *Laths* or *Spars* (supported by *Pillars*) in *Oats* for drying *mault*, the only use of them, and in truth I think a very good one too, for beside they are no way liable to fire, as the *wooden Laths* are, they hold the *heat* so much better, that once being *heated*, a small matter of fire will keep them so, which are valuable advantages in the *Profession* of *Maulting*'.[277]

** 'Great brick' was used in medieval documents to indicate large thin bricks (e.g. 11 x 12 x 2 inches). In the eighteenth century it probably referred to a large brick. Richard Neve in the *City and County Purchaser & Builders Dictionary* of 1726 describes a 'great brick' of 12 inches by 3 inches by 6 inches and recommends its use for gardens. John Harris, *Lexicon Technicum,* **2**, 2nd ed. (1710) suggests that they are used, 'to build Fence Walls'.

---

277 Plot, R., *Natural History of Oxfordshire,* (1677), 251-252. Kingman, M.J., 'The Long Brick', *BBSI*, **129**, (2015), 8-9.

*** The 'skew' or 'skewback' is a 'backward sloping voussoirs at the springing of a flat arch'. Brunskill, 108.

**** There is a type of brick known as a 'king closer'. This is 'a three-quarter bat with a half header exposed as a closer'. Brunskill, 103. Such a brick would be an exceptionally sophisticated product at that time particularly from a relatively remote Staffordshire Moorlands brick kiln. The term is more likely to refer to its large size.

***** Windsor brick. An early reference to their use is as a lining in a Bristol copper furnace in 1696. They may have originated in the Thames Valley but it is hard to envisage their carriage to the Midlands. It may be a generic name for hard furnace bricks. Jenkins, R., 'The Silica Brick and its Inventor, William Weston Young'. *Transactions of the Newcomen Society,* **22**, (1941), 139.

The Price of Bricks

How far was the decision to build in brick influenced by its price? Tables 5 and 6 are a collection of documented prices paid for Midland brick. At first sight the information seems somewhat random with no clear pattern and wide variations in price. There is an obvious temporal bias in that the sources are much richer after the Restoration than before. This imbalance not only reflects the increasing popularity of brick after 1660, but also the extensive evidence of brick production or purchase on large aristocratic and gentry estates whose agents usually kept very detailed estate accounts. In some estate building, although the accounts are detailed, the cost of the brick is subsumed in the total cost of brick, bricklaying and lime, for example in the Derbyshire estimates for Robert Revel at Carnforth Hall in 1727 and for a small house for the Countess of Oxford in 1747.[278]

---

278 NA, D184/3/48-73, DD4P/70/45.

Table 5: The Price of Estate Produced Bricks (per 1,000)

Date	Estate	Price per 1,000	Notes
1580	Paget, Beaudesert	2s 6d	+ £11 for 'digging earth', own timber, 300,000 fired
1642	Earl of Huntingdon	5s	Earl provided clay,' coales or woods for fewell', straw, sand and moulds
1677	For Sir Edward Skrymsher of Aqualate Hall	7s 5d	Brickmaker to provide fuel and its carriage
1689	Bellbroughton	6s	
1699	Anson, Shugborough Hall	10s	
1697	Burley-on-the-Hill	5s 6d	The estate provided hovels, straw, pit coal, sea coal and furzes
1700	Paget, Beaudesert	10s	Bricks as rent of estate kilns
1705	Bagot, Abbots Bromley almshouses	10s	
1706	John Edwards	7s 6d	Purchaser to provide 30s towards cost of 'hovill'
1716	Greswold, Malvern Hall	5s	Greswold purchased bricks from local brickmakers and seems to have built a tile and a brick kiln on his estate
1718	Greswold, Malvern Hall	9s	9s for 3,450. In 1721 26,000 at 8s 6d
1720	Gower, Trentham	4s 9d	Gower provided clay, coal, moulds, etc.

Year	Estate	Price	Notes
1721	Powis Attingham	14s, 7s	14s for 'well burnt' 7s for poorly produced
1725	Herrick Estate	3s 6d	Estimate for 250,000 bricks
1726	Portland Estate	6s	Welbeck Abbey
1729	Ingestre Estate	10s	For a house at Alton
1731	Jervis, Meaford Hall	12s	Included carriage
1732	Wolesley Estate	9s	
1734	Chetwynd	5s 3d	150,000 of 'good brick'
1737		5s 6d	+ £2 14s 4d for oven and clay
1739	Edge of Srelley	7s	Produced on Longnor Estate
1749	Winkburn Hall	4s 6d	Also to provide coal, sand and water for brickmaker, John Hobson of Sheffield
1751	Gough Estate, Edgbaston	12s 6d	
1753	Gough Estate, Edgbaston	10s	'from my own brick kiln'
1753	Edge Estate, Sherborne	6s	
1755	Earl of Stafford	10s	
1755	Hatton Vicarage	5s 6d	12,700 purchased
1760-65	Sir Edward Littleton, Teddesley	10s-10s 6d	In these years 1,079,225 bricks were purchased
1762	Bradford Estate, Castle Bromwich	10s 6d	
1773	Penbury Estate, Salop	8s 6d	Repairs to a barn
1785	Edge Estate kiln	7s 6d	With extras actually 9s 2d
Late 18th c	Barford Estate of Richard Wright	18s	

Table 6: The Price of Non-Estate Produced Bricks (per 1,000)

1483	Nottingham	£1 3s 9d	Only 14 bricks for repairs to the Crown Inn. For the chimney?
1485	Nottingham	8s 4d	400 bricks for a chimney
1575	Paget Estate	9s 1d	Also recorded 9s 4d and 10s from 'Marston of Lychfyeld'
1576	Stratford	30s	Includes large element of carriage
1593-4	Leicester Borough	£1 5s	'23 doson of bricke to mend the said chimney 7s 8d'
1589	Walsall Manor	7s 1d	Records of the Persehouse family who were stewards of the Manor
1629	Marchington	16s 8d	Will evaluation of John Budworth
1632	Nottingham	20s	Borough records, for sewer
1634	John Cottril	25s	Walsall brickmaker
1639	Barrow Church	16s 8d	Church repairs
1646	Shrewsbury	18s 4d	Battlement repairs
1660	Lichfield	12s	Inventory of Denis Napper 'brickmaker'
1663-65	Coughton Court	5s, 15s, 16s and 20s	Prices paid to various brickmakers
1665	Newcastle-under-Lyme	10s	Municipal kiln. In 1742-4 for the Hospital bricks still cost 10s
1671	Wolverhampton	8s 6d	8,900 bought
1677	Leicestershire	16s 8d	House repairs

Year	Place	Price	Notes
1678	Derby	7s	Inventory of John Squire, 'Brickmaker'
1679	Hanbury	20s	200 bought. Churchwardens' accounts
1684	Yoxall Court House	10s	9,950 purchased
1688	Thomas Astbury	12s 2d	Fired by John Edwards (of Burslem?) probably includes carriage
1689	Belbroughton	6s	Agreement for 40,000 bricks for Humphrey Perrott
1689	Shifnal	20s	200 purchased for disbursement to a poor townsperson
1692	Swynnerton	10s	Thomas Astbury, barn?
1693-97	Appleby Magna School	8s 6d	Purchased by Sir John Moore
1696	Warwick	15s	Rebuilding of Warwick houses. 7 different suppliers
1698	Stratford-on-Avon	20s	Parcels of 750 and 250
1700	Little Wyrley	10s	Inventory evaluation of Thomas Green
1701		16s	500, includes carriage
1703	Nottingham	11s 6d	4,500 purchased by Nottingham Borough
1705	Newcastle under Lyme	8s 6d	107,500 for John Fenton's house. Fired by Daniel Edwards of Burslem
1710	Beaumanor William Herrick	12s 9d	
1710-12	Rectory at Checkley	8s-10s	Subsidised building of kiln, price initially 10s and later 8s
1717	Repair of Stoke Bridge	11s 8d	1,200 bought

1717	House repairs	8s 6d	Lichfield, repairs of Dyott family
1717	Inventory	9s	Roger Smith of Hea Carr, Wolstanton
1728	Great Bolas	10s	'Common brick' for church rebuilding
1728	Great Bolas	12s 4d	'drest brick' for church rebuilding
1730	Warwickshire	14s	Brewhouse
1731	Lichfield	12s	1,000 for repair of a chimney of Bishop's Palace
1734	Church House, Betley	10s	3,600 for repairs?
1734	Edge of Strelley	9s 6d	Barn and chimney at Longnor, Salop
1736		8s 4d	87,500 bought
1738	Ludlow Corporation	Stock Bricks 12s, Clamp bricks 10s	Corporation lease at fixed prices
1742	'Mr Doniston'	11s	Worksop
1742	Richard Harrison Babworth, Notts.	6s 4d, 7s 8d and 10s.	Inventory of 3 separate kilns
1752	Newcastle	10s	'Mr. Bucknalls Workhouse' and carriage
1754		12s 6d	Included carriage
1755	Stivichall Hall	18s	Initially 50,000 bought, subsequent payment of £146 3s 3d for bricks, 162,000?
1755	Lichfield Close	10s	6,000 supplied by James Orton
1757	Edgbaston	9s 6d	Gough Estate, Reddons Farm
1760	'Harry Lankford gentleman'	11s 6d	100,000 bricks fired by William Fearnihough, 'Brickmaker'

1763	'Mr Doniston'	11s	3,000 brick fired at Worksop by Wm. Plant
1767	Greasley	10s	For garden wall
1770	Beesthorpe Hall	14s	From three separate brickmakers and own kiln
1771	Nottingham	17s	Borough purchase of 25,000
1772	Sawley	13s 3d	Delivered by boat
1775	Ludlow	15s Front brick 12s 'common hard brick'	Corporation lease
1780	East Bridgeford	20s	Building contract, 'no more than 20s'

In general estate produced bricks before the Brick Tax of 1784 rarely cost more than 10s per 1,000, although prices may be distorted in a variety of ways. Apparently low prices may mask subsidies provided by estate owners or even small-scale purchasers who provided one or more of the hovel, fuel, clay, carriage or unskilled labour. On the Whitworth Estate in 1737 Moses Hulme was paid 5s 6d per 1,000 for 'Burning of 43,600 Brick'. The estate accounts reveal that he was given a further £1 towards the cost of 'an Oven' and £1 14s 4d for casting clay. These additions raised the price to about 6s 7d per 1,000. But even this may not be the true cost as the estate also paid the cost of coal for firing the kiln.[279] Contracts for large numbers of bricks were often based on discounted prices. In 1720 Lord Gower signed contracts for 1,150,000 bricks, at only 4s 9d per 1,000 from five separate producers for whom he provided clay, coal and moulds.[280] In 1749 the owner of Winkburn Hall, Notts., agreed with:

John Hobson of Sheffield to make 200,000 bricks in the paddock at 4s 6d per thousand. He to find all the tools etc. to work with. I to find coal, sand

---

[279] WSL, 26/15/22.
[280] SRO, D593/N/2/2/3/17. An Inclosure plan (nd. but eighteenth century) shows brick kilns at Northwood Common and Toft Green. SRO, D593/H/3/238.

and water for 2 months and nothing else, all to be well burnt and full 10 inches long when burnt, five broad and 2½ inches thick.[281]

Such a size was extravagant. Prices may also be distorted by the undescribed quality or function of purchases hidden under the general term 'brick'. For bricks produced by independent brickmakers the price paid was approximately 50% higher than that from estates. Particularly noticeable were the high prices paid by municipal authorities who were perhaps supporting friends and colleagues. As early as 1632 Nottingham Corporation paid the equivalent of 20s per 1,000 for bricks for sewer work. At Shrewsbury in 1754 the price was 13s per 1,000.[282] Specialist bricks could also be expensive, in 1769 Josiah Wedgwood paid 27s 9d for 700 bricks for the 'Well Sough' at Etruria.

On most estates the brickmaker was not a full-time employee but was hired for a particular building or project. Bricks could only be made for six months per year and as 'casting' clay took only another month there was rarely sufficient demand for continuous employment. At Welbeck in the 1730s Reuben Lee was paid as a tile maker but for some years the accounts show payments only for ploughing and harrowing.[283] The brickmaker negotiated a price and within that formal contract the provision of clay, coal and carriage was the responsibility of either the brickmaker or the purchaser. Where the brickmaker was an estate employee then brick prices tended to be even lower. On the Edge Estate at Sherborne, to which coal had to be carried a considerable distance, in 1753 the brick was priced at 6s per 1,000, ten years later the price was identical. In 1726 at Kelham Hall 106,150 estate produced bricks cost 10s 3d per 1,000 and a further £32 6s 2d to carry them to the Hall. Their price was higher because the kiln was fired by gorse and heather which cost £11.

The true costs of production can be difficult to define, but it is probably fair to say that the landed estates with their range of resources and materials and extended production runs were able to produce brick at below market prices, therefore for their owners the crucial disparity in prices was an obvious economic incentive to build in brick. For example, Sir Thomas Paget paid 9s per 1,000 for bricks in 1575 and in 1580 in the 'Bricke Kilne' accounts only paid 2s 6d

---

281 Jansenn J., 'The Transformation of Brickmaking in 17th c London', *Construction History Society Newsletter,* **71**, (May 2005), 4.
282 SA, 3365/659/25a, 3365/661/388.
283 NA, DDP5/1/1.

(although not all costs were included). On the Herrick Estate at Beaumanor bricks were priced in 1710 at 12s 9d and in 1725 at 3s 6d.[284] The apparent disparity between commercial and estate fired bricks may be exaggerated for additional costs, such as fuel deliveries, wages and transport were not always included.

Apparently high prices may be the result of purchases of very small quantities of brick; at Barston, for example, the churchwardens in 1702 purchased 100 bricks and 18 'hipps' for 3s at a price equivalent to more than 20s per 1,000.[285] At Knowle in 1708 the churchwardens paid 15s 2d for 400 bricks, equivalent to almost 38s per 1,000.[286] At Hanbury in 1683 they 'pd for laying downe 2 Grave Stones & laying of brick 0 1s 4d'. These were probably for brick lined graves. A mason's bill of 1774 for a brick grave at Temple Balsall included 10s for 600 bricks.[287] Brick lined graves were an increasingly good market for brickmakers. At St Nicholas', Gloucester, in 1786 the authorities declared, 'No person shall be buried in the church without having a Brick Grave as … it will prove very ruinous to the Foundations'.[288] As late as 1884 many glebe terriers reveal that the fee paid to the incumbent for ordinary burials was only a few pence and slightly more if a coffin was used. A brick grave cost a minimum of £1 1s and at Dresden (Staffs) the burial fee in a brick grave ranged from £3 3s to £6 6s. In contrast, as late as 1852, the Fitzherbets of Tissington ordered the sexton/parish clerk 'not to permit any graves or vaults of brick or stone to be built'.[289]

Most commonly high prices could also reflect the inclusion of the costs of transport. On the Jervis Estate in 1726 Edmund Bagely was paid 12s per 1,000 specifically for 'brick and carriage'.[290] One rare opportunity which allowed independent brickmakers to raise prices was that provided by the need for urgent repair work following a fire or other disaster. At Warwick 'after the late dreadful fire there in September 1694', for the rebuilding by the Edge family of two houses in Sheep Street in 1696, bricks were bought at the high price of 15s per 1,000.[291]

---

284   ROLLR, DG9130, DG9/2136.
285   WRO, DR(B) 46/140.
286   Downing, 299.
287   NA, DD/E/98/292.
288   Gloucester Archives, P154/15CW2/3.
289   DRO, D239M/E5011.
290   WSL, 49/44/36. 16.
291   NA, DD/E/117/1.

For purposes of comparison the prices quoted are restricted to the prices paid for 'brick' or 'common brick' and exclude prices paid for the more sophisticated products such as 'front', 'fire' or 'dressed' bricks. However even within the general classification of 'brick', variations in quality were reflected in a range of prices. At Coughton Court, where the building of an extension began in 1663, 'Clamp bricke' was supplied at 4s 8d per 1,000 with the brickmaker also paid for clay and his initial accommodation. In 1665 a different brickmaker was paid 5s per 1,000 plus the cost of the clay. Later that year brick, tiles, gutters and crests were obtained from three other brickmakers; Edward Vize of Spernall provided bricks at £1 per 1,000, Joseph Vise's bricks cost 16s and Robert Bibb's bricks at first cost 16s 8d but latterly 15s, with a few early bricks sold at 7d per 100 (5s 10d per 1,000).

The variation in prices suggests that some were inferior and only used internally.[292] On the Powys Estate at Attingham, Shropshire, the steward, Charles Hunt, reported in 1721 that 'there is above 100 thousand bricks left but the last kiln is good for very little it being not have burnt. There is about eighteen thousands of them, they are worth not above seven shillings per thousand. The others in general are very good bricks. He bids to the full value for them at fourteen shillings per thousand'.[293]

The main problem faced in compiling the price of brick is the lack of data for the late medieval and early Tudor period. At Kirby Muxloe Castle, built in 1481-3, the detailed building accounts reveal that bricks were carried at 5d or 6d per 1,000, lime cost 7d per quarter and bricks were laid at 14d per 1,000. Frustratingly no brick prices are given, although at Tattersall Castle, whose builders may have worked at Kirby Muxloe, the price of bricks was 18d per 1,000. An aberrant price was that of 4d paid for 14 bricks (£1 3s 9d per 1,000) in 1483 by Nottingham Council for repairs to the Crown Inn.[294]

There are virtually no prices available for the period 1500-1560, although Nicholas Moore has suggested that nationally 'the open market price for bricks from 1400 to 1550 (was) between four and five shillings the thousand'.[295] For the remainder of the sixteenth century sources are limited to the Paget and Persehowse Estate papers in which the prices recorded are inconsistent. In

---

292 Moore, 'Coughton', 12-14.
293 SA, 112/2/275.
294 *NBR*, **II**, 391.
295 Moore, 'Bricks', 225.

1560-62 Sir William Paget proposed to pay 5s 2d per 1,000 for bricks for a new house at Burton.[296] In 1575 Thomas, Lord Paget, paid 9-10s per 1,000 for bricks from Lichfield and Brereton.[297] The accounts do not reveal if this was the market price or if it included the cost of transport to Beaudesert. This high price may have been the incentive for his investment in an estate kiln. His accounts suggest that the cost of the estate-produced bricks was only 5s 2d per 1,000 in 1580, although a further £11 for clay extraction would suggest a truer figure would be nearer 5s 11d.[298] In 1589 the Persehowse Estate paid 7s 1d per 1,000 bricks.[299]

If all these numerical difficulties are stripped out of the overall picture, the generally accepted market (rather than estate) price profile, per 1,000, of common brick in the Midlands would seem to run from about 7-8s per 1,000 in the 1580s, to 8-9s in the late seventeenth century[300] and about 10-11s in the first half of the eighteenth century. Over a period of approximately 200 years, from 1580 to 1780, the average price of basic building bricks rose by about 45%. Over the same period the Phelps Brown and Hopkins Index suggests that the daily wages of building craftsmen more than doubled as did the price of a basket of consumables.[301]

The fall in the real price of bricks was not however associated with a significant increase in brick building at all levels of society. The dramatic rise in the prices of agricultural products was mainly confined to the Tudor and early Stuart period when brick building was less popular. The expansion in brick building coincided with a period during which agricultural prices were relatively static or even fell, 'Over the period 1640-1750 as a whole, agricultural prices in general changed by only a few percentage points, compared with the

---

296 SRO, D(W)1734/2/3/27.

297 SRO, D(W)1734/3/4/93. Thorold Rogers wrote that 'in the later part, i.e. the last thirty years (of the sixteenth century) the price of bricks was about double that of the earlier average'. Thorold Rogers, J.E., *A History of Agriculture and Prices*, **IV**, Oxford: Clarendon Press, (1883), 441. There are relatively few examples of Midland prices but those which do survive do not confirm such a rise in prices.

298 SRO, D(W)1734/3/4/119.

299 SRO, D260/M/F/1/5.

300 In nearby Leicestershire for the Wren designed school at Appleby Magna, its sponsor, Sir John Moore, paid 8s 6d per 1,000 bricks in 1693-97, McWhirr, 48.

301 Phelps Brown, H. and Hopkins, S.V., *A Perspective on Wages and Prices*, Methuen, (1981), 11, 29-30.

sixfold increase recorded in the preceding century and a half'.[302] Assuming a rise in brick prices from 8s 6d in the 1690s to 10s per 1,000 by 1750 gives an increase of 17.5%, over a period during which grain prices declined by an average of approximately 12% and livestock prices increased by almost 18%.[303] The rise in brick prices was therefore roughly in line or even slightly lower than the general price trends of the period.

There is no evidence of Midland brick prices rising to reflect increases in the cost-of-living. Most contracts were short term and often for less than 100,000 bricks. In these circumstances the producer had less bargaining power and presumably had to absorb any increase in costs. For most of the first half of the eighteenth century the market price of bricks was static at about 10s per 1,000, for nearly 50 years the builder and developer could rely on what was almost a fixed price. This may have provided them with a confidence in anticipated costs and have been an incentive to invest in brick. How was this price level maintained for such a lengthy period? For much of the period for building craftsmen and labourers this was a time of rising real wages, there was thus little or no wage pressure on costs of production or building.[304] In the Midlands, between 1660 and 1750, the average daily rate for building craftsmen varied over the whole period from only 16 to 18 pence and that of building labourers from 9 to 12 pence.[305] Wage rates thus exerted little pressure on overall building costs.

Of significance is the fact that Midland brick prices were considerably lower than those of London, the South-East and East Anglia. In those areas bricks were burnt either by increasingly scarce furze or mainly by expensively imported coal and there were frequent complaints about its quality and price. Linda Clarke has estimated the following London ex-kiln commercial brickmaker's prices, per 1,000 as, 1670-1710, 9s, 1750, 11s, 1790, 18s. There are many references to prices higher than these, particularly in Admiralty contracts. Neve, in his *City and Country Purchaser* of 1726, quoted 16-20s. These higher prices were probably due to the cost of the coal.

---

302   Bowden, P.J., 'Agricultural prices, wages, farm profits and rents', in Thirsk, J. ed. *Agrarian History,* **V**, 1640-1750, (1985), 1.

303   Bowden, 1.

304   Lindert, P.H., 'English Population, Wages and Prices, 1541-1913', in Rotberg, R.I., and Rabb, T.K., *Population and History*, CUP, (1986), 54.

305   Woodward, 256-258. Even when there were sudden, short-term surges in the demand for labour, for example following a major fire, Woodward could find no evidence of wage rates rising in response.

The great advantage of the Midland brickmaking industry was its ready access to fuel, although it has been suggested that Midland prices could also have been lower because of over-production: in 1711 many of the Nuneaton kilns closed because of lack of demand.[306] The net result was that it was considerably cheaper to build in brick in Midland England. Even if the aristocracy or the very wealthy chose to build in stone they could substantially reduce the overall cost by using brick for the foundations, as at Meriden Hall where bricks which cost at least £66 (but 'not all included') were used in the cellars, or stuccoed brick for the internal walls as at Keddleston. At Milton House, Northants, the first two items of the specifications are: 'There will be required to build this front 300 Tun of Ketton Stone'. A note at the foot of page one states, 'N.B. The Brick work will take 250 Thousand of Bricks'. The total cost was £6541.15s.[307] At the stone-built Stivichall Hall the bricks cost £191 3s 3d which represents about 220,000 bricks. The total cost was £5,961 8s 8d.[308] Paul Foley, an extremely wealthy ironfounder, built the palatial Stoke Court apparently in stone but his records include the purchase of 709,100 bricks in 1696 and 845,000 in 1698.[309] The Foleys also owned the brick-built Prestwood Hall.

There is a need to put aristocratic building costs into an overall financial perspective. Between November 6th and December 31st 1739, Sir William Wolseley spent £48 15s 6d on lottery tickets whilst his accounts include a skilled brick mason at 2s 8d per day, a half year's Window Tax at 15s, 191 elm trees for £7 5s and 2 locks for 2s 4d.[310] Similarly the steward of Sir Humphrey Greswold in 1716 paid £2 13s 6d for 10,700 bricks and 'pair of stockings for my master £1 5s 6d'.[311] It must be emphasised that people of power were literate and able to contribute material to archives and that the quality and price of brick may reflect their perspectives. The use of brick by others may have not been recorded.

---

306 Gooder, E., 'Clay Working in the Nuneaton Area: A Historical Background to the Pottery Industry through the Ages' in Mayes, P., and Scott, K., 'The Pottery Kilns of Chilvers Coton', *Society of Medieval Archaeology,* Monograph **X**, (1984), 13-18.
307 Northants RO, F (M) Charter/2327.
308 SBT, DR10/1518.
309 Peacock, R., *The Seventeenth Century Foleys, Iron, Wealth and Vision, 1580-1716,* The Black Country Society, (2011), 145.
310 SRO, D (W)1781/17/1.
311 WRO, CR1291/292.

The Quality of the Brick

The quality of the brick produced varied according to the plasticity of the clay, the temperature achieved in the kiln or clamp and the skill of the brickmaker. Many of the bricks were identified not by shape or size but by quality and contracts frequently included the right to refuse imperfect products. In 1689 a contract between Rowland Heathly, brickmaker, and Humphrey Perrott required Heathly to 'dresse the same well and Workman like and allsoe Burne them Workman like … and to deliver to Hum: Perrott such Bricks as by a workman shall be ajudged good and new'. In an agreement of 1706, Thomas Allen agreed to 'paying to the sd John Edwards 7s and 6d per thousand for all such bricks as the said Tho Allen shall like and approve'. Similarly for tiles 'Tho: Allen shall … give the sd John Edwards leave to sell or otherwise dispose of what he refuses as unfit for use'.[312]

There was also a potential variation in quality between kiln and clamp produced bricks. In Francis Smith's estimate of 1722-3 for the building of Ombersley Court, he included '120,000 Best Brick at 18s p 1,000d' and '500,000 Clamp Brick at 9s p 1,000d'.[313] Attached to a note entitled 'Account of Brick and tyle made at Stretton 1730' are several small scraps of paper with details of repairs and purchases. On one of these is an unusual reference to 'brick ends' with a 'load' costing 3s. Their low price suggests that they were of inferior quality, perhaps either broken or over-burnt.[314] Green bricks which were not properly dried and which contained residual moisture often shattered in the early stages of firing.[315]

Poor quality bricks could lead to bitter dispute between maker and purchaser. In 1770 Josiah Wedgwood was involved in an acrimonious argument with the architect Joseph Pickford concerning the quality of the facing bricks at Etruria Hall, the result of the 'carelessness, or something worse, of your bricklayers'.[316]

---

312 SRO, D(W)1742/4.
313 Gomme, A., *Smith of Warwick, Francis Smith, Architect and Master-Builder*, Stamford: Shaun Tyas, (2001), 567.
314 SRO, D1057/J/2/30. They may have been used for house foundations.
315 Smith, 'Medieval Brickmaking Industry,' 114. 'The time for drying bricks varied, depending on the weather and the type of firing: bricks fired in a kiln took less time than bricks fired in a clamp, since it did not matter, with kiln-burning if the bricks were not thoroughly dry; for firing in a clamp, where full heat was attained immediately, the bricks had to be fully dry or they would 'fly to pieces' when fired'.
316 Saunders, E., *Joseph Pickford of Derby, A Georgian Architect*, Phoenix Mill: Alan Sutton, (1993), 98.

It was eventually resolved by Wedgwood agreeing to obtain the replacement brick himself and buy the scaffolding poles from Pickford.[317] In 1770 at Stafford Infirmary Samuel Wyatt cancelled his contract with brickmaker Charles Clarke, who had 'made several Bricks there which are found improper for the purpose'. The contract was rewarded to a Mr Berrington who erected 2 kilns 'one of them which is the larger is … to be built of burnt brick'. Clarke paid compensation of 12,000 bricks and 5 guineas.[318]

By the mid-eighteenth-century brick had become a sophisticated product purchasable in a variety of forms and at a wide range of prices. Midland patrons did not have the extensive range available to London purchasers but could, by the middle of the century, choose from bricks with at least 30 different names, although local vocabulary must have led to some duplication. The increase in the volume of bricks produced was not the result of mechanisation, or of any significant refinement of the manufacturing process, but from an increase in the number of kilns and clamps meeting increased demand. Between 1737 and 1746 the Trentham Estate purchased bricks from eight separate brickmakers. Sir William Gough at Perry Hall between 1733 and 1760 received bricks from 20 different suppliers.

The making of brick was still closely associated with the construction of the building which was to use them. Contracts were individually negotiated to meet a particular demand, but this was not a contract between equals. On the one hand was the often illiterate and seasonal brickmaker or bricklayer and on the other hand the wealthier and socially more prominent purchaser. The cost of brick was therefore maintained at a traditional and familiar level. Essentially brick production was an innately unadventurous, small-scale and seasonal industry. Any investment in large scale, permanent brick kilns required at the least a regional market for bricks and therefore an appropriate transport system. Prior to 1780 and the opportunities afforded by the canal network for a widening market, large scale investment in brick production was rare. There were almost no brick works at which potential purchasers could make spontaneous purchases. Brick was rarely produced in anticipation of demand until the coalfield-based brick kilns were built in large numbers in the late eighteenth and nineteenth centuries.

---

317   Wedgwood Archives, E25-18292.
318   SRO, D1778/634/80.

Chapter 5

THE FUELS EMPLOYED IN BRICK PRODUCTION

IN THE period under study there were five basic methods of firing clay. The least effective, given the Midland climate, was that of baking bricks using the heat of the sun. There is little evidence of its use, although an excavation in 1990 of a medieval house at 41 Guildhall Lane, Leicester, reported 'painted walls, probably on sun-dried bricks'.[319] This method was not unknown in other parts of the country – in 1588 the Spanish ambassador reported 'that they were raising bulwarks at Portsmouth made of sundried bricks and faggots, to serve for defence in case of need'.[320] As late as 1803 a letter to John Frewen of Cold Overton Hall, Leics, mentions the poor quality of sun-dried bricks at Fisherton Angar near Salisbury.[321]

A fuel for which there is some Midland evidence is the burning of brick using turves or peat, as was common on the Lancashire moss lands.[322] Peat is of low calorific value and was commonly used for domestic heating in areas with poor timber or coal resources, but recent research into the uplands of Derbyshire has revealed the scale and importance of an intensive industry within the local economy.[323] A Peak District agreement in 1655 included 'in consideration of

---

319 Liddle, P., 'Archaeology in Leicestershire and Rutland, 1990', *TLAHS*, **65**, (1991), 103.
320 *CSP, Spain (Simancas), Simancas: April 1588, 11-20*, **4**, 1587-1603, 263-269.
321 East Sussex RO, FRE/2471.
322 Barker, T.C. and Harris, J.R., *A Merseyside Town in the Industrial Revolution: St. Helens, 1750-1900,* London: Routledge, (1994), 7.
323 Myers, A.M., *An Archaeological Resource Assessment of Modern Derbyshire (1750 Onwards)*, 6.

£8, of a house, bay and peathouse'.[324] It is difficult to identify its use for firing bricks, but further south there are scattered references, such as an indenture of 1683 at Meir in mid-Staffordshire which included a 'turfhouse', a 'backhouse or kilnhouse' and an 'oven'.[325] Samuel Garbet in the 1750s noted that in Wem, 'The most profitable subterranean earths are clay for making bricks … and peat or turf for firing'.[326] The brickmaking accounts at Staunton Harold Hall of 1766 include a single reference to 'Cutting Turfs 600 at 6d-3s',[327] and the Edge brick accounts at Sherborne for 1755 include the purchase of '1 doz turf bricks'. As late as 1830 W.O. Foster, the owner of an iron forge at Hampton Loade, used peat in conjunction with charcoal. The peat was dug from the recently purchased 200 acres of turbary on Whixall Moss.[328]

The earliest evidence in the Midlands for the use of fern and furze as kiln fuels is derived from the archaeological investigation of Bradgate House, which was built around 1490-1520 and where in three excavated kiln or clamp sites very fine ash suggested the use of fern.[329] The scale and importance of fern and gorse (also known as furze) is reflected in many manorial records, for example in a Derbyshire final concord of 1573 by Thomas Stanhope, Earl of Harrington which included 2,000 acres of 'furze and heath'.[330] Astley Manor, Warwickshire, in 1658 also had 2,000 acres of furze.[331] The amounts required for brick burning are rarely listed but an undated mid-eighteenth-century letter which gives the dimensions of a small kiln, probably in Sussex, producing 5,000 bricks per firing, states that '300 goodsized Furze bushes or two loads of Bran straw will be sufficient for burning a Kiln'.[332] Wood and coal with their higher calorific value were the later dominant fuels but furze continued to be used well into the eighteenth century. In the 1698 glebe

---

324 DRO, D4573/2/5.
325 SRO, D543/C/4/2/1.
326 Garbett, S., *The History of Wem and other Townships,* (1818), 7. (Garbett died in 1751.)
327 ROLLR, 26D53/2506.
328 Mutton, N., 'The Forges at Eardington and Hampton Loade,' T*SalopAHS,* **58, pt3**, (1967-68), 241.
329 Ramsey, D., 'Bradgate Kiln or Clamp sites', *TLAHS,* 61, (1986) 92. As late as 1668 the Treasury Commissioners allowed ferns to be used to fire bricks in Richmond Park. CSPD, Charles 11, 1668-69, (1898), 45-86.
330 DRO, D518/MF/2.
331 WRO, CR0136/C185.
332 Centre for Buckinghamshire Studies, D-LO/6/9/4.

terrier of Rolleston-on-Dove the churchwardens listed a 'furze or gorse-house anciently a kiln house'.[333]

The inventory of the brickmaker John Law of Market Harborough in 1699 reveals that the fuel he used was straw and 'ffurs'.[334] Gorse was a traditional source of fuel and noted as a potential source of urban fires.[335] In Nottingham in 1697 the Council warned of the potential danger of the Bakers' 'Gosse-hovells and Gosse-stacks'.[336] William Woolley in his *History of Derbyshire* of 1712 noted that 'Nun Green (in Derby) belongs to the free burgers and is made use of by the bakers to lay there stacks of gorse by the carpenters to lay timber and brick-makers to make and burn bricks'.[337] The Malvern Hall brickmaking accounts of the Greswold family in 1718 included the purchase of 'Thorns' at 4s per 'load'.[338] In 1726 the accounts of the Duchess of Rutland at Kelham Hall included building 'a New Brick Kiln to burn with Gorse and light firing' and the payment of £11 for 'Cutting & Kidding Whinns (furze or gorse) for the Brick Kilne'.[339] The Lockington Hall brickmaking accounts of 1756 included 'getting Turf & Gorse 0 2 6', although coal was also purchased from Coleorton.[340] As late as 1772 in Warwick the Bridge End Coal Charity was established to compensate inhabitants for the loss of furze traditionally collected from the recently enclosed Warwick Heath.[341]

In central England during the sixteenth and most of the seventeenth centuries the usual fuel for both kilns and clamps was wood. Neve suggested that '500 faggots would burn a kiln of 10-11,000 Statute-bricks'.[342] (A faggot was defined as 4ft long and 100 to the ton). Wealthy owners of wooded estates therefore had the considerable advantage of being able to exploit their own resources. At Kirby Muxloe, immediately following entries about a 'Newe

---

333   Watts, S., ed. 'Staffordshire Glebe Terriers 1585-1844', *SHC*, **XXII**, (2009), 100.
334   McWhirr, 48.
335   Historical Manuscripts Commission, 'The Corporation of Shrewsbury: Municipal Registers', in *The Manuscripts of Shrewsbury and Coventry Corporations [Etc.] Fourth Report, Appendix: Part X* (London: 1899), 9-25.
336   *NBR*, **V**, 394.
337   Woolley, W., *History of Derbyshire,* (c.1712) ed. Glover, C., and Riden, P., *Derbyshire Record Society*, **VI**, (1981), 30.
338   WRO, CR1291/292.
339   NA, DP70/1.
340   ROLLR, DE1536/164.
341   *VCH, Warks*, **8**, (1969), 545.
342   Neve, 49.

kylne', Lord Hastings' accounts record 'paid for felling and Breykyng of 78 loode of wood', the price 'lood ffellyng and Brekyng' was only 1½d per load. Other estate resources reduced the overall costs, for example, quarried sand was only 1d a cart load for digging and 3d a load for carriage. The transport of the brick from the kiln to the castle site was only 5d per 1,000. Sir William Paget, the owner of the coal-rich Cannock Chase, when planning a new house at Burton in 1560-2, emphasised the value 'of my own wood':

> *Item for the burning of and making of 300,000 bricke allow is the 1,000 and for the felling, makinge and carriage of 200 loads of my own wood for making of the same bricke allow 12d the load ... 47li 10s. Item for 300,000 tyle burning (the woods being my own) [crossed out] allow 3s 4d the thousand for the felling making and carrying of 150 load of wood being my own allow xiid the load 57li 10s. Item for lathe and tyle pinnes made of my own wood 40s.*[343]

This gives a price of 5s 2d per 1,000 brick which was cheaper than the market price of externally produced brick based on local suppliers of fuel and carriage. In 1575 Lord Paget's accounts recorded the purchase of non-estate bricks at 9s per 1,000.[344] Some indication of the considerable scale of timber consumption in large scale brickmaking is apparent in a document of 1578, entitled 'The charges of makynge of Bryckes this yeare'. At Beaudesert, Paget's receiver, William Warde, listed a payment of £8 2s 'payed for fallinge and cutting of fyve hundred and foore score loades of wood and for sawinge'. His accounts also include, 'given to the wayne man to drynke that gave the carriage of sixe scoore and Twelve loades of wood to the Brycke Kylne at iiijd the wayne'.[345]

The Pagets were only one of many aristocratic Midland families with huge timber supplies, in 1642 the Marquis of Newcastle on his Nottinghamshire estates had timber valued at £2,000.[346] Crown forests also supported brickmaking – a survey of the Needwood Forest in 1658 included an area called 'Brick Kilnes' valued at £56 18s.[347]

---

343   SRO, D(W)1734/2/3/27.
344   SRO, D(W)1734/3/4/106.
345   SRO, D(W)1734/3/4/106.
346   NA, 157DD/P/42/36.
347   Madge, S.J., *Domesday of Crown Lands,* London: Routledge, (1938), 380.

THE FUELS EMPLOYED IN BRICK PRODUCTION

By the seventeenth century there was a change to coal as the main fuel for firing brick, although this is difficult to date with precision. Whitehead, in his study of West Midlands brickmaking, suggests that coal 'was not generally used for making brick until the late seventeenth century'. This he attributed to the small output of the mines and the 'technological problems which made coal a difficult fuel to use'.[348] Yet in Southern England, as early as 1609, the steward of Hatfield House, Hertfordshire, an area with no local coal deposits, reported to Robert Cecil that 'With respect to the charge of bricks at Hatfield. The intention is now to burn them with sea coal instead of wood'.[349] In 1618 the Venetian ambassador reported on:

> *their excellent method of baking bricks … At the bottom of the kilns … when they pile the bricks and tiles they place a layer of coal dust between each tier in succession up to the very top of the kiln, so that when the furnaces below are lighted, the fire spreads throughout.*[350]

These examples reflect the manufacture of brick using coal expensively imported from the North-East. In those Midland counties with much easier access to coal it may have been used extensively well before the 'late seventeenth century'. At Castle Donington in 1642 The Earl of Huntingdon ordered 100,000 bricks, fired by 'coales or woods for fewell'.[351] In 1658 the inventory of Michael Biddulph, the extremely wealthy owner of houses at Lichfield and Elmhurst, includes a 'brickclampe' and 'coles and other fuell'.[352] 'Coal' as opposed to 'sea coal' or 'pit coal' could refer to charcoal but this is unlikely as it would have been a very expensive fuel. At Coughton Court in 1665 the accounts include 'cole for the Clamp' and '8 cordes to make Scales to weigh Coale'.[353] Dud Dudley, who owned estates and ironworks in Staffordshire recommended in his *Metallum Martis* of 1665, 'Fifthly that no pit coal be exported, seeing that wood, fuel and timber is decayed for building; and instead thereof brick making (formerly

---

348 Whitehead, 44.
349 *Calendar of the Cecil Papers in Hatfield House*, **21**, 1609-1612, Historical Manuscripts Commission, January 1, 1608-9.
350 *CSP, Venice, 1617-1619*, **15**, September, 1618, ed. Hinds, A.B., London: HMSO, (1909).
351 McWhirr, 55.
352 Vaisey, ed. 'Probate Inventories', 112.
353 Moore, 'Coughton', 13.

spending wood but now coals) is much in use'.³⁵⁴ Plot, writing in 1686, with no indication that this was a new process, stated that, 'In the glass-houses, Salt works and Brick-clamps they use the raw coal as brought from the pit ... and for burning a Clamp of 16,000 bricks they use about 7 Tunns of coal'.³⁵⁵

One ton of coal produced the equivalent heat of two tons of dry wood, so the fuel employed was determined by relative price. The qualities and properties of coal varied regionally – the most expensive burned slowly and was used mainly for domestic heating, soap boiling and glassmaking. Sulphurous coal, such as that of the Wyre Forest Coalfield, burned with a higher temperature and was more suitable for activities such as brickmaking, lime-burning and dyeing, but with the disadvantage that it produced sulphur dioxide fumes and therefore was a generally inferior product with a higher proportion of spoilt bricks. Balthazar Gerbier in his *Counsel and Advise to all Builders* of 1663 claimed that when coal was used 25% of the firing could be wasted.³⁵⁶

By the early eighteenth century there are increasing references to the use of coal. In 1701 William Anson of Shugborough recorded in a pocket almanac, devoted to his brick accounts, '12 May pd 3 loades Coales'.³⁵⁷ In the Giffard accounts of 1728-9 a page was specifically headed 'An Acct of Coals for Burning the Bricks for the Building at Wolverhampton'.³⁵⁸ A page in the Hawkstone accounts of 1725 is headed 'Coles to Burn Brick & Tile'.³⁵⁹ Where coal was not immediately available then its transport costs could add substantially to the costs of brick manufacture. One solution was to burn a mixture of fuels – in a brickmaking contract of 1697 at Burley-on-the-Hill, the Earl of Nottingham agreed 'to such pitt coals, seacoals and furzes as should be necessary for the making and bavins (brushwood or firewood) to kindle the fire'.³⁶⁰ The surviving accounts for a brick kiln at Meerbrook (Staffs) in 1750 include many references to the carriage of coal and include the transport of 37 loads of timber from Grattage Wood. Such a quantity may indicate the use of a dual-fired kiln.³⁶¹

---

354   Dudley, D., *Metallum Martis*, (1665), ed. Bagnall, J.N., London, (1854), 46.
355   Plot, 128.
356   Gerbier, 52-3.
357   SRO, D615/P/(A)/1/5.
358   SRO, D590/634. Unfortunately, the account was not completed.
359   SA, 112/1/2775.
360   *VCH, Rutland,* **1**, (1908), 233.
361   SRO, D 1028/2/1.

Where wood was available, it may have continued to be used for reasons of quality or innate conservatism. As late as 1690 the inventory of Robert Garnett of Nuneaton refers to 'The Brickkiln at Bedworth, wood Brick and Tyle there £5 0 0', suggesting a wood fired kiln in an area well known for the quality of its coal.[362] Martin Baylie's account to Sir Willoughby Aston, Lord of the Manor of Nuneaton, in 1691-2, included the expenses of building a brick-house and kiln and amongst the payments is the cost of carrying six loads of wood from Stockingford. In the 1690s at Eccleshall, Nicholas Tindon was described as 'Brickmaker and Wood Collier', such dual occupations might indicate that he used wood as his primary fuel.[363] At Edwall, Cheshire, in 1726 John Perry issued a receipt for 10s 'for cutting cordwood for burning bricks' to the estate brickmaker of the Tyrwhitt-Drake family.[364]

Precise information of the fuel employed is not always available. This may be because it was the responsibility of the brickmaker to obtain the appropriate fuel, so its cost and type are hidden in the overall charge. At both Aqualate Hall in 1677-8 and in Thomas Allen's contract of 1706 the brickmaker was responsible for providing the fuel.[365] In other contracts it was the responsibility of the purchaser to provide the fuel. Such provision could be reflected in the price of the brick. At Trentham a contract of 1720-21 stated that '… also he the said John Lord Gower … will find provide & lay down at the Oven or Ovens coals necessary for burning all the said Bricks'.[366] This subsidy was reflected in the contract price of only 4s 9d per 1,000 bricks. There was thus an incentive to use the cheapest coal and some records distinguish between 'coal' and the cheaper 'slack' used for burning poorer quality bricks. At Attingham in 1721 the bailiff, Charles Hunt, wrote that he 'hopes to burn Powy's at 12s 6d the thousand or less. The slack burnt brick will be useful for building the new kiln. They hope to burn fifteen hundred thousand in the summer'.[367] In the Jervis Estate papers for 1728-39 is a detailed account of 'The Fire Engine and Coal Mine at the Woods', the records of George Sparrow's mining enterprise, based on a Newcomen engine, at Hawarden, Clwyd. Here

---

362 SRO, L, B/C/11, Robert Garnett, (June 1690).
363 Spufford, M., 'Poverty Portrayed: Gregory King and the Parish of Eccleshall', *Staffordshire Studies*, (1995), **7**, 135. They could also indicate the manufacture of bricks in the summer months and charcoal in the winter.
364 Cheshire RO, packet H, DTD/27/48.
365 SRO, D(W)1788 P47B2. SRO, D1742/46.
366 SRO, D593/N/2/2/3/17.
367 SA, 112/2/275.

'slack' was used to fire a brick kiln, in 1728 there were used '12 barrels of Slack and one Ton of Coale for the burning the Brick 12s 4d'.[368]

Documentary evidence of the cost of fuel as a proportion of the cost of manufacturing brick is rare. Where brickmakers were responsible for the total price of production they almost always calculated the total cost and even when fuel costs are separately listed their relationship to the number of bricks burnt is rarely clear. The Hawkstone Estate coal accounts for brickmaking of 1725 list the purchase of 20 tons 18 cwt of coal between 13th July and one week before the legal end to the brickmaking season on 22nd September. The total cost was £12 7s 6d. The 19 separate deliveries by 10 different carriers are recorded in 'loads' and of interest is that the weight of each 'load' was given such as '1 tun 3 hun' or '19 hun'. Presumably, as at Coughton, some form of primitive balance was available. The cost of the brickmaking coal was 10s per ton, but the number of bricks fired is not given.[369] In 1786 Thos. Fletcher paid £5 10s for 20 'loades of coal laid down at Domvilles for the use of Thos. Jones,' the brick account specifically refers to 'therty fowre thousand Eight hundard are burned' as the 'Number of Bricks Made at the Domvils'. This might suggest that one load of coal at 5s 6d would fire 1,740 bricks which is 3s 2d per 1,000, about 30% of the total cost, but whether the 'load' was consistent over time and region is uncertain.[370] At Trentham in the single year of 1742 the estate paid £34 8s 0d 'for carriage of Coals to the Brickkiln' and for 176 'Stacks of Coales to the Brickkiln'.[371] The Giffard family records of 1728 include 'An Acct of Coals for the Burning the Bricks for the Building at Wolverhampton', collectively £67 18s 6d (6.3%) was spent from a total price for the exceptional combined chapel/house of £1,069 2s 2½.[372] Houghton in 1684 estimated that for southern England wood for a timber fired kiln contributed about 3s (22-25%) to a final price of 13-14s per 1,000.[373] At Arley, Cheshire, in 1752-65 the cost of coal from South Lancashire was about half the total cost of manufacturing bricks on a estate which had no other resources.[374] Such proportions were lower in the Midlands where timber and then

---

368 SRO, 49/44/50.
369 SA, 112/1/2775.
370 SRO, D(W)1788 P44/10.
371 SRO, D593/F/3/2/16-17.
372 SRO, D590/633.
373 Houghton, 398.
374 Foster, C., *Seven Households: Life in Cheshire and Lancashire 1582 to 1774,* Arley Hall Press, (2002), 211.

coal were readily available on many rural estates and enabled the aristocracy and gentry to fire bricks at below market prices. In 1694 William Anson purchased 94,000 bricks, 4,000 tiles and carriage of them from Lichfield for £51 1 5d, a price of approximately 10s. per 1,000. From his own kiln in 1699 the cost was 5s per 1,000.[375] Coal, timber, clay, carriage and labour were available at below market prices on large and well-resourced estates and were important factors in the willingness of the landed gentry to invest in brick building or rebuilding.

Coal was also required in considerable quantities for the making of plaster for the interiors of brick houses. As early as 1485 the Nottingham civic accounts include 'Item paid, the same tyme, for coles and wodde to brenne the same plaster wtt iis'.[376] The materials and techniques used for plastering range from the bottom layer of clay and chopped straw spread over a wattle base in poorer houses to the much finer lime plasters used over a screen of oak laths in the superior houses of the seventeenth and eighteenth centuries. The traditional method of making plaster involved burning the limestone and then mixing it with sand and water to make a mortar which hardened as the calcium hydroxide became converted to calcium carbonate.[377] Increasingly in this period, smooth plaster walls which could be painted or even wallpapered replaced either wattle and daub or the more expensive wooden panelling. In 1705 John Fenton purchased wainscoting for his expensive new house but 24 years later the estimate for a cheaper and smaller estate house at Ingestre included plastered walls. In almost all eighteenth-century contracts there are references to the purchase of laths and of either straw or more usually hair which were used to bind the plaster together. For all houses in which the walls were plastered, coal was required at some stage in the process. The result of the demand for coal for brickmaking and the production of plaster was a marked expansion in the machinery of distribution. For example, a document entitled 'Teams to be asked to Lord Chetwynds Coal Carriage' in 1737 includes 19 separate names.[378] This was obviously a substantial trade.

Coal and its Impact on the Brick Industry
Early coal mining is generally poorly documented. John Hatcher, in a survey of the Midland coal industry, comments on 'the want of colliery accounts' and

---

375 SRO, D615P(A)/1/1, D615/P/(A)/1/5.
376 *NBR* **III**, 231.
377 Hudson, 46.
378 SRO, D1789/HM/Chetwynd105. The coal trade also included domestic demand.

the 'ill-documented' production side. But he estimates, based on 'informed guesswork,' that in the Midlands there was a considerable rise in production founded on increased domestic and industrial demand.

Table 7: The Estimated Output of British Coalfields, 1560s-c.1700[379]

Area	1560s (tons)	c.1700 (tons)	Growth Rate (fold)
Leicestershire	5,000	40,000	8
Nottinghamshire and Derbyshire	15,000	75,000	5
Shropshire	12,000	230,000	19
Staffordshire	15,000	150,000	10
Warwickshire	3,000	45,000	15

Between 1550 and 1700 regional production rose to about 540,000 tons. The size of the collieries varied considerably, for example on the Warwickshire Coalfield generally the main method of production was working at the outcrop on the exposed coalfield in a succession of short life shallow bell pits whose depths were governed by the length of a ladder. Exceptionally there were also large and heavily capitalised mines at Bedworth and Griff. The 'great mine' at Bedworth for example, employed 500 men and produced 20-30,000 tons annually in the 1630s, but geological and transport problems prevented continuous production. Between 1599 and 1710 the large colliery at Griff was only in operation for 39 years. These two pits illustrate a major problem in Midland coal production that only where the coal seam approached or crossed a navigable river could large-scale workings be consistently profitable.

The Warwickshire Coalfield generally had two major problems, it was a 'wet' field and required a smaller labour force than that needed than in other coalfields. The collieries progressed along the narrow, exposed coalfield in short life pits that were exhausted after a year or so. On this field and in most others the size of the units was small, with a small labour force, few producing more than 5,000 tons p.a. Any rise in production was therefore generated by a proliferation of many small units. Stephen Glover in his *History of the County*

---

379   Thatcher, J., *The History of the British Coal Industry*, **1**, *Before 1700: Towards the Age of Coal*, OUP, (1993), 68.

of Derby of 1829 lists over 250 collieries, mainly in Derbyshire, of which half had been 'worked formerly'.[380] At Goyt Moss Colliery on the small Buxton field there were over 200 shafts with no more than three used at any one time.[381] In Central Derbyshire, 'the view that there were no pits of any size in this part of the coalfield is borne out by the earliest Derbyshire Land Tax records'. Those for the year 1779 mention only the two collieries at Shipley and Stanton.[382] The level of investment for such pits was relatively small. Is another explanation for the limited number of coalpit-based brick works the lack of capital of men investing in mines alone? Did small-scale investors in coal not have the wealth to invest in both bricks and coal? It was also possible that the temporary and seasonal nature of brick production meant that coal pit owners had little incentive to invest in buildings or expensive equipment. Precise costs of the capital required to build a brick kiln are rare and as previously described are erratic varying from a few pounds to the £31 18s 1d paid in 1726 by the Duchess of Rutland for a 'New Brick Kiln'. For the aristocracy or gentry, the kiln usually provided bricks for the estate. The small-scale producer, seeking a more general market, was handicapped by the added costs of buildings, labour, tools and the transport of brick to a potential purchaser.

In terms of economic development Hatcher concluded that in Staffordshire, despite the lack of navigable rivers and the competition from the Leicestershire, Warwickshire and Shropshire Coalfields, 'these disadvantages did not impose a strait jacket upon development since, to an extent greater than almost anywhere else, central Staffordshire was an industrializing region where a wide range of coal-burning industries flourished close to the mines'.[383] As previously noted, Plot in 1686 referred to its use in 'glass-houses, Salt works and brick clamps'. An example of a little-known salt works is the one at Preston on the Weald Moors which incorporated a brickworks and were held between 1721 and 1730 by local mining interests. It later used coal from nearby Wombourne before its closure in 1799.

Porcelain manufacture, initially established in London far from clay and coal supplies and based only on the demands of fashionable society, began from the 1760s onwards to move northwards. By 1787 there were no porcelain

---

380 Glover, S., *History of the County of Derby,* Derby, (1829), 53-56.
381 Barnatt, J., and Leach, J., 'The Goyt's Moss Colliery, Buxton,' *DAJ,* **117**, (1997), 56.
382 Hopkinson, G.G., The Inland Navigations of the Derbyshire and Nottinghamshire Coalfield, 1777-1856. *DAJ,* **79**, (1959), 23.
383 Hopkinson, 149.

manufacturers operating in London and all production was taking place at centres away from the capital, with a special emphasis on the Midlands. This was in part brought about by ease of access to coal measures as a source of fuel, to the presence of a growing and skilled workforce and to improvements in transport brought about by the canal network and turnpiked roads.

For brickmaking the picture is somewhat different with the documentary evidence not fully supporting Hatcher's assumption of coalpit-based brick works. One of the most intriguing features of some coal mining leases of the eighteenth century is the refusal of the landowner to grant permission for large scale brick production alongside the extraction of coal. Although in the nineteenth century the integration of coal mining and large-scale brickmaking was commonplace, before 1780 there are surprisingly few references to its obvious advantages. Limited integration did occur, an early example is one of 1551 at Broseley where there was 'the house called a Tylehouse next le Cole Pyt there'.[384] An exceptional survival is a mining account book of 1748 which includes an entry for '7,400 bricks from the Star at 9s per thousand £3 7s'. Star Wood, near Alton, was a traditional mining area.[385] On the other hand an undated (1720s?) draft agreement between Burslem Sparrow, a mining entrepreneur, and landowner John Robins for a lease of mines at Stowheath required 'That Mr Sparrow shall have Liberty to make Bricks upon the Premises for the use of the Mines only therein'.[386] In 1743 the Ellesmere churchwardens leased land to Joseph Lee which allowed that 'J.L. may within the first 5 years raise clay on the premises and make brick with it provided bricks should not exceed 40 thousand'.[387] A mining agreement between Samuel Bamford of Cheadle, and four others in 1774, allowed Bamford 'the liberty to get slack to take to lime kilns to be exchanged for lime for the improvement of their own lands, to carry away with horses carts and wagons. Also to make bricks for his own use but not for sale'.[388] Near Oswestry the lease of a coal mine in 1750 allowed the lessee 'to get and carry away all coals and slack under the arable and pasture lands and to stack them on the banks, to dig pits, to drive soughs, to dig clay to make bricks and burn them for the use of

---

384 *Patent Rolls, 1549-1551*, 213.
385 Chester, H.A., *The History of the Cheadle Coalfield*, Ashbourne: Landmark (2002), 31.
386 SRO, D1798/666/171.
387 SA, P256/Q/5/9.
388 Chester, 43.

sinking pits'.[389] A lease of 1773 at Priorslee specifically granted 'all mines of clay for making brick or tile for the sinking of pits (but not for sale)'. In Derbyshire in 1767 on the aristocratic estates of the Dowager Duchess of Portland, a lease of £20 p.a. secured 'all coal in (the) common called Grassmoor, (p. Chesterfield) and stone and clay to make bricks required for shafts or soughs'. The pits had to be filled up or rendered safe at the end of the lease and the lessees were granted the right to inspect the work. As late as 1805 a lease at Pontesbury allowed free coal only 'for burning brick for erecting buildings for the use of the colliery only'.

Even on a smaller domestic scale brickmaking could be restricted, in 1734 at Broseley, Richard Beard leased 'a messuage and a little pit or wasteland before the house with liberty to make brick on the premises for the use of the premises only'.[390] In 1750 an agreement concerning coal workings at Wolstanton granted permission to carry bricks *to* the mine.[391] In all the above examples brick making was limited to the use of the clays exposed when these small scale mining enterprises sank their shafts or opened shallow pits.[392]

It is difficult to explain the above restrictions imposed on the natural integration of coal mining and brick manufacture. The enormous emphasis placed on the restoration of the land on the completion of the lease suggests that many landlords feared the environmental impact of clay extraction and regarded as essential the need to return the field to agricultural use. In Ludlow in 1694 the Corporation:

> *Graunted then licence to Mr Nicholas Fothergill to rayse claye upon the towne lands in his possession in Gaolford to be imployed onley in buildinge and repairing the houses and buildings bellongeinge to this corporation in his possession and not elsewhere provided it be noe nusance to the towne and make good and soyle when finished.*[393]

Detailed land restoration is implicit in an Ellesmere lease of 1723 which stated that it was:

---

389   SA, 2868/175.
390   SA, 1224/3/503.
391   SRO, D4452/1/14/10/3.
392   SRO, D1798/666/171.
393   Roberts, K., ed. Ludlow Historical Research Group, 'Resources', 89.

> *Lawful from Edm. Bullock to raise clay for the making of brick and to burn bricks in that corner and part of the demised premises only, which is between the town of Ellesmere and the place where the first gate now is, always leaving a sufficient road for such as claim a way through the premises, and carrying off all pieces of brick and other rubbish at end of lease and levelling and reducing to good order for pasture land all banks and pits made on that part of the premises.[394]*

At Atherstone a brick kiln lease of 1763 specifically required the top soil to be kept 'at end of town'.[395] The environmental impact of large scale brickmaking could be obvious, as at Chester in 1658 where a brick pit associated with a complaint against 'poisoning the water' was measured as 71 yards wide by 203 yards long.[396] At about the same time, the City Council received a:

> *Petition of the Constables and other inhabitants of St John's ward, who have suffered by divers persons building houses and workshops on the waste land of the City near Cowlane gate and have dug deep holes and pits to get clay to make bricks, Edward Gray, bricklayer, had dug up about 60 yards of ground.[397]*

Where common land was to be dug often the local authorities insisted on a licence and fee as in the petition of Nicholas Fothergill in 1700 at Ludlow.[398] The incidental dangers of brick pits were obvious, in 1705 William Morton of Redditch was presented for keeping a disorderly alehouse and selling drink on the Sabbath, particularly to John Mitchell who, full of drink, drowned in a brick field.

Environmental damage was not restricted to clay working, but also could be inflicted by coal mining. In 1746 a lessor of a coal mine at Stretton, Derbyshire, complained that the lessees:

> *Have carried and laid very great quantities amounting to more than One Thousand Loads of Deads, (unusable coal) earth, dirt, slack and rubbish*

---

394 SA, P256/Q/5/3.
395 WRO, CR2581.
396 CRO, ZA/F/34/34.
397 CRO, ZA/F/34/34.
398 SA, LB/4/3/2115.

raised out of the said coal mine into the Common King's highway leading from Chesterfield towards Derby. Whereby the same is becoming dangerous.[399]

Lord Middleton in 1731 had to pay compensation to 12 tenants for damage by coalmining at Trowell.[400] However, relative to clay extraction, restoring the damage caused by coal workings was comparatively easy to accomplish and was often a requirement of the lease. At Ansley in 1723 a ten-year mining lease at £50 p.a. allowed John Farmer 'to erect inns, reckoning houses, shops, barns or stables, but must be removed within 9 months of the determination of the lease'.[401] A 1730 Apedale agreement required the 'sd George Berks Shall & will fillup all his or their Pitts immediately after he has left of using them. Also to pay tenant farmers for any damage'. At Uttoxeter in 1754 Richard Dudley was presented 'for breaking the Lords soil in Uttoxeter heath, getting clay and not filling up the pits 13s 4d', he, William and Thomas Dudley were all fined for same offence in the following year.[402] In 1766 a lease of coal and ironstone pits at Morley Park required John Hurt 'to fill up the pits and to make good the damages to tenants'.[403]

The Trowell contract described above required '2 pickmen to fillup and level' on completion. When the coal was exhausted or the lease expired then the pit could be back-filled with spoil, any buildings removed, and in a few years all that would remain would be the saucer-shaped hollow so characteristic of bell pits. The scale of such industrial enterprises varied considerably, some mines were often very small. An extreme example is a 1684 agreement on the Edge Estate at Strelley for a pit entrance limited it to 7 feet long and 6 feet wide.[404] At Salterwood, Derby, bell pits were found which measured 16 feet by 10 feet at the top and 20 feet deep. Many were obviously less shallow but still were small-scale workings, the deepest pit in Leicestershire at Measham in 1722 was only 75 feet deep. Most pits employed only a small labour force, for instance the colliery accounts for a pit at Bilston for 1750-51 suggest

---

399 Hopkinson, G.G., 'Stretton in the 17th and 18th Centuries', *DAJ*, **71**, (1951), 64.
400 Aley, S., *The Nottingham Landowners and their Estates*, unpublished PhD, Nottingham Univ. (1985), 294.
401 DRO, 231/M/E/5153.
402 SRO, D1504/2/2.
403 DRO, D2535/M/3/66.
404 NA, DDE/46/80.

that only four labourers were employed.⁴⁰⁵ Such small-scale workings left the landscape relatively unscarred. Where brick was fired at a coal mine there could be greater damage to the land surface. A mining agreement of 1723 for a large Nottinghamshire mine rented at '£1,200 p.a., also £100 per acre of coal over the former sum, and £25 per acre of soft top coal, and 1/6d for every 1,000 bricks made' included compensation of '£2 10s for every acre of land spoilt'.⁴⁰⁶

Compared with coal mines a clay pit could cause lasting environmental damage as it covered a much wider area, removed the topsoil and thus reduced the future agricultural potential of the land. Gerbier in his *Counsel and Advise* emphasised that those 'who love to keep their Park and grounds even and handsome, they may take notice that in the number of twenty Thousand of Bricks bought or made, there is not above six shillings & eight pence difference' – arguing that to protect the appearance of the estate bricks could be purchased at only a slightly higher price.⁴⁰⁷ Such a limited price differential is very optimistic, but it does suggest an awareness of the damage created by brickmaking. In 1762 a lease of the lands of the Earl of Lichfield specified the mining of 'all mines, veins of coal, ironstone, limestone, or other minerals, and clay for making bricks, *except the Park and Gardens of Ditchley*'.⁴⁰⁸

Coal fired brickmaking was also a source of environmental pollution – in 1687 a Treasury warrant granted the right to make bricks for the repair of Windsor Castle 'but with a proviso that care be taken not to burn bricks when the Court is at Windsor for avoiding any offence which may be given by the smoke thereof'.⁴⁰⁹ In 1768 the Chester city council protested against the use of a piece of waste land for brickmaking, 'the ground in front of the house … was in unseemly condition, with several pits of unwholesome stagnant water. The smoke occasioned by the brick burning cause great annoyance to the inhabitants'.⁴¹⁰ The filth and disruption created by the brick kiln was neatly summarised in the choleric verses of an anonymous visitor to Cheltenham:

---

405   SRO, D1798/666/171.
406   Nottingham University Library, D231M/E5153.
407   Gerbier, 52.
408   Oxford History Centre, E36//1/1/D/14.
409   *Calendar of Treasury Books* **8**: *1685-1689*, ed. Shaw, W.A., London: HMSO, (1923) 'Entry Book: December 1687, 21-31'.
410   CA, ZA/B/4 [262].

'Verses, written by a Phthisicky visitor, after hemming up an ounce of brick-dust, on an evening walk':

> *Where Taste erects a classic cot*
> *To suit some sickly peer,*
> *Envy, with diabolical zeal*
> *Will build a brick-kiln near!*
>
> *While at one wing the genial breeze*
> *Wafts health, as poets tell us;*
> *On t'other side the smoke obtrudes,*
> *And clogs the pect'ral bellows!* [411]

The restrictive attitude was not common to all landowners for some entrepreneurs were able to see the obvious advantages of combined production and many were apparently willing to accept environmental disturbance to their lands and required only its restoration after clay extraction had been completed. In a lease in 1721 of three acres of land by John Persehowse, of Reynolds Hall, to Thomas Wood, 'brickmaker' at a rent of £5 p.a. Wood was allowed 'to digg cast up earth and clay and convert the same into Brick or tiles and to have take see and dispose of the said Brick and tiles to his or their own proper use'. Wood had also 'to fill up and make level the holes and pitts that shall be wrought … and the soyle that shall be cast up shall lay upon the surface of the said demises', i.e., the surface soil had to be retained and replaced. However further leases in 1731, 1744 and 1766 all to Thomas Wood, 'Brickman and husbandman', of the same field specifically prevented Wood from 'working clay, stone or other minerals'.[412] At Ludlow in 1732 'William Back, who had made Brick on his lands in Goalford with (out?) ye license of the Corporation be forgiven the offence and has liberty to make brick there under the above conditions'. In 1754 the Corporation minutes recorded 'Mr Back, Brickmaker, given notice to make land good in Gaolford or be sued for the waste committed'. A lease to William Hand in 1775 required that 'The land is to be used for making brick for the first seven years after which

---

411 *Morning Herald*, (4th July, 1809).
412 SRO, D260/M/E/ 425/1-7.

the tenant will fill up holes etc. and lay it with clover or grass seed on pain of payment of £10 per acre. He is not to break it for tillage without licence on pain of same sum'.[413]

If the land was not restored, it could continue to be rented out to other brickmakers or on aristocratic estates the clay pits could be transformed into a feature of formal parkland such as a fishpond or ornamental water. In 1724 the steward of the Attingham Estate reported that 'John Holford and his men are now making a fish pool where all the bricks have been made'.[414] It was often difficult to create the ornamental ponds or lakes which were so desired by aristocratic gardeners and landscape improvers. Only in areas of impermeable clay, of which there were many in the Midlands, was it a relatively cheap and straightforward process. By the early eighteenth century large-scale displays of water had become a feature of the formal landscape and whatever the scale, lakes were a significant expenditure. A small lake for Wrightson Munday at Osbaston, Leics, cost £319 13s 11d and between 1787 and 1790 the Duke of Newcastle spent £3,000 15s 9d on an extension to the lake at Clumber Park. Building an artificial lake was expensive so the re-use of a redundant brick pit could make a considerable saving.[415]

Whilst production of brick at the building site reduced transport costs, if coal was not immediately available then the cost of its transport added to the overall cost of making brick.[416] Poor weather and badly surfaced roads would hinder the carriage of coal. In the summer of 1725 the Hawkstone Estate steward reported that 'the brick and tile is not yet made … and if the brick had been made the roads have been and still are so bad that the coals cannot be had to burn them'.[417] A further problem, hinted at in some leases, was the effect of heavy loads of bricks on the surface of local roads and for which there was a legal duty of repair. A Manchester Cathedral lease of 1761 describes the resulting restrictions, 'The Lessee may make brick on Newton Common … not prejudicing the roads or highway in any way, such bricks to be employed … in the walling of pits, water

---

413 Roberts, *Ludlow*, 117, 130, 138.
414 SA, 112/1.2550.
415 Roberts, J., 'Well Temper'd Clay: Constructing Water Features in the Landscaped Park', *Garden History*, **29**, **1**, (2001), 12-28.
416 Barker, T., and Gerhold, D., *The Rise and Rise of Road Transport, 1700-1950,* Cambridge: CUP, (1993), 5. 'The cost of carrying coal overland for ten miles at least doubled pithead prices'.
417 SA, 112/1/2717.

ends or dams, in the erection of buildings … and for no other purpose'. In 1737 the Worcestershire Quarter Sessions issued a 'Certificate that the road from Mr Hadley's brick kiln in Yardley to Lea Ford towards Castle Bromwich, being the Solihull to Sutton Coldfield Road is in good repair'.[418]

Prior to the use of brick, timber was required for lining the mine shaft and for pit props. An important investigation of early coal pits at Coleorton, some of which were 100 feet deep, revealed some 300 timber lined shafts whose supportive and carpentered oak frames were set roughly 3 feet apart along the shafts which were about 4 feet by 5 feet in cross section. Dendrochronology has revealed that those of fifteenth century timber exceeded in size and quality those of the late sixteenth century suggesting that timber was increasingly expensive and in short supply.[419] Brick linings resolved the problem. Plot describes the specialist bricks produced for coal mines:

> *To a sort of arched-Bricks they make about Wednesbury, bent round to fit the Eyes of their Cole-pits, which are generally about 2 yards in diameter, by which they are secured from colting in, much better than by timbers, as I saw some pits near that Town, thus wall'd up with them for two yards deep.*[420]

At Broseley, archaeological research into this once rich coal mining area revealed shafts at Fishouse Colliery, Stocking ironstone spoil and Cockshutt spoil heap – each of which contained evidence of the exposed tops of shafts with three or four courses of brick with a diameter of around five foot.[421]

A rare survival of a contract with a London engineer for construction of a colliery pump at Bilston in 1692 also includes a reference to a brick lining.[422] A similar reference is contained in a letter of 1739 from the Rev. D. Wardle in which he mentions a mine with pits bricked and timbered being available for lease and no longer in 'precarious & inconsiderate conditions' as it had been previously.[423] As Plot hints, the lining of the coal pits with brick increased

---

418   Worcestershire Record Office, (Worcs. RO) 1/1/315/18.
419   Hartley, R., 'The Tudor Miners of Coleorton, Leicestershire', *Bulletin of the Peak District Mines Historical Society,* **12**, **3**, (Summer, 1994), 91.
420   Plot, 358.
421   Hudson, S.C., *Industrialisation and an Early Modern Town: Broseley in Shropshire 1600-1820,* M.Phil. Thesis, University of Birmingham, (2017), 326.
422   WSL, Hand Morgan (Robins), uncatalogued, 34/6/1.
423   SRO, D3359/12/1/30.

their efficiency. A deed of 1751 which concerned a mine at Wood Farm in Little Fenton specifically arranged for a 'fire engine' (atmospheric pump) and 'a bricked pit to be provided so that coal can be got out at a lower level'.[424] Shaped bricks used for lining coal shafts were of obvious value, a lease of coal lands at Heanor in 1799 included the requirement 'also to pay 2s. 6d. for each 1,000 bricks to be taken out of another pit there'.[425]

This chapter does not argue that the natural integration of brick and coal production was rare, but rather that many mining enterprises were small-scale, under-capitalised and for environmental or financial reasons were unable to exploit their potential. Larger coal mines could be extensive businesses burning and employing brick for outbuildings, public houses, engine houses, accounting rooms and for public sale. As early as 1634 Lawrence Benthall had sunk coal pits in Benthall Marsh, and it was said that 30,000 tons were annually shipped along the Severn. He also promoted the manufacture of bricks at the mine site.[426] The lengthy inventory of the South Normanton mine owner Godfrey Hazelhurst in 1698 valued his estate at £1,228 and included 20,000 bricks 'In Ye Brick Kill' and 'Coals' valued at £108.[427] A lease at Little Dawley in 1733 required the tenant to pay 1s per stack of coal (40 cwt) or 1s for every 10s 6d of coal sold on the banks of the pit or at Severn side, 1s for every dozen of 11 strikes of ironstone, 1s for every 1,000 of bricks, 1s 6d per 1,000 of tiles and 3d a dozen of crests, gutters, kiln bricks (fire bricks?) and quarries. This was obviously a totally integrated enterprise.[428] In 1760 a lengthy pamphlet by Gabriel Holland, a Swannington 'Coal-Master', sought to justify his debts and explain the failure of promised investors to support him. The letter describes a sophisticated complex of two pits, 'deep coal', the process of 'waggoning' and a 'Fire Engine'. 'There is also a new pit … of elliptical section set with bricks' – presumably shallow and drained by gravity. He notes a type of coal peculiar to Swannington 'of excellent use … for the burning of brick'. Holland also adds that he had built

---

424 SRO, D1798/HM39/20. Clark, G., and Jacks, D., 'Coal and the Industrial Revolution', *www.econ.ucdavis.edu/faculty/gclark/papers/Coal2006*, suggest for the later period of c.1850 that bricks represented about 10% of mining capital.

425 NA, DD/CH/36/6, 1799.

426 *VCH, Salop,* **10**, 247-257.

427 SRO, B/C/5/1692/3.

428 SA, 1681/183/2.

several houses for his workforce.[429] Other entrepreneurs also saw the obvious advantages of integration, Joseph Wilkes (1733-1805) climbed to fortune and celebrity by investment in coal mining, cotton mills, banking, the Ashby canal, turnpike roads and early Boulton and Watt engines. He supported many of his enterprises with bricks from his brickworks at Measham where the famous Wilkes 'Gobs' or 'Jumbies' were produced.

The role of the coal pits as consumers of brick is not well referenced, but the limited sources are sufficient to suggest that the expansion of the coal industry provided a stimulus to brick production. An early mining contract of 1668 between three Cheadle landowners included an agreement with a neighbouring landowner which allowed the building of a sough or drain under his land. That sough, accidentally revealed in open cast mining in the 1960s, was brick-built.[430] The soughs represent sophisticated drainage engineering and were often of considerable length, for example the stone built Hillcarr Sough in Denby Dale, built in 1766, was over 6,100 yards long and cost £30,000. In coal mines they were usually built of brick and their cost equally added to overall production charges. 'John Oliver's Sough' driven in 1708 was 320 yards long and measured only 8 inches wide and 10 inches high, it cost £63. Goyts Moss Sough of c.1750 was driven 'at considerable expense'.[431] Many brick-built soughs were built at a substantial charge for 'dewatering' in the years before the Newcomen and later, Boulton and Watt pumping engines were regularly employed for drainage. On the South Derbyshire Coalfield, in the 1720s, John Barnes estimated a price of £500 for a sough at Barlow, near Chesterfield.[432]

Brick soughs became increasingly popular as the demand for coal increased and as mines were worked at deeper depths. An agreement on the Isle Estate in 1793 provides a detailed picture of the sophisticated bricklaying expected of three 'contractors' for a brick sough of 300 yards in length and 18 inches in diameter, at a cost of £152. It was to be built in a 'firm, substantial,

---

429 Baker, D., 'Swannington Coal-Master Seeks Capital: Gabriel Holland in 1760', *The Leicestershire Historian,* **3**, **1** (1982-3), 5-12.

430 Chester, 21.

431 Heathcote, C., 'Coal Mine Soughs Draining into the Rivers Goyt and Sett in North-West Derbyshire,' *Mining History, Bulletin of Peak District Mines Historical Society,* **16**, **4**, (Winter, 2006), 25.

432 Hopkinson, G.G., *The Development of Lead Mining and the Coal and Iron Industries in North Derbyshire and South Yorkshire, 1700-1850,* (1958), White Rose Theses Online.

expeditious and workmanlike manner', with the sponsor, Foliot Sandford, providing 'timber, lime, sand and carriage'. Work was to start on 29th July and be completed by 29th of November in the next year.[433] It was claimed that the sough 'drained one of the largest pieces of water in the county' and significantly increased the value of the estate.[434]

The evidence suggests that coal became the main fuel for burning brick earlier than has previously been believed. It was easily accessible and in conjunction with Triassic and Carboniferous clays, produced bricks to meet an increasing demand for domestic and industrial use. A complex relationship ensued in which mined coal was used to burn clay and the bricks produced supported the increased efficiency of coal mining. Landholders, increasingly aware of the financial potential of clay-rich estates, had to make crucial decisions on the prospective profits from the short-term manufacture of brick and the consequent damage to their land, against the extraction of coal with its limited and repairable impact.

---

433   SA, 465/399.
434   Blakeway, J.B., 'History of the Shrewsbury Hundred or Liberties – The Isle', *TSAS*, **IX**, (1897), 224-5.

Chapter 6

TIMBER AND BRICK AS BUILDING MATERIALS

MOST MIDLAND houses were neither timber-framed, brick nor stone but of much poorer building materials. 'Mud' was probably the most common building material. In Nottinghamshire Thoroton noted 'how often, even at this distant period, do we meet with wretched dwellings in some of our villages … two parallel dirt walls, a dirt floor and thatched roof constitute the abode that shelters human forms, almost without cloathing, from the inclement seasons of each revolving year' and at Edwalton, 'the parsonage … is one of the most wretched habitations I ever beheld: the walls are of dirt or of materials equally as graceful … once honoured with thatch covering now partly removed by the wind … near it is a brick barn which serves as an elegant contrast'.[435]

In Elizabeth's reign, 'saltpeter men' were legally allowed to break down mud walls and earthen floors to recover potassium nitrate for gunpowder manufacture. The extent of earthen buildings is suggested in a petition by Leicester Council in 1590 to the Earl of Huntingdon, 'there ys a saltpetre maker within the towne who reporteth that he will throw down our mudde walls … will be in damage to the towne a thousand markes'.[436] In 1583 the City's accounts include 'making

---

435 Thoroton, **2**, 3-16, 123.
436 Fosbrooke, T.H., and Skillington, S.K., 'The Old Town Hall of Leicester', *TLAS*, **13**, (1923-4), 59.

of the florthe ageyn in the kitchyn of the hall after the salte petre man'.[437] The saltpeter men also visited local villages, in 1601 the constable of Repton recorded 'It(em) spent with the saltpeter men ii d'.[438] Their work proved so vexatious that in 1646 they were restricted to 'Saltpeter in all Pigeon-houses, Stables, Cellars, Vaults, empty Ware-Houses and other Out-houses, Yards and places likely to afford that earth'.[439] Interestingly, as early as 1561, the entrepreneur Gerard Henrick, who built five gunpowder mills for Queen Elizabeth, suggested that saltpeter could be obtained by scraping 'New Brick' set in lime mortar.

The diarist John Evelyn recorded in 1654:

> *Went to Uppingham, the shire town of Rutland, pretty and well-built of stone which is a rarity in that part of England where most of the parishes are built of mud and the people living as wretchedly as in the most impoverished parts of France, which they much resemble, being idle and sluttish. The country (especially Leicestershire) much in common.*[440]

An undated report to the Duke of Newcastle described the building of the traditional 'mud and stud' buildings, 'a bay to be made up a wall with Splents uprites & Clay … and the Splents are all worked in whart are made Comonly of split halfes sallows or willos and not of timber'.[441] In Leicestershire a similar 'Mud and Frame' building combined a 'basic' timber framework with solid mud lower walling. William Cobbett described the 'miserable sheds' of a Leicestershire village as 'hovels made of mud and of straw with old off-cast windows … bits of glass stuck into the mud walls'.[442] At Lye Waste, near Stourbridge, there were so many earth-built cottages and houses that this

---

437 *RBL* **III** 292. In 1627 a Royal Proclamation declared that, 'When a house in London or 3 miles round is pulled down, notice is to be given to the Saltpetre men at Southwark, who may remove what earth they choose'. Crawford, J., '*Biblotheca Lindesiana, Bibliography of Royal Proclamations of the Tudor and Stuart Sovereigns,* Oxford: Clarendon Press, (1910), 178.
438 Cox, J.C., 'The Registers and Churchwardens' and Constables' Accounts of the Parish of Repton', *DAJ,* **1**, (1879), 36.
439 Acts and Ordinances of the Interregnum, 1642-1660, HMSO, (1911), 828-830.
440 Evelyn, J., The *Diary of John Evelyn,* (online), **1**, 294.
441 NA, DD4P 64/14/16.
442 Cobbett, W., *Rural Rides,* (1830), Nelson, (1934), 541.

squatters' settlement was nicknamed 'Mud City'.[443] In 1830 the Archdeacon of Stafford's Visitation noted that the parsonage of Thorpe Constantine was 'small, ill-built, house-walls partly brick, partly mud'.[444] Even later in 1865 Dr H.J. Hunter, the Medical Officer of the Privy Council, condemned the 'dilapidated and miserable hovels' of the Midlands.[445] Although most mud-walled hovels were demolished by the newly created Sanitary Commissions after 1871 some, particularly in Nottinghamshire and Leicestershire, have survived hidden behind superficial brick facing and are the remnants of what was perhaps the most frequently employed building material.[446] For many of the poor of the rural Midlands, clay and poor-quality wood were the building materials of necessity and brick therefore represented a level of investment only rarely employed.

For some of the Midland poor, the easily workable Sherwood Sandstones provided cave dwellings. A sketch by William Stukeley in his *Itinerarium Curiosum* of 1724 is entitled, 'Ruins of Settlement of Cave Dwellers near Nottingham'. The site occupied by these 'troglodytiae' was on the Park Estate of the Duke of Newcastle. In 1740 the City Council ordered that the 'Rock Holes' should be pulled down.[447] Similar dwellings existed at Mansfield, where in 1654 John Evelyn observed 'a diverse people who live in rocks and caves'. They were also present at Kinver, (Staffs), Anchor Church, (Derbys) and Bridgnorth.

The Relationship between building Timber and Brick
The traditional opinion that the popularity of brick was determined by its falling price and the rise in the price of building timber is shared by several historians. For A. Clifton-Taylor, 'it was not until the last quarter of the seventeenth century that, thanks to falling prices, the taste for this material really gathered

---

443 Cochrane, D., *A Brief History of Lye & Wollescote, Part II,* Waterloo Design and Print, (2013), 14-16. The cottages dated from the 1650s. Most were single-roomed, but a nineteenth-century photograph of the last surviving house shows a four-roomed house with two upper rooms.
444 Robinson, D., ed. 'The Visitations of the Archdeaconry of Stafford 1829-184', *SHC.,* **X**. 26.
445 *Parliamentary Papers* **XXVI**, HMSO, (1866), Medical Officer of the Privy Council, seventh report, (1865), 12.
446 *VCH, Leics.* **4**, In Fleckney 'were the mud-and thatch cottages of the brickmakers, four of which stood in front of the pinfold on the Arnesby Road and were demolished shortly before 1956', 84.
447 *NBR,* **VI**, 166.

momentum'.[448] R.J. Brown has a similar view, 'Slowly the use of brick gained momentum for whilst the price of timber was rising the price of brick was falling'.[449] Anthony Quiney also agrees with this interpretation, 'In fact the cultivation of timber fell into desuetude as brick and stone rose in general esteem and fell in relative cost'.[450] This chapter investigates the price and availability of timber, it considers and modifies the previously commonly held view that traditional building timber was increasingly unavailable and that therefore there were no alternatives to brick for the would-be builder, purchaser or improver.

How far and with what ease was brick able to replace the previously traditional building material of timber? For some historians the apparent coincidence, after 1660, of the increased use of brick and reduced building in timber has suggested a direct relationship. Mercer in a description of 'late framing' of the seventeenth and eighteenth centuries, states that:

> *Everywhere timber was replaced by brick and stone for the homes of the wealthy, but it continued to be used by poorer men. The timbers are of small scantling, and their diminution in size was probably due to several causes. In the first place there may have been a shortage of timber due to its prodigal use for iron smelting and ship-building.*[451]

Palliser in his *Staffordshire Landscape,* in the context of a discussion of Broughton Hall, concludes that, 'well before 1637 a combination of fashion and timber shortage was encouraging the use of brick in the Vale of Trent'.[452] For Brunskill, 'brickwork made most headway in those counties in which structural timber was becoming scarce but timber for firing the abundant brick earth was still available'.[453]

The likelihood of a scarcity of building timber in the early seventeenth century is however open to some doubt. For example, in the 38 parishes administered by the Stafford District Council there survive 193 timber-framed buildings of which 'the majority ... are of 17th century date although a few are

---

448 Clifton-Taylor, 215.
449 Brown, R.J., *English Farmhouses*, Robert Hale, (1993), 231.
450 Quiney, A., *The Traditional Buildings of England,* London: Thames & Hudson, (1990), 149.
451 Mercer, E., *English Vernacular Houses,* RCHM, HMSO, (1973), 125-6.
452 Palliser, *The Staffordshire Landscape*, London: Hodder & Stoughton (1976) 97.
453 Brunskill, *Houses,* 178.

earlier'.[454] In Welford-on-Avon, Warwickshire, are '(some 30) small timber-framed buildings, apparently none earlier than the 17th century'.[455] This would suggest that building timber was readily available in the seventeenth century. Airs agrees with this assessment:

> *It seems that the generally accepted thesis of a growing shortage of timber in the late sixteenth and early seventeenth centuries must be modified to a certain extent in its application to the building industry … it seems that a large number of country house builders, particularly … in the north Midlands completely escaped the effects of any shortage.*[456]

Whitehead has argued, in the contexts of the West Midlands and the late sixteenth and early seventeenth centuries, that, at least for the landowning gentry, building in brick was not because of the shortage of alternative materials 'or even fashion … but rather the availability of fuel which enabled brick to be burnt inexpensively'. He has suggested that building in brick was a piece of 'prudent estate management' and that paradoxically by using readily available underwood and loppings as fuel, valuable mature trees were saved.[457] This very point was made forcibly by the London brickmakers as they sought a charter of incorporation from Charles I in c.1634.[458] In 1686 Plot repeated this view when he wrote that 'the Underwood will pay them (landholders) better for its growth than their Timber ever would'.[459] In 1649 the Parliamentary Survey of the 'Lands and Possessions of the Dean and Chapter of Worcester' laid great emphasis on the value of coppiced wood. It calculated that coppice growth per acre at 17 years growth was worth £7 with slightly less for fewer years. The Survey also recorded attempts by the Chapter to divide its woods into separate areas which could be coppiced in rotation.[460]

---

454 Shryane, J., *Timber Framed Buildings of Staffordshire, Stafford District*, Staffordshire County Planning and Development Department, (nd. 1984?), 7.
455 *VCH, Warks*, **5**, 189.
456 Airs, 121.
457 Whitehead, 44.
458 Thirsk, J., 'Agricultural Policy: Public Debate and Legislation' in Thirsk, J., ed. *The Agrarian History of England and Wales*, **V**, *1640-1750*, CUP, (1984), 374.
459 Plot, 382.
460 Cave, T., and Wilson R.A., eds. *The Parliamentary Survey of The Lands and Possessions of the Dean and Chapter of Worcester,* London: (1924), xvii, xxiv.

Proponents of the view that there was a decline in timber supplies with a consequent rise in prices have attributed these to a variety of causes. One suggestion is that the sequestration of wooded estates during the Civil War and the felling and sale of the timber by new owners uncertain of their ability to hold the estates permanently had significantly affected its availability. Joan Thirsk has concluded that during the Commonwealth, 'the timber resources of the nation had been extravagantly and, indeed, wastefully used'.[461] Pennington and Roots agree with this national picture but have reservations about its application to Staffordshire:

> *The Interregnum is commonly regarded, probably quite rightly, as a period of ruthless and unthinking onslaught on the timber resources of the country as a whole in order to meet short-term demands in the military and naval sphere, to provide ready cash for purchasers of estates or simply as plunder. This does not seem to have been the case in Staffordshire during the first Civil War. The County Committee conceived one of its duties to be the preservation and control of the timber resources of sequestered estates. Goring (Commissary of Timber) dealt with it at every stage to the best advantage of the state, and also, one suspects, of the delinquent owners themselves.*[462]

On many estates due regard seems to have been given to the season of the year, the age of the trees and 'the commodity of the bark'. In Staffordshire, there is some evidence of punitive felling, for example at Brewood Park, leased by the devout catholic Giffard family, the sequestrators calculated that iron working would 'advance the sale of the wood'. In 1649 Peter Giffard, the lessee cut down 110 trees with a value of £300.[463] On estates held by ex-royalist aristocracy confiscation and felling could be extreme. On the Earl of Derby's estates in Nottinghamshire and Derbyshire all his timber was sold on the instructions of the Parliamentary commissioners.[464] The Earl of Newcastle similarly lost woodland worth £45,000 and of his eight hunting parks only Welbeck survived with the others 'defaced and destroyed'. At Clipston 'there

---

461   Thirsk, 374.
462   Pennington, D.H., and Roots, I.A., eds. The Committee at Stafford, 1643-1645, *SHC*, (1957), xliv.
463   *VCH Staffs*, **5**, 26.
464   Coward, B., *The Stanleys, Lords Stanley and Earls of Derby 1385-1672*, Manchester UP, (1983), 69.

being not one timber tree in it left for shelter'. In Nottinghamshire by the end of the seventeenth century the woods were 'mere remnants'.[465] Civil War sieges also led to trees being felled to provide timber for defence or to clear a line of fire as at Warwick castle in 1642.[466]

Enhanced demand for timber for shipbuilding and for wood as an industrial fuel have been proposed as significant causes of a national shortage. There is however some disagreement as to their effects on timber supplies. Parliament, composed mainly of landowners, frequently debated timber supplies during the late seventeenth and eighteenth centuries and proposed a variety of remedies for the shortfall they perceived to exist. Unsuccessfully the disafforestation of some crown forests, including Needwood, was proposed.[467] The urgency and passion of the above discussions and debates would suggest that timber supplies were generally thought to be insufficient and that the integrity of the Royal Navy was at risk from an inadequate supply of shipbuilding timber. Other historians disagree with this view. For Oliver Rackham:

> *the belief that shipbuilding timber was scarce depends on complaints or forebodings of shortage from the sixteenth century onwards. These concern timber for building warships and are not to be taken at face value: had there been the slightest difficulty in finding timber for the tiny fleet that defeated the Armada, it would have been utterly impossible to build the sixty-fold larger fleet that defeated Napoleon. Civilian dockyards were bigger builders of shipping than the navy but bought timber at market prices … Naval dockyards were parsimonious and wasteful: they were short of funds not trees … Not until about 1780 did its (shipbuilding) growth begin to catch up with the supply of trees.*[468]

The traditional view that the woods were largely destroyed by felling for fuel, especially for the charcoal iron industry, has also been subject to reassessment.

---

465 Bishop, Baddeley and Mordan, 4.
466 Tennant, P., 'Parish and People; South Warwickshire and the Banbury Area in the Civil War', *Cake and Cockhorse*, **11**, No. 6, (1989-90), 125.
467 SRO, D(W)1778/V/1176. The estate papers of George Legge contain many references to the timber on his estates at Sandwell and Patshull. They also include an abstract of a scheme for furnishing the Navy with timber and an outline of a bill for the increase and preservation of timber in Needwood Chase.
468 Rackham, O., *The History of the Countryside,* London: Weidenfeld & Nicolson, (1987), 91.

In a famous quotation Dud Dudley wrote in his *Metallum Martis* that in 1665 'within ten miles of Dudley Castle there be near 20,000 smiths of all sorts, and many ironworks decayed for want of wood'.[469] There is no doubt that the charcoal burning iron furnaces of the Midlands consumed huge quantities of wood. Lord Paget's ironworks on Cannock Chase, between 1577 and 1585, burnt 85,600 cords of wood to produce 1,700 tons of iron.[470] Dudley's pessimistic evaluation however may well be an exaggeration for charcoal continued to be produced in large quantities.[471] Philip Riden has identified 38 separate charcoal fired furnaces in the Midlands after 1660. At least eight furnaces in Staffordshire and Shropshire stood on sites active for more than a 100 years and their persistence would suggest that wood supplies were not an important problem. He has concluded that, 'the final phase, roughly 1660-1750 is no longer seen as one of decline in which a growing shortage of fuel led to falling output, but a period in which production reached a higher level than ever before'.[472] In 1737 Edward Knight told a Committee of the House of Commons that Shropshire had an excess of wood, and that in recent years the price of a cord of wood had fallen from 16d to 7d. Abraham Spooner, giving evidence to a similar Committee a year earlier, had suggested that there were sufficient stocks of wood in the Midlands to allow a significant increase in iron production.[473] Hammersley has calculated that 'Twenty-two thousand acres of such coppice would therefore have supplied all the needs of the British iron industry for a year' and 'that as the trees are constantly growing, 650,000 acres of woodland, less than 2% of the land surface of England and Wales, could have sustained the maximum output of the British charcoal iron industry for ever'.[474] After the experiments at Coalbrookdale, coke gradually replaced charcoal for the large-scale production of iron but there were industries where timber was still an important fuel. Pococke in his diary noted that at Newcastle-under-Lyme, a china manufacturer, 'has a great quantity made here

---

469 Dudley, *Metallum Martis*, 7.
470 SRO, D(W)1734/3/3/240.
471 SRO, D1798/664/106-108 are agreements for the sale of timber for charcoal in the 1690s. SRO, D260/M/E /425/7 includes a Walsall agreement as late as 1757.
472 Riden, P., 'The Charcoal Iron Industry in the East Midlands, 1580-1780', *Derbyshire Archaeological Society,* **111**, (1991), 64.
473 Flinn, M., 'The Growth of the English Iron Industry 1660-1760', *Economic History Review*, **11** (1958), 149.
474 Hammersley, G., 'The Charcoal Iron Industry and its Fuel', *Econ. Hist. Rev.* **26**, (1975), 593-613.

for the oven, but he cannot bake it here with coal, which turns it yellow, wood being the fewel which is proper for it'.[475]

The arguments of Rackham, Hammersley and others would suggest that the belief that woodland was dramatically reduced in the period 1550-1750 is exaggerated and that therefore it was not a crucial factor in the decline of timber-framed building. Defoe touring through the counties of the south observed the landed estates and wrote 'There in my opinion are no signs of the decay of our woods or of the danger of our wanting timber in England'.[476] In the Midlands, Staffordshire, for example, was generally regarded as a well wooded county. Celia Fiennes wrote of the view from Harts Hill that, 'all the country which (is) in this part of Staffs is full of woods and inclosures and good land except Kank (Cannock) Wood, which is but barren heath ground but good wood'.[477] Eight years later Dr Plot noted 'that in generall the timber of this Country (though much of it has been destroyed of late years) is as large and good perhaps as in any part of England. Not to mention the great quantities of excellent timber, to be seen in many other parks all over the county'.[478] In the royal Needwood Forest there is some evidence of a typical but minimal loss of timber, a survey of 1684 showed 47,150 trees surviving compared with 57,290 counted in the 1650s. The surveyor added however, that the quality of the wood was 'excellent and particularly 'fitt for shipping … And much of the rest of the said tymber is very good and fitt for building'.[479] There was also sufficient timber for James II to grant 125 tons of wood from the Forest for the building of the Franciscan Masshouse in Birmingham in 1687. In Wem, Samuel Garbett wrote, in 1751 'Wood is nowhere very scarce, but in some places plentiful, being chiefly used for fuel in country houses during the summer season' … although this was qualified by 'Timber for building is not yet wanting but it grows dearer and in some ages will fetch double to present

---

475 Pococke, R., ed. Cartwright, J.J., *The Travels through England of Dr Richard Pococke*, **1**, Camden Society, (1889), 7.

476 Defoe, Vol. 1 140.

477 Fiennes, 147.

478 Plot, 223. The Bagot records include an account of a single elm tree which it was estimated produced 97 tons of timber. SRO, D4038/F29.

479 Mosley, O., *History of The Castle, Priory and Town of Tutbury*, London, (1832), 297-299. The surveyor commented on the 'greate waste committed … aboute the skirtes of the foreste, where the poorer sort of people having been permitted to erect small tenements and cottages doe generally chip and cutt the trees round that are neare their dwellings'. Presumably these were timber-framed cottages.

rates since the trees planted bear no proportion to those that are felled … In the parish of Wem there were formerly several large woods of which little now remains' (felled for charcoal).[480]

Building timber and firewood were not scarce but supplies needed to be carefully managed. At a domestic level a lease on the Whitton Estate, Salop, in 1682, specifically required the tenant to use '20 horse-loads of pitt coal for the saving of wood'.[481] The steward to the Duke of Newcastle wrote in an undated letter from Haughton, 'I shall want a little New Bay about 5 Yards Square to be built of brick therefore will save an abundance of wood'.[482]

Celia Fiennes' comment on 'Kank Wood' is given added weight by a recent comparative study of Elizabethan ironmaking in Cannock Chase and the Churnet Valley.[483] This analysis has demonstrated the considerable *local* impact of charcoal making. Chris Welch has calculated that 24,000 acres of woodland in Cannock was reduced by 91% between 1554 and 1588.[484] A vigorous regime of coppicing would have ensured that the trees regenerated over time. Unfortunately, that attempted was insufficient for sustainability and the effect was therefore severe. In the Churnet Valley iron production was less successful but more in balance with the charcoal supplies, 'while the woodland may not have been as productive as had been hoped, the industry may not have been short of sustainability'.[485]

For the crucial period after 1660 some of the larger forests, such as Sherwood Forest, had almost disappeared, but the owners of smaller estates attempted to take advantage of rising prices by investing in timber. Plot, in 1686, mentions the example of the estate of John Offley at Madeley where 'the timber that surpasses all in the County' was worth £20,000. In Stockerston in 1685 the standing timber in a small wood was valued at £2,000, with yearly profits of £150.[486] A survey at Norbury Park in 1710 estimated that there were 734 oak trees which contained 1,119 tons of timber, i.e. sufficient for 30-35

---

480   Garbett, 8.
481   SA, 11/448.
482   NA, DD4P/64/16.
483   Welch, C., 'Elizabethan Ironmaking and the Woodlands of Cannock Chase and the Churnet Valley, Staffordshire', *Staffordshire Studies*, **12**, (2000), 17-74.
484   Welch, 33.
485   Welch, 40.
486   VCH, *Leics.*, **5**, 305.

houses, with each ton valued at 30s.[487] Rodgers had proposed that between 1653 and 1702 timber rose in price by about 40%. This figure requires some qualification for much of his evidence was derived from southern England where there was greater demand. For the 1680s and 1690s Rodgers suggested an average price of 38-39s per ton. In the Midlands prices were lower. For the rebuilding of Lichfield Grammar School in 1683 oak was purchased at 30s per ton.[488] A private Leicestershire agreement in 1686 recorded the sale of 8 oak timber trees for £15 10s, a price well below Rodger's calculation.[489]

Considerable evidence survives to support the overall impression that there was a very real awareness of the worth of second-hand reusable timbers to maintain older buildings. At Elford, for example, on the Bowes Estate, the steward specifically headed a page in his notebook 'Material from the Old Building pulled down at Elford Hall appropriated to the Repairing of Several farm Houses at Elford July 7th (1758) as follows' and included, 'Thomas Leese 2 wall plates 15' long … To Richard Smith for a bay of building at the End of the House for a new stable …'.[490] The agent of the Beresford Estate in Derbyshire c.1700 recorded 'A note what Timber Mr Beresfords house will take & what it is worth', the timbers included 18 principal posts, 4 main posts with 'collars at each end' and what would seem to be the timbers of a three gabled frontage, the total value was £55 15s.[491] In the Anson manuscripts a page in the steward's records for 1710 is headed, 'an account of saved timber in ye barn' and lists 'wal plats, beames, 2 pare of blads and other wood to the value of £18 8s 6d'.[492] In John Fenton's extremely detailed financial record of his house building at Newcastle he notes that he, 'pulled down ye 2 old Houses, abt Lady Day 1702 and that for the houses I pulled downe were better than £5 … for spending of any timber (for it was almost all my owne and counts not into the acc(ount)'.[493] At Ludlow the Corporation recorded in 1705:

---

487 SRO, D(W)1788/P3/B8.
488 SRO, LD53/1/1.
489 North, T., 'A Leicestershire Pocket-Book, 1686', *LAAS*, Vol **VI**, **pt 1**, (1882), 25.
490 BLAC, Elford Mss., 633.
491 DRO, D158/2/145.
492 SRO, D615/E/8/17.
493 SRO, D(W)1788P/25/1.

> *That Edward Wilding have liberty to plucke downe the little old house near Lower Galford by him held as tenant of this corporation, the materialls whereof are to be disposed of to ye use of the corporation and ye money thereby ariseing to be payd to the hands of Mr Bayliffe Karver for ye corporations use.*[494]

In 1738, having surveyed various properties, Sir Walter Bagot's steward, Samuel Ingram, wrote, 'but the Homes is ready to fall has not been inhabited for severall Years and I believe if all the materials were sold they would more pay for takeing down'.[495] An agreement in 1729 for the rebuilding of Alcester parish church required old timbers to be re-used if approved by Francis Smith.[496] In 1771 a gossipy letter from Thomas Weston to Ann Willes noted that 'The repairs were so expensive because the old timber could not be reused'.[497] This awareness of the value of building materials is found at the highest levels of society. The will of Sir Frances Smith of Wootton Wawen in 1628 included, 'to my wife stone brick and timber about my house at Ashbie (Ashby Folville) or to my sonne Sr Charles or to either of them shall think fit to bestow in building my house at Ashbie'.[498] In 1737 the will of Mary, Countess of Bradford, daughter and co-heir of Sir Thomas and Elizabeth Wilbraham of Weston-under-Lizard, included the gift of 'all building materials at Weston' to her son, Thomas.[499]

One little considered advantage of timber-framed buildings was their flexibility and the opportunity to easily dismantle and rebuild them. In Ludlow in 1600 the Corporation:

> *ordered that Mrs Baldwinge (Baldwin) may remove her little house that we buylded upon the bylet belonginge to the towne mills called the Castle Mylls now in her tenure and the same to be sett upp in Corve Street upon the tenement in the tenure of the said Mrs Baldwin beinge the Townes ground.*[500]

---

494 Roberts, *Ludlow*, 96.
495 SRO, D(W)1721/3/215.
496 WRO, DR0360/33/1.
497 WRO, CR4141/5/150/12.
498 Cooper, W., *Wootton Wawen, its History and Records*, Whitehead, J., (1936), 28.
499 Bridgeman, E.R.O., and Bridgeman, G.C.O., 'History of the Manor and Parish of Weston-under-Lizard,' *SHC*, (1899), 192.
500 Roberts, Ludlow, 10.

In 1614 Sir Thomas Holte agreed that his steward should take down a house 'wherein Dorothy Oldham widow did dwell in Aston with three bays of barninge and two bays of housing and sett up the same where he should thinke good in the further lamstede ffield' and that he would pay £30 towards the cost of so doing.[501] During the Civil War as part of the defences of Stafford, Leicester and Coventry timber-framed houses were taken down with the implicit idea that they could be re-erected. Leicester petitioned that 120 houses had been demolished to improve the defences.[502] In Shrewsbury, Castle Gates House was moved to its present position c.1702 by the Earl of Bradford, its original site being developed as what is now the Guildhall.

The Persistence of Timber-framing
Brick was a material of fashion and the general pattern of its diffusion after 1530 was from royalty to aristocracy to wealthy gentry to the more modest landowners. But this was not a consistent pattern, individual fancy, innate conservatism, tradition and availability often influenced the choice of style and materials. Tim Clayton has explained such conservatism as 'old money could assert its pedigree by displaying its ancient seat'.[503] The King Edward VI Grammar School at Nuneaton, a symbol of great civic pride, in a district of considerable clay working, was rebuilt 1596-99 mainly in timber, only 34s was spent on brick in a total of £119 4s 11d. The brick was probably for chimneys.[504] Pevsner has commented on the clothiers of Shrewsbury that 'it is perhaps worth some stress that they did not change from timber to stone as they grew richer … but from stone to timber. To them timber was the more welcome material because it made a more ostentatious display possible'.[505] Whether this argument applies to the rural Midlands is less certain but balanced against an increasing number of smaller brick farm and manor houses was the consistent building of timber houses. In Shropshire, to which brick, according to Pevsner, 'was a late arrival', elaborately decorated and substantial timber houses continued to be built well into the seventeenth century, for example the huge Boscobel House (1632),

---

501 BLAC, Holte Mss., 46b.
502 Stocks, *Leicester*, 89.
503 Clayton, T., 'Publishing Houses: Prints of Country Seats', in Arnold, D., *The Georgian Country House*, Sutton, (2003), 48-49.
504 WRO, H0001/25.
505 Pevsner, *Shropshire*, 27.

Cherington Manor House, Berrington Manor House (1658), Minsterley Hall built in the latest London double pile style in 1653 and Chirbury school (1675). Bridgnorth Town Hall (1648-52) was rebuilt in timber from an old barn given by Lady Bertie.

Many conservative builders or those with access to cheap supplies continued to build in timber despite the social advantages of brick building. In Derbyshire, Mickleover Old Hall was erected in 1648 and Wadley Manor in 1662.[506] In Staffordshire substantial manor houses were built at Haselour in about 1600, at Boughton (the old part) in 1637 and at Madeley Old Hall in 1647. In Leicestershire dated examples have been recorded at Husbands Bosworth (1712), Bruntingthorpe (1714) and Swinford (1718).[507] In Warwickshire, except for Packwood House and the rebuilding of Middleton Hall, there are few Elizabethan or Jacobean timber-framed mansions. In a county in which there are a great many timber farmhouses and small manor houses, did the aristocracy and wealthier gentry not wish to be associated with the common vernacular style?

The change from timber-framed to brick-built may not have been as dramatic as some historians have suggested. The shift from common building materials and the craft tradition to national 'polite' architecture needs to be qualified by elements of continuity. Lodge Farm at Hollington, Derbyshire, is a cruck-framed house of the seventeenth century, it was built reusing cruck trusses dendrochronologically dated to the fifteenth century.[508] In 1709 at 'Hardywick' (Hardwick near Sandon?) an extremely well-drawn plan for a timber-framed barn and kitchen was drawn which required 'For kitchen one pair of blades 12½ foot long 11 inches broad at the foot 8 inches at the head … to stand upon ye wallplate of ye old timbers,' and reads very much as a pair of cruck trusses.[509]

Many householders were conservative and comfortable in their old houses. At Sinai House, Burton-on-Trent, the Pagets in 1700 built a complete timber-framed extension to their ex-monastic/Jacobean hunting lodge. At the Domvilles in 1783 the carpenter was required to find, '120 ft of skirting of

---

506 English Heritage ID: 81294.
507 Smith, 'Smaller Domestic Buildings', 62.
508 Bond, R., Wittrick, A., and Miele, C., 'Lodge Farm, Hollington,' *English Heritage*, (1996), 5-6.
509 SRO, D1798/664/231.

Oak to match the Old'.[510] The Cheshire landowner, Roger Whitley recorded in his diary in 1693, 'Kerison (a tenant) came to desire that he might build his house of wood rather than brick'.[511]

There are many examples of complete timber-framed houses being built well into the eighteenth century. Upper Farm House, Rushton, Wroxeter, is timber-framed with a contemporary chimney stack dated 1675. In Northgate Street, Warwick, is a timber house of 1688, at Ashford Carbonell is a house dated 1677, Walton Grange, Gnosall, bears the date 1695 and at Rolleston on Dove, Ferndale Cottages are a row of three cottages which were built in the early eighteenth-century. In Staffordshire there are at least nine buildings which incorporate timber dendrochronologically dated to later than 1660.[512] In Warwickshire, at Stoneleigh, a semi-detached pair of timber-framed cottages were built between 1727 and 1731.[513] At Clifford Chambers, Pevsner has identified Hines House Farm as built c.1720 of timber with an integral brick frontage.[514]

Improvements or repairs were necessary but did not always require the complete demolition of the house. At Weston-under-Lizard the churchwardens reported in 1694 on, 'the parsonage house containing three bayes of building tiled one end and stone and brick, the other part is intermixt with timber'.[515]

In other houses traditional carpentry techniques were maintained in conjunction with brick, for example in Coachman's Cottage, Whittington, a new estate cottage of c.1700, the brick exterior hides a primitive upper cruck.[516] Half cruck buildings in the Midlands suggest that timber frame technology persisted, all be it in combination with brick, well into the eighteenth century. In Newark, an upper cruck at Potter Dyke House is dated to 1730 and in Millgate there is an upper cruck of the early eighteenth century.[517] In Peters'

---

510 SRO, D(W)1788P44/10.
511 Stevens, M., and Lewington, H., eds., *'Roger Whitley's Diary 1684-1697'*, 101, Bodleian Library Ms Eng Hist C711.
512 Index of Tree-Ring Dated Buildings in England, County List, *Vernacular Architecture Group,* **47**, (2016).
513 Alcock, N.W., 'Innovation and Conservatism: the Development of Warwickshire Houses in the Late 17th and 18th Centuries', *TBWAS*, **100**, (1981), 148.
514 Pickford, C., and Pevsner, N., *The Buildings of England, Warwickshire,* New Haven and London: Yale UP, (2016), 191.
515 SRO, L B/V/6 W15.
516 Personal observation by the author of this unrecorded and unlisted building.
517 *Archaeological Research Nottinghamshire,* 5.

survey of farm buildings he notes that within the barns, 'timber framed closed bays continued to be built into the second half of the 18th century, the last dated example being 1758 of Village Farm, Seighford'.[518] In Stafford examples of timber-framed internal walls have been noted in high status brick houses of the early/mid-eighteenth century at nos. 37 and 38 Greengate Street, nos. 7 and 8 St Mary's Grove and no. 15 Tipping Street. An interesting brief in the Staffordshire Quarter Sessions records of 1794 contains the plea of Thomas Jones of Wolverhampton, carpenter. He sought compensation for timber and tools destroyed in a fire of the new and unfinished dwelling house of the Rev. G.H. Hampson at Great Saredon. Jones claimed he was to be paid £500 12s 6½d when he was finished. Although it was traditional to exaggerate losses, such an enormous sum surely cannot be the cost of the timber content of a stone or brick house and may therefore have been, even at this late date, the cost of a new timber-framed house?[519]

The Cost of Timber-framed Buildings

There are very few records which contain the costs of building a new or late timber-framed house, the little evidence which survives is mainly confined to low status cottages and farm buildings.[520] Machin suggested that nationally a timber-framed house would cost the average farmer £5-6 per bay in the late sixteenth century rising to £50 per bay in the mid-eighteenth century.[521] In Nottingham in 1479 an urban house of 18 feet broad cost £6 paid in four instalments of 30s.[522] In Leicester 18 'masons and plasterers' were employed in 1587 to discover decays in tenements that had belonged to the dissolved

---

518 Peters, J.F.C., *The Development of Farm Buildings in Western Lowland Staffordshire up to 1880*, Manchester UP, (1969), 97.

519 SRO, Q/SB/Trans, 1794. By comparison a plan of a 'newly erected' parsonage at Bromshall in 1800 shows 3 large ground floor rooms, 2 bedrooms, an attic, cellar and barns and stables around a fold yard. The builder's estimate was £343 6s and the eventual mortgage was £326. LRO, B/V/6 B25.

520 Hutchison, R., and Tringham, N.J., 'A Medieval Rectory House at Clifton Campville, Staffordshire', *TSSAHS*, **XXXII**, (1990-91), 83-84. The authors quote a survey of 1453 in which 'a cottage in the vill of Clifton is beyond repair and needs to be rebuilt 100s'. The materials to be employed and the size of the cottage are not mentioned. A dovecot in a similar condition was to be totally rebuilt at a cost of £6 13s 4d.

521 Machin, R., 'The Mechanism of the Pre-Industrial Building Cycle', *Vernacular Architecture,* **8** (1972), 816-7.

522 *NBR*, Vol. II, 389.

colleges, hospitals, guilds and chantries. They found 235 houses in 'decay' and that 406 buildings, commonly called 'bays of houses', had the timber, plaster and slates 'wasted'. At the rate of £6 a bay they would require £2,436 and that to rebuild each bay would take 8 tun of timber which with carriage at 10s a ton would total £1,624. Four tons of timber at £465 'would scarce repair each of the 235 houses in decay'. Carriage of wood from H.M.'s wood at Hinckley would be £598, at 3s 4d a tun and that the total cost of repairs would be £5,123 6s 8d with each bay requiring '8 tuns of timber'. 'Some who hold leases for 10 years ought to do their own repairs'. For yearly repairs of houses that are still in good condition they cannot name a sum with accuracy … 'but think £390 would be approximate'.[523] It is difficult to identify costs in a convoluted and confusing report but building costs seem not to have risen significantly. In 1621 John Alcock of Hanbury left 'one baye of building ready framed and valued at 40s, Plaster 3s, Wood and timber logs 40s'. Allowing for the fact that these are inventory evaluations, a bay of timber-framing may have been about £4 to £6.[524] At Hanbury in 1639, the Overseers of the Poor provided what was probably a single roomed house for a man called Berke at a total cost of £5 9s 9d.[525] That the frame needed 'raising' suggests that this was a new timber house. At Griff in 1614 'one bay of a barn converted into a dwelling' cost £18 but only £7 on its resale in 1620. A slightly later example from about 1661 amongst the accounts which related to the sale of coal-bearing lands of Lord Mansfield to Thomas Pyot of Huntley gives a price per bay of £14 5s, 'Cost Thomas Pyott and his father in building upon ye misses Five Bays & a half built by him and a Bay & an half by his Father & bought all ye timber well worth £100'.[526] In 1693 on the Jervis Estate the carpenter's bill 'for building ye barne 4 bayes, thrashing floor betweene £17 10s, another bay to the bakehouse £2 10s', suggests a price per bay of £2 10s to £4 10s.[527] These examples give some indication of the considerable difficulty in comparing the price, quality and size of houses. In 1736 the churchwardens of Hatton recorded a Memorandum concerning the building of 'a bay of building for Thomas Granger at a cost to him of £8 to be paid in twice yearly instalments

---

523 *RBL*, III, 239-240.
524 Woolley, 40.
525 SRO, D1528/4/1.
526 Chester, 19.
527 WSL, 49/44/39. Such a building would not, of course, include decorated doors or windows.

to the churchwardens and overseers who are to provide the building'.[528] In 1709 a contract to build a barn of two bays, a kitchen and a kitchen chamber 'of timber frame' was agreed at £40.[529]

Medieval and post-medieval timber-framed buildings were maintained, repaired and extended in the period when brick was becoming increasingly important. Timber was available by a process of cannibalisation of older and decayed buildings and from the extensive woodlands of the major landowners. Robert Towers of Knipersley in Marchington Woodlands recorded in his will 'to be careful of my woods and not to fall or suffer to be felled but for necessary of buildings belonging to my messuage'.[530] The steward of the Duke of Newcastle wrote in 1711, 'I have been with Edward Marling (Morling?) to see after his Repaires and doth find an old Backhouse of very little use and the tenant is willing to have it taken down to help Repair the rest of his houses … it will save the Cut of sum timber if taken down'. A later letter stated 'they must do their repairing very substantially and not be wasteful of ye wood'.[531]

The allowance of timber to tenants for repairs is an important part of the explanation for the survival of timber-framing in the rural Midlands. The identification of responsibility for repairs was a central feature of many landlord and tenant agreements. In those contracts which specifically named the landlord as responsible for the provision of the materials for repair and where there was no brick kiln on the estate or where increased rents would not result from improvements, it was cheaper to provide timber 'in the rough' usually from that growing on the estate. In 1657 a lease of corn and paper mills at Cossington included a memo that the 'leasor will provide timber for repairs'.[532] As late as 1737, for some of their tenants, the Giffards were still only providing timber in spite of the changing forms of construction.[533] In about 1750 their steward defined an estate house entirely in terms of its constructional timbers, '3 Sommers (bressumers) 20' x 11" x 13", 78 Sparrs 14½' x 3" x 3", 18 joyce 8½' x 5" x 7", etc.' A similar undated seventeenth-century survey of an unknown timber-framed house in the Needwood Forest

---

528   WRO, DR0123/2.
529   SRO, D1798/664/231.
530   Woolley, 40.
531   NA, DD64P/64/14/15-16.
532   ROLLR, 2D31/112.
533   SRO, L. D590/599.

provides an equally detailed record of all the timbers in the house.[534] Even in the towns and cities the cost of new timbers does not seem to have been excessive. The accounts of the Warden of the Lichfield Conduit Lands Trust in 1690 suggest that important constructional timbers could be purchased at prices equivalent to two or three days wages of a building craftsman.

Table 8: The Price of Constructional Timbers, 1690

door fratheme	5s 0d
a sill	4s 6d
2 wall plates	4s 0d
2 beames	4s 0d
1 Ridg Tree	2s 0d
12 sparrs	9s 0d

The total bill, which included a door, ironwork, other timbers and 'workmanship' was £2 6s 4d.[535]

How much timber would have been required to build new timber-framed houses? According to a detailed investigation by Oliver Rackham of Grundle House, Stanton, West Suffolk, a timber-framed house of c.1500 with an originally open hall and two cross wings revealed that the house, as initially built, contained about 730 timber parts. Measured and cubed up these amount to 1,230 true cubic feet of timber, which in the green state would weigh about 24 tons. He estimated that a total of 332½ oak trees were required, 251½ of which were of relatively small diameter. In terms of woodland acreage Rackham's rough calculation is that the timber used to construct the farmhouse is the equivalent to 50 year's growth on 5.7 acres of woodland or one year's growth on 286 acres. (It must be remembered that when a tree was felled it would almost certainly be replaced, often by re-growth from the stump.) At Mapledurham, a cruck house of c.1335 required 111 trees, 75 of which came from immature trees of less than 6 inches in diameter and only 6 from large branching trees. Rackham estimates that the house would have used the

---

534 SRO, D1721/3/23a. 'These are all the dementions of Mr Ward building What Ever'.
535 SRO, D12111/2.

growth of 1¼ acres of woodland, and the oldest trees would have been about 50 years in age, the smallest about 10.[536]

What are the implications of this research? If it is assumed that the basic structure of a late timber-framed house would require say 30 tons of green timber and without allowing for sawing, shaping and carriage then the net cost of the raw timber for one house would be about £45. The number of bricks which would be required to build a new house of dimensions similar to those of Grundle House is difficult to estimate precisely for only its combined length (67 feet) and the average width (20 feet) are given. An informed guess might be that 58,000 bricks would be required to build a similar house at a price of about £29.[537] On the Littleton Estate the building of Wharstone Farm in 1756 required at least 62,000 bricks, a 'Dovehouse and Cowhouse' used 65,850 bricks.[538] The building of Acton Mill in 1764-65 needed over 100,000 bricks at a cost of over £50.[539] Carriage and labour costs would be similar at between 35%-60% of the total cost. But all brick-built buildings would require timber for the roof trusses, floors and door frames etc. so the total cost of a brick house may have been higher than that of a timber-framed house. A builder's estimate book of a mid-eighteenth-century date held in the Essex Record Office reckoned that a building costing £95 in brickwork would cost about £82 in oak or about £70 in fir.[540] In a recent study of building in Hertfordshire, Paul Hunneyball suggests that 'Brick was more expensive than timber and even use

---

536 Hilts, C., 'Peasant Buildings in Midland England', *Current Archaeology*, (2013), 279.

537 An informed guess might be that the total area of bricks employed was approximately 3,500 square feet. In 1793 a local calculation was that '4,500 bricks go to a rod and 272 square feet of a brick and half, is a rod of statute measure'. SA, 587/68. This would suggest that a brick farmhouse equivalent in size to Grundle House would require 58,000 bricks. In 1720 for a house at Meriden, Warks, Francis Smith estimated a price of £1 per rod of brickwork, so the cost of bricklaying etc. for the hypothetical farmhouse might be about £13. Gomme, *Francis Smith*, 576. Smith's estimate should be treated with caution for this is the price of the brickwork alone. The overall price per rod of walling, including windows, doors and ironwork etc. could be much higher. In Shropshire in 1793 'workmanship' was calculated at '£28 or £30 per rod', SA, 587/68. For the restoration of Chester Castle in 1684 the 'brickwork' was calculated at £4 per rod, SRO, D742/M/4/5. Variations in price could be the result of the detail required in the walling, i.e. the number of arches or window openings or differences in the materials.

538 SRO, D260/M/E/116.

539 SRO, D260/M/E/116.

540 Quoted in Lucas, R., 'When Did Norfolk Cross the Brick Threshold?' *Vernacular Architecture* **28**, (1997), 75.

for lower-class chimneys was restricted until the late seventeenth-century'.[541] As late as 1775, Nathaniel Kent, in his *Hints to Gentlemen of Landed Property* suggests that a small two storey labourer's cottage could be built in brick for £56 and in timber for £58 whilst a larger cottage could be built for £66 10s in wood and £70 in brick and tile.[542] Peter Guillery quotes an account from Norfolk, where in 1775 it was estimated that a cottage cost £116 to build in timber and £132 in brick. He argues that even in London 'it probably remained cheaper to build in timber until the end of the eighteenth century, the margin perhaps shrinking until the 1780s … the cost factor joined more effective legislation and the percolation of fashion to see off timber building, though not decisively before the Building Act of 1774'.[543]

It may well be that the price advantage of brick, so frequently claimed by historians, has been exaggerated and that it is inaccurate to claim that brick replaced timber out of financial necessity. Indeed, it may well be that timber allowed economies to be made in the use of brick when it was incorporated in brick houses as reinforcement. To avoid or minimise distortion, particularly in hastily erected buildings, many brick walls incorporated longitudinal timbers. This use of 'bond timbers' was common and was described by James Smith in *The Carpenters Companion* of 1733.[544] As a method of apparent support this was not fire resistant and often created structural problems. Although it was regulated by several London Acts between 1708 and 1774, its dangers were ignored in many provincial buildings.

It is not suggested that there was enough timber within the region to build all the large number of structures erected between 1660 and 1780, but it is important to stress that timber was readily available and, in conjunction with brick, was employed in all the houses, workshops, engine houses, churches and other new buildings of the period. The Newcomen steam pump, for example, so representative of the early industrial economy, was contained within a brick

---

541 Hunneyball, 14.

542 Kent, N., *Hints to Gentlemen of Landed Property*, (1793), 233, 235.

543 Guillery, P., *The Small House in Eighteenth Century London*, Yale UP, (2004), 7. The building of wholly timber houses in London continued in spite of Post-Fire legislation. 'Up to the mid-eighteenth-century houses in and around the square (Wellclose Square, between Wapping and Whitechapel) were built or rebuilt in timber. These were not modest houses and they incorporated fashionable classical embellishments'. Ibid., 70.

544 Hurst, L., 'The Rise and Fall of the Use of Bond Timbers in Brick Buildings in England', *Proceedings of The Second International Congress on Construction History*, **2**, (2006), 1633-1654.

skin but was structurally based on massive oak timbers.[545] When the Rev. Thomas Allen built his brick house at Stoke-on-Trent in 1706 its cost was £233 9s 7d. Of that total, £41 19s (18%) was spent on timber and £11 11s (5%) on its carriage.[546] When the 'school house' at Lichfield Grammar School was completed in 1683 the total cost of the rebuilding was £102 4s 10d. Of this £43 11s 10d (42%) was spent on timber and on the carpenters and £29 10s (29%) on masonry.[547]

Lucas, in his study of the 'brick threshold' in Norfolk, strongly emphasises the importance of timber within houses:

> *It has to be said at the outset that the first reason, that the timber shortage encouraged the introduction of brick, does not stand up to argument ... it has to be recognised that building construction put more timber into floors and roof structures than into walls and that if timber scarcity was critical, it would have led to no building whatsoever.*[548]

Oak, the traditional building material, continued to be available. At Trentham in 1701 the steward identified 120 'oaks for building', 'about 20 for laths' and '2 large oaks in the park for sashes for windows'.[549] For the rebuilding of Swinfen Hall in 1756, its builder/architect, Benjamin Wyatt, particularly emphasised the purchase of 'very fine, very dry English oak boards'.[550] The cost of the oak was 4d per foot. Oak continued to be a popular and available building material throughout the eighteenth-century.

The building contract for Handsworth Parsonage House in 1782 specifically required 'The Timber for the floors and Roof to be Oak'.[551] John Phillips wrote in 1793 that 'timber of all kinds, and especially oak, of which there are many large woods near the intended course of the canal, (Trent and Mersey) that, for want of a proper conveyance to sea-port towns, where timber is much wanted

---

545 See the example at the Black Country Museum, Dudley.
546 SRO, D(W)1742/46.
547 SRO, L D53/1/1.
548 Lucas, 75.
549 SRO, 868/9/55.
550 SRO, L D44/3.
551 SRO, L B/V/6 H4.

for shipbuilding, are sold in the neighbourhood for a low price'.[552] Phillips also notes that James Brindley, in the building of the canal, used 'some thousands of oak piles' and that the proposed canal would encourage the transport of timber for 'houses'. There is also evidence of the use of cheaper and alternative home-grown woods. In the above contract Wyatt purchased poplar boards at 2d per foot and elm at 1½d per foot. For Samuel Peake's house at Yarlet in 1759, the carpenter charged 1¼d per foot for poplar boards and 3d per foot for oak.[553] But as late as 1793 George Whitfield of St Thomas's Hospital wrote to his brother in Shropshire, 'Oak timber in the country may be cheeper than Fir or deale'.[554]

The Use of Foreign Timber

Closely associated with the increasing use of brick was the use of foreign timber. Although some oak was imported from America, Germany and the Eastern Baltic, the majority of timber imports were of soft woods.[555] The largest source of timber for the British market was Norway, which in the eighteenth century exported large quantities of redwood (Scots Fir) and whitewood (Common Spruce). The poorer quality whitewoods were used for cheap furniture, pit props and box making. The redwoods were employed in shipbuilding and house construction. The advantages of the redwoods were their cheapness, the saving in manufacture by mechanical sawing by wind or waterpower and their consequent import as 'Die-square timber', cut perfectly square, into lengths as required and immediately useable in buildings as joists and trusses.[556] Such softwoods were appropriate for interior construction and painted could be used for windows and door frames, but they were unsuitable for exterior and exposed framing. They required the protection of stone, or more usually brick, walling. To keep down costs cheaper wood could be used but that dictated the necessity of brick and tile to protect it from the weather. One advantage of imported softwoods, and introduced from Italy, was the 'stressed' truss in

---

552 Phillips, J., *A General History of Inland Navigation*, (1793), 165.
553 SRO, D1798/HM39/10.
554 SA, 587/68.
555 SRO, L D20/4/3, the Churchwardens' Account Book of St Mary's, Lichfield, includes a payment in 1760 'to put up a canopy of Norway oak'.
556 Kent, H.S.K., 'The Anglo-Norwegian Timber Trade in the Eighteenth Century', *Econ. Hist. Rev.*, 2nd series, 8 (1956), 62.

which a 'king-post' is suspended from the top of the principals, picking up the dead load weight of the tie beam at its base. This, in combination with the great lengths available in the imported softwoods, gave the ability to bridge wider spans with roofs of low pitch. The king-post and its variant, the 'queen-post' truss, was much used during the eighteenth century with the addition of iron straps and tension bolts. Ironically, given that one of the arguments in favour of brick was that of greater protection from external fires, the internal use of softwoods added to an increased risk of fire damage within the house. In 1816 Whitaker commented on 'the increased danger since builders had turned from English oak to imported timber'.[557]

Specific references to the origins of timber are scarce and in the Midlands the price of imported timber would have been slightly more expensive than in coastal areas since the costs of water transport via the Severn, Weaver or Trent and then overland would have been higher. The carrier John Salt's bill to Lord Chetwynd for the 'Newhouse' at Betley specifically included, '32 Dale (deal) planks from Chester which weighed a ton three hundred (weight) & half at 1s 2d per hundred'.[558] In 1706 William Smith, the builder of Sandwell Hall, wrote to Lord Dartmouth that he had 'put of going to Hull to by wanscoot and Deall for the finishing of may Lord Gowars house'.[559]

Such increased costs were not necessarily a deterrent to building, but simply added to its costs. The Giffard accounts for the building of the Mass House, Wolverhampton, for example, make specific reference to 'Norway wood' whilst the Dyott accounts for repairs at Sadler Street, Lichfield in 1717 also refer to the purchase of 'half inch Norway B(oards)'.[560] In Birmingham, equally remote from coast and navigable river, Chalklin claimed that 'the quantity imported was considerable' and 'Its use was widespread in Birmingham in the 1740s'.[561]

The shift to brick-based building was subtle and gradual with timber continuing to be employed and re-used where appropriate. The change was not dramatic but slow and piecemeal. Nef believed that the 'brick threshold' i.e. when most customers and builders chose brick, had been reached in England

---

557 Quoted in Beresford, M.W., 'Prometheus Insured: The Sun Fire Agency in Leeds during Urbanisation', *Econ. Hist. Rev.*, 2nd series, **35**, (1982), 373.
558 SRO, D1789/HM/Chetwynd 105.
559 SRO, D(W)1778(V)1325.
560 SRO, D661/21/4/1c.
561 Chalklin, C.W., *The Rise of the English Town 1650-1850*, Cambridge: CUP, (2001), 190.

by 1700.⁵⁶² But timber and brick seem to have existed side by side well into the eighteenth century. In South Staffordshire Peter's fieldwork suggested that 'brick did not completely displace timber framing from the outside of farm buildings until about 1760 nor from the interior for another twenty years'.⁵⁶³

Large town houses may have been built of brick by the end of the seventeenth century but this does not mean necessarily that the same was true of tenement property, for the dwellings occupied by the artisan and labouring classes cost alone was the crucial factor and poor quality timber was probably always cheaper than brick.⁵⁶⁴ The chronological point at which brick replaced timber varied from town to town.⁵⁶⁵ In Birmingham for example, local clay was abundant and such grants as 'Liberty to dig clay therein for the making of Brickes to be used in the sd Building' often were included in leases.⁵⁶⁶ The environmental impact of brickmaking could however be severe and similar liberties do not seem to have existed in the gentrified towns of Derby, Nottingham and Warwick, whose citizens perhaps did not wish to see clay spoils in the street.

This analysis of brick prices and timber supplies suggests that it is too simplistic to suggest that the transition from traditional building materials to brick was the result of either a significant decline in timber supplies or the marked price advantage of brick. The price paid for 'building brick' in the period 1660 to 1780 did not fall but rose slightly and was then maintained at about ten shillings per 1,000 for the early and mid-eighteenth century. Building timber seems to have been readily available and there is considerable evidence for the erection of timber-framed buildings throughout the period under review.

Documentary evidence and that provided by surviving buildings suggest a continuity of timber-framed building rather than a decisive and dramatic shift to brick building. The two materials were used in parallel for a century. Bricks

---

562 Nef, J.U., *The Conquest of the Material World,* University of Chicago, (1964), 188, Chalklin, 259-60.
563 Peters, 213-4.
564 Guillery, P., and Herman, B., 'Deptford Houses: 1650-1800', *Vernacular Architecture,* **30**, (1999), 58. In Deptford, Kent, a documentary search suggested that 'Most of the town's ordinary housing before 1750 was slight and timber built'.
565 Chalklin, 189.
566 Carter, W., ed., 'The Records of King Edward's School Birmingham', **II**, *Publications of the Dugdale Society,* (1928), 110.

held no obvious price advantage and despite the evidence, contemporaries seemed quite secure in their belief that brick houses were more expensive than those built in timber. This would suggest that the explanation for the choice of brick was not determined simply by economic factors but could be based, perhaps even unconsciously, on an awareness of the values and messages reflected in a brick dwelling. As Lucas has suggested, 'The only credible explanation is that eighteenth-century builders were moved to build in brick by the esteem accorded to brick construction'.[567]

---

[567] Lucas, 71.

Chapter 7

THE TRANSPORT OF BRICK

BRICK PRODUCTION in the pre-canal era was on a relatively small scale – transport on farm carts was expensive and hindered by poorly surfaced roads, so where carriage was necessary it contributed significantly to the overall cost of most buildings. Contemporaries were aware of the economic difficulties created by the lack of appropriate transport – in the Needwood Forest in 1587 there were more than 74,000 mature trees but few were used by the expanding iron industry, probably because they were 14-15 miles from the navigable part of the Trent.[568] In 1704 Edward Repington wrote to Thomas Coke, 'Poetry and pockets are at a low ebb in these parts (Tamworth). We have neither wine to raise our fancies, nor navigable rivers, nor passable roads to convey our commodities when they may take a price'.[569] Damage created by brick carts was also a problem, in 1711 a memorandum to the Lord High Treasurer about the state of the Fulham Road noted, 'As for the brewer's drays and brick carts, which had always done the greatest damage, there was no preventing it'.[570]

This is not to suggest that the market for brick was confined to sites adjacent to the kiln or clamp but rather that transport costs became a factor in the decision to select brick as the building material of choice. In July 1788 Thomas Ward, the steward of the Kingstone Estate of Earl Talbot, reported to his master that:

---
568 *VCH, Staffs,* **10**, 43.
569 Edden, P., and Jones, H., *The History of Alvecote,* Warwick, (1968), 29.
570 Worcs. RO, 1/1/315/18.

> *I have Inspected into Materials Wanting for Harises House at Thorney Lanes and find it will take about 6,500 of Bilding Bricks and 1,200 of Floor Bricks and Considerable Quantity of Timber for Cilling which Metearals all ly at a distance. Haris has No Team Nor is not able to Hier the Caridge. Be Pleased to Send … What I must do in the Afaer.*[571]

In 1676 when Parson Roades purchased a timber-framed house at Blithfield, he describes in his diary its appalling state but despite that he was 'parsuaded to take it becase we had no Brick mad at that time within les than 2 miles and these very small and dear'.[572] The implication is that the costs of the carriage of brick and tile, even for only two miles, could be an important part of the overall expenses incurred in building a brick house.

Much brick was made on the building site as immediate access to supplies of brickearth or clay and the ability to build a clamp or kiln adjacent to the proposed building provided an important financial advantage. Nathanial Kent advised in 1775, 'Upon most estates, of any considerable size, brick-earth, or clay, may be met with; and, where this is the case, they (bricks) may be always made, and burnt in clamps, for one third less than they can be bought at the kilns'.[573] At Mapperley, near Nottingham, brickmakers were consistently fined for digging on the Common, for example in 1683, 'it is this day ordered by the Councell that the severall persons that dig Claye upon the Playnes shall be this day discharged and theire kills and hovells pulled down forthwith'.[574] The 'Clay Stealers' persisted because transport costs to the City were low and their price gave them a ready market. Extra costs would have of course been incurred by any substantial transport of coal and lime. On the Warwickshire Estate of the Edge family in 1782 lime which was priced at only 11s (plus '6d his man as custom') cost 2s 6d in turnpike costs, i.e. 23% extra.

Recent research has suggested that there was considerable transport of bricks by road in the period before improvements to the Trent, the Derwent, the building of the Trent and Mersey canal and the creation of the Midland canal network. A table (Table 9) has been constructed based on 20 contracts which clearly identifies the cost of bricks for specific undertakings and the

---

571 SRO, D240/E (C)1/15/74.
572 SRO, D1386/2/1/5.
573 Kent, 166.
574 *NBR*, **V**, 323, 356.

additional costs of their carriage as a proportion of the cost of the brick and as a proportion of the overall cost of brick and carriage. The table is based on a limited range of evidence, for in most contracts the individual costs of brick and carriage are rarely identified. Most frequently they were combined with the brickmaker taking responsibility for delivery. A typical example is that of new felt hat workshop built in Newcastle-under-Lyme in 1753, the accounts included:

15,410 Bricks and Timber £16 16 0 3,000 Bricks and carriage 1 16 0
Job Hulse for carriage of Brick 0 7 0
Wm Bayley for carriage of Brick 0 8 6
Benj Whiston for carriage of Brick unpaid 0 19 0.[575]

Table 9: The Costs of the Carriage of Brick in the Midlands, 1560-1780

Date and Place	Number of bricks purchased	Cost of bricks £ s d	Cost of carriage £ s d	Carriage as % of cost of brick	Carriage as % of cost of brick and carriage
1578 Beaudesert	4,600	13 0	4 0	31%	24%
1588 Persehowse accounts	1,800	1 7 0	16 0	59%	37%
1664 Lapley	100 'quarie' and 83 tile	1 0 9	11 0	53%	43%
1671 Chirbury	600 for church 'alley'	16s	5s	31.25%	23.8%
1681 Hanbury	80	1s 8d	1s 0d	60%	37%
1693 Sandon	'8 load of brick'	£1 7s 6d	£1 0s 10d	75%	42%
1693 Sandon	'3 load of brick'	10s 0d	10s 0d	100%	50%

---

575 SRO, D(W) 1788/59/6.

1696-7 Warwick	13,000	£8 18 9	16s 3d	9%	8.3%
1710 Checkley	3,000	£1 10s	6 0	20%	17%
1720 Giffard Estate, Brewood	27,500	£13 12s 6d	£6 16s 3d	50%	34%
1727 Jervis Estate, Chartley	3,000	£2 10s	6s	12%	11%
1729 Whitworth Estate	22,000	£11	2s 6d per 1,000	25%	11%
1730 Congreave Estate	9,200	£4 2s 9d	£2 6s	55%	35%
1736 Chetwynd Estate, Betley	3,000	£1 10s	£1 2s 6d	75%	32.5%
1739 Edge Estate, Longnor	4,000 brick 4,000 tile	£7 12s	£1 4s	16%	14%
1753 Newcastle	2,950	15s	2s per 1,000	40%	28%
1753 Edgbaston, Gough Estate		10s per 1,000	1s per 1,000	10%	9.1%
1756 Hilderstone	4,500	£2 5s	9s	20%	17%
1756 Littleton Estate	22,000	£11	2s 6d per 1,000	25%	20%
1760 Gough Estate	3,600	£2 2s	17s 6d	42%	29%

The 20 examples collected suggest that on average the cost of the carriage of brick was over 40% of the cost of the brick itself and 27% of the combined cost of the brick and its carriage. Given that brick was the most important single cost of any of the building materials of smaller houses then its carriage contributed significantly to the overall cost of many buildings. Thus Parson Roades, in 1710, paid, 'For carriage of bricks-viz 7,000 00-16s-00', i.e. he paid 2s 4d for the carriage of every 1,000 bricks. He had been given the bricks by his patron Sir Edward Bagot of Blithfield Hall, so the distance over which the bricks were carried was not more than 1-2 miles. Similarly in 1712, Roades paid £1 10s for 'Carriage of brick from kiln to hall' when rebuilding the church and hall at Checkley.[576] In that spirit of scientific enquiry which was so characteristic of the Enlightenment, Lord Harrowby began the rebuilding of Sandon Hall, newly acquired in 1778, with a series of investigations into the weight and carriage of brick. He reported that he had:

> *Weighed three bricks pretty exactly. The largest weighed seven and a half pounds, the next seven and a quarter pounds and the smallest six and three-quarter pounds … I should from this experiment calculate the common weight of bricks to be about seven pounds … or three tons and a half for 1,000 bricks.*[577]

The author's personal evidence would suggest the heaviest estimate is more accurate, with circa sixteenth bricks weighing 5-6 lbs and circa seventeenth bricks weighing 6-7lbs. John Harris, in his *Lexicon Technicum* of 1723, proposed slightly lower weights in that '407 in Number are a Tun weight' and that 1,000 bricks weighed 5,500 pounds, i.e. 2.4 tons. Bricks varied considerably in size and weight but using the Sandon calculations suggests that for a very moderately sized building of say 35,000 bricks then over 100 tons of bricks would need to be moved to the building site and for a substantial farmhouse and outbuildings of 300,000 bricks then over 1,050 tons of bricks would be required.

Evidence for the size of 'loads' is scarce.[578] At Swynnerton in 1693 Thomas Astbury's accounts include adjacent entries for 1,000 bricks and for 'carreing 3 loads of brick' for 10s, this would suggest that a load was about 330 bricks (approximately 1 ton).[579] In 1717 the Dyott accounts included two references to, '6 load of Bricks … 4020,' possibly in this case a 'load' was 670 bricks weighing around 2 tons.[580] At Stretton in 1730 an 'Account of Brick and Tile made' includes a reference to '600 to the load in att guisey bank to blackmoor'

---

576 SRO, D1386/2/1/5.
577 Sandon Hall, Harrowby Mss. **437**, Doc. 67. For all the Harrowby Mss. references I am indebted to Appleby, J. 'Lord Harrowby's Home Farm at Sandon', unpublished D.Phil. thesis, University of Nottingham, (1997).
578 Kingman, M., How large was a load of bricks? Some Staffordshire evidence and its implications'. BBSI, **106**, (2008) 4-12.
579 SRO, D5909.
580 SRO, D661/21/4/1c.

(1 ton 15 cwt).[581] At Meerbrook in the Staffordshire Moorlands, where the hills were steeper, a load seems to have been between 400 and 500 bricks (between 1 ton 4 cwt and 1 ton 9 cwt). These figures are derived from kiln records of the 1750s where the bricks were listed as 'loads' with a number immediately below, for example for August 19th 1750, '10 loads 4 thousand' and for September 2nd, '5 loads 2 thousand'.[582] At Beesthorpe, in East Nottinghamshire in 1770 the load size seems to be about 875 bricks.[583] Load size could vary considerably. The detailed building accounts of the Curzon Estate at Breedon-on-the Hill in 1761 include, under the heading of 'Little Bricks', 'carriage of 500 bricks on July the 26th, 28th, 30th and August 2nd, 3rd, 4th and 13th'. On 4th August 2,500 bricks were carried 'by my own Teame' and between the 10th and 30th August a further 27 journeys were made mostly by 'My Team'. The loads carried were 500 bricks (x 6), 1,000 (x 6), 2,000 (x 1), 600 (x 5), 1,200 (x 1), 400 (x 2), 300 (x 1). Bricks from a general carrier, Warrener, in loads of 600 also seem to have been delivered three times per week.[584] Depending on the demands of the terrain and the size of carts used, a hypothetical house of 35,000 bricks would require between 52 and 87 journeys just to bring the bricks.[585]

Extra payment was occasionally recorded for the loading and unloading of the carts. The Littleton accounts for 1754 record, 'Rogers wife unloading bricks 4s 6d' and a year later the 'Lad' received 2s 6d for 'Loading Brick'.[586] Usually however the cost of the carriage and unloading of the brick was included in the overall contract. The loading and unloading of brick carts however could delay completion and add to the overall cost of the building. Lord Harrowby was aware of the costs of transport as the total cost of the newly rebuilt Sandon Hall was over £2,000 and included, 'for extra allowance … upon account of

---

581 SRO, D1057/J/2/9. The Persehowse Memorandum Book of the late sixteenth century includes several references to the purchase of bricks in lots of 600. SRO, D260/M/F/1/5 f.4.

582 SRO, D1028/2/1.

583 NA, DD/BB104 /20.

584 ROLLR, DE1536/164.

585 The size of the load presumably varied with the capacity of the cart and the number of horses available. In Dorset the diary of a farmer, James Warne, in 1758 includes many references to the carriage of 'Brix'. A load was 800 bricks and usually required five or six of the nine horses kept on the farm. James, E.F., 'Farming in Dorset, The Diary of James Warne, 1758', *Dorset Record Society*, **13**, (1993), 50, 52, 55, 73.

586 SRO, D260/M/E/116, 60-61.

extraordinary hard work in carriage for new buildings £24 6s 8d'.[587] Harrowby instituted a time and motion study in which his servant Shord 'observed that the time a cart took in going … was 43 minutes … with a load of bricks, and 35 minutes in returning … I observed the time they took in unloading the carts … 4 men … 3 carts … less than 30 minutes … that is less than 10 minutes per cart'.[588]

If cost was not a significant factor in the decision to build, then materials could be carried for long distances. Samuel Wyatt restored Fisherwick Hall in 1757-8 for its new owner Samuel Hill. His detailed accounts included the purchase of '21 tons of Westmoreland Blew Slate at £2 10s per ton, delivered at Bristol £52 10s, freight from Bristol £7 11s 6d … For carr(iage) of the above slates to Fisher £33 12s 7d', with a total cost of £4 9s 3d per ton. A later reference to a 'Quantity of slates from Bewdley' suggests that the price of £7 11s 6d may relate to the cost of shipping along the River Severn and the greater amount to the cost of land carriage from Bewdley to Fisherwick.[589] In 1770 Wyatt, who was restoring the east wing of Blithfield Hall, also received '11 ton of fine Westmoreland Slate d'livered at Burton at £4 15s (per ton), £52 5s 0d'.[590]

After improvement in the mid eighteenth century the Trent was navigable by the broad beamed boats of the Burton Boat Company both upstream and downstream from Burton. The Trent and Mersey Canal had been opened from Wilden Ferry to Shugborough in 1770 and the specific mention of delivery to Burton rather than to Blithfield suggests that either the Trent or the canal was used to transport the slate. Surprisingly the cost per ton of using the canal or river was slightly higher than the total cost of the lengthy sea journey to Bristol, the transport along the Severn and the overland haul from Bewdley.[591] The completion of the Trent and Mersey Canal and its feeder network was an important factor in the distribution of building materials. John Philips wrote in 1793 in his promotion of the canal, 'In the neighbourhood of Burslem,

---

587 Harrowby Mss. **438**, Doc 67.
588 Harrowby Mss. **438**, Doc 76.
589 BLAC, 628 Elford Mss.
590 SRO, D1721/3/215. (What Mathew Boulton called 'Wyattacising') When Betley Hall was repaired in 1785 the contract also specified 'Blue Westmoreland Slates'. SRO, D(W)1788P56B25.
591 Jackman, W.T., *The Development of Transportation in Modern England*, 2nd ed. Cambridge: CUP, (1916), 449, 'the cost of canal carriage normally did not exceed one-half, and in most cases was from one-fourth to one-third of the cost of land carriage'.

bricks and tiles are made of blue colour, which are so vitrified as to be harder than stone used in building; and these articles will find a demand through the whole course of the canal'.[592]

The cost of transport was obviously influenced by the length of the journey although this information is only rarely included in any surviving accounts. But at Betley in 1737 the Churchwardens' Accounts include entries for the purchase of bricks (3,600 for £1 16s), tiles and crests (2s) and the cost of 'drawing the tile and crests from Madeley Heath to Betley Churchyard' (7s).[593] The distance from Madeley to Betley is approximately 4 miles. Journeys of similar lengths are recorded for the building of many small and medium-sizes houses. The Gough Estate at Perry Barr between 1733 and 1757, for example, purchased bricks from as many as 18 different suppliers with the longest distance being 5-6 miles.[594]

In general the distances over which brick was carried were short. In most of the Midlands brick clays were readily available and most builders were able to take advantage of local access to the basic raw material. Much brick production, particularly in the countryside, was site specific. Chaloner and Musson emphasise that in the hinterlands brick making remained in the hands of the craftsmen due to the high cost of transport.[595] The trade in specialist bricks could however involve their carriage over extended distances. Although there was a highly productive brick kiln at Meerbrook in 1750, its records show that floor brick for Birchwood Park was imported from Uttoxeter about 25 miles away.[596]

Transport costs were also of importance in the decision to build in stone. At Milton in 1754 Ketton stone was priced at £300 at the quarry but £150 was needed to transport it.[597] In Derbyshire many substantial houses are of stone derived from very local sources. Craven and Stanley have suggested that because bricks were cheaper than stone for very large buildings this allowed the builder to afford the transport costs of high-quality stone for edgings and quoins, for example the dressings at Sudbury Hall are of Sherwood Sandstone

---

592 Phillips, 168.
593 SRO, D689/PC/1/2.
594 BLAC, Gough Mss, 3145/262/2.
595 Chaloner, W.H., and Musson, A.E., *Industry and Technology*, Vista Books, (1963), 14.
596 SRO, D1028/2/1.
597 Northants RO, F (M) Charter) 2327.

from the famous Hollington quarries, a distance of 12 miles and the paving came from Breadsall, a distance of 16 miles.[598]

The season of the year and the consequent state of the roads could also influence costs. In the summer of 1752 William Bucknell paid 10s per 1,000 for bricks and their carriage for his 'workhouse'. In October the cost was 12s per 1,000.[599] This distinction between summer and winter rates was officially recognised and accepted as a legitimate explanation of differences in price.[600] Transport costs were also increased by the need of the carrier to use a turnpiked road. The Shropshire Estate papers of the Penbury family include a note from George Penbury to his son concerning estate repairs in which George allowed him 8s 6d for 'bricks and making the oven' and 1s 6d for 'carriage and turnpike'.[601] The very detailed building accounts for Penn Vicarage in 1778 include a carriage bill for waggoners of £2 13s and 'at Turnpikes £2 18s'.[602] The turnpikes did however generate substantial benefits, road quality was improved, food supplies could be carried more economically, land values were raised and urbanisation, and therefore housing, encouraged. Building materials could be carried more speedily and for longer distances and particularly the market for coal was widened.[603]

An unusual document from Yoxall entitled 'Charges about the Building & repairing of the Co(u)rt house Barne cowhouse and other necessaries about the House 1683 1684 & 1685', provides rare evidence of the sources and costs of its building materials.[604] As Figure 1 (overleaf) indicates, most of the materials were obtained from farms and estates within a radius of 2-3 miles. Only 2,400 'playne tyles' and 20 'Ridging Tyles' from Abbots Bromley (5-6 miles) and nails from Rugeley (7 miles) involved longer journeys (the origin

---

598 Craven M, and Stanley, M., *The Derbyshire Country House*, Breedon Books, (1991), 8.
599 SRO, D(W)1788/59/6.
600 SRO, L, D103/6/31/6. 'Rate of Carriage of Goods', 1784. The Quarter Sessions agreed to a price rise of 6d per cwt from Michaelmas to Lady Day for goods transported 'by waggon' from London to all Staffordshire towns. There were also seasonal variations in the cost of transporting lime, Kingman, 164.
601 SA, 938/450.
602 SRO, L, B/V/6P5. The accounts also include 'Entertainment to (waggoners) at the Rose & Crown & White Hart £2 14s'.
603 Bogart, D., 'The Turnpike Roads of England and Wales', https://www.campop.geog.cam.ac.uk/research/projects/transport/onlineatlas/britishturnpiketrusts.pd
604 SRO, D603/F/3/1/13. In 1722-23 when further repairs were made to the Court House Henry Shipton paid £8 5s for 15,000 bricks and £3 15s for their carriage.

BRICKMAKING AND BRICK BUILDING IN THE MIDLANDS (1437-1780)

Figure 1. Sources of Building Materials for Yoxall Court House, 1683-1685

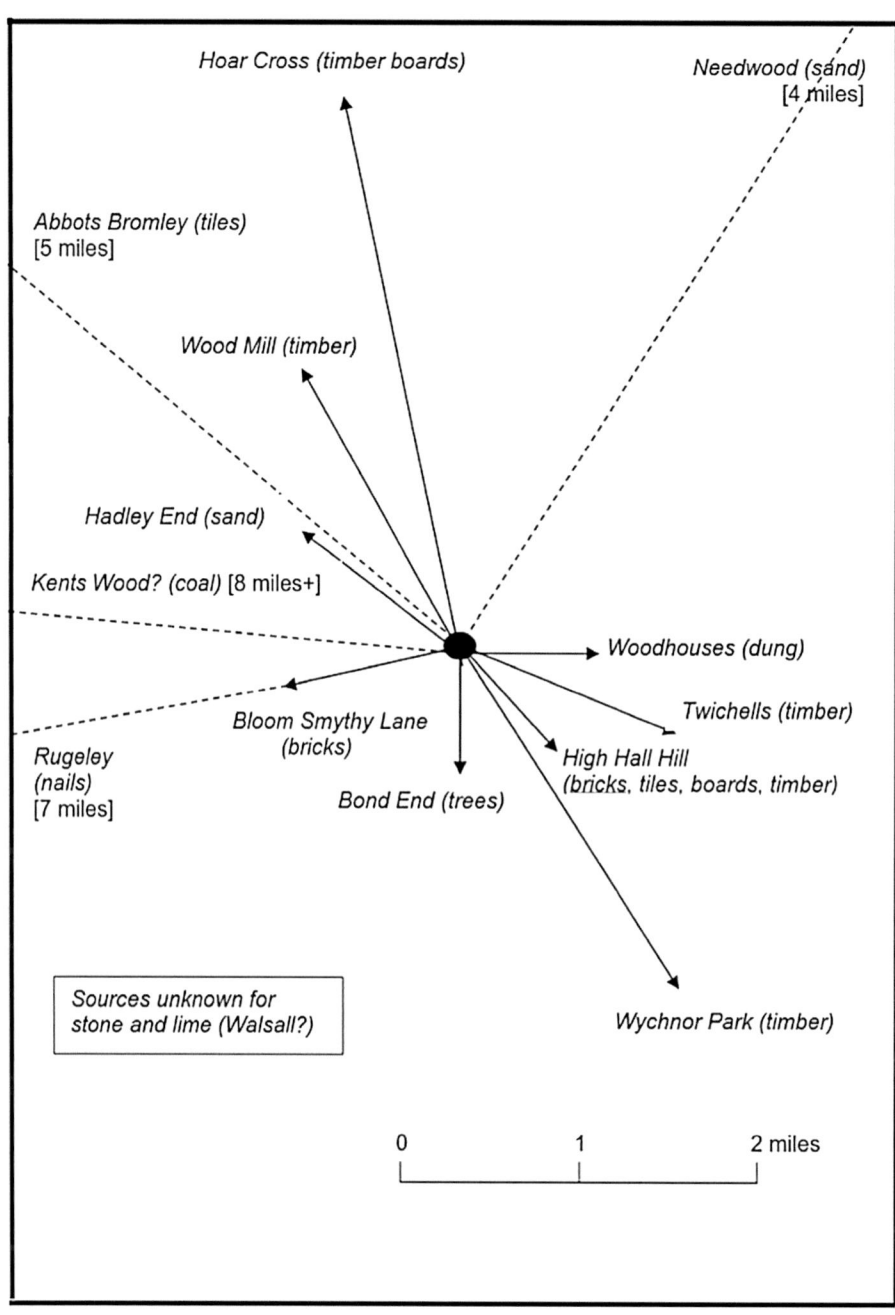

of the stone and lime is not recorded). The total cost of the building works was £70 2s 4d, of which sum the specifically listed costs of carriage were at least £9 18s (14.5%). A further £11 17s 9d was spent on coals, lime, plaster, thatch, nails and bricks where the cost of transport was included. These sums would suggest that approximately 25% of the total cost of the building work was consumed in the carriage of very heavy materials in relatively small loads.

The sheer volume of road traffic generated by the building industry has been little discussed. To take two examples, the building accounts for Betley 'Newhouse' in 1736-37 do not include the total number of bricks purchased but their cost was £99 18s. The supplier, John Lockett, in other accounts of Lord Chetwynd, was charging 5s per 1,000 bricks so a reasonable estimate would be that the house and outbuildings required approximately 400,000 bricks.[605] To carry those bricks at about 650 to each load would need over 600 journeys from the kiln at Madeley Heath a distance of 4 miles. Allowing for empty return journeys to the kiln the carriage of the brick alone required 4,800 cart miles. Added to this was the cost of the carriage of sand, lime and timber. The cost of the transport of lime was at least £25 whilst some timber deals were fetched from the port of Chester. An even more extreme example of the impact of the carriage of brick is that created by the purchase of almost 1,000,000 bricks in 1720-21 by Lord Gower. These were fired in Burslem and transported to Trentham Hall, a distance of approximately five miles. In that one year, assuming 650 bricks per load, a minimum of 1,540 single journeys would have been required to carry the bricks to Trentham. The total cart miles including return journeys would have been 15,000 miles.[606]

Traditionally, research into the road traffic of the seventeenth and eighteenth centuries has emphasised aspects such as turnpiking, long distance carrier and coach routes and their networks. A more regionally focused analysis of road traffic has extended consideration to private carriers and the transport of stones and minerals. David Hey, for example, discusses the carriage, in Derbyshire and South Yorkshire, of coal, lead, millstones, lime and salt. He suggests that where the quantity to be carried was considerable, special arrangements were made

---

605 SRO, L, D1798/HM/Chetwynd105. The accounts include a further payment for 'Bricks and Tiles' of £51 6s. Chetwynd also paid for two kilns and some labour so the average cost per 1,000 was actually higher than five shillings.
606 SRO, D593/N/2/2/3/17. There is a further unsigned contract for 200,000 bricks so the total may have been considerably larger.

with local farmers and that carrying was often a by-occupation at times when horses were not needed on the farm.[607]

It should, however, be emphasized that brick building and brickmaking were predominantly Spring and Summer activities, i.e. at a time when there was greatest demand for carts for agricultural work. A detailed account of bricks and carriage charges for 'Mr Mason to Wilmcote' from Stratford-on-Avon gives some indication of the complexity of brick carriage; in total between 8th April and 20th May, 1720, 39,300 bricks were carried: there were 24 journeys of 1,000 bricks at 5s each, 20 journeys of 500 bricks at 2s 6d, one journey of 800 bricks at 4s and two of 1,500 bricks at 7s 6d each. There were 11 separate carriers who undertook 47 journeys. The Midland evidence suggests that to this traffic should also be added competition from a large-scale local trade in other industrial materials such as coal, timber and lime. Phillips, in 1793, in his support for canals argued that 'the great quantities of fine hard bricks fit for floors and blue tiles … from Staffordshire and Shropshire are conveyed at great expence by land carriage'. He calculated that 'the price of land carriage, in the neighbourhood of the canal, is upon an average about nine shillings per ton for ten miles'.[608] The building materials employed were heavy, cumbersome and expensive to transport, even over short distances. Such additional costs were borne by the builders and their clients and for some would-be purchasers these marginal expenses may have delayed or even have prevented the ready acceptance of brick buildings.

At the end of the period under study are documented the first references to canals as important carriers of bricks and to the regional and national markets they developed. The huge brick structure built by the Board of Ordnance between 1804 and 1809 was deliberately sited at Weedon, (Northants), on the Grand Junction Canal so that building materials could be brought easily to the site of Britain's first inland armoury. Red bricks were made from local brick earth, but pale bricks were brought by canal from Brinklow, (Warks), thirty miles away.[609] An integrated network of rivers and canals extended the market and reduced the costs for heavy weight and low value building materials. The

---

607 Hey, D., *Packmen, Carriers and Packhorse Roads; Trade and Communication in North Derbyshire and South Yorkshire*, Leicester UP, (2001). Carriers were also required for the transport of pottery, iron, coal and cloth. Edwards, P., 'The Horse Trade in Tudor and Stuart Staffordshire', *Staffordshire Studies*, **13**, (2001), 38.
608 Phillips, 148, 171.
609 Gibbs, L., 'Understanding the Development of the Site', Conservation Plan for Storehouse Enclosure, Royal Ordnance Depot, Weedon Bec, Northants., (2005), 7.

records of the Staffordshire and Worcester Canal include reference to the carriage of Coalbrookdale bricks via the Severn, a network of Midland canals and the Trent to Gainsborough in Lincolnshire.[610] One investor in the canal, Sir Edward Littleton, used it to import building materials from Evesham and North Wales.[611] The Midland rivers added to the available transport network – in Nottinghamshire the Trent, both upstream and downstream, required deepening but was then used extensively for bricks and tiles. At Sawley, where there was no bridge over the Trent, bricks were delivered by boat in 1733 and for the building of a nearby school in 1771-72.[612] For the building of his grand mansion at Burley-on-the-Hill, the Earl of Nottingham imported deals and marble chimney-pieces from London along the Fossdyke which linked the Witham and Trent.[613]

In regions without access to navigable rivers the canals were able to reduce the cost of coal, an important contributor to the overall costs of producing brick. Charles Foster has examined the Arley Hall Estate (Cheshire) accounts of Sir Peter Warburton at the time of its rebuilding in 1752-65. They reveal that coal for brickmaking was usually purchased from Haydock (South Lancashire), and brought overland by road. Following improvements to the River Weaver and the building of the Sankey and Bridgewater Canals, the price of coal fell.[614] There was fierce competition between suppliers and the Arley Estate purchased coal from six different agents. The price of the bricks made at the Hall was 11s per 1,000. 'Lump' coal for firing facing bricks cost 6s per 1,000 bricks and 'slack' coal for firing ordinary bricks cost 5s per 1,000, so that coal and its transport was half the total cost of the bricks.[615] Any reduction in the price of coal would therefore have a significant effect on the total cost of manufacturing bricks.

With the canals, local building materials began to be superseded by mass produced brick and tile. The first year's accounts for the Staffordshire and Worcestershire canal in 1772-73 include tolls for 'Floor Brick', tiles, crests,

---

610 Trinder, B., *The Industrial Revolution in Shropshire*, Chichester: Phillimore, (1973), 113.

611 Peters, J.E.C., *Development of Farm Buildings in Western Lowland Staffordshire up to 1880*, Manchester UP, (1986), 215.

612 DRO, D779B/T420. Redman, K., 'Accounts for the building of Sawley School, 1771-2', *Derbyshire Miscellany*, **15 pt 3**, (Spring 1999), 66-70.

613 ROLLR, Finch Mss., DG 7/1/129.

614 Willan, as early as 1760-61 14 tons of bricks were carried along the river. By 1765-66 the total was over 91 tons. In 1772-73 quite exceptionally over 2,500 tons were carried, 209-212.

615 Foster, 208-215.

gutters, building timber and a reference to 'Brickiln locks'.[616] The canal companies themselves were major producers of brick – in 1777 the relatively short Chesterfield Canal of 46 miles had 15 brick kilns and a tunnel at Norwood which required 3 million bricks.[617] Telford's second Harecastle tunnel required 8,814,000 bricks and Brindley's earlier tunnel of 1777 must have needed a similar number.[618] (John Phillips in his history of canal navigation recorded an imaginative – but doubtless failed – attempt by James Brindley in 1756, 'to erect a steam engine, near Newcastle-under-Lyme upon a new plan: the boiler of it was made of brick and stone instead of iron').[619]

---

616 SRO, D1386/1/8/1/17.
617 Richardson, 57.
618 Telford, T. ed. Rickman, J., *Life of Thomas Telford ... written by himself,* London: J. and L.G. Hansard, (1838), 311.
619 Phillips, 91.

1. St John's Almshouses, Lichfield, built in 1495. Photographed with kind permission of the Trustees.

2. 'Ancient Brick House at Lichfield', sepia drawing by J. Buckler, 1807. Reproduced by kind permission of the Trustees of the William Salt Library.

3. Diaper work forming a Christogram 'JHC' on Abbot Penny's Wall at Leicester Abbey, c.1500.

4. Bridge Chapel House, Derbyshire, built in the 17th century with medieval stone chapel to rear. Courtesy of the Trustees.

5. *Dual Hearth and Room Divider, 1675, at Middleton Hall, Warwickshire. Photographed with kind permission of the Trustees.*

6. Wreake Valley style 1686 at Brick Cottage, Syston, Leicestershire. Photographed with kind permission of the owner.

7. Friar Gate, Derby, built following the Improvement Act of 1768.

8. Pear Tree Farm, Yoxall, brickwork of c.1700, c.1740 and c.1780 fronting a medieval house.

9. Church Street, Ashbourne. 17th century/18th century houses in 'one of the finest streets in Derbyshire', Pevsner.

10. False front at Bridge Farm, Yoxall, Staffordshire. Photographed with kind permission of the owner.

11. Bradgate House, 16th century ruin, Bradgate Park, Leicestershire. Image © NotFromUtrecht, licensed for reuse under the Creative Commons Attribution-Share Alike 3.0 Unported license.

12. Hawkstone Hall, near Shrewsbury. Image © Steve McShane, licensed for reuse under the Creative Commons Attribution-Share Alike 2.0 license.

13. Hodsock Priory gatehouse, Nottinghamshire. Image © Enchufla Con Clave, licensed for reuse under the Creative Commons Attribution-Share Alike 4.0 International license.

14. Nave and tower rebuilt 1726-29 at Great Bolas Church, Salop. Photographed with kind permission of the PCC.

Chapter 8

FIRE AS A FACTOR IN THE ADOPTION OF BRICK

AFTER 1660 brick was increasingly adopted by the middling classes, as in Stobart's words, 'leisure and consumption gained a new centrality in the lives of many in the upper and middle ranks' of town dwellers.[620] The problem for the historian is in teasing out the motivation for its adoption. Price, availability, fashion, and safety are possible explanations but none of these are discrete but are entwined in complex relationships. For example, to insert a brick chimney may have provided increased comfort and protection from fire but it may also have provided heated upper rooms which enhanced the social status of the owner and presented an opportunity to display newly acquired domestic goods.

One major argument for the adoption of brick is that proposed by Jones and Falkus. They have suggested that the numerous urban fires in the seventeenth and eighteenth centuries provided positive opportunities for rebuilding in a material which they regarded as considerably more fireproof:

> *Such substitution (of brick for timber) was well in evidence before the turn of the eighteenth century and can be traced in a growing number of towns from the time of the Restoration. In effect, the brick building involved the reshaping of the urban landscape throughout the country, and by about 1750 there were few towns of any size that had not experienced considerable*

---

620 Stobart, J., 'Shopping Streets as Social Space; Leisure, Consumerism and Improvement in an Eighteenth-century County Town', *Urban History*, **25**, 1 (1998), 3.

> *reconstruction in this manner. There can be no doubt that the frequent fires that occurred in the closely clustered timber and thatch dwellings in so many medieval and Tudor and Stuart towns provided a major opportunity for such reconstruction, and their reduction a major incentive for it … the reconstruction of town centers (sic) with brick and tile, was largely completed by about 1750.*[621]

Jones and Falkus thus offered a pragmatic explanation for the rebuilding in brick of 'so many medieval and Tudor and Stuart towns'. In 1615 James I, when applauding the change in London from 'stickes to brick', described brick as 'being a material farre more durable, safe from fire and beautiful and magnificent'.[622] It is significant that in his list of the characteristics of brick that its fire-retardant qualities are recorded ahead of its aesthetic merits. In a gossipy letter of 1702 Richard Hill of Atcham wrote, 'I hope care is taken to arch the chimneys everywhere with stone or brick, so as to have no timber near the fire'.[623]

Fire and its potentially ruinous effects was an everyday part of the consciousness of all members of English society in the period before 1780.[624] From William III and Mary who observed the burning of their palaces at both Whitehall and Kensington to the petition of William Blicke of Barford who in 1629 experienced 'a sudden and fearful fire … which burnt his dwelling house to the ground … whereby he is almost undone and become utterly destitute for himself, his wife, and six small children,' almost everyone was aware of the danger to life and property occasioned by accidentally created fires.[625]

In many houses there are vertical tear-shaped smoke marks on the wooden beams which traditionally have been described as the result of careless handling of candlesticks. More recently these taper marks have been defined as deliberate and superstitious attempts to insure against domestic fires. The existence of hundreds of these ritual marks, many found on the fireplace lintel,

---

621 Jones, E.L., and Falkus, M.E., 'Urban Improvement and the English Economy in the Seventeenth and Eighteenth Centuries', in Borsay, P., ed., *The Eighteenth Century Town, A Reader in English Urban History*, London: Routledge, (1990), 120-121.

622 Cooper, N., *Houses of the Gentry, 1480-1680*, Yale University, (1999), 172.

623 SA, 112/1B/1/1-72.

624 SRO, 5350. The diary of Richard Wilkes, (1690-1760), a physician of Willenhall, is a good example of the obsession with fires. It contains references to fires all over Europe.

625 Ratcliffe, S.C., and Johnson, H.C., eds. *Warwick County Records*, Vol. 1, *Sessions Order Book 1625-1637*, Warwick, (1935), 98.

confirms the fear of fire.[626] Similarly houseleeks (*sempervivum tectorum*) were grown on some roofs as a protection against lightning.[627]

In their churches the congregations were often reminded of the precariousness of property and life as churchwardens made collections for communities which had been damaged by fire, flood and tempest. 'Briefs', which sought charitable donations, were licensed by local Justices and sent all over the country from communities in Britain and Ireland.[628] Of similar purpose to the 'brief' was the 'Letter of Request' in this case representing an individual's need for financial compensation for disaster. These methods of raising funds were widely adopted and must have formed a topic for general discussion and gossip. Pepys recorded, 'Lords day. To Church where we observe the trade of Briefs is now come up to so constant a course every Sunday that we resolve to give no more to them'.[629] It is conceivable too, that the existence of a firm of 'farmers' of the briefs at Stafford resulted in the success of an above average number of applications, from the Staffordshire-Shropshire region.[630]

Churchwardens' accounts include many references to parish collections for towns, villages and individuals affected by fire. At Hanbury in 1665, 3s 3d was 'collected for Chalbury, Oxfordshire, for a fire'. In 1685 1s was 'Given to James Starrat of Stoake who had loss by ffire' and 1s and 9d was 'Given to John Hone of Packington for a great loss by fire'.[631] Destruction by fire varied from a single building, like the messuage 'partly burned downe' at Longdon in 1669 to the large-scale urban fires.[632] In 1657 at Desford, the loss by fire of the church and other buildings was costed at £2,159 3s 6d.[633]

---

626 Dean J., and Hill N., 'Burn marks on Buildings, Deliberate or Accidental? *Vernacular Architecture* **45**, (2014), 1-15.

627 'Sky-high houseleeks and lightning strikes', *SPAB Magazine,* (Autumn 2020), 56-58.

628 SRO, D3361/5/3. Is a letter from the Staffordshire Quarter Sessions to the Lord High Chancellor asking for a brief for the restoration of Baswich church. Altogether 10,053 briefs were 'laid' at 4d per paper (10d in London) and £575 16s 10d was raised. SRO, D3361/2/1.

629 Pepys, S., *The Diary of Samuel Pepys,* (Sunday, 30th June 1661), Online.

630 Jones, E.L., Porter, S., and Turner, M., 'A Gazetteer of English Urban Fire Disasters', *Historical Geography Research Series,* **13**, (1984), 7. The briefs also included bogus requests for 'the repair of the ancient Chapel on Mt. Golgotha' and 'for the releife of the Archdeacon of Jerusalem'. Laithwaite, P., 'The Parish Briefs of Bilston', *SHC,* (1938), 208.

631 SRO, D1528/4/1.

632 Laithwaite, 203-26.

633 Lucas, F.G.L., *History of Campsea Ash,* (1909), 45. A Brief was recorded in the parish register of this Suffolk village.

At Rugeley, the churchwardens noted, 'The fier began in Ridgley ye 20 May, 1649 and Burnt 29 dwelling houses', its briefs raised £340 1s.[634] On Saturday 19th February 1709 there 'happened a dreadful fierce fire in ye West end of Rugeley'. The fire began (perhaps unsurprisingly) in the workshop of Richard Jaxons, 'a blind baker', fired adjacent thatch and did 'damage to 10 habitations 8 Barns and Cow houses'. It was of course the presence of adjacent thatched and timber-framed buildings which encouraged damaging conflagration. The Quarter Sessions of 1709 were informed that the total value of goods and buildings lost was £808 11s. The testators to the value of the goods and the 31 bays of buildings destroyed were 3 carpenters and 3 masons.[635] Doubtless self-assessments and partial valuations exaggerated the scale of the damage, at Baswich 'able and experienced workmen' calculated the costs of rebuilding the unstable church at £1,695 12s, the actual cost of rebuilding (in brick) was £336.

It was particularly the towns and cities which were vulnerable to fire. Closely packed timber-framed houses with thatched roofs stood close together along narrow twisting streets with clusters of thatched outhouses, barns and workshops behind them. Defoe defined succinctly their vulnerability, 'the houses all built of timber, lath and plaister, or, as they were properly call'd paper work'.[636] Thatched roofs mixed unhappily with the naked flames used for lighting, heating and industrial processes. A combination of burning thatch and a strong wind could spread flames across the streets to consume whole quarters of a town. As early as 1652 Parliament recorded that 'fire could be stayed' by means of brick houses, that brick preserved timber, prevented incumbrances to the streets by the building out of jetties on the first storey, prevented the excessive breeding of vermin in wood houses and added to the honour and beauty of the capital city of the commonwealth.[637]

In the Midlands there were significant urban fires. At Nantwich in 1583 150 houses were destroyed and all that survived were the brick chimney stacks. The Queen gave £1,000 for the rebuilding. In 1591 the Earl of Shrewsbury asked the Justices to organise collections for the relief of Shifnal 'where both

---

634 'Rugeley Parish Register, 1569-1722', *Staffordshire Parish Registers Society*, (nd.), 96.
635 SRO, Q/SR 474. The use of masons, carpenters and bricklayers as valuers of burnt buildings was common, see for example the valuations made at Wem in 1677. SA, 484/240.
636 Defoe, Vol. I, 325.
637 CSPD, Interregnum 1651-52, (March 1652), 164.

the town and church have been almost entirely consumed by fire'. Similarly, the Duchy of Lancaster in 1599 gave 80 trees for the repair of houses burnt at Uttoxeter while 11 citizens were named as 'persons who have repaired parts of their houses and purchased wood at their own cost'.[638] There were fires at Stratford-on-Avon in 1594, 1596 and in 1614 the town Council obtained an order from the Privy Council that all houses should be roofed in tile or slate. From a fire in 1641 damage was assessed at £8,816 19s. It was alleged that the fires 'had their beginninges in poore Tenements and Cottages wch were thatched wth Strawe, of which Sort very many have byn lately erected there'.[639] At Market Drayton a fire in 1651, again started in a bakery, consumed much of the town. From a further fire in 1661 the consequent briefs included losses of £24,000 'and upwards'.[640] At Newport, Salop, in 1665 156 families lost their 'habitations' because of the 'Great Fire'[641] and in 1677 at Wem, 140 houses were lost at a value of £14,769 10s with destroyed goods valued at £8,918 13s 1d. At Tuxford, Notts, in 1702 almost the whole town was destroyed.

At Warwick in 1694 according to the 'Book of Estimates', 157 houses were lost. The consequent Fire Act required that replacement buildings should show a uniformity of façade, that there should be a standard house of 2 storeys each of 10 feet plus garrets and/or cellars and that the roof should be hipped and parallel with the road. Some streets were widened with compensation paid to those disturbed. 'The Fire', destructive as it was, thus provided the opportunity for the development of a uniform collective townscape. The building regulations nominated the building materials, and the Commissioners determined the price of brick and stone.

C.R.J. Currie has modelled the attrition of old houses based on a study of the village of Swavesey in Cambridgeshire. He argued that fire was a 'more significant cause of destruction than previously thought' and that 'the cumulative effect of small fires on the housing stock may have been as great as that of the rarer major ones'. The model is based on an analysis of fires reported in the newspapers of the nineteenth and twentieth centuries and concluded that there 'was between three and four houses (burnt) in fires occurring at three-to-four-year average intervals'.

---

638 ROLLR, 23D6621.
639 Porter, S., 'Fires in Sixteenth Century Stratford-on-Avon', *Warwickshire History* **3**, (1976), 97-105.
640 Southam, H.R.H., 'Briefs for Shropshire Churches', *TSalopAS.* **43 pt2**, (1926), 218.
641 SA, P207/A/1/1.

For the period before newspapers when houses were rebuilt in timber and thatch, Currie suggests 'an average of three houses burnt down in fires occurring at, on average, three-year intervals'.[642] In the Midlands such fires were often formally unrecorded and are discoverable only as asides in other documents. In Rugby is a lease of 1728 of a 'new built messuage' replacing one 'lately burnt down,'[643] and in 1734 was recorded 'the cottage being newly erected in place of a butchers shop and gatehouse burnt down in the fire at Southam'.[644] Ironically the very building process itself was often a cause of fires. Many houses were destroyed by fire from stoves used to melt the lead for weights in sash windows or roofs, houses therefore often caught fire before they were completed. In 1750 Horace Walpole suggested an Act of Parliament making master builders liable to pay for any fire damage caused by fire before the workmen had left.[645]

Municipal legislation aimed to control thatching and to support the limited technology of fire-fighting. As early as 1474 Coventry prohibited the use of thatched roofs and in 1493 banned the construction of wooden chimneys.[646] At a local level a typical example is that in Stowheath where in 1617 were recorded the 'Pains laid at the Great Leet and Court baron for the better avoyding and preventing … of those dangers which happen to the Towne by fyre (except it shall please god)'. It notes, that 'losse may there upon grow by one negligent person' and ordered 'Robert Smith, Naylor repair the Smythie Chimney before the feast of Saint Andrew the Apostle'. It threatened the removal of a cottage 'or that there be sufficient chimney made' and ordered that 'the some chimneys to be seene viewed and Certified by the homagers to be sufficient'. In Lichfield Street, Wolverhampton, Thomas Tomkys was ordered 'to remove the chimney forge to some other more convenient place or else make the same in such sufficient order'.[647] Similar legislation exists for many other towns and cities.

---

642 Currie, C.R.J., 'Time and Chance: Modelling the Attrition of Old Houses', *Vernacular Architecture*, **19**, (1988), 1-7.
643 WRO, CR0240/27a-b.
644 WRO, CR1470/Box 5/Bundle 2.
645 Stone, L., and Fawtier Stone, J.C., *The Open Elite? England 1540-1880*, Oxford: Oxford U.P (1984), 369.
646 *Leet Book*, 389, 549.
647 SRO, D 3212/1/4.

FIRE AS A FACTOR IN THE ADOPTION OF BRICK

The Insertion of the Brick Chimney

Sir, he made a chimney in my father's house and the bricks are alive at this day to testify it. Henry VI, Pt 2, Act 4.

The motives for the insertion of the brick chimneys into timber houses and later as important features of brick houses have traditionally emphasized their value in reducing the risk of fire. There was danger of conflagration in houses which did not contain a chimney and where the fire was contained in a free-standing fire box or was laid on the floor itself. Smoke was conducted out of the building through a small gablet in the thatched roof (or even a 'headless barrel'), through purposely built louvres or via a 'smoke hood' or 'smoke bay' constructed of timber and daub.[648] Even in those smaller timber or clay and stud houses which possessed a chimney it might well have been constructed of timber or of a timber/clay mixture. Examples of a hooded chimney of lath and daub still survive in a mud-walled farmstead at Great Dalby and of a timber-framed chimney at The Thatch, Cropston. (p. Thurcaston), Brook Cottage, Longdon, Thimble Hall, Yoxall, 56 Clifton Road, Nottingham and Bleasby Hall, Notts.[649] Such structures could be dry, brittle and comparatively fragile although Anthony Quiney has argued 'that wood fires were encouraged to burn slowly and radiate a warm glow rather than burn furiously … so timber chimneys were not as impractical as they sound.'[650] One method of reducing the risk of fire was by 'torching', in which a small fire was lit in the chimney to produce a carbon lining on the timbers – the Chamberlain's Accounts for Leicester in 1555 include payment for 'gronsellyng the wholl house and torchyng the chimney … old hey to torche with 1s 8d'.[651]

Smoke bays or smoke hoods rarely survive as they were generally replaced by a more fireproof source of dispersal. For example, in Wolverton Manor, a

---

648 Mason, R.T., *Timber Framed Buildings of England*, Coach Publishing, (1974), 87. The 'smoke bay' was created by the construction of a small bay, four or five feet long but extending across the full width of the house. It is generally post-medieval and is normally found only in two-storied houses.
649 One survives at 'The 'Old Medicine House', a timber-framed house of c.1600, originally in Betley, the timber posts of the firehood remain on the ground floor and the wattle and daub infill of the flue survives on the first floor. The house was demolished and re-erected at Goostrey, Cheshire. Mercer, E., *English Vernacular Houses*, (RCHM, 1975), 200.
650 Quiney, A., *Period Houses*, London: Hamlyn, (1989), 103-4.
651 Bateson, 156.

medieval hall-house at Eaton-under-Heywood, the development of heating can be traced from a typical sequence of an open hearth, a smoke bay of c. 1570 and finally in c.1660 a brick chimney.[652] The blackened and encrusted condition of the roof timbers of many medieval houses is evidence of the confinement of smoke and the long-term discomfort it must have created. One solution was the addition of brick chimneystacks on the exterior walls of the house or their insertion into its core. As early as 1467 the Worcester Ordinance declared that 'no chymneys of Tymber ne thacched houses be suffred wtyn the cyte but that the owners do them away and make them cheymneys of stone or bryke'.[653] In 1485 the Nottingham Council accounts recorded the building of a timber house but with brick used on the chimney 'reredose'.[654]

How far the use of brick was generally applied is uncertain for there are many references to the presence of wooden or mud chimneys. In 1649, the Parliamentary Survey of Hampton in Arden recorded 'a house of 1 roome and a wodden chimney'.[655] In Nottingham in 1626 the Bridge Wardens Accounts included, 'Paid for … with other woods for two chimneys xiis iiiid' and 'Bricke to make the hudde (Chimney top) straye (straw) and thacking (coarse grass) with workmanship xiis vid'.[656] As late as 1734 in Nottingham, the Constable Jury presented 'Christopher Wrigley for his Mud Chimneys being out of repair and dangerous for fire'.[657]

Other explanations have been added to the essentially practical reason for building in brick. After the 1530s there was a sharp cooling period in the weather. The seventeenth century particularly was a period of prolonged climatic instability characterised by a sustained fall in temperature, increased precipitation, restricted tree growth and fewer sunspots. For decades after 1645 there was virtually no sunspot activity. (Although recent research now attributes climatic instability more to volcanic disruption and fluctuations in the global atmosphere than to their absence.) In the seventeenth century most decades had at least three winters described as 'severe', 'very severe' or

---

652 Moran, M., *Vernacular Buildings of Shropshire,* Almeley: Logaston Press, (2003), 309.
653 Wight, 90.
654 *NBR,* **IV**, 258.
655 BLAC, L/acc 511984.
656 *NBR,* **V**, 11.
657 *NBR,* **VI**, 145.

'extremely severe'. 'The twenty years between 1680 and 1700 were remarkable for their cold, unsettled weather at the end of a century of generally cooler temperatures and higher rainfall'.[658] At a local level Jonathan Jenner, the vicar of Alrewas, recorded in 1683, without apparent irony, the 'vehemence and severity' of freezing such that 'carts and wagons … were generally ffrozen within doors insomuch that many suffered great loss in their drink … and many of ye richer sort were forced to drink water'.[659] Was the insertion of a brick chimney a response to falling temperatures?

At the same time as the cooling period the population rose and there was increased demand for firewood for both domestic and industrial use. This also may be part of the explanation for the increased number of chimneys as homeowners moved to use domestic coal rather than high priced firewood. There is no direct documentary evidence, but domestic logic would suggest that the insertion of brick chimneys, with more hearths burning a cheaper fuel, making a more comfortable house and warmer bedchambers would be sensible. Such economy was reflected in many leases, for example, a Shropshire lease on the Whitton Estate in 1682 required the tenant 'to use 20 horse-loads of pitt coal for the saving of wood'.[660]

Historians have traditionally associated the building of brick chimney stacks with the insertion of floors into open-hall houses. Logically it would seem sensible at a time of rebuilding to erect a chimney whilst additional floor supports were being introduced and when some means of expelling smoke would be required because of the obstruction caused by the new floors. In his study of Hertfordshire houses, J.T. Smith, however, concluded that:

> *Examination of vernacular open-hall houses showed that upper floors inserted in halls are frequently earlier than the existing brick chimney stacks which, in theory, should be of the same date. The floor is commonly late 16th century and the stack about 100 years later.*[661]

---

658 Fagan, B., *The Little Ice Age,* Basic Books, (2001), 132. The coldest years were: 1675, 1684, 1688, 1692, 1694, 1695 and 1698. Manley, G., Central England temperatures, monthly means 1659 to 1973, *Quarterly Journal of the Meteorological Society*, (1974), 393.
659 Stubbs, N., *A History of Alrewas,* Hailwood Enterprises, (1987), 81.
660 SA, 11/462.
661 Smith, J.T., *English Houses, 1200-1800, The Hertfordshire Evidence*, RCHM, (1992), 185.

At Garthorpe Vicarage a diary of building alterations made between 1672 and 1759 by two successive members of the Turner family described a three-bay building with upper chambers with a great bay added at the east end in 1672, a middle bay built in 1706 and 'partitions' in the great chamber, entry and buttery in the following year. It was not until 1707 that a chimney was also added to 'the parlour' which was socially the most important room.[662] At Yoxall as late as 1700 inventory evidence suggests that 'a very few upper chambers had heating'.[663]

The building-in of chimneys was a long process which might exhibit three phases of development – open hall, conversion to smoke bay and a later construction of a brick chimney. Mason concludes that 'the building in of chimneys ... was not completed until about 1700'.[664] In poorer cottages the date may be even later. Richard Gough in his unique *The History of Myddle* (c.1701) describes the widow Chidley not by her personal characteristics but as, 'living in a little house in Newton that had no chimney'. On her death the new tenant, Richard Clarke, 'built a chimney in this house'.[665] At Attingham in 1722, 1,200 bricks were ordered for a 'new chimney' and 3,000 bricks for a chimney in a house 'burnt to the ground'.[666] The latter case would seem to be unusual as only the chimney is to be of brick suggesting the house was rebuilt as a timber-framed house?

The building of gable-end chimneys may also have been an incentive to build in brick as they needed to be set in something more substantial than a stud-work end wall.[667] The presence of brick gables on timber fronted houses has also led to some possible misinterpretations. M. Moran, in her study of the vernacular buildings of Whitchurch, describes two such early eighteenth-century houses as 'representative of the transitional period between timber framing and brick construction'. A more prosaic explanation is that the brick

---

662 Varley, J., 'Episcopal Records', *TLAHS* **46**, (1970-71), 58-59.
663 Stuart, D., ed., *A Social History of Yoxall in the Sixteenth and Seventeenth Centuries*, Keele UP, (1990), 85.
664 Mason, 87, Quiney, A., *The Traditional Buildings of England*, London: Thames & Hudson, (1990), 97, concurs with this view. In the context of 'Chimney stacks in the Midlands', he states that 'while there was plenty of clay for brick ... in many parts of the Midlands, they were applied to house building very slowly'.
665 Gough, R., ed. Razzell, P., *The History of Myddle*, Caliban Books, (1979), 175, 177.
666 SA, 112/1/2406, 112/1/2407.
667 For example, Ashley Farmhouse, Loggerheads, a timber-framed house with brick gables.

gables were necessary for the four chimney stacks which served both ground floor rooms and the bedrooms.[668]

In larger or more prestigious houses brick chimney stacks were earlier, more sophisticated and frequently spectacularly ornate. Pevsner describes the chimneys of Plaish Hall, Shropshire of 1580 as 'gloriously overdecorated'.[669] There, local legend has it that the owner, Sir William Leighton, found he had condemned to death at Shrewsbury Assizes a craftsman who could make ornate chimney shafts. He was released, completed the work and was then hung! Similar examples to Plaish are shown in the drawings included in Plot's *Natural History of Staffordshire,* of the timber-framed halls at Sandon, Chartley, Madeley, Tixall and Broughton. One advantage of these multi-shafted chimneys, as against the earlier shaftless masonry flues, was that the smaller flues reduced down-draught and increased domestic comfort. Such impressive chimneys also served as an indication of status and wealth, as at Upton Cressett Hall, refaced in brick about 1580 for an important county family.

The visual effect was often more important than domestic comfort. Olive Cook has observed that the number of shafts did not always correspond to the number of fireplaces.[670] In this she was echoing Plot's comments of 300 years earlier on the houses at Tixall and Chillington, 'It is observable likewise that the *tunnels* (shafts) of the *Chimneys* in both these houses are very numerous, the Hall *chimney* at *Chillington* having no less than 8 *tunnells* to one hearth'.[671] Similarly at Willington Hall where, in the Hearth Tax returns of 1666, the house was assessed at 28 hearths (only 5 less than Trentham) the assessors noted that 'And shee (Mrs Parkes) returned 40 under her owne hand into the Exchequer and hath but 28 but refuseth to pay soe many'.[672] At Shugborough Hall the collectors recorded, 'William Anson Esquire nine (hearths) formerly returned

---

668 Moran, M., *Vernacular Buildings of the Whitchurch Area and their Occupants*, Fir Cone Books, (1999), 67. The two houses are Ellesmere House and Barkhill House. The concept of a 'transitional period' in which houses were built of external timber framing and brick *at the same time,* and where the front of the house is timber is not generally accepted. Houses with brick fronts and timber gables are known in many areas.

669 Pevsner calls it 'The earliest use of brick in the county', *Shropshire*, 228, a view no longer accepted. Mercer, E., and Stamper P., 'Plaish Hall and Early Brickwork in Shropshire', *TSalopAHS*, 66 (1989), 90-96, suggest a later date of c.1580 which is now generally accepted, for the monogram of Henry VIII painted on the ceiling has now been identified as a 'fake'.

670 Cook, O., *English Farmhouses and Cottages*, London: Thames & Hudson, (1982), 97.

671 Plot, 359.

672 The Staffordshire Hearth Tax, Seisdon Hundred, *William Salt Archaeological Society*, (1923), 96.

two too many by mistake'.[673] Possibly more status was gained by paying more tax and thus implying the possession of a larger house? The number of ornamental and high-quality brick stacks erected was relatively small and although they indicate a high degree of bricklaying craftsmanship, were insufficient to have been an important factor in extending the brick industry.[674]

In less important houses timber chimneystacks could serve one fireplace or two back-to-back, but not fireplaces on different floors. This was an important limitation and a pressing motive for the adoption of brick chimneys. In those houses in which a higher standard of comfort was demanded and where the ground floor was used for industrial or retail purposes then the first-floor rooms could serve as dining and recreational rooms.[675] Some indication of the spread of brick chimneys is provided by reference to the specialist trade of 'chimney sweep'. The earliest Midland example may be that of the Nottingham Chamberlain's Accounts for the Guild Hall in 1558 which include the sum of 1d paid for 'sweppyg and dressing the chimney'.[676] In 1699 Thomas Harrison of Eccleshall was listed, his main employment was probably at the Bishop of Lichfield's Palace.[677]

To improve the draught above the lintel, early brick stacks usually batter inwards on three sides. By the late seventeenth century this batter, visually obvious at first floor/second floor level, was regarded as ugly and often, as general bricklaying skills improved, the face of stack was made vertical. In the middle of the seventeenth century there was considerable improvement in the design of chimneys, perhaps connected with the use of coal as the main fuel. As coal became the preferred fuel for domestic housing then the hearths and chimneys needed to be of brick to resist the higher temperatures. The notion of a 'timber famine' has been discussed and generally dismissed, but it is possible that there were local or regional shortages of affordable local firing. High densities of population tended to coincide with low densities of woodland

---

673   The Staffordshire Hearth Tax, Pirehill Hundred, *WSAS*, (1921), 60.
674   SRO, D593/R/1/2. The opportunity for decorated brickwork may explain the purchase of 1,100 bricks 'for topping of the chimney' at the stone-built Trentham in 1634.
675   Vaisey, 252. The inventory of Richard Harrison of 1676 describes 'the dining roome over the parlour'. The first-floor dining room of the timber-framed 'High House' on the High Street, Stafford was wall-papered in the mid-eighteenth century.
676   Cullingford, B., *The British Chimney Sweep*, New Amsterdam, (2001), 7.
677   Spufford, M., 'Poverty Portrayed: Gregory King and the Parish of Eccleshall', *Staffordshire Studies*, **VII**, (1995), 106.

and therefore adjacent to urban centres there could be a timber shortage and an incentive to use coal. The use of coal and the need that was evidently felt for first floor fireplaces led to the adoption of grates which in turn led to the building of smaller brick stacks with more flues. A study of the medieval Pear Tree Farm, Yoxall, has revealed a massive, sophisticated and multi-flued stack of the sixteenth century which is battered on all four sides, an external stack probably of the seventeenth century and a stack inserted at first floor level in the eighteenth century.[678] The addition of chimneys on external walls is common. At Wellesbourne (Warks), there is a timber-framed house with a brick house, (The Little House, dated 1699), about a metre to its left, the external chimney stack serves a ground floor hearth in the timber-framed house and a first-floor hearth in the brick house! Another cottage in the village has an external stack sufficiently large to accommodate a garden bench. Brick also provided the opportunities for specialist hearths and fireplaces. At Middleton Hall (Warks) there is a rare survival of a wedge-shaped structure of two hearths set against an external wall whose apex formed the end of a brick dividing wall. Built in 1675 this fashionable structure heated two rooms and used one chimney shaft.

Skilled and experienced bricklayers could produce elaborate chimney stacks, but untrained bricklayers, perhaps recruited from estate workers, could lack skills and training. A problem experienced by many clients was that of the smoking chimney where insufficient draught prevented ready smoke dispersal. Many contracts included the requirement that the chimney must draw well, for instance Thomas Allen's contract of 1706 agreed to pay the bricklayers 4s per 1,000 bricks but 'the chimneys to carry smoke'.[679] The publication of specialist guides reflects the need for advice, in 1715 Nicholas Gauger translated and published a work by J.T. Desaguliers, *Fires Improved or a New Method of Building Chimneys*. In 1776 James Anderson wrote *A Practical Treatise on Chimneys* which pointed out that a tall chimney gives a better draught than a low one.

An analysis of Lichfield inventories has identified 26 houses between 1641-1680 as possessing upstairs rooms in which grates and fireside equipment imply the existence of a chimney or in which a chimney is specifically mentioned.[680] Although there is no precise evidence, such a chimney, being in

---

678 Personal observation of the author.
679 SRO, D(W)1742/46.
680 Vaisey, A typical entry is that of (73) William Nicholls, 1664, 'one grate' in the chamber over the hall and 'one grate, one paire of bellows and landirons' in the chamber over the parlour.

an upper room, was almost certainly of brick and almost undoubtedly was so constructed where the inventory refers to newly built rooms. The average value of the post-1643 inventories of those who had a chimney (26) was £174 2s 6d. The average value of the post-1643 inventories of those who did not have a chimney, or where a chimney is not recorded or implied, (131) was £62 18s.[681] Even allowing for the well-known difficulties of using inventory valuations, such a discrepancy must support the unsurprising view that, at least before 1676, the possession of a (brick) chimney was a reflection of above average personal wealth. What percentage this might be of the total number of houses in Lichfield is difficult to estimate but Gregory King counted 655 houses in Lichfield in 1695. The majority of these were owned, or more probably rented, by the very poor, a class who did not leave inventory evidence and the physical evidence of whose buildings was destroyed by attrition, redevelopment and the moral certainties of the late nineteenth century Urban District Councils. The number of chimneys per decade suggests that chimneys were becoming more popular after 1660 but were present in only a small proportion of the total number of houses in what was a popular and relatively wealthy city.

Table 10: Lichfield Houses with Inventory Evidence of Chimneys, 1641-1680

Decade	1641-50	1651-60	1661-70	1671-80
Number of inventories of houses in the City	17	12	37	65
Houses with inventory evidence of chimneys	4	5	5	12

A similar pattern of a relatively slow adoption of the brick chimney is revealed in the inventory evidence from Stratford-on-Avon where, not until the end of the seventeenth century, are they found in significant numbers.

---

681 The total value of the 26 post-1643 inventories where a chimney is recorded was £4,526 16s 8d. The total value of the 131 post-1643 City inventories where a chimney was not recorded was £8,245 8s 8d.

Table 11: Stratford-upon-Avon Houses with Inventory Evidence of Heated Upstairs Rooms/Chimneys, 1626-1699

(Note: these exclude houses in those rural settlements which are in Stratford parish. eg. Shottery, Luddington and Clopton but include the adjacent Old Stratford, Bridgetown and exclude 16 which were damaged and undecipherable by the editor)

Decade	1621-1630	1631-1640	1651-1660	1661-1670	1671-1680	1681-1690	1691-1699
Number of inventories of houses in the town	14	20	5	20	20	24	42
Houses with inventory evidence of chimneys	3	2	1	3	6	12	9

The above tables suggest that the pace of adoption was slow even when there were early precedents. In Lichfield as early as 1495 eight tall brick chimneys were incorporated in the St John's almshouses and formed a visually impressive model. Why then were they not commonly built in the city?[682] A purely economic explanation would suggest that the price and availability of brick were the determining factors. Mathew Johnson, in a study of 'housing culture', has suggested that 'the disengagement from the craft tradition in terms of both layout and technical system is most obviously apparent in the use of different building materials'. Based on a regional study of housing he concludes that:

> *Domestic architecture in western Suffolk underwent a fundamental transformation between the 15th and 17th centuries … Purely economic and typological explanations were found to be inadequate, (to explain the change). Instead cultural change was postulated to be at the core of the underlying changes in domestic space.*

---

682 The delay in inserting chimneys was apparent in other towns. John Persehowse, an extremely wealthy landowner in Walsall, only added chimneys to his son's house as late as 1634. SRO, D260/M/F/1/5.

For him the explanation for the inserted chimney and the consequently heated upper rooms lies not in convenience or the availability of new building materials but in changing social relationships, perhaps in the enhanced social status derived from an increased number of rooms, a perceived need for privacy or changes in the relationships with servants.[683] His explanation for variations in the speed of adoption is therefore an innate conservatism and resistance to cultural change by some townspeople.

In all towns and cities some brick chimneys were erected. The presence of hearths in upstairs rooms provided further opportunities for decoration and the approval of visitors for the wealth and awareness of fashionable style they demonstrated. Anthony Quiney has suggested a more pragmatic explanation for the emphasis on the chimney piece. He argues that the widespread adoption of coal led to a revision in the form of the fireplace. Coal fires were smaller than those of wood, but the grate needed to be raised to enable the ash to fall away, 'A coal fire could easily have been fitted in a grate only one-foot square … Traditionally, a fireplace was the focus of a room, and so the diminution of the fire with the advent of coal made an imposing chimney-piece a necessity'.[684]

Inserting or improving the chimney was a practical response to soot and smoke and reflects changing conceptions of comfort. In terms of cooking this was marked by the decline in use of round bottomed pots, previously hung over the fire, and their replacement with flat bottomed saucepans. The use of hearths where brick could be damaged by intense heat also encouraged the use of cast iron, decorated firebacks. These became familiar domestic objects, in 1674 the vicar of Cleobury Mortimer, Robert Goodwin, recorded the 'summe of tenne shillings for an iron plate behind my fyre at Hopton'.[685]

The chimney piece provided a focal point in the room and a feature where paintings or looking glasses were often hung.[686] The inventory of Elizabeth Bagot of Cannock in 1685, for example, included 'Dutch ware' over the chimney.[687] Delft tiles were particularly fashionable, the accounts at Trentham

---

683 Johnson, M., *Housing Culture*, London: UCL Press, (1993), 53-54, 157-8.
684 Quiney, 147. A prestigious chimney piece could be important even in relatively low-level housing. Corner Cottage, Penkridge, for example, has a chimney piece with plaster foliage decoration and is dated 1680.
685 Childe, F.C.B., 'Extracts from the Note-Book of a Shropshire Vicar, 1656 to 1691', *SAJ*, **28 pt 2**, (1905), 196.
686 Fiennes, 82, 106, 140, 171. Fiennes often refers to the use made of the chimney piece.
687 SRO, B/C/11, Elizabeth Bagot, (4th November, 1685).

include for 1739, 'paid for ye Carriage of a box of Dutch tyles from Warwick to Trentham'.[688] Much further down the social scale, Pear Tree Farm, Yoxall, a medieval farmhouse refronted in brick in the early eighteenth century, also possesses two first floor fireplaces decorated with Delft tiles.[689] In 'The Lodge', Hopwas, 'newly erected' in 1731 there were three rooms with 'Dutch Tiles' and two specific references to 'A Stafford Grate'.[690] In most building accounts the fireplaces were highlighted by elaborate chimney pieces, for example, the accounts for the Herrick house at Beaumanor in 1725 include, 'Harth Stones & Chimney Peses £10, A Marble Chimney Pese £5'.[691] The size of the hearth could also be reflected in the appearance of buildings. William Chambers in his *A Treatise on Civil Architecture* of 1759, declared that 'the size of the chimney must depend on the dimensions of the room wherein it is placed'. He also recommended that chimney stacks should not be placed on outside walls where they were more likely to collapse.[692]

Fire provided new opportunities for the replacement of traditional building materials by a sophisticated and socially desirable resource which also contributed to increased overall safety and domestic security. The dangers of fire were not totally redeemed by brick building. The Exton Hall accounts for 1778-79 include 'payments to 64 men helping when the chimney was on fire at the Hall'.[693] Nevertheless Jones et al. concluded that 'The steep fall in the scale and incidence of provincial town fires after 1760 is the result of fire-fighting improvements but above all because of the effects of brick barriers to the spread of fires'.[694] This essentially pragmatic explanation is important but does not provide a full explanation for the adoption of brick. As this study demonstrates economic, cultural and social factors were of equal importance.

---

688 SRO, D593/F/3/2/13. At Wolseley Hall, Sir Charles Wolseley purchased two chimney pieces from William Anson at Shugborough, SRO, D(W)1781/17/1. At Newcastle, Thomas Allen's building contract required the bricklayers to make 'two handsome' chimney pieces, SRO, D(W)1742/46.

689 The social importance of the Delft tiled fireplace in a first-floor parlour is illustrated in the reconstruction of James Gibbs' No. 11 Henrietta Street (1727-34) in the Victoria and Albert Museum. There are also Delft tiled ground floor fireplaces at Gregory Stonynge's house (previously Lichfield Public Library) and in the timber-framed 'Tudor Café' in Bore Street, Lichfield.

690 SRO, D170/M/120, 160/2.

691 SRO, D(W)1734/2/3/27.

692 Chambers, W., *A Treatise on Civil Architecture*, London, (1759), 150.

693 ROLLR, DE3214/5953/1.

694 Jones, Porter and Turner, 'Gazetteer', 61.

Chapter 9

WHY DID PEOPLE BUILD IN BRICK 1660-1780?

IN HER novel *Mansfield Park*, Jane Austen wrote:

> *By some such improvements as I have suggested … you may give it higher character. You may raise it into a place. From being the mere gentleman's residence, it becomes by judicious improvement the residence of a man of education, taste, modern manners, good connections. All this may be stamped on it; and that house receive such an air as to make its owner be set down as the great land-holder of the parish.*[695]

This was the social and cultural explanation for brick building, that new or refronted houses were a very visible expression of wealth and social prominence to the casual observer who walked the streets of towns or travelled the countryside. On a more prosaic level Benjamin Franklin wrote in *Richard's Sayings*, 'Now I have a sheep and a cow, everybody bids me good morrow', making the same point as Jane Austen, that social identities are constructed around the way in which wealth is demonstrated.

Reconstructing how purchasers imagined their own acts of consumption is a daunting challenge for few people committed their motives to paper and issues such as social value and the desire for novelty are particularly elusive. In 1676 Parson Roades of Blithfield bought a house which was in an appalling condition:

---
695 Austen, J., *Mansfield Park,* Penguin, (2003), 224.

> *… very bad, but one chymney below stares and but one very mean one above staires the floors below were dirt and clay … those above of plaister sadley worn. Above a third part of ye house had no Floore over it. (Open Hall house?) … every body concluded it had bene an ould kiln. I had a mind to a sould it off ye ground as it stud. I got it at 60 pound Value and was bid but 50 and parsuaded to take it becase we had no Brick mad at that time within les than 2 miles and these very small and dear … Laid out in all about my house 350li of which I heartly Repented for I might a built a new tile brick house big enough for Blithfield parsonage and more convenient for ye Same money. In 1678 he began a series of improvements, I began to build ye south west end of ye house, in January 1680 he recorded, I began to repair ye rest of the house … all that I added to ye Bigness of ye house was room for ye east staircase a passage to ye well yard & a large Jetty at ye south east end to make it answerable to that on ye south west side.*

Roades was thus responding to the fashion for a symmetrical façade. By 1710 he had spent £426 and had enclosed the house in brick – 'To the Mason and Bricklayer for casing the parler end of the House and Hewing a Facies (Facia) of Stone and setting it up in the brickwork £2 15s 4d'. 7,000 of the bricks were provided by his patron. Over a period of 34 years Roades had invested heavily in meeting the demands of fashion and comfort.[696]

Doubtless for some to build in brick was a totally pragmatic and sensible decision determined by its price, availability and inherent qualities, but increasingly historians are emphasising the social context of consumerism in the late seventeenth and eighteenth centuries. The debate has been mainly conducted in terms of the diffusion of a widening range of domestic and luxury goods within the middling classes and the meanings of their purchases. It could be argued that the purchase of a new house, or the rebuilding of an old house in a new style, using a relatively new material, is an act of consumption which parallels the purchase of ceramics or furniture or printed calicoes. The house has a greater importance because it provides the fundamentals of warmth and shelter, provides the social setting for the display of newly acquired material goods and, more importantly, is obvious evidence of the purchaser's wealth and understanding of style and architectural idiom. John Benson has

---

696   SRO, D1386/2/1/5.

identified consumer societies as those 'in which choice and credit are readily available, in which social value is defined in terms of purchasing power and material possessions, and in which there is a desire, above all, for that which is new, modern, exciting and fashionable'.[697] For Benson, consumption is based on an economic background where cash or credit is available and a decision to purchase is not necessarily based on use and need but rather on the impression which is created amongst others. For many patrons brick building was therefore exciting and stylish, and timber framing was outdated and unfashionable, for example Kedleston Rectory, prior to its demolition in 1759, was described as 'an Ancient and decayed building being only lath and Plaister'.[698]

Historians of consumerism have traditionally argued that conspicuous consumption and emulation were central to any understanding of the relationship between individuals and objects of material culture. In 1982 Neil McKendrick wrote that emulation was the spur to 'an unprecedented propensity to consume' that gathered force over the course of the eighteenth century. 'Spurred on by social emulation and class competition, men and women surrendered eagerly to the pursuit of novelty, the hypnotic effects of fashion, and the enticements of persuasive commercial propaganda'.[699]

More recently research has suggested that the motivation to consume is more complex and more variable. The 'emulation thesis' in which copying one's betters appears as the chief motive for consumption has been modified in several ways. Bourdieu, for example, has demonstrated that consumption activities may not be motivated by emulation, but by differentiation, whereby each class strives to distinguish itself from others.[700] In her research on women

---

697 Benson, J., *The Rise of Consumer Society in Britain, 1880-1980*, Longman, (1994), 4.
698 SRO, L, B/C/5, (Faculty papers of the Bishop's Consistory Court).
699 McKendrick, N., 'The Consumer Revolution', in McKendrick, N. Brewer J., and Plumb, J.H., *The Birth of a Consumer Society*, Bloomington: Indiana Press, (1982), 101.
700 Bourdieu, P., *Distinction: A Social Critique of the Judgement of Taste*, (1979). Bourdieu, an important French philosopher, argued that all our acts are led by social pressures. Taste therefore is determined by social background and becomes a social marker. He argued that the dominant class asserts its lifestyle (based on refined, distinguished pleasures) as the benchmark of 'good taste' to which others must aspire, and in so doing legitimises class differences. Taste is an acquired 'cultural competence' whose function is to make social 'distinctions'. Usually 'cultural competence' was demonstrated by the adoption of new materials and new styles. It could however be demonstrated by a refusal to adopt new ideas. In the mid-nineteenth century many of the wealthy rejected the cheaper gas lighting, preferring the more expensive candles. Later they did however welcome the much more expensive electricity 'as a status marker that the cheaper gas never could have been.' Flanders, J., *The Victorian House*, London, (2003), 171.

and ceramics Moira Vincentelli suggests that gender is an important factor, 'Gender affects people's relationship to the material world, hence men and women have different attachments to different objects corresponding to the gender roles 'scripted' by society'.[701] Laura Weatherill, in a study of consumer behaviour in the North-East of England, regards emulation as a simplistic explanation. Her evidence suggests that consumption patterns did not neatly dovetail with the social hierarchy and that there were 'outstanding differences between urban and rural patterns of consumption'.[702] Maxine Berg thinks 'social emulation is a facile behavioural explanation' and that 'consumer response must be connected to incomes and the regional location of the purchasers'.[703] It may be true that the concept of emulation requires refinement, but human nature is a powerful force. The anonymous author of *A Discourse shewing the Great Advantages that New-Buildings, and the enlarging of Towns and Cities do bring to a Nation* of 1678 had no doubt that:

> *There are two great Causes of Labour and Industry, Necessity for Food and Emulation … Emulation provoaks a continued Industry, and will not allow no Intervals or be ever satisfied … Every Neighbour and every Artist is endeavouring to outvy each other, and all men by a perpetual Industry are struggling to mend their former condition: and thus the People grow rich.*[704]

Berg has written that 'Fashionable furniture was set off by lighting and mirrors which were amongst the most rapidly diffused goods'.[705] For example an inventory of James Humberstone of Melton Mowbray in 1688 included, 'In ye great Chamber 6 Chairs a looking glass a Table a grate fire-shovel and Tongs 1 10 0'.[706] At Wigwell an inventory of the manor house in 1684 included in the 'Purple Chamber' a 'stand' for a mirror.[707] At Hopwas in 1731 the 'new erected building' contained a 'Best Chamber with a 'large looking glass'.[708] A

---

701 Vincentelli, M., *Women and Ceramics, Gendered Vessels*, Manchester UP, (2000), 110.
702 Weatherill, L., 'Consumer Behaviour in the North-East of England, 1670-1730', http://seastorm.ncl.ac.uk/invs/paper1.
703 Berg, M., *Luxury and Pleasure in Eighteenth-Century Britain,* Oxford: OUP, (2007), 206.
704 Quoted in Earle, P., *The Making of the English Middle Class,* London: Methuen, (1992) 9.
705 Berg, 114.
706 Hoskins, W.G., 'A History of the Humberstone Family, 1688', *TLAHS,* **20**, **pt2**, (1938-39), 274.
707 Wigley, D., 'Wigwell Grange' *Derbyshire Miscellany,* **3**, No. 8, (1966), 641.
708 SRO, D170/M/120.

typical example of such diffusion from gentry to yeoman farmer lies within the accounts of Edward James of Penkridge who, between 1694 and 1701:

Pead for a grate fire shule and tonges 9s, 13 cheares & carridge of them £1 14 6, table and 2 standes £1 3 0, for a glas (mirror?) £1 4 0, glasing the Hall top £1 4 0 and 6 knives & 6 forckes 11s 0.

The context for all this domestic improvement was the purchase of 47,400 bricks and 5,500 tiles and the rebuilding of his farmhouse.[709] At nearby Caversall another farmer, George Parker in 1700, recorded:

Pd to george knolls 5s in part for ye chimney peise for ye parlour Chamber which he brought this day Pd to James Saunders for glazing ii windows 8s 0, Carrage of 22 bags of lyme £1 10 0. (replacing the wainscoting?)

Ten months later he 'Pd to George Senally for ye chimney peise & hearth for ye bed chamber £4 10 0'.[710] In the house of this provincial farmer, the insertion of fireplaces in two upper rooms clearly reflects the aristocratic emphasis on the first floor, the *piano nobile*, of a grand house.

Mathew Johnson has described how the transition to Georgian architecture is clearly demonstrated at Temple Balsall, Warwickshire, where Temple House, brick-built in the 1730s, deploys many of the elements of Georgian style and arrangement. It was the residence of the well-regarded Evetts family who had previously lived at the timber-framed Old Hall, a traditional vernacular house. The switch from unfashionable to fashionable residence was marked not just by the houses but also by the way in which they chose to prepare and consume food, drink and tobacco. Excavation of the cellar of the Old Hall revealed a great mass of rejected material, including plates, wine glasses and beer mugs, etc., most were unbroken, discarded presumably because they were unfashionable.[711]

In Pepys' diary there are many references to the copying of new styles of dress and furnishings, for example, 'he was planning a fine new bedroom and wanted to have an exact copy made of the bed belonging to the Duke of York's secretary,

---

709   SRO, D1798/HM/27/2.
710   SRO, 3806.
711   Johnson, 161-163. Gooder, E., 'The Finds from the Cellar of the Old Hall, Temple Balsall, Warwickshire', *Post-Medieval Archaeology*, **18**, (1984), 149-249.

Mathew Wren who obligingly allowed it to be viewed'.[712] At Alderson House, Warwick, built in 1696 after the Fire, the front door and fan light are a direct copy of those at 10 Downing Street which had been installed in about 1688. In 1773 the extremely detailed building instructions for the 'Rose and Crown', Derby, required 'the portico to be the same as Mr Cooke's House' (Cooke was a neighbour).[713]

Style was a key element in establishing social norms and social identity. Evidence for the emulation of style and fashion survives in the personal instructions of the gentry and clergy. In 1712, Thomas Allen, the rector of Stoke-on-Trent, signed a 'memorandum' with two bricklayers, Joseph Hemmings and John Tame, 'to well and truly build a certain piece of Building … the Brickwork to be entirely as closely laid as Mr John ffenton's is in Newcastle by his now dwelling house'.[714] The request for fine layers of lime mortar pointing between brick courses, ('closely laid'), was not for structural reasons but was an expression of fashion. Delicate joints emphasised the smooth uninterrupted façade of the house and at the same time informed the viewer that money had not been saved by deep and inelegant pointing. A groove in the horizontal and vertical joints was filled with lime putty to give the appearance of uniform brickwork with a thin precise network of joints which could be as fine as ¼ inch wide or even thinner.[715]

An excellent example of this 'gauged work' was observed by James Granger on High Pavement, Nottingham, 'undoubtedly one of the finest examples of the bricklayer's art to be found anywhere … the joints are practically as thin as it is possible to make them'.[716] Such ingenuity is an indication of the degree to which brick was manipulated in the interests of fashion. This fashion was taken to extremes by the development of the more expensive 'tuck' pointing in which pigmented surface mortar was followed by a thin white ribbon of plaster. In other houses the mortar could be made-up of brick dust as well as lime and sand, to give a colour as close as possible to that of brick. This effect could also be achieved by painting the pointing red, a rare survival of this can be found at 46 Friar Gate, Derby.[717]

---

712 Tomalin, C., *Samuel Pepys, the Unequalled Self*, Penguin, (2003), 272.
713 DRO, 195/2/133.
714 SRO, D(W) 1742/46.
715 Brunskill, 62. Clifton-Taylor, 237. In earlier Tudor and Stuart buildings because the brick was often irregular and misshapen, broad mortar courses were essential.
716 Granger, J., *Old Nottingham its Streets, People etc*, Nottingham, (1902), 54-55.
717 Another rare example is at Church House, Presteigne.

There was an obvious obsession amongst the provincial 'middling classes' with the fashions of London. Their records contain many personal and domestic references to the urgent need to be dressed, furnished or housed in the most fashionable styles. These could be as simple as Elizabeth Gell's request to her brother in 1670, 'are laced shoes out of fashion?'[718] Or a letter of Sir John Mordaunt in 1698 in which he expresses his need for a new black suit, remarking that 'the king's return is liable to bring in a new fashion trend'.[719] In 1728 Bishop Hough of Worcester wrote to Lady Kaye:

> *Our Friend in Town tells us of two very comical fashions, that the Lady's wear ruffs and the men hoops, the former may be for ought I know becoming, at least a little use … they are warranted by Precedents of great Authority but the other is entirely new and fantastical.*[720]

In 1760 Robert Shirley wrote to William Herrick about the fashionable colour for 'Post Chariots' which was blue, 'but I have not seen one of that colour since I came to town only a few Green with Ogee's gilt. Pompadour with ye Ogee's gilt is the next fashionable colour but then your shield should not be crimson'.[721]

More important in terms of building are the letters of Lady Mary Bridgeman of Castle Bromwich. Writing in 1688 to her architect, William Winde, fashion dominates her correspondence:

> *I beg the favour of your further opinion, whether you think the fashion as to the form of them (chimney pieces) may be of long continuance or likely to alter much, for if the fashion may be liykely to last, I do incline to buy too more.*[722]

In a further letter she is very aware of the cost of the Closet which 'may be handsome with as little charge as may be'. Winde replies that for a small closet

---

718 SRO, D 256/38/11/7.
719 WRO, CR1368 Vol. 11/4a.
720 SRO, D(W) 1778/1/ii/611.
721 ROLLR, DE10/2497.
722 Barre D.E., and Chaplin, R.A., eds. *William Winde: Advice on Fashionable Interior Decoration*, 2nd, letter, University of Birmingham, (1983).

'Painting should do better more a Lamode' (à la mode).[723] Her letters reflect an obsession with style and modernity which was shared by many. John Evelyn's diary includes many references to houses which were 'moderne', e.g. Kirby Hall visited in August 1654. Perhaps the most obvious example of cultural inspiration was Nuthall Temple (Notts) built in 1757 for Sir Charles Sedley, this bore a close resemblance to the 'Rocca Pisana' (1578) by Palladio's follower, Vincenzo Scamozzi, and was very similar to Lord Burlington's famous house at Chiswick. It was demolished in 1929.

The context for the whole debate about the nature of seventeenth and eighteenth-century consumerism has been conducted mainly in terms of the purchase and possession of material objects. The argument of this chapter is that the selection of brick was at least in part determined by fashion, style and social pressures. A brick house was a symbol of status and social acceptance for investing in property, erecting houses and equipping interiors were three of the most significant acts of consumption in the eighteenth century. This is clearly demonstrated in a letter of 1705 held within the records of the Herrick family of Beaumanor, Leics, in which Mrs Brayne declared that she was not angry but criticised her daughter for marrying a man about whom she knew so little and without Sir Edward Clarke's advice. She was angry at the state in which she had allowed her brother to be sent out to Jamaica but says that he is now accepted in the best of company. Her daughters had built themselves a 'brick house and had a new carriage'. They refused all offers of marriage as they were able to support themselves.[724] This is a letter about social values and the ability of her family to present evidence of their wealth and social standing. These qualities are demonstrated by the son's acceptance in Jamaican high society and her daughters' erection of a brick-built house. The house was not built of brick because it was cheap or fireproof but because of the social and economic information it presented to the public.

The mechanisms through which style and fashion, and therefore brick building, were diffused throughout the region were by personal observation, visits, discussion, pattern books and the employment of architects and builders who were familiar with the new styles. Domestic and estate records reveal a network of friendship and patronage that lay behind the creation and rebuilding of the

---

723   Barre and Chaplin, letters 5 and 8.
724   ROLLR, DG9/2443.

houses of landowners. The journal of Nathaniel Ryder, 1st Baron Harrowby, is particularly illuminating on the aristocratic network in Staffordshire. Harrowby had purchased Sandon Hall in 1776 and began to demolish the brick building and replace it with stone. In detail he records discussions and visits undertaken with a group of local gentry and aristocracy who were united by marriage, an interest in garden and house design and a commitment to estate improvement. The group included members of the following families, Anson, Leveson-Gower, Curzon of Hagley Hall, (Rugeley), Talbot of Ingestre, Mills of Barlaston, Bagot of Blithfield and Littleton of Teddesley. His journal begins with a comment on his own inadequacies, 'Memo: I must endeavour to acquire a taste for paintings, architecture, the furniture of the house and the laying out of gardens'.[725] That education was achieved by visits and critical analysis:

> *Sir John Cust went with me to Belton where Lady Cust his mother lives … the house built by J. Brownlow of good stone in the form of an H, in length 150 feet … the garden … in the old taste and I think very ill contrived even in that manner …*[726]

In 1756 he visited 'Lord Burlington's house at Chiswick … the house is built of very beautiful taste'.[727] Nearer home he visited the Curzon Estate at Hagley Hall, Staffordshire, 'Saw Mr Curzon's offices and made many observations on them … the kitchen floor was made of tiles like those which my offices are paved here at Sandon'.[728]

Harrowby's journal reveals the process of architectural diffusion at work. Through visits and discussions new ideas were absorbed, buildings were erected and they in their turn became models for others to copy. This is illustrated in an unsigned letter, in appalling handwriting, in 1697 to Sir John Chetwynd which describes the process where friends and neighbours were consulted prior to the employment of a builder:

> *After I had bargained with him I found him a very fuddling fellow which he will be and was exceedingly troubled thereat, but upon very great Enquiry*

---

725   Sandon Hall, Harrowby Trust Mss., **343**, Doc. 39.
726   Sandon Hall, **434**, Doc. 44.
727   Sandon Hall, **434**, Doc. 39.
728   Sandon Hall, **CXXIV**, Doc. 195.

after him from severall persons he had built for was incouraged to employ him and think him as able … as any man living: I was incouraged upon my (damaged) by Sir Humphrey Foster, Mr Philip Foley, Sir Humphrey Wrack and Sir William Ellis and others of whom I enquired concerning him.[729]

Personal recommendation was often the means by which builders gained contracts. In 1767 Mr Parry, the Tamworth estate agent of Viscount Townshend, wrote:

Mr Lees spoke to me today to enquire for a person understanding in Architect and Building to wait on yr Lordship at Rainham since when I have seen on Mr Pratt a very ingenious man & reasonable who I believe will wait of your Lordship.[730]

Prior to 1760 much Georgian architecture was anonymous but plans and drawings were made which could be shared with other would-be builders. For Cubbington Vicarage in 1721 there survives 'the Draught for building ye Vicarage House' a 'grand plan' and accounts.[731] For Beaumanor the building agreement includes plans of the ground and first floors and a coloured elevation of the house front.[732] Beesthorpe Hall building accounts of 1770 included, 'To Drawing design for the whole Building £1 5s, To Measuring the Brick and plaister work £1 0 0, Jorneys to set out the Buildings and give direction to the Workmen £3 0 0', (the workmen were given 3s for 'Christmas Boxes'). In total the plans cost £5 5s of a total cost of £205 18s 2½d (2.5%).

There were men who combined the roles of architect, builder and craftsman of whom Francis Smith, (1672-1738), and his brother William (1705-1747) supplied many brick buildings including Dudmaston Hall, Stanford Hall, Davenport House and Umberslade Court. Dudmaston Hall provides an excellent example of the process of emulation, it was probably built for Sir Thomas Wolryche by Francis Smith, the family of Sir Thomas's aunt, Elizabeth Wrottesley, also employed Francis Smith to build Wrottesley Hall in the 1690s. In 1695 Sir Thomas's father-in-law, George Weld, wrote to

---

729   SRO, D(W)1744/18/4.
730   SRO, LD187/2/2/46.
731   WRO, DR0452/22, accounts /25.
732   ROLLR, DG9/2135.

Andrew Archer of Umberslade Hall, another early Francis Smith house which was very similar to Dudmaston:

> *Having had ye hon(ou)r to sitt with you in the House of Commons makes me soe bold to beg of you that if you have a moddell of your House you will lend it to Sir Tho. Wolryche my Son in Lawe for some time, and I will carefully Returne it to you againe, if you have not such a model, that then you will let this bearer take a platt (plan) of ye same.*[733]

Smith modelled his houses on Belton House as an H plan in brick with sandstone window surrounds, a plan frequently employed.

The Smith business was passed on to William and David Hiorn, the builders at Edgbaston Hall, Joseph Pickford, the builder of Etruria Hall, was an agent for David Hiorn. This network of contractors, supervisors, craftsmen and builders was extended by the Wyatt family of Weeford and the Trubshaws of Colton. William Baker's account book for 1748-1759 illustrates the range and nature of the professional work of a man who was, like Benjamin Wyatt and Richard Trubshaw, architect, builder, supplier of materials and in the eighteenth-century term 'inspector of works'. Baker was based at Highfields near Audlem on the Cheshire/Shropshire border and worked on many of the important houses of the West Midlands. He was not usually the main designer but often contributed plans for stables and other outbuildings. He provides important evidence for the transmission of architectural style from London to the provinces. Baker was an associate of James Gibbs, the architect of the Radcliffe Camera, and was strongly influenced by him. At Patshull Hall Gibbs was nominally the architect but it was Baker who designed and built the outbuildings, stables, chapel, parlour and flanking pavilions for a favourite client, Sir John Astley. At Catton Hall Gibbs was the architect but it was Baker who supervised the erection of the building. Baker's own buildings also clearly demonstrate the influence of forms and decorative features derived from Gibbs' *Book of Architecture* (1728).

Local architects and builders were aided by the profusion of pattern books that were available. These were required because the Georgian style was thought to be more demanding to put into practice than the vernacular

---

733   Garnett, O., *Dudmaston*, National Trust, (2002), 27.

or English Baroque, as it was subject to more rules of taste. The architect James Gibbs realized this, stating that his *Book of Architecture* of 1728 was for, 'gentlemen who might be concerned in buildings, especially in remote parts of the country, where little or no assistance for design can be procured'.[734]

Gibbs' influence is most obvious in Baker's best work, the Ludlow Butter Cross. In 1743 Lord Herbert and two other gentlemen donated 200 guineas towards the proposal. The Corporation paid three guineas to two men to draw up a plan for pulling down the Cross and, in 1744, contracted Baker for the large sum of £860.[735] Baker's accounts also contain rare references to the purchase of London pattern books. In 1752 he bought 'halfpennys books and Chinese books' for 17s 6d. Possibly this was William Halfpenny's *Twelve Beautiful Designs for Farm Houses* (1750) or his *Useful Architecture* (1752). His clients included men of high social standing and influence, for example he planned outbuildings for the Earl of Stamford at Enville and built Wood Eaton for the Headmaster of Repton. Such men readily accepted his ideas and, as importantly, the building materials he proposed. He was a timber merchant and supplied the wood for many of his projects.[736] But more importantly at Highfields he owned a brick kiln from which he supplied nearby projects. Baker must have responded to the preferences of his clients, but where he had the freedom to suggest the building material to be used then brick was his obvious and logical choice. At Tixall Baker provided '81 rods of Brick-work in the new building' and '16 rods of Brick-work in walls to Court'.

The cost of transporting brick from Audlem to South Staffordshire would have been prohibitive and presumably local supplies were obtained but Baker must have been sympathetic to the employment of brick. For example, Baker did considerable work for the Littleton family at Teddesley Hall and at their new house, 'The Coppice', in the 1750s. The Littleton Estate records for those years include many references to the manufacture of huge numbers of bricks for the house.[737]

Two of Baker's commissions were for the restoration of parish churches. At Seighford he rebuilt the tower and nave in brick and at Penn he encased the

---

734 Gibbs, J., *Book of Architecture,* (1728), Introduction, 1.
735 Roberts, *Ludlow,* 124.
736 Oswald, A., 'William Baker of Audlem', *SHC,* (1950-51), 129. Baker supplied deals etc. to a Mr Crocket at Johnson Hall, Eccleshall in 1758.
737 SRO, D260/M/E/116.

tower in the same material. At Seighford Church he used one rather peculiar decorative device by giving the pilaster quoins of the tower tall deep rectangular panels, similar work survives on the tower at Seighford Hall (dovecote?) and on a tower at Oakley (near Tutbury). A recognisably personal style of brick building was also developed by Baker for farmhouses. Of three bays and two storeys, Baker decorated the buildings with crenellated parapets, examples can be found at Lady Dorothy's Cottage at Enville, (1748-50), Wood Eaton Hall, (1753-56), Burnhill Green Farmhouse, Patshull and in Shropshire, Woodhouse Farm, Peplow, (1754-58).

Most architects, builders 'inspectors of works' or 'contrivers' were men but there are some rare references to women as the designers of buildings. Plans drawn by Lady Elizabeth Wilbraham for the restoration of St Andrew's Church in 1700 are believed to be the first architectural plans to be drawn by a woman.[738] Barrells Hall, Warks, was remodelled in brick by Lady Luxborough in the 1730s and Castle Farm, Worksop, was designed by the Duchess of Norfolk in 1758. When husbands inconveniently died whilst building, often these elite wives assumed responsibility. Chesterton House, the site of a glorious brick gateway, was rebuilt between 1657 and 1662 mainly under the supervision of Elizabeth Peto. Lady Bridgeman similarly supervised the construction of Castle Bromwich Hall.

Hundreds of houses were built or remodelled in the late seventeenth and eighteenth centuries and frequently employed brick as the main building material, but not all owners were excited by new façades. In 1765 George Lucy wrote from his Elizabethan brick house at Charlecote, refusing to allow a Mr Standbridge to copy a painting, in silver, which he had seen at Lord Plymouth's, 'But what have I to do who am so happy to have a good old house but to make it decent and to content myself with that, as it is already design'd'.[739] Other builders rejected the restraint of the typical brick house and built with exuberance. In Brewood is the Gothick Speedwell Cottage, called by Pevsner 'a peach' and 'a delectable folly'. Folklore suggests that it was built following a winning bet on a horse in the Derby, a similar house is at Stourbridge. (At Bridgnorth Low Town, Diamond Hall was built by a Roger Pope (d.1710) from the 2,000 guineas prize won by his horse *Diamond*.) In North Wheatley, (Notts), is the

---

738 SRO, 12857/8/5.
739 WRO, L06/1473.

Old Hall of 1673, described by Pevsner as 'a wonderful specimen of decorative brickwork' with brick mullions and transoms, Ionic pilasters which don't carry anything, obelisks in flat relief and a broad frieze of modillioned lunettes and half-lunettes.[740] North Wheatley, like other villages in the Retford area such as North Leverton, possesses houses and cottages whose gables are emphasised by brick 'tumbling' where courses of bricks are laid at 90° to the slope of a buttress, chimney, gable or other feature and form a series of triangles.

One encouragement for brick was the assertion that brick houses were drier and healthier. In 1652 the London brickmakers claimed that the substitution of brick for timber would reduce the occurrence of plague but Paul Slack believes that what caused the great plague of 1665 to be the last, was not an improvement in housing with brick and tile replacing timber, but the successful quarantining of ships from abroad.[741] James Sharpe thinks 'The alleged connection between the end of the plague and better housing and sanitation … seems unconvincing. The living conditions of the poor did not improve so dramatically after 1665 as to make their residences inhospitable to rats'.[742]

The Window Tax of 1696, (The Duty on Lights and Windows Act), may also have led to restricted ventilation with windows boarded and limited in number. The American economists W.E. Oates and R.M. Schwab have described the tax as having 'pernicious health and aesthetic effects'. Originally the tax was levied at 2s per household and 4s for houses with more than 10 windows and 8s for houses with more than 20 windows. The level was changed several times and in 1747 was set at 2s per house and 6 pence *for every window* in a house with 10-14 windows, 9 pence for houses of 15-19 windows and 1s for over 20 windows. The result was that the occupant paid no tax with only 9 windows but with 10 he or she paid for every window i.e. a total of 60 pence. The authors' analysis of tax data, mainly from Ludlow, is based on 496 houses and unsurprisingly shows a distorted distribution of the numbers of windows per house with 9, 14 and 19 as the most popular.[743] In 1766 when the tax was

---

740 Pevsner, *Nottinghamshire,* 213. Wrongly called 'Manor House'.
741 Slack, P., *The Impact of Plague in Tudor and Stuart England*, Oxford (1990), 322.
742 Sharpe, J.A., *Early Modern England, A Social History, 1550-1760,* London: Hodder Arnold, (1997), 54.
743 Oates, W.E., and Schwab, R.M., 'The Window Tax: A Case Study in Excess Burden', *Journal of Economic Perspectives,* **29**, 1, (2015), 163-180. See also Glanz, A.E., 'A Tax on Light and Air: Impact of the Window Duty on Tax Administration and Architecture, 1695-1851', *Penn History Review,* **15**, (2008), 18-40.

extended to houses with seven windows and upwards, the number of houses in England and Wales having exactly seven windows was reduced by nearly two-thirds.[744] There was thus a causal relationship between the tax and architecture.

The avoidance or reduction of the impact of the tax led to the blocking of windows in some houses with consequent effects on the provision of light and air (the blocking of windows was made illegal in 1747). It is commonly accepted that blocked windows in buildings between 1696 and 1851 were an effort to avoid the Window Tax, but it should be remembered that what were known as 'blind' windows, were a common design feature of Georgian architecture in which symmetry was paramount. The most extreme example of this may be St Michael's Vicarage, Madeley, built during the incumbency of Jeremiah Taylor (1709-1728), where only 2 of the 12 window openings on its face admit light. It has been suggested that this was a dramatic action to avoid the Window Tax although others have proposed that the brickwork was inserted in the nineteenth century to prevent the house being overlooked by children from the National School!

In the mid-nineteenth century Edwin Chadwick recorded that:

> *The new dwellings of the middle-class families were scarcely healthier, for the bricks tended to preserve moisture. Even picturesque old country houses often had a dungeonlike dampness, as a visitor could observe: if he enters the house he finds the basement steaming with water-vapour; walls constantly bedewed with moisture, cellars coated with fungus and mould; drawing rooms and dining rooms always, except in the very heat of summer, oppressive from moisture; bedrooms, the windows of which are, in winter, so frosted on their inner surface, from condensation of water in the air of the room, that all day they are coated with ice.*[745]

Many houses built or refaced in brick and tile experienced problems with damp. Inexperienced builders ended the line of the tiled roof flush with the gable end of the house so that water ran down the brick gable. With the previous thatched roofs there was almost always a rainwater overthrow. Builders contrarily claimed that walls constructed of porous brick and lime mortar

---

744   George, D.M., *London Life in the XVIIIth Century,* Penguin, (1989), 77.
745   Chadwick, E., *The General History of the Principles of Sanitation,* (1889), 10.

plastered with lime were 'breathable'. In the winter months, the combination of large open fires and draughts from ill-fitting windows and doors kept a flow of warmed air running through a building and so enhanced the evaporation of moisture from walls and floors. The result could be a dry building with little sign of damp internally.

The False Front

The most obvious and important visual evidence of the choice of brick being a statement of status is the false front. Houseowners unable or unwilling to totally rebuild their comfortable vernacular buildings but wishing to give them a fashionable face-lift, could have the façade partially or wholly re-fronted. The building of a single or double-plane brick façade on a vernacular house had little structural value, indeed by trapping water between the brickwork and the timbers it may have led to the more rapid deterioration of the woodwork. Richard Neve in *The City and County Purchaser* also warned that the lime in the pointing would cause the timbers to decay. Even when completely removing the old timber front, constructing a water-tight joint between the new walling and the older and often distorted side timbers was difficult and at its worst required large amounts of expensive lead work.

These problems were further compounded where the houses stood at right angles to the street and rainwater collected in guttering between the gables. This water had to be discharged either in the middle of the new walling or led through lengthy gutters to the building's edges. The water was collected at a relatively low level between the buildings. The newly fashionable parapet had to be sufficiently high to hide the ridge of the gables, so the drainpipes and hoods had to be fixed well below it, creating an unsymmetrical and unbalanced façade. The absence of an overhanging roof also allowed rainwater to run down the façade of the building and many of the projecting string courses and cornices soon required extra protection by the addition of lead coverings. There was also a general lack of understanding of lead's tendency to expand and tear in heat and of the problems which arose from using lead in sheets too long or too wide. Adding walling to the gable ends of houses similarly created a problem where there were existing windows in the gables. These had to be either completely covered, or if window frames were set into the new walling blank windows had to be constructed to maintain symmetry. Despite these drawbacks the false front was widely popular.

One advantage of the plain parapet was the use of the leaded area between the roof and the façade as an observation point. After dining, house guests could retire to the roof for the new and fashionable social activity of 'leading'. Predominantly a London activity, Celia Fiennes also noted the practice at Nottingham Castle and at Beaudesert Hall.[746] On the country house the flat leaded area served as an observation point for spectators of hunting.[747] The earliest recorded example of the use of lead 'flats' is probably that of Papillon Hall built by the property speculator, David Papillon at Lubbenham in 1627.[748] For some houses lead itself was an expensive contribution to overall building costs – at a modest Francis Smith house at Meriden in 1720 the cost of the lead and its carriage was £162 out of a total expenditure of £860.[749] The precise cost of the lead is often difficult to determine for it was usually subsumed in the overall plumbing costs.

An elegant single-plane brick façade filled with symmetrical sash windows and perhaps a classical ornament, such as a pilastered or pedimented doorcase, was a sufficient statement of fashion and their popularity transformed many townscapes. Property demolition was radical and expensive, re-fronting was practical and economical. Refacing could be defined as a pragmatic compromise between the vernacular and a completely new brick house. For many houses the addition of a brick façade was not a process of renovation or improvement but was primarily constructed as a deliberate statement of the social priorities of its owner. Fashion is a public phenomenon – Richard Neve wrote in 1726, 'let not the Front look a squint on a stranger but accost him right at his entrance. Uniformity and Proportion much pleaseth the eye'.[750] The façade constituted the public face of the house; this was an unavoidable advertisement as to how an owner or occupier wished to be perceived in local society. An unfashionable vernacular frontage could have a debilitating impact on social position and status. The Nottingham historian Charles Deering wrote, probably before 1744, that 'Soon after the Restoration, Nottingham put on quite a new Face, since which time many of the Inhabitants have taken

---

746 Fiennes, 87, 229.
747 Mowl, T., *Elizabethan Jacobean Style*, Phaidon, (1993), 185.
748 Airs, M., 'David Papillon: Architect, Military Engineer, Developer, Author, Jeweller'. *The Georgian Group Journal*, **XXV**, (2017), 4.
749 Wilson and Mackley, 192.
750 Neve, 69.

to new Fronting their Houses after the newest Fashion, some with Parapet Walls'.[751] Robert Thoroton, in the context of the refacing of houses in the town, described it as the 'dance of building new Fronts in the Town'. County House for example was refaced in 1728-33.[752]

The building of a false front was thus a cultural action reflecting both personal and social values. Such values are often implicit and rarely described but the building may reflect a cultural desire to make a declaration about wealth or an understanding of fashion. Because the contrast between old and new was so obvious, owners with social aspirations replaced the fronts of their vernacular houses to make a statement that they were abandoning traditional materials and craft skills and embracing national or 'polite' architecture. Sometimes fashion outweighed the practical, Hines House, a timber-framed house in Clifford Chambers, was refronted in brick in 1720, its:

> … *most surprising feature is that what was clearly the front … reasonably enough faces away from the farmyard, but it also faces away from the access road to the farm and would have been unusable for all practical purposes. The modest amount of 'show' … would have been invisible in the house's daily use.*[753]

A similar oddity is at Millichope Court (later Upper Millichope Farm, p. Munslow) which was rebuilt c.1730 in stone except for a brick façade which strangely faces away from the road.

In the towns civic permission was required for intrusion into the street, for example at Nottingham in 1725 where it was, 'Ordered that James Hornbuckle do pay 6d p.a. for an Incroachment of a Brick a breadth'.[754] At Shrewsbury a covenant of 1732 declared 'that John Spark as soon as he conveniently might, at his own cost, is to build a new brick front to the house and make 2 convenient cellars under it, and take down two old chimnies and rebuild the same with

---

751   Deering, C., *History of Nottingham,* Section 1, (1751), 6.
752   Henstock, A., *County House, High Pavement Nottingham a Georgian and Regency Town House, TTS,* **78**, (1974), 54-67.
753   Alcock, N.A., 'After the Stamp Collecting, The Context of Vernacular Architecture'. *Transactions of the Ancient Monuments Society,* **46**, (2002), 9-17.
754   *NBR,* **VI**, 99.

brick'.⁷⁵⁵ Brick was therefore a symbol of the withdrawal from a body of previously shared values and cultural forms. The fact that the house, or at least the refronting, was new was often emphasised by the insertion of 'datestones'.⁷⁵⁶

In many houses the side walls and rear were left unaltered leading, in Lutyen's famous phrase, to 'Queen Anne fronts and Mary Anne behinds' and suggesting that a brick front, the public face of the house, was a socially sufficient statement. In those houses which were completely built or refaced in brick the emphasis on the visually obvious frontage was reinforced by expensive 'front bricks' and the use of cheaper 'common bricks' for the sides. The distinction between the front and rear of a building could also be emphasised by different roofing materials, for example Priory Farmhouse, Ratcliffe on the Wreake, is a red brick house of 1707 with pantiles on the front and Swithland slate on the rear. Even for a simple stone wall, appearance was crucial. In 1635 William Fetherston ordered for a house in Warwick that the mason must use 'lime mortar outside and clay mortar inside'.⁷⁵⁷

The false front masking old timber-framed façades is evidence of the status afforded to brick and brick building and there are hundreds of examples throughout the region.⁷⁵⁸ It was a most powerful symbol of the considerable pressures on house owners to conform to the socially created demand for a flush façade based on proportion and symmetry. At the highest social level, it is present at Middleton Hall, Warks, Odstone Hall, Warks (which was 'new cased in brick' in 1686) and Brand Hall, Salop, a timber-framed building with a brick front of c.1700. At farmhouse level there are examples at Manor Farm, Kibworth Harcourt, 1702 and Manor Farm, Houghton-on-the-Hill, 1718. At

---

755   SA, 3890/3/1/.

756   For example, Brook Farmhouse, Leigh, is dated 1694 in vitrified headers. Gorsty Manor House, Wolverhampton, is dated WS 1683. There are many other examples. Particularly rare are datestones with the date and name of the builder. There are two examples in Shenstone Parish. A barn on the Chester Road carries the inscription '1727 John Smith' and a barn at Lower Stonnal is inscribed 'John Smith 1747'. At Rolleston-on-Dove a farmhouse in School Lane carries the initials and date of its first owner I(saac) E(mery) 1707. Its string course is similar to those at No. 11 'Willow Cottage' and Nos. 5 & 6 'Bladon's Yard' (also dated 1707). This suggests they were erected by the same builder.

757   WRO, CR 2981 Billiard Room/Commode/Drawer 3/1/43. R.

758   It should be noted that in some isolated areas where good building stone was readily available and clay and coal less obtainable, then timber-framing was sometimes hidden behind stone façades. For example, in the Shropshire parish of Cardington where there were easily quarried sources of gritstone, Greensand and limestone, several timber-framed houses were refaced in sandstone in the seventeenth and eighteenth centuries. *VCH, Salop,* **10**, 22-44.

a lower social level, the need to demonstrate an awareness of the value of brick is demonstrated at South View, Burton Overy, a timber and mud cottage with just one brick gable dated 1739.

Considerable technical difficulties had to be overcome in refacing, for example, where the house was jettied then it had to be either cut back to the line of the ground floor or extended forward to the line of the top storey.[759] Refronting could be expensive, Hackwood in his *History of West Bromwich* (1895), quotes the example of the landowner and millowner Nicholas Ryder who suffered severe financial difficulties as a result of the extravagant rebuilding and re-fronting of Ryder's Mill following his marriage in 1663.[760]

The willingness to accept and respond to fashionable but structurally unnecessary demands is well demonstrated by the addition of brick fronts to stone buildings. At Middleton on the Leics/Northants border are several cottages of marlstone with brick fronts. At Longnor in the Staffordshire Moorlands most old buildings are of stone, yet the Crewe Harpur Arms has a superfluous eighteenth-century brick façade to an elegant stone building. The complete refacing of stone houses can be observed at The Tinsmith's Cottage at Wirksworth, Derbys, and at a house now called Cabin Knoll at Calwich Park, Ellastone, which has a seventeenth-century stone core and was remodelled in brick in the eighteenth century. Other examples are at Limes Farm, Breedon, where there are extensive stone quarries, at Jury Street House, Warwick, which was refaced by the architect Sir Simon Archer, at Parwich where the limestone manor house was refaced only on the front and sides in 1747 [761] and at Lord's Place, Leicester, an urban aristocratic Elizabethan stone house with eighteenth century brick cladding.[762] The Manor House at Stanton Long, Salop, has a stone wing with the gable on the street front in brick. In Melbourne where there were several quarries of Millstone Grit some cottages had rubble stone side walls and brick fronts, for example, 24-26 Potter Street.

For the more conservative of the social elite who still wished to use easily available stone, money could be saved by building the façade in stone but

---

759 Cheshire RO, ZA/B/3/205v-6v. A petition of 1713 to the Chester Assembly seeking permission to build in brick level with the 'jetting over' of the first floor of a house in Parsons Lane.
760 Quoted in Dilworth, D., *The Tame Mills of Staffordshire,* Phillimore, (1976), 158.
761 Hutton, 47., *VCH. Warks,* **8**, 427-434.
762 Courtney, P., 'Lord's Place, Leicester, An Urban Aristocratic House of the 16th Century', *TLAHS,* **65**, (1991), 103.

using brick for the side and back walls, as at Welland House of 1694 in Market Harborough, and similarly the superior Stanford Hall, built in 1690 at a cost of £2,137 10s 7d, has a stone façade and cheaper brick side walls.[763] As early as 1588 Sir Francis Willoughby built the magnificent Wollaton Hall apparently from Ancaster stone but a surviving contract for 1585 includes the purchase of 186,000 bricks. These were used as the cores of interior walls and to line underground passages to the water supply.

At Burley-on-the-Hill, the Earl of Nottingham between 1696-1708 was personally responsible for the decision to build the carcase of the house, which Pevsner calls a 'palace', in brick and to face it in Clipsham and Ketton limestone. He was apparently advised by Sir Charles Shere, the Surveyor of the Ordnance, that brick was 'more durable and a lighter burden to the foundations' and 'stone work ripens by slow degrees in comparison to brick, that the one in a year or two may afford a tolerable habitation, while the other (stone) in thrice the time will continue green, moist, cold and unfit to dwell in'.[764] The appearance of stone could also be achieved by money-saving deception. The Anson records contain two letters of June 1749 which contain advice on painting brick to imitate stone.[765] Hilton Hall, probably built by Richard Trubshaw, has painted ashlar on a brick façade.

The fashion of the brick fronted house began as an urban phenomenon and is understandable as a response of the community to new styles and fashions in building. As Borsay has observed, 'to contemporary observers brick became a powerful symbol of a community's architectural status and economic prosperity'.[766] The demand for visual conformity and uniformity spread quickly to the rural Midlands, suggesting an almost immediate awareness and diffusion of fashion and style. As early as 1676 Whitmore Hall was refaced in the Artisan Mannerist style. At a much lower social level Bridge Farm, Yoxall, is a small, isolated seventeenth-century timber-framed farmhouse, yet it has an early eighteenth-century brick façade. Adjacent to the Needwood Forest where timber was readily available, the probable explanation for the façade is one of imitation of urban models. A similar example exists at Foxhole Farm near Wem. They provide excellent illustrations of the influence and diffusion of fashion and style.

---

763 ROLLR, DE2399.
764 Habakkuk, *Rutland Record*, **10**, (1990), 350.
765 SRO, D615/PS/1/3/1749.
766 Borsay, *Urban Renaissance*, 200.

WHY DID PEOPLE BUILD IN BRICK 1660-1780?

Brick Nogging

'Nogging' or 'noggin' is best defined as bricks which have no structural responsibilities but are merely decorative infill in panels of timber-framing. The traditional and common form of infill was wattle and daub, or as it was described in 1704 'for Claying ye walls'. Its replacement by brick has been generally recognised as dating from the late fifteenth-century to the eighteenth-century. The reasons for replacement have emphasised the erosion of clay and timber over time and its poor insulation qualities. It has been argued that brick was more weather resistant, required less maintenance and could provide more security against burglary and pests,[767] yet examples of medieval wattle and daub have survived into the twenty-first century. This would suggest that, provided it was kept dry, it was durable and robust and if it decayed it was easily and very cheaply reinstated. Alec Clifton-Taylor has suggested that the enhanced comfort derived from the replacement of wattle and daub by brick is 'a delusion'. Brick overburdens the timber frame, causes structural problems and the brick is often more porous than good and well-rendered daub. His explanation for its replacement by brick is that by 'the end of the seventeenth century good daubers were already becoming scarce', their skills replaced by those of bricklayers.[768]

The most authoritative study of nogging is that of John McCann who provides evidence of fifteenth and sixteenth century nogging in Essex and disproves the previously held general view that there was no convincing evidence for nogging before 1650.[769] In some buildings, particularly in the south of England, the nogging is presented in decorative forms such as herringbone or some form of basket-weave. This would suggest that display and presentation were a significant reason for its use. In the Midlands, although herringbone framing is not uncommon and spectacularly demonstrated at 28 Wymeswold Rd., Hoton, (Leics), most brick infill was laid in a conventional stretcher bond or a more haphazard and irregular arrangement.[770] Such infill, although it rejected decorative patterning, did add the dramatic colour of the brick to houses which were traditionally built of unpainted timber and clay panelling. In most cases brick replaced earlier material, but David Smith has claimed

---

767 Clifton Taylor, 47.
768 Clifton Taylor, 47.
769 McCann, J., 'Brick *Nogging* in the Fifteenth and Sixteenth Centuries, with examples drawn mainly from Essex', *Transactions of the Ancient Monuments Society,* **31**, (1987), 106-133.
770 Smith, D., 'Smaller Domestic Buildings', in Pevsner, *Leicestershire,* 52.

that 'elsewhere, as in a group of late C17 and early C18 houses in South Leicestershire, it was undoubtedly the original infill'.[771] Pevsner provides the examples of Orpudds Farm, Ashby Parva, which is timber-framed with brick panels, one carrying the date 1695. In Husbands Bosworth in Honeypot Lane is 'a timber-framed house clearly built for brick-nogging with timbers sawn against the grain, and TBD 1712 in blue headers'.

Brick nogging is most difficult to date, as rarely is the brick so narrow that an early date can be confidently suggested. An attached date is equally rare although Webster's Farm, Swinford is timber-framed with brick nogging dated 1718 in blue headers.[772] For almost all of the examples described by the editors of the *Victoria County Histories* or the Department of the Environment's *Listed Buildings*, the nogging is 'later' than the timber-framing and although it is never precisely dated they imply an alteration sometime in or after the later seventeenth century.[773] Nogging thus coincides with the period of full or partial encasement of timber-framed buildings in brick. This coincidence suggests that the explanation lies less in the decay of wattle and daub but rather in the need for householders, even at the lower (cottage) end of the housing market, to make a statement about the social value of brick. For instance, at Diseworth, Leics, at 14-16 Lady Gate (Cherry's) are a pair of eighteenth century half-timbered cottages. The end nearest the road has brick nogging the other panels are plaster. With limited financial resources they were emulating as best they could those who could afford to completely encase their houses in brick or build a new dwelling. Brick nogging was a statement of an awareness of a building material not an expression of a desire for enhanced insulation.

Care must be taken in identifying 'nogging' in estate documents. The term seems also to be used for general plastering and insulation work. At the Hanmer Estate at Pentre Pant where between 1704-6 brick was purchased as part of 'an account of what was layd out in the making of Robert Moris his new house', payments were made for 'nogging ye walls of ye stable stoves & courtyd about ye henhouses' and for plastering noging & whitening when ye

---

771 Smith, 52.
772 Such brick was used at The Old Manor House, Lapley and would seem to date from the sixteenth century. It may, of course, have been reused.
773 E.g. 'in Wheaton Aston … from the last quarter of the 17th century onwards there was much rebuilding in brick. Several of the smaller cottages were encased entirely; in other cases the panels only were bricked up', *VCH., Staffs*, **4**, 145.

tenant came to pentr pant'.[774] Repairs carried out to the tenants' holdings in 1712 at Attingham included 'Nogging' and 'brick work'.

Estate records often reveal the sale of very small parcels of bricks, and such small quantities might suggest that they were used for brick panelling, (although they could equally have been used for paving floors or for chimneys). In the Anson accounts of 1699-1701 there is a pocket book specifically devoted to brick sales with a sub-heading 'Noging bricks', which includes a number of sales of parcels of about 300-500 bricks, with some purchases as small as 50 bricks.[775] It is difficult to define the exact nature of a 'noging brick'. To contemporaries it was obviously recognisable. The account book of Thomas Astbury of Swynnerton for 1688 includes payments to John Edwards for 'tenn Thousand Brick £6 2 0' and 'noging brick 0 8 0'.[776] As the nogging brick was not load-bearing perhaps it was of inferior quality? The purchase of small quantities of brick is found on several estates. From the Antrobus Estate at Rushton James there survives 'An Acct of Brick which Mr Arnett had & sold in Rushton James in the years 1755 & 1756'. This account covers the distribution of 12,500 bricks which were sold in the following parcels to tenants of the estate, 100 (3), 200 (2), 250 (1), 300 (2), 350 (1), 750 (1), 1,000 (1), 2,150 (1), 3,000 (2).[777] The building accounts of Richard Wright at Barford in the late eighteenth century of the 'Charges and Expences of the taking down of the Old House Hovells etc. and the Rebuilding the House Walls Hovells etc.' include in one corner 14 different names with payment for a number of bricks varying from 100 (2), 200 (1), 300 (1), 350 (1), 400 (1), 500(1), 600 (1), 1,000 (1), 1,200 (1), 1,500 (1), 1,600 (1), 3,000 (1), 4,000 (1), 4,800 (1), 12,000 (2). Such a pattern would suggest that some bricks at least were being used for panelling.[778] On Lord Chetwynd's estate in 1736 he recorded the receipt of 87,900 bricks from John Locket of Burslem, 83,000 were retained for 'my New House' and the remainder distributed to seven tenants, mostly in parcels of between 200 and 700.[779] There is no indication of payment by the tenants in these accounts and they may reflect a policy

---

774 SA, 894/334.
775 SRO, D615/P/(A)/1/5.
776 SRO, 5909.
777 SRO, D(W)1909/K/2/6/4.
778 WRO, CRO, 574/116/3.
779 SRO, D1789/HM/Chetwynd 105.

of making holdings more attractive to tenants or the fulfilment of tenancy agreements. Such a policy may also be indicated in the estate accounts of an unknown Staffordshire landowner kept between 1723-1755. His records contain several references to tenants who received an allowance of a small number of bricks against their rent.[780]

Mention should also be made of alternatives to brick as infill for timber-framing. In Leicestershire, Smith notes that 'at Castle Donington and Loughborough stone or slate pieces were used on some of the more important buildings'.[781] Unrecorded and previously unknown is a unique replacement for wattle and daub at Walsall where in 1774 the accounts of the Earl of Mountrath included a payment to Samuel Bagley 'for filling up the sides and ends of the Barn and Raming (ramming?) Them with Cinders and Engine Ashes'.[782]

Brick provided material comfort but the evidence of specialist 'front bricks', false fronts and other elaborate ways of displaying brick, emphasises that fashion and social acceptance dominated much of the seventeenth and eighteenth centuries. The brick house was crucial evidence in defining the social standing of its inhabitants. Georgian England is frequently characterized as an era where emulation of the fashions, tastes and behaviour of the elite was all-important. It is the period of what is termed 'polite society', a belief that members of the upper classes and sections of the middle classes could group together, whilst respecting the strict social structures in place. To belong to polite society was to hold in common the correct taste in objects, design, fashion and food.[783]

The consumption of cultural goods transmitted social identity. As Kant put it, 'No one in complete solitude will decorate or clean his house; he will not even do it for his own people (wife and children), but only for strangers, to show himself to advantage'.[784] The architectural language of status is subtle and may be presented not only in the external appearance of the building, but also in its plan, amenities and structure. Such aspects are difficult to decipher

---

780   SRO, (W)1082/F/12.
781   Smith D., 62.
782   SRO, D1287/G/15.
783   Wilson, R.J., 'The Mystical Character of Commodities: The consumer society in 18th-century England', *Post Medieval Archaeology*, **42/1**, (2008), 144 156.
784   Quoted in North, M., *Material Delight and the Joy of Living*, London: Routledge, (2008), 2.

but may be present in, for example, the height of the rooms or in the use of the first-floor rooms as dining rooms in imitation of the aristocratic *piano nobile*.[785] But the external appearance of the house, viewed by every passer-by, is the obvious expression of status and wealth. Borsay, for example, writes of the 'unavoidable advertisement as to how an owner or occupier wished to be perceived in local society. To possess a frontage that was out of vogue could have a debilitating impact on social position and status'.[786] Prestige could be obtained by the size of the house, but in the towns and cities large building plots were rarely available. Ornament, idiom and material were the basis of social respect.

---

785 Tall rooms were not merely status symbols, they were considered 'much more healthful than low ones, and when disorders occur … they are less infectious'. Waistell, C., *Designs for Agricultural Buildings*, (1827), 21. Quoted in Machin, R., *Rural Housing*, London, (1994), 40.

786 Borsay. P., 'The Early Modern Landscape', in Waller, P., ed., *The English Urban Landscape*, Oxford: OUP, (2000), 105.

Chapter 10

THE COST OF BRICK BUILDING

A PREVIOUS chapter considered the availability of timber and the use of bricks as an alternative building material and suggested that the selection of brick was not the result of a major timber shortage nor of its marked price advantage. Intensively managed woodland and the reuse of medieval timbers allowed the continuation and repair of timber-framed building well into the late eighteenth century. Even in the grandest houses reused timber was extensively used. At Blithfield, Wyatt's accounts for his carpenters included, 'Streightening Old Timber, Sawing Old Timber' and 'Altering Old Doors'.[787] In all the Lichfield diocesan parsonages rebuilt or restored after the 1777 Act, independent surveyors ensured the value of reusable timber was built into all financial consideration. At Handsworth in 1782 the builder, Solomon Smith, was allowed £36 10s from a bill of £480 for 'Olde Metearills on the Primmisoes' in accounts counter-signed by the Bishop of Lichfield. References to such surveyors are rare but the Longford, Salop, terrier of 1781 at a time of the parsonage rebuilding for £225 1s includes, 'Mr John Jones appointed Nominee to direct and inspect certain buildings at the Parsonage of Longford … in which it was agreed to pay the said sum when the said building shall be covered with tile'. If old timbers were not available, then compensatory imports of softwoods provided internal bracing and roof structures.

This section seeks to examine in detail the contributory costs of brick buildings. It concentrates mainly on housing, but it should be remembered

---

787   SRO, D(W)1721/3/215.

that the period also saw the erection of churches, chapels, mills, schools, garden paths and walling, and a wide range of other buildings. It is assumed that every building was based on a carefully considered decision of great concern to those making it. The purchaser might have wished to meet social pressure, have been a husband wishing to impress a new wife, a speculator/builder hoping to take advantage of a rising market or a householder wishing to improve his/her house. If the investment was a rational and logically founded decision then the expansion of housing stock should reflect one or more of these factors: the purchaser's savings, his/her surplus income, which in some cases arose from a run of good harvests, his/her ability to borrow through loan or mortgage and the current rate of interest. It presumes a personal and optimistic view that investment was a sensible decision. If indeed these are the factors which influenced the decision to purchase a house, then if the requirements of size and location were met, its cost should be of crucial significance.

The cost of building grand and prestigious houses was frequently recorded in detail by conscientious and responsible estate stewards. As early as 1560-2 William Paget specifically estimated the cost of his proposed new house at Burton at £1,104 8s 0d.[788] The actual cost of the Masshouse built by Peter Giffard at Wolverhampton between 1st August 1729 and 1st January 1734 was precisely recorded, down to the last halfpenny, as £1,069 2s 2½d.[789] Thoroton claimed that the cost of rebuilding Nottingham Castle between 1680 and 1683 was £14,002 17s 9d. The total cost of the Newcastle-under-Lyme Hospital, built in 1742-4, was £898 17s 1d.[790] Stivichall Hall, a large mansion, was built for £5,961 8s 8d. Woodhouse, built for the Mostyn-Owen family, cost £2,373 13s 5½, with 'Planting and Draining £448 18s 11d' and 'the new Road £196 9s 8d', the total 'Disburst in Building and Alterations' was £3,019 2s ½d.[791] Newnham Paddox was rebuilt by 'Capability' Brown between 1768 and 1781 at a cost of £7,529 2s 9d.[792] In negotiating building prices the aristocracy had considerable power. At Beaumanor William Herrick

---

788 SRO, D(W)1734/2/3/27. The house was initially to be of 102 bays but a later reference is to 44 'bayes for timber work'. It was estimated that 300,000 bricks and 300,000 tiles would be required with the total bill for labour or 'workmanship' being £376 16s, (33.3%).
789 SRO, D590/634.
790 SRO, D1798/HM/Bourne/29/2.
791 SA, 3890/3/2/35.
792 WRO, CR2017.

negotiated a contract for £1,020 with the builder John Westley, Westley had spent £930 when he withdrew from the contract having previously asked for £200 to finish the building.[793]

The information contained in Table 11 is complicated by the fact that no regular format of building accounts was employed. Some were extremely detailed whilst others provide only summaries of expenditure. Thomas Allen for example, the Rector of Stoke-on-Trent from 1697-1732, kept the most meticulous accounts with all sums recorded under one of 12 headings, namely 'Bricks, Bricklayer, Glazier', etc.[794] Others, such as the steward of Lord Chetwynd, produced itemised accounts for all purchases of materials but paid one man, Richard Jackson, £222 11s (35% of the total), he was presumably the master mason and responsible for all the unrecorded labourers and craftsmen employed.[795] In the Dyott accounts all the labourers and carriers are recorded by name but their exact skills and roles are unlisted.[796] At Standon, Thomas Astbury did not define the 'building' he erected. At only £22 6s 1d with no payments for glass and with a thatched roof it may well have been a barn, but it did stand on the site of a demolished old house, and this is unusually detailed evidence for the erection of such a building.

The value of the record lies in the detail of the two-year building process and incentives provided for the workforce in terms of the food and drink offered to the workers in 1692 and 1693. Detailed building costs were also recorded in the surviving accounts of the Rev. Thomas Nelson for the building of Hatton Vicarage between 1751-1755. In at least 90 separate documents are listed the initial clearing of the land (£1 14s 8d), legal expenses (16s 10d), the purchase of bricks (approx. 181,000), coal for their firing, tree cutting in a saw pit, food for the workers and lime from 15 different carriers.[797] Similarly 'An Estimate by Mr Jackson of the Building the house at Allston' provides a valuable model of

---

793   ROLLR, DG9 2134-41.
794   SRO, D(W)1781/17/1.
795   SRO, D1789/HM/Chetwynd105. A Richard Jackson is recorded as the mason responsible, with Richard Trubshaw, for the rebuilding of Baswich church in 1741-42. SRO, D3361/5/3. In 1730 he served as builder, architect and advisor on costs to Derby Corporation for the building of the Guildhall. He probably built 'The Friary,' Derby, for the banker, Samuel Crompton. This house closely resembles Walton Hall, Walton-on-Trent, built by Jackson in 1730. Craven, M., 'Derby's Eighteenth-Century Guildhall,' *DAJ*, **125**, (2005), 138-151.
796   SRO, D661/21/3/11.
797   WRO, CR3134/17/1-90.

building expectations in the early eighteenth century. It was compiled for the Ingestre Estate of Lord Talbot in 1729. The size of the building is not given but '9 door cases', '8 doors', '12 window frames' and 35,000 bricks would suggest a modest house of about six rooms with a front and rear door. The presence of casement rather than sash framed windows suggests that the house was not the most fashionable although all its walls were plastered. The estimate of £75 18s 8d also includes a reference to the reuse of old timbers, 'Note the Doore Cases & Window Cases to be made of old Stuffs'.[798] The estimate would seem to be for the house alone and does not include any outbuildings. A larger farmhouse might require 60-70,000 bricks. In 1793 George Whitfield of St Thomas's Hospital wrote to his brother:

> *I am sorry to hear of the farm house being burned down … if you should alter your mind and build a farm house, I can give you some information respecting the workmanship and value of the materials that will be wanted; fourteen or fifteen rod of bricks would build you a good farmhouse, 4500 bricks go to a rod and 272 square feet of a brick and half, is a rod of statute measure, workmanship £28 or £30 per rod. Oak timber in the country may be cheeper than Fir or deale. It is very easy to calculate the expence by knowing the dimensions of the buildings of a farm house in length, breadth and height. A Good Cellar in a farmhouse is a very material thing.*

Whitfield is suggesting 63-67,500 bricks and building costs of about £420.[799]

It is generally assumed that a brick building would be cheaper than its equivalent built in stone, for example in 1737 two plans for a five-bay, four-storey house near Doncaster were priced at £1,035 in brick and £1,485 in stone.[800] Of particular interest are two building estimates in 1747 for a house at the Clipstone Park Estate of the Countess of Oxford. One marked 'brick' on the reverse is for £224 0s 10d, the other, for an identical house, marked 'stone' is for £218 1s 2d. The difference is part explained by the reuse of 'Materials of ye Old Building for Pulling Down Excepting ye Wood' and a difference in the crucial transport costs, for the stone house 'Carriage of all Materials at £1

---

798 SRO, D(W)1788 P25/1.
799 SA, 587/68.
800 Wilson, R., and Mackley, A., *Creating Paradise, The Building of the English Country House 1660-1880,* CUP, (2000), 264.

4s 0d per Rood'. 'Duble Brick' was carried at £1 11s.[801] The usual differential favoured brick and was reflected in the estimates for the rebuilding of Baswich church, in 1733 Richard Trubshaw's appraisal for a replacement in stone was £1,695, the cost of rebuilding in brick was £336.[802] Where stone quarries were adjacent to the building site, the implication of some leases is that brick or stone was a matter of individual choice. At Sheinton, Salop, a covenant of August 1736 'to build a good and substantial house … with at least 2 rooms on ground and 2 over' allowed a choice of 'brick or stone', this generous lease required completion by Michaelmas 1739.[803] A further lease in 1739 was for a bay of building in brick or stone.[804]

The cost of a new brick-built farmhouse or town house with details of materials, wages and transport was much more rarely recorded.[805] Overall costs are sometimes given but without the size of the building. As early as 1628 a Shrewsbury lease stipulated that '£100 be spent on building' an undescribed house.[806] In 1649 a lease at Bridgnorth of a plot 18 feet by 40 feet required a house of 'brick or stone' costing £30.[807] In 1658 at Leamington Priors, William Olney signed a lease for 21 years and covenanted that he would within 6 years build a house near the place where the old house stood for £47. The lease is endorsed, 'Mr Beaufoy's lease to William Olney after the house was burnt'.[808] A letter of 1723 from the Rev. John Salt of Betley about his holding in the Town Field, 'the worst land in all the Parish', stated that 'I was bound to build upon it. I have built two houses on Buckley Croft cost me near £300 and I have built Mr Lathans a house which cost me near £700'.[809] At Bridgnorth, the four daughters of William Haslewood 'spent £600 on building a new dwelling house'.[810]

A few leases are more informative. On the Neville Estate in Nottinghamshire, an undated eighteenth century proposal for a three-storey house in brick and

---

801   NA, DD4P/70/44, DD4P/70/45.
802   SRO, D3361/5/31, D3361/2/1. Other records suggest £400, SRO, D4182/26.
803   SA, 2089/1/7/40.
804   SA, 2089/1/740.
805   SRO, D(W)1788P18/9.
806   SA, 3614/5/1/61.
807   SA, 775/242.
808   WRO, CR4141/5/82.
809   SRO, D(W)1788P18/9.
810   SA, 3614/2/2/19.

stone, 54 feet long, 15 feet wide and using old materials, was costed at £260.[811] These dimensions would suggest a house of six-eight rooms and attics. Among the most detailed is a Coventry agreement of 1720 for the demolition of an 'old house' and its replacement with a 'New dwelling house' 16 feet wide with two cellars 20 feet by 15 feet, three first floor rooms each 10 feet deep and 8½ feet high, the second storey rooms (attics)were to be of identical floor space and 3½ feet high. The ironwork and doors were also fully described. The cellars were lined in brick but the house may well have been a very late example of a timber-framed house, for it was to be 'Of the same Timber materialls demensions manner and forme as herein after mentioned'.[812] In 1777 a tenant, Joseph Clark of Tillyvelly, petitioned the Savile Estate against having to build a farmhouse 50 feet long, 16 feet broad with sidewalls 7 feet high.[813] An undescribed house of unknown size on the Beesthorpe Hall Estate cost £205 18s 2½d and employed about 38,250 bricks.[814] In 1696-97 the total cost of two houses in Sheep St. Warwick, after 'the dreadful fire' was £323 2s.[815] A rare agreement for the building of a brick house and brewhouse at Church Stretton in 1775 fully describes all the rooms. The frontage was 32 feet 3 inches with the main building 20 feet deep and 20 feet high, the parlour was 11 feet 8 inches by 11 feet 6 inches, the cellar was 8 feet deep with a passage of 18 feet, there was also a kitchen, a closet, a staircase, three bedrooms and garrets. The brewhouse, with bread oven, was 11 feet by 11 feet by 10 feet with the total price for this moderately sized provincial town house estimated at £200.[816] In July 1779 an 'Estimate to Build a New House upon the Churchyard in Allesley' containing '30 feet by 17; And 18 feet high: to the Wallplate all Materials workmanship carriage included' was £89 7s 7d with £17 12s 'Deduct for Old materials', i.e. £71 15s 7d. In addition, 'to take off Roof and raise Wall three feet high' was £15 15s and 'to make new little house (lavatory), alter the stairs make good Chambers floors to alter Pantry & new back door' a further £4 9s 5d. The Agreement includes the maintenance of quality by a disinterested examination. 'The Materials of which shall be viewed

---

811 NA, DD/N/231/16.
812 Coventry RO, 811 Bundle 6/1.
813 NA, DD/FJ/11/1/7/319.
814 NA, DDBB104/1-52.
815 NA, DDE117/1.
816 SA, 1045/469.

by a Person appointed & if any of em are not perfectly good and approv'd of the(y) are to be exchanged and not put into the Buildings which are to be completed by Michaelmas next', i.e. within 2 months.[817]

Detailed research has revealed a sufficiently large number of accounts of brick buildings to enable analysis of the contributory costs to be made.

Table 12: Constituent Costs of Selected Brick Buildings

Place	Date	Overall Cost	Brick	Timber	All Materials	Notes
Yoxall	1683-1685	£70 2s 4d	11.2%	9.2%	36.3%	'Court House'
Standon	1692-1683	£22 6s 1d	29.2%		42.7%	Barn?
Newcastle-u-Lyme	1705	£266 13s 8¾d	17.1%	3.2%	50%	House
Stoke-on-Trent	1706	£229 9s 11d	17.6%	12.6%	50.1%	House
Beaumanor	1725	£1,297 5s	22.2%			Labour not included, estimate
Great Bolas	1726-1729	£331 18s	16.8%	17.2%	60.3%	Rebuilding Church, bricklaying at 6.8%
Alston	1729	£75 18s 8d	23%	13.9%	67.2%	House estimate.
Warwickshire?	1730?	£61 3s	33.5%	25.6%	85.8%	'Mr Divith's house' 2 bays, 30' x 12'
'Busbyes Bill' Newnham Paddox	c1730	£28 4s 7d	24.3%	33.8%	84%	Warks brewhouse, mason charged £4 10s

817 WRO, DRO452/25.

THE COST OF BRICK BUILDING

Freeford	1732	£436 7s 9d	14.8%	10.5%	48%	House, (SRO L D661/2/1, gives £354 2s)
Stafford, Drakelow	1749	£308 18s 10d	16.1%		36.9%	House financed by naval prize money
Beesthorpe Hall Estate	1770	£205 18s 2½d	14.5%			12,000 old bricks also purchased for 16s
Sawley School House	1771-1772	£47 15s*	41.4%	25.2%	81.3%	*Includes £7 5s 6d for bricklaying and 'loading'
Penn Vicarage	1778	£206 17s 6d				Mortgage of £140 plus value of timber on glebe land
Cubbington	1779	£89 7s 7d	47.3%	29.7%		Price reduced by £17 12s for use of 'Old materials'. Alterations and extensions added at price of £20 4s
Handsworth	1782	£496 10s				Parsonage
Barford	Late 18thc	£761 7s 11½d	14.9%			Rebuilt farmhouse

The above table would suggest that brick was on average at least one quarter of the cost of the average house and the cost of all the building materials was about 55% at a time when the price of common brick seems not to have fallen, but to have stabilised at around 10s per 1,000 for most of the early eighteenth century. Of particular interest is the proportion of the costs spent on timber, for here the aristocracy and gentry could have an advantage derived from their own estates. Arthur Gregory's accounts for the building of Stivichall Hall in 1755-62 include under the heading of 'Valued my own … Timber used in Building £100 0s 0d, Work of my own team £150 0s 0d', although these were relatively minor contributions to a total bill of £5,961 8s 8d.[818] In January 1701 John Hill wrote to his brother Richard, 'I have sent you a draft of the building you propose to be done at Hawkstone, the charge of which although you have timber of your own, the workman says will amount to near £300'.[819] On a much smaller scale John Fenton's accounts for 'Building my house at New Castle' (under-Lyme) in 1705 includes, 'for spending of any timber (for it was almost all my owne and counts not into the acc)'.[820]

The Building Trades

Within some of the few surviving building contracts a common feature was the responsibility of the purchaser to provide scaffolding and ropes. For the building of Meriden Hall in c1720 the owner, Martin Baldwin, agreed to 'find all Scaffalling and Ladars'. Woodward noted that 'in most cases it (scaffolding) was supplied by the employing institution'.[821] The sums were small, but their significance lies in the evidence they reveal about the professionalism of the bricklayers. The need for the sponsor of the building to provide ropes, poles, scaffolding boards and often building tools, and the fact that the bricklayers did not possess such equipment, suggests that the workforce was not committed to full time employment in the building industry. Even in London Campbell noted in 1747 that 'they (bricklayers) are out of Busines for five, if not six months of the year'.[822] In his study of northern building craftsmen, Woodward concludes that 'most (building) labourers were not specialists'. Locock at Castle Bromwich found that bricks were laid by tenant farmers from the estate at slack parts of the farming year.

However it would be a mistake to regard all bricklayers as unskilled, Campbell noted 'his Skill consists, considering him as a mere bricklayer only in ranging his Brick even on top of another … But a Master Bricklayer thinks

---

818   SBT, DR10/1518.
819   SA, 112/1B/10/7.
820   SRO, D(W)1788P25/1.
821   Woodward, 50.
822   Campbell, 159.

himself capable to raise a Brick House without the tuition of an Architect'.[823] The quality of the craftsmanship was variable ranging from the ornate panelled chimney stack at Ram Hall, Berkeswell, to those houses where cracks and subsidence indicate that the weight of the frontage is carried only by the window frame. The Midland building accounts suggest that many of the workforce were only casual workers. Josiah Wedgwood in 1770 wrote to the architect Pickford with an offer to share the cost of removing 'bad bricks' from the Etruria buildings, 'to ease the loss you (Pickford) sustain by the carelessness, or something worse, of your bricklayers ... Mr Gardiner (builder?) estimates takeing out the bad brick at 6d p yd includeing the whole outside'.[824] Bricklaying as a secondary employment is confirmed in a humorous and enigmatic entry from the parish register of Eccleshall for 1748:

> *Joseph Cheshire Parish Clerk by trade a mason happened to lay bricks from July 20 to September 9 which is the reason of this hiatus in the Register, but if the good people of the parish of Eccleshall will forgive him this one crime he promises faithfully never to lay bricks again so long as he lives. Witness my hand Joseph Cheshire.*[825]

For some individuals bricklaying could be an occupation with status. In 1777 Wedgwood produced a medallion for the Etruria bricklayer Edward Bourne, such a portrait was produced for personal rather than commercial reasons as an indication of the estimation in which he was held. (Bourne and his team may have been responsible for laying 330,000 bricks at 18d per 1,000 for £24 15s and 331 yards of 'front laying' for £5 10s 4d.) An assignment to a London bricklayer, Robert Gay of Camberwell, includes reference to Diana, his wife, who was the daughter of Richard Keelinge of 'Kings Swinford, gentleman'. The nomination was by Edward, Lord Dudley and Ward.

---

823 Ibid., 159.
824 'I would have wrote ... but Mr Pickford coming here to settle his accounts prevented me. Thate business took us a whole day & a good part of another, & after deducting about £200 of his false and most unreasonable charges and submitting to pay £150 in my wrong, I have finally closed his account and pay'd his £142 bill ... cleared my head and hands of one dirty affair although I have made a considerable pecuniary sacrifice in doing so. I will give you one instance ... I have paid him for 70,000 bricks and laying of 21/p/yard ... more than he will account for me the bricks ... although he did not buy one from any other person'. Wedgwood Archives, E25 18369.
825 I owe this reference to Richard Totty of 'Friends of Staffordshire and Stoke-on-Trent Archives'.

There was a lack of demarcation in the building trades. At Blithfield, in 1770, the bricklayers were employed in digging foundations, tiling roofs, laying laths, pargetting, laying floors and assisting the carpenters.[826] In a rural economy bricklaying was often a part-time occupation. Thomas Allen in an agreement of 1707 agreed to provide scaffolding and declared, 'they are at liberty to work els where provided I am not prejudiced thereby nor the oother workmen hindered if it is to be done in May & June'.[827] At Betley, in a letter of July, 1737, the steward wrote, 'The first week I was here Betley Fair & haymaking detain'd the Bricklayers the best part of the week & not so much as a stone layd for Foundation'.[828] In 1722 the steward of the Shropshire Estate of the Hon. Richard Hill reported that, 'the paver has done the lower court. When finished he will desire to go home for a fortnight to get in his harvest, and then return to continue with more paving'.[829] With building confined mainly to the late Spring and Summer months such relaxed attitudes delayed completion and added to the costs of building. The rebuilding of the Court House at Yoxall began in May, 1683 and was not completed until the Summer of 1685. The relatively small house at Snails Green was begun in May, 1759 and finally finished in November 1760 and the much larger house at Betley took two years to complete as did the small barn or house at Standon. At Weston-under-Lizard the great house of the Wilbrahams was begun in 1671 and not completed until 1688.[830] At Sheinton two building covenants of 1736 and 1739 allowed exactly two years for the erection of two four-roomed houses.[831] At Sandwell Hall a wonderful series of letters from the estate steward, William James, to Lord Dartmouth describe the procrastinations of the builder, William Smith, and the steward's unwillingness to provide stage payments for

---

826   SRO, D(W)1721/3/215.
827   SRO, D(W)1742/46.
828   SRO, D1798/HM/Chetwynd105.
829   SA, 112/1/2420.
830   Bridgeman, E.R.O., and Bridgeman, C.G.O., 'History of the Manor of Weston-under-Lizard', *SHC*, (1899), 142.
831   SA, 2089/1/7/28, 2089/1/7/40. At Bristol the contract for a merchant's house in 1724 specified three years. Bold, J., 'The design for a house for a merchant', *Architectural History*, 33, (1990), 76.

completed work.⁸³² For many purchasers there was an air of resignation about building delays. In 1725 William Shaw wrote to Richard Hill at Attingham:

> *I wish I could tell you the workmen had left your house, which … they now promise me to do by the end of next week; I fear they will not be so good as their words in that, and will compound with … them to be gone the week following. They have found more to do than was expected. I visit them every day, to preach up expedition to ye workmen and patience to your servants.*⁸³³

In 1801 Sir Henry FitzHerbert of Tissington reported resignedly that 'his own building goes on as is always the case when you get into the hands of carpenters and bricklayers'.⁸³⁴ Such delays were not acceptable to all purchasers and some of them insisted on penalty clauses being inserted into building contracts. The extremely detailed contract for the rebuilding of Handsworth Parsonage house in 1782 included the requirement for the house to be completed 'within the space of eight months' with a penalty of £100 for any delay.⁸³⁵

The time taken to erect a house varied with commitment, resources and the number of labourers employed. At Forton the contract was dated 24th June, 1664 with a completion date of 1st November, 1665.⁸³⁶ At Church Stretton in 1775 the articles of agreement were specifically designed 'for building a house within 7 months'.⁸³⁷ The detailed building accounts of Richard Drakelow for his house at Stafford erected in the summer of 1749 demonstrate that with the employment of a large team of labourers a house could be easily, if expensively, built in a relatively short period of time. Excluding sawyers and masons, Drakelow paid for 909 days work from his 'workmen' over a period

---

832 SRO, D(W)1778(V)1325. The letters commence in 1704 with the assurance to Lord Dartmouth that 'the works goes on very well … Mr Smith hath had in all £390 I suppose he is within compass'. In July 1705, 'Mr Smith talkes of having the new undertaking Covered by Michelmas'. In August 1705, 'Mr Smith hath nott yet performed his word … and still says he will cover the whole building next Michelmas'. In December 1705, 'Mr Smith is very pressing for money'. In January 1706, 'I have not seen Mr Smith'. In May 1706, 'Mr Smith had hath of me £1,200 … he is extraordinary pressing for money'. The final payment of the total of £1,400 was made in December 1706.

833 SA, 112/1/1852.

834 DRO, D239/M/E/12288.

835 SRO, L B/V/6 H4. The cost of the house was £496 10s.

836 SRO, D(W)1788P16(2)1.

837 SA, 1045/569. The total cost was £200.

of only 16 weeks, this average of 56 days work each week suggests a minimum of eight labourers per week. This figure is likely to have been much higher in some weeks. For example, between 30th July and 12th August the workmen were paid for an equivalent of 210 days' work.

The accounts were maintained for a five-day week, but many labourers were paid for seven days per week. Some workmen even received payment for eight days per week, presumably some form of bonus payment. The total cost of the house was £308 18s 10d. Of this sum the labourers' wages were approximately £45 (15%), the cost of the masons was £93 (30%) and other labour costs for sawyers, lime work and the weekly 'drink' probably raised the overall cost of labour to nearly 50%.[838] At Beaumanor in 1727 the owner, William Herrick hired 'such men as he thinks fit in order to finish the house by the contract date' and compelled the builder, John Westley, to pay for the extra materials and labour.[839] On the dowager Countess of Mountrath's demesne estate at Walsall in 1765, the bricklayers received extra rewards for their efforts:

July 9 Paid for Ale for the Bricklayers at Wid Newton's Building working very late at Night 0 2 0.
Aug 19 Paid the Bricklayers when sinking the Cellar at Woodward's House for Working very hard and late 0 1 0.
Sept 7 Gave the Bricklayer to be carefull and Work up all the Brickends 0 1 0.
Oct 31 Paid for a Pound of Candles for the Masons the days getting short.[840]

Alcohol was a consistent bonus for building workers. Charles Trubshaw recorded in his notebook, 'gallon of Gin for Raniere 8s 0d, drink for my men at ye Dog & Doublet'. George Denson's accounts for a house at Worksop include, 'For Beer for ye Work at ye Rate of 2 pr (per) day Each man for 45 days 0 7 6'.[841] The accounts for the building of Hatton Vicarage between 1751 and 1754 include many references to 'Bread and Cheese' and 'food for workers'. The bonus of food and ale did not directly contribute to the family

---

838   SRO, D1798 H.M. Drakelow/19. Woodward calls the provision of food and drink at the workplace the 'traditional buffer against privation', 12. In 1692 at Standon, food and drink were nearly 10% of the total building costs.
839   ROLLR, DG9/2139.
840   SRO, D1287/G/6 (temporary reference).
841   NA, DDN/212/75.

income and were unlikely to be shared by wives and children. Wives or other women could provide their own building materials. In 1704 the Malvern Hall accounts recorded, 'bought of Coles wives hare (hair) the first time eight ounces at 5s per ounce £2 0 0, this time four ounces £1 0 0'.[842] The hair was used to bind the plasterwork.

Within the overall building price measuring the costs of bricklaying is hindered by the variety of ways in which it was recorded. The most straightforward payment was just laying a number of bricks as at St Mary de Castro, Leicester, where in 1721 bricklayers were paid 5s per 1,000 bricks laid.[843] In 1716 at the Malvern Hall Estate, Humphrey Greswold recorded 'all the masons work belonging to ye new stables at ye rate of laying seventy thousands of brick at seven groats p thousand which amount to £8 3s 4d – gave one shilling in earnest'.[844]

In some contracts pay was per 'perch' of walling which seemed to be, in the eighteenth century, about 3s. In other contracts brickwork was paid by the 'rod', in others by a fixed contract or by a 'day's work'. A 'rod' of brickwork was 4,350 bricks or 272 square feet. At Woodhey Hall Lady Elizabet Wilbraham, planning its restoration, was quoted per rod, 20s 'for bricke & halfe', 26s 'for ye same', 15s 'for ye same', 43s 'Measuring over all & per all Thicknesses', 43s 'for a bricke & halfe' and 4s per … 'thousand viz 18s per Rod'.[845] Other examples maintain this variety, at Sheep St. Warwick in 1696 'brickwork belonging to the front building', i.e. the superior frontage, was 18s per rod.[846] For the Countess of Oxford in 1747 a building estimate included '36 Roods of Double Brick' and carriage at £1 11s a rod, '52 Roods of Brick and half' with carriage was £1 4s a rod.[847] At Nottingham in 1764 the price was only 3s. For Newark Town Hall the agreement with the two bricklayers was 'Brick Work reduced to Standard Measure or a Brick and a half work measuring all the Apertures in brick Work and for turning the arches over the Windows … and providing whatever Scaffolding … the sum of 18s a Rod and to all Chimney Tunnels the

---

842 WRO, CR0299/536.
843 *VCH, Leics,* **4**, 166-187. In this case the bricklayers were to provide scaffolding themselves, and to provide their own drink, which in many cases was provided by employers.
844 WRO, CR299/536.
845 Hewlings, 23.
846 NA, DD/E/117/1.
847 NA, DD4P/70/45.

sum of 12p a yard', the bricklayers were also paid day rates of 2s per day for 'demolition of houses and outbuildings'.[848]

The cost of brickwork varied considerably with the degree of difficulty or ornament, and the amount of support given to the bricklayer. At Carnfield Hall, Alfreton, an estimate of 1727 was only 2s 6d per rod, but the owner, Robert Revell, covenanted 'to prepare the foundation and to find stone, brick, lime, sand, water, scaffolding, ropes, etc. (except that Clarke is to pay for all stone got upon the High Moor or East Moor)', with the 'Proviso that Clarke shall not be obliged to slate or cover the building or do work other than that in the table' (the estimate).[849]

At the other extreme at Edgbaston in 1752, David Hiorn was paid for brickwork measured in three different ways, 'For laying 11,000 of Bricks and parging the Chimneys £4 2 0, 25 Rodd ½ of Reduced Brickwork in all the Walls at £5 10s a Rodd, Brickwork 5½ Square at 4s 6d a Square'.[850] The 'Square' was 100 square feet and in 1742 *The Modern Builder's Assistant* produced a variety of house plans all of which were expressed in 'squares'.[851] An undated (1740s?) Shropshire document records stonework and brickwork in cubic yards and compares their respective costs for the rebuilding of Mytton Bridge, stone was 6s 9d per 'cubical' yard, lime was 1s per yard, carriage of sand and stone was 5s, making a total of 12s 9d per cubic yard. Brick could not be procured for under 20s per 1,000 as there was 'very bad clay for the purpose', 400 bricks will make a cubiclal yard, which at 20s per 1,000 will amount to per cubical yard = 8s 0d. Carriage of ditto to the bridge = 1s 0d. Laying a cubical yard = 1s 6d. Lime for a cubical yard, carriage included. Carriage of sand, the centre = 2s 6d. Total 13s 0d (per cubic yard).[852] This was another example where the assumed price advantage of brick was not present.

In the eighteenth century there were three contractual arrangements in use. Sir Christopher Wren told the Bishop of Oxford, 'There are three ways of working: by the Day, by Measure, by Great'.[853] 'Building by the great' was where

---

848 NA, DDT/1347.
849 DRO, D/184/3/50.
850 BLAC, MS2126/EB3/3.
851 Wilson and Mackley, 259.
852 SA, QS/6/4/478.
853 Quoted in Woodward, 35. Woodward adds 'a fourth, hybrid method of setting labour to work: key workmen were given contracts, usually for a year, and were paid a small salary which obliged them to work whenever required, usually for the going daily rate', 35.

the whole work, or discrete parts of it, was contracted separately. 'Building by measure' required contracting usually for parts of the work at a fixed price and the work then measured by an independent surveyor or architect. 'Building by day' refers to a contract for payment at day rates, the direct contract. All three forms were employed for house building but any clear distinction between them is blurred by the fact that in some contracts materials were provided by the patron. Thus at Forton the agreed price for the building of the whole fabric of the house was £100, but 'The sd Gerald Skrymsher doeth on his part promise to bring all the materials to the place'.[854]

The majority of houses were built 'by the day' and thus the incentives to complete the work quickly were much reduced.[855] John Fenton's agreement with his bricklayers specifically includes the phrase 'for laying brick by day wage'.[856] Evidence of building 'by Measure' is not uncommon. As early as 1482 the master bricklayer, John Corbell was paid at 18d per 1,000 whilst ordinary bricklayers received 3d per day.[857] At Abbots Bromley Almshouses in 1701 the accounts include 'laying the brick at 3s per 1,000' and on the Gough Estate in 1760 payment was made for '64 yards of brickwork at 4d per yard'.[858]

Payments for bricklaying by measure varied considerably perhaps based on the difficulty of the work, the need for a high-quality finish or the provision of food and drink. At Weston Hall in 1671, interior brickwork, which would be covered by plaster, was paid at the rate of only 6d per yard whilst foundation brickwork cost 18d per yard. For Thomas Allen's house at Stoke-on-Trent, between 1706 and 1712 the bricklayers were paid 4s per 1,000 for erecting the chimneys, 6s per 1,000 for a six feet high single brick wall and for other building they received 3s 6d per 1,000.[859]

The quality of the house building was ensured in many contracts by external examination and consequent penalties, as early as 1479 a Nottingham agreement for building a timber-framed house 18 feet broad had to be finished

---

854 SRO, D(W)1788P16(2)1.
855 There is a precise summary of architectural and building practices in the context of the rebuilding of Keele Hall in 1761 in Saunders, 40-44.
856 SRO, D(W)1788P25/1. In 1664 at Lapley the 'Brickman' was paid at 4s per 1,000 for laying tiles. SRO, L B/V/6.
857 Hamilton Thompson, 205.
858 SRO, D4038/F/3. BRL, 334/7. In 1712 the Rector of Checkley paid 3s 6d per 1,000 for laying bricks. SRO, D 1386/2/1/6.
859 SRO, D(W)1742/46.

by 'Whitsuntide next upon forfeiture of xli' (£10).⁸⁶⁰ At Church Stretton the cost of the house was £200 with stage payments 'subject to the approbation of Samuel Scoltock, surveyor'. Here any disputes were 'to be referred to 2 indifferent persons who understand building'.⁸⁶¹ At Walsall the Montrath accounts of 1767 include a payment of 2s 6d to 'Edward Lycett joiner and carpenter for valuing and inspecting Jos. Wood's New House and Buildings at Heyhead to see if finished properly'.⁸⁶²

As with the entrepreneurial brickmakers, so some skilled and adventurous bricklayers seized the opportunity to invest in an expanding house market. It is implicit in many surviving leases and mortgages that bricklayers were developers of and investors in new premises. In 1737 Richard Warr, bricklayer, leased land in Litchfield Street, Birmingham and in 1741 mortgaged a messuage in the same street. In a deed poll of 1742 John Hands of Birmingham, bricklayer, acknowledged a debt of £40 to Thomas Pickard of Birmingham, gent., being a further charge on mortgaged premises in Birmingham at Upper Gosty Green, land adjoining Lichfield Street, Whitealls Lane, Steelhouse Lane and a messuage in Lichfield Street.⁸⁶³ In Derby in 1776 a lease 'for lives or 99 years' to Henry Moore of Derby, mason and bricklayer of a messuage in the Cornmarket known by the sign of the Rose and Crown, at a rent of £7 included an agreement 'to pull down the present building and rebuild it, in one calendar year, according to the attached plan and specification'.⁸⁶⁴

Wage Rates
For most of the first half of the eighteenth century the commercial market price of bricks was fairly static at about 10s per 1,000 with estate produced bricks often cheaper. It was not a period of falling prices, as some have claimed, but for nearly 50 years the builder and developer could rely on what was almost a fixed price. This may have provided them with a confidence in anticipated costs and have been an incentive to invest in brick. How was this price level maintained for such a lengthy period? For much of the period for both brick producers and building craftsmen this was a time of rising real wages. Craft

---
860 *NBR*, **II**, 389.
861 SA, 1045/569.
862 SRO, D1287/G/4.
863 BLAC, MS 3530/11.
864 DRO, D1955/2/133.

and Mills suggest that between 1660 and 1780 real wages rose by 0.45% p.a.[865] There was thus little or no wage pressure on costs of production or building.[866] For the city of Chester, Woodward has compiled a series of wage rates which suggest that the craftsmen's daily wage rate rose from 6d per day in 1548 to 16-18d in 1751, while labourers' rates rose from 4d per day to 12d over the same period. In both cases the period of greatest increase was from approximately 1550 to 1650. In 1628 the Shropshire Quarter Sessions declared a wage rate for master craftsmen of 6d 'with dyett' and 12d 'without dyett', only 12 years later these had risen to 8d and 14d.[867]

The rise in wages was not universal for in Rutland for the working months of Easter to Michaelmas master carpenters were daily allowed 8d in 1563 and the same sum in 1610, without food the assessments were 12d and 14d.[868] Between 1660 and 1750, Woodward indicates that the average daily rate for building craftsmen varied over the whole period from only 16 to 18 pence and that of building labourers from 9 to 12 pence.[869] In the Midlands the wages of craftsmen and their labourers were relatively static during the period of much more intense brick building. In Warwickshire in 1672 the Quarter Sessions determined 'the particular rates of all manner of artificers, labourers and servants'. A master bricklayer was to be paid 6d per day with food and drink or 12d without food. Building labourers were to receive 4d or 8d. In 1685 these exact wage levels were repeated in an Act determining 'the rates of wages of all manner of servants in Warwickshire'.[870] Midland evidence of wages for building craftsmen and labourers is erratic but the following have been recorded.

---

865 Crafts, N., and Mills, T., *The Race between Population and Technology: Real Wages in the First Industrial Revolution*, Cage Working Paper, (2020), 1.

866 Lindert, P.H., 'English Population, Wages and Prices, 1541-1913', in Rotber, R. I., and Rabb, T. K., *Population and History*, 54. 'Real wages of construction workers in England were relatively static between 1700 and 1800'. Clark, G., *A Farewell to Alms: A Brief Economic History of the World*, Princeton, (2007).

867 Reed, M., 'Early Seventeenth Century Wage Assessments', *SAJ*, **55**, **pt2**, (1955), 140.

868 *VCH, Rutland,* **1**, 220.

869 Woodward, 256-258. Even when there were sudden, short-term surges in the demand for labour, for example following a major fire, Woodward could find no evidence of wage rates rising in response. 204.

870 Nichols, J., The rates of wages of all manner of servants in Warwickshire 36 Car II, *Archaeologia* 1st. Series, **XI**, (1794) 208-211.

Table 13: Midland Evidence for Building Wage Rates

Date	Craftsmen (pd)	Labourers (pd)	Place
1481	8d	4d	Kirkby Muxloe
1552-3		8d	Leicester Borough
1595-8		6-7d	Nuneaton
1628	12d		Shropshire Q S
1634		8d	Staffs
1640	14d		Shropshire Q S
1664	14d		
1671?	15d	8d	Wolverhampton
1684-5	14d	8d	Staffs
1690-1740		10-12d	Leicester
1693		9d	Ripley
1704		12d	Pentre Pant
1706	16d		Rugeley
1715	14d		Leicester
1722	14d		Chillington
1728	14d		Chillington
1740-60		12d	Leicester
1742	17-20d		Staffs
1745	10d		Notts
1749	14d	12d	Staffs
1750s	20d		Leicester
1754	16d		Staffs
1755	18d		Shifnal
1759	20d	18d	Yarlet
1768	17-20d	16d	Staffs (building vouchers)
1770	21d	14d	Staffs
1770		14d	Notts
1771		10d	Derbys

The wage rates recorded above are essentially provincial and local rates. For specialist workmen they could be higher. The building accounts for Chatsworth House include detailed protests by its skilled workers against the level of wages agreed:

> *And this Defendt. doth confesse that workemen & provisions are generally cheaper in Derbyshire than in London but saith that artist skilfull and able workmen (of which sort this Defendt. carryed very mafly from London) are scarce and deare in those parts.*[871]

To provide the social context for these wage rates, between November 6th and December 31st, 1739, Sir William Wolseley spent £48 15s 6d on Lottery tickets.[872] At Shifnal Court Leet in 1755 the cost of '18 Gentlemen eating' was 18s and 'Wine Ale & Tobacco' £1 5s.[873]

The above evidence would suggest that, just as with brickmaking, the semi-skilled bricklayer tied to an estate, without personal tools, receiving a low wage subsidised by food and alcohol and, perhaps, by a tied cottage did not add significantly to building costs. Bricklaying was rarely a full-time occupation and labourers may have been grateful for the security of agricultural employment during the winter months. For large scale building bricklaying made a relatively small contribution to overall labour costs. Wilson and Mackley's analysis of the building costs of ten substantial country houses suggested that labour costs averaged 57% of the total expenditure but a high proportion of that was for specialist craftsmen who produced chimney pieces, panelling, sculptures, etc.[874] In Leicester, for which substantial evidence survives, carpenters were paid 2d per day more than bricklayers.[875] Similarly for Drakeford's house at Stafford in 1749 the sawyers as craftsmen were also paid 2d more than the labourers. In smaller cottages and houses with little decoration labour costs may have been lower.

The evidence above suggests that the contributory costs were a factor in the decision to build in brick. This was particularly true for those owners of estates

---

871 Hart, W.H., 'Proceedings in the Court of Exchequer respecting the Chatsworth building accounts', *DAJ*, **3**, (1882), 7-54.
872 SRO, D(W)1781/17/1.
873 SRO, D641/2/G/1/6.
874 Wilson and Mackley, 256.
875 North, T., ed. *Accounts of Churchwardens of St. Martin's*, Leicester, (1884), 25, 44.

who could harness the estate's resources of wood, clay, labour and transport. But why should the owner of an estate house or a substantial timber-framed town house decide to build or reface in brick? That decision was decided not by price but rather by the social appreciation for those who gained status by using this new material.

Chapter 11

MUNICIPAL SUPPORT FOR BRICKMAKING AND BRICK BUILDING

CIVIC APPRECIATION of brick was present in many towns. In Nottingham the medieval church of St Nicholas, devastated in the Civil War, was rebuilt in brick between 1671 and 1682 as the parish church of the fashionable quarter of the city. In 1690 the churchwardens of St Martin's church, Birmingham, prominent in the central Bull Ring, 'dressed the church in brick' encasing all but the spire in three layers of brick.[876] In her *Journeys*, Celia Fiennes hints at a contemporary viewpoint that buildings which were timber-framed reflected a community which was staid, lacking in imagination, uninspiring and not moving with the times. She is generally, although not consistently, condemnatory of towns which were timber-framed and complimentary about those which were brick-built, thus at Norwich 'all their buildings are of an old form … but none of brick' whilst Newcastle-upon-Tyne is 'a noble town … its buildings … of brick mostly'.[877] Similarly, Defoe found in Coventry that 'the buildings are very old and in some places much decayed', whilst Warwick was 'rebuilt in so noble and beautiful a manner'.[878] In 1654 John Evelyn entered in his *Diary*, 'to the old and ragged city of Leicester … despicably built'.[879] William Hutton, the eighteenth-century historian of Birmingham, was perhaps aware of

---

876 The inspiration was probably Wren's post-Fire London churches. Little, B., *Birmingham Buildings, The Architectural Story of a Midland City*, Newton Abbot, (1971), 9.
877 Fiennes, 137, 176.
878 Defoe, *Tours,* ii, 83, 84.
879 Evelyn, *Diary,* **1**, 294.

this contemporary opinion when he defended old houses, 'It may be objected that the buildings are ancient. But there is no more disgrace in an old house, than in an old man; they may both be dressed in character'.[880]

It is argued in this study that provincial brick production before 1780 was traditional in operation, hindered by transport costs and served a market which was too small to act as a spur to large-scale capital investment. How did would-be builders obtain bricks in communities which did not possess a resident brickmaker? In many towns or cities, the responsibility for ensuring a supply was taken by the municipal corporation. To encourage the settlement of brickmakers within their community councils guaranteed them either subsidies or a market at a fixed price. In Southampton in 1569 the Council complained about 'foreigners' bringing bricks and clay into the city. Its solution in the following year was to lease a considerable holding of Council land at £3 8s 4d to a brickmaker on condition that he provided brick of an agreed size for the townspeople.[881] At Sudbury (Suffolk) in 1610 a lease of land by the borough to a brickmaker allowed him to build a brick house or houses and to carry brick and tile toll free through the borough.[882] In Nottingham in 1615, the county justices ordered a cottage to be built at Sneinton for John Griffin, 'an expert in the art of making bricks and tiles', with the intention of inducing him to settle.[883] In Leicester the Common Hall declared in 1697, in an early reference to bricks in that city, 'that Edward Broughton should have leave to exchange a piece of land held by the Corporation for one on which to make bricks'. The Corporation presumably thought the land to have little value for it was described as 'it being ground not fit for grazing'.[884]

In Ludlow, the corporation allowed brickmaking only under licence and strictly controlled the price of brick and the restoration of the land, in 1679 it 'Granted to Thomas Watson liberty to take clay out of the warrant field for ye making Bricke he paying the halfe of the profit to ye Bailiffes for ye time being'. In 1732 it was 'Ordered that Morgan Lloyd having petitioned this Corporation to have Leave to make Brick in his Lands at the Sandpitts that

---

880   Hutton, W., 2nd ed. *An History of Birmingham,* (1783), 298.
881   Speed, J., ed. Aubrey, E.R., 'The History and Antiquity of Southampton', c.1770, Southampton Record Society, **8**, (1909), 92.
882   Suffolk RO, EE501/6/53.
883   NA, QSM, 17th April 1615.
884   Thompson, J., *History of Leicester* **II**, Leicester, (1849), 242.

he have leave accordingly he levelling and making ye Ground Good and that Such Leave continue only dureing the pleasure of this Corporation'. A lease to William Hand in 1775 stated that 'He will deliver to the Corporation best Front bricks at 15s a thousand and best hard brick at 12s a thousand, as many as they need for buildings in Ludlow'.[885]

At Gloucester the municipal authorities adopted a different policy, the siege of 1643 had destroyed at least 240 houses and at the end of the Civil War there was an urgent need to replace them at a time when there was a shortage both of building timber and of horses to carry stone. The city had no tradition of brickmaking and after surveying local resources of clay and alluvial deposits it recruited two Worcestershire brickmakers, William Swayne and his son. The Corporation gave them £10 to establish their brickworks and granted generous leases of suitable Corporation lands. By 1685 Phillip Greene, who succeeded them, had at least four permanent kilns.[886] In Northampton two brick kilns are recorded in 1755 as part of a large-scale business owned by wealthy residents but let to a brickmaker.[887] In all the above examples the brick kilns or clamps were built by the brickmaker himself either from his own resources or with a financial contribution from the corporation or its citizens and the price of the brick was either guaranteed by contract or subsidised by payments for labour and raw materials.[888]

Brick was not only chosen for its social message; its selection could be a political decision. In Bristol the introduction of brick was the result of political chicanery by its Town Clerk, John Romsey. Bristol Corporation at the end of the seventeenth century was corrupt and bankrupt. Romsey had the idea of redeveloping an area of marshland owned by the Corporation and insisting that all buildings should be of brick. He thus isolated his political opponents,

---

885   Roberts, *Ludlow*.
886   Broadway, J., 'The Probate Inventory of Philip Greene: A Restoration Brickmaker in Gloucester, 1685'. *Trans. Bristol, Gloucs Arch. Soc.* **121** (2003), 233-241.
887   Atkins, R., 'Brickmaking in St Sepulchre's Parish', *Northampton Archaeology,* **30** (2002), 83-100.
888   In Scotland in 1755 it was suggested to Cupar Town Council that a brick and tile works should be set up, using the local clay and 'furnishing the towns people at as easy a rate as anywhere else by which the carriage will be save'. In 1764 permission was granted 'for building and erecting a kiln and shade thereon … The petitioners shall be obliged to sell their brick and tile to the inhabitants at as reasonable a rate as sold for at other brick and tileworks'. Local people would retain rights to graze cattle and dig clay for their personal use. Martin, C.J., and Martin, P.F., de l., 'Vernacular Pottery Manufacture in a Nineteenth Century Scottish Burgh: a Kiln Deposit from Cupar, Fife', *Tayside and Fife Archaeological Journal*, **2**, (1996), 27.

the traditional craftsmen/builders of Bristol who had a monopoly of plaster and Pennant stone construction. Romsey also had a friend who probably owned the only brickworks then existing in Bristol.[889]

In Staffordshire there survives the detailed documentary evidence of the different approaches taken by two relatively small towns. Tamworth in the mid-seventeenth century possessed few of those qualities which would suggest that it had the potential to develop into an attractive and prosperous market town. Its position, straddling the county boundaries of Staffordshire and Warwickshire, denied it any regional administrative functions, and there is little evidence of any substantial industry, the northern end of the adjacent East Warwickshire Coalfield was exploited on only a small scale and the town stood remote from any navigable river. Its population was small at below 1,000 and its major building, the Castle, which might have served as a centre of consumption was, between 1688 and 1754, ignored and neglected by its two successive owners. Yet by 1760 this unprepossessing little community, so typical of what Dyer has called 'the smaller and more nondescript inland settlements', had through improvements, refurbishments, new welfare institutions and civic buildings significantly enhanced its physical image. The chief element of this urban redevelopment was the improvement in the environment as building styles were translated quite deliberately from the vernacular to the classical. The most obvious feature of this change of emphasis was the replacement of timber-framing and thatch by brick and tile. The overall aim was to attract a larger number of wealthy visitors and residents who would stimulate demand for goods and services and invest in the community.[890]

There is little evidence of the use of brick in Tamworth before 1660 other than in the Moat House of 1572 and a limited rebuilding in the Castle. The Moat House in 1591 reverted to William Comberford on the death of his aunt. It was the principal residence of this ambitious and aggressive politician who in the 1590s made determined attempts to gain the prestigious position of Lord of the Manor of Tamworth, on the grounds that Tamworth and Wigginton had once been joined when they were held by the Hastings

---

889 Mowl, T., *To Build the Second City*, Redcliffe Press (1991), 11-12. Mowl describes the brick houses of Queen Square as 'unworthy', 'haphazard' and lacking 'movement and power'. This he attributes to inexperienced craftsmen and the inferior quality of the bricks.

890 Kingman, M., 'Civic Improvement and the use of Brick: A Case Study of Tamworth, 1572-1760'. *TSSAHS* **42**, (2008), 68-80.

MUNICIPAL SUPPORT FOR BRICKMAKING AND BRICK BUILDING

family and that he was the Lord of the Manor of Wigginton. The dispute with the bailiffs of Tamworth was violent and reflected a deeper dispute between the Ferrers family of Tamworth Castle, an ancient stone building, and the Comberfords, owners of an elaborate and elegant brick building. In 1619 when James I visited Tamworth he rested at the Castle, but Prince Charles stayed in the brick house. By 1620 William Comberford appears to have come to terms with Tamworth's borough council. That year he built a new brick wall to divide his estate, 'Moate Croft', an area of six acres, from Tamworth Green.

A deed of October, 1668, included a barn called 'Brickbarne near Motehall' and it being so identified would suggest that the use of brick made it a distinctive and unusual building. Yet in 1698 when Celia Fiennes visited Tamworth, she described it approvingly as 'a neate town built of brick and mostly new' which 'look'd like Litchfield but not a quarter so big a market town'. Her comments suggest that noticeable building and rebuilding had already taken place, but the portrayal of the town as 'built of brick' and 'mostly new' is almost certainly an exaggeration. The town's Common Hall minutes contain many references to 'old' and 'decayed' houses still standing in the years following her visit and as late as 1829 Etienne Hamel's lithograph of Cole Hill shows a mixture of timber and brick houses.

The detailed minutes of the decisions of the town's Common Hall and the leases of property granted between 1667 and 1760 demonstrate how considerable investments in social and commercial amenities such as Market Street, the Town Hall, centrally placed shops, schools, an almshouse and in private and communally owned housing significantly transformed the appearance of the town. There was a small fire in the town in 1664 which might have been a spur to brick building but the earliest unambiguous documentary reference to the use of brick is that of 1682:

> *Whereas Mr William Ashley is about to pull down his dwelling house in Church Street and a Tenement late belonging to John Shemonds deceased in the same street adjoining and intends to rebuild it with brick which will be an Ornam(ent) to the towne, that he shall have free and full liberty and licence to lay his foundation for better raising of this building soe farr as is needed.*[891]

---

891 Tamworth Borough Records, (TBR) XII 1 34.

The concept of new brick houses as an 'ornament' to the town is not unique to Tamworth for similar references are also present in both Henley-in-Arden and Warwick. At Nottingham in 1703 the Council was asked 'whether or no the Toll House or Engine House be pulled down for the better Ornament of the Markett place'?[892] Thomas Guy's lease of 1704 with 'three good substantiall, messuages, burgages, dwelling houses or Tenements with Tymbre Brick Stone and Tiles' was described as 'for the Ornament and grace of the said Towne of Tamworth'.[893] The willingness of the Tamworth Common Hall to support the demolition of municipal properties and their replacement by brick houses is important evidence of its opinion that brick added status to the community.

The Corporation also attempted, wherever possible, to impose planning controls on the new houses to achieve a uniform façade or front onto the street. As early as 1668, Robert Woodcocke was encouraged 'to build the said house and stables proportionable to the building of Robert Harthills house neare thereunto and as good'.[894] In 1696 a proposed lease had sought to control the height of buildings by including a restrictive covenant 'not suffering the Houses to grow to high'.[895] Maintaining an imposing even height was obviously an important element of town policy. In 1700 Richard Russell was allowed to 'build and erect a brick house in the kind full as high as Mr Weamans & as well',[896] and in 1708 John Wallis was to build his new house 'hansomily with Timber and brick three storeys high to the satisfaction of the Burgesses and Corporation'. The latter's formal lease required him to build a 'sufficient, hansome, uniform substantial building'.[897]

The policy of uniformity applied equally to lesser buildings, and in 1716 William Farr was allowed to erect some barns in the town, 'what he build to be built with brick & all his buildings be sufficiently Tiled & not thatched … must be built to form of Common pound and make sufficient form to the Common pound'.[898] The overall appearance of the streets was also controlled, in 1704 Jonathan Backhouse was required 'not to build as … farre in any

---

892 *NBR*, Vol. VI, 25.
893 TBR, 10/22.
894 TBR, XII 1, 33.
895 TBR, XII 1, 66.
896 TBR, 1, 108.
897 TBR, 1, 176. TBR, 10/23.
898 TBR, XII 1, 221.

ground that is prejudicial to any highway & that he take care that these be a good foot away from the side'.[899]

This desire for uniformity was present in other towns – as early as 1593 a Ludlow lease of a tenement in Lokers Row contained a clause that 'within three yeres next ensueing' the tenant must 'newe build the same in such sorte as the next building is now built'.[900] In 1622 William Burton in his *The Description of Leicestershire* denounced the town of Hinckley as the 'streets and buildings thereof I cannot greatly commend, having no uniformity or neatness in them'. At Bridgnorth in 1691 a new house was 'to be built as high as the howse wherein the said John Bankes doth now dwell'.[901] In 1722 in the same town James Farrington covenanted to build one or two houses of:

> … *stone, brick and sawn timber and to cover the same with good burnt tyle, the said building to the street shall be built to the Walplatt (wall plate) of the same height as William Whitmore Esqr's house is next adjoining with a Partition wall at the south end adjoining to the messuage of the said Mr Whitmores and with two convenient sellars and the lower rooms shall be at least 8 ft high to the top of the summer and chambers 7 ft high or thereabouts.*[902]

At Stratford-on-Avon a lease of the 1670s to Simon Smart was made 'Uppon this Condicon that hee build two bayes with bricke too the fronte of the Streete … the height of the house to bee built too raynge with Arthur Lane's'.[903]

Although there was a degree of inconsistency in the policy of the Tamworth Common Hall, as indeed might be expected from a body some of whose members benefited from lengthy leases of timber-framed houses and shops, there is little doubt that within its membership was a modernising lobby which encouraged redevelopment, sought to impose uniform, high-quality buildings, and laid down restrictions on their materials, size, height, and the maintenance of their façades. Other members, more pragmatically, encouraged partial rebuilding using timber and reclaimed materials or even the complete

---

899   TBR, XII, 153.
900   Roberts, *Ludlow*, 5.
901   SA, 796/100.
902   SA, 775/239.
903   VCH, *Warks*, **3**. SPBT, ER3/4.

re-erection of old buildings. In 1701 it was 'Ordered that … the old houses and buildings that are now to be taken down that stand between the ground where the old Towne Hall stood and William Alcocks have (for making roome for planting the new hall) been set upp & placed in Gunngate'. In 1713 Henry Sketchley was given permission 'to pull the old house down & … to erect & build two good substantial bays of building to be with Timber brick and Tile'. The timber may have been employed in a brick-fronted house to stiffen its side walls. A detailed archaeological investigation of No. 6 Market Street revealed just such a house with its brick façade dated to 1695, but with side walls which contained re-used timbers of the fourteenth and fifteenth centuries as well as new ones.[904] Bricklayers had the curious notion that by adding timber plates in internal brickwork they would somehow reinforce the masonry. Whilst 'bond' timber may well have been useful to support paneling, rainwater penetration could lead to its weakening and rotting and when totally decayed would leave a hole in the wall. Where this happened, the walls bowed out and split into two separate layers. Many brick buildings in the eighteenth century employed such bond timbers. At Bridgnorth a lease of 1720 specifically describes this process of combining timber with brick; Richard Goolden was to have 'liberty of fixing any timber in the 'sheire' end of the house-with sound well-burnt brick and tile'.[905]

The Tamworth Common Hall and individual developers were very aware of the value of reclaimed building materials. In 1700 Richard Russell was permitted 'to pull down the house and all the buildings' and the agreement allowed him 'to have all the old materials'.[906] Thomas Guy, 'our incomparable benefactor', may have personally paid for the costs of the new Town Hall, but the agreement of 1700 for the demolition of several shops and houses on its site allowed him 'libertie to dispose of the materials of the old hall at his pleasure'. In 1703 it was agreed that 'William Ashley pay forty shillings for the materials of a house in Eldergate Lane'. In 1743 Lord Weymouth was granted the materials from 'pulled down cottages' on the site of the proposed workhouse. Possibly one way in which the building costs of brick houses could be reduced was through recycled materials.

---

904   Meeson, R., and Kirkham, A., 6 Market Street Tamworth, *SSAHT*, **33**, (1991-2), 42-48.
905   SA, 796/101.
906   TBR XII 1, 108.

Amongst the references to the use of brick in Tamworth in both public and private spaces are those approvals granted for the building of brick walls. In 1693 Thomas Guy was given permission to build a brick wall in Gungate, Philipp Cooke, a 'taylour', was given the right 'to put upp a brick wall' in 1699 and in 1704 Viscount Weymouth was allowed to build a brick wall in Lichfield Street. It is possible that urban tenement boundaries, previously based on ditches and light fencing and frequently a source of dispute, were better defined by permanent and immovable brick walling. High brick walls could, of course, be an inconvenience during a fire and in 1736 Elizabeth Mouseley obtained from her neighbours the 'Right of safe drop over the wall she is now building'.[907]

Between 1680 and 1740 the civic records include many references to specific building activity within the town and describe the demolition of old and 'decayed' buildings and a 'dangerous Thatched house'. New shops were built in the Market Place, John Mainwaring's lease of 1711 mentions adjacent buildings including, 'Also another two lately erected houses & shops', and buildings 'erected in the place where formerly two decayed shoppes and Chambers over them stood'. Altogether there are dozens of references to building, rebuilding and the refronting of houses and shops.

Parallel with the improvements in housing, the Common Hall in partnership with local philanthropists and private capital, also encouraged investment in the public and institutional space within the town. In 1674 permission was granted for another bay of buildings to be added to the schoolhouse. The Free Grammar School was opened in 1677 and demonstrated the positive preference which the council members had for the use of brick in municipal buildings. The men's almshouse was built on land granted in 1692 to Thomas Guy on a site adjacent to the women's almshouses. Slightly earlier, Lord Weymouth had given a barn and a yard to be converted into a 'school for poor children'. In 1740 the Corporation officers were ordered 'to turn out all those paupers who live in Corporation Houses', and in 1743 a workhouse was built by Lord Weymouth on the site of the pulled down cottages. The materials from the cottages were granted to him and as with Thomas Guy and other developers the old materials thus subsidized the rebuilding of the town.

Although the aesthetic benefits of rebuilding were widely appreciated, one result of building in brick for a uniform and classical façade was to emphasize

---

907 LRO, D187/493.

the social stratification of the town, 'Those who could not comply with the requirements to use brick-and-tile and who were too poor to choose to do so were likely to be edged into older, poorer cottages outside the best streets, perhaps outside the borough bounds'.[908] Spatial differentiation was emphasized by rebuilding in brick in a cultural idiom that was not easily understood by the uneducated. Brick building added a cultural dimension to age-old inequalities and gave a sharper edge to patterns of social stratification. Such social engineering is difficult to identify readily in the small Midland towns, but it may perhaps be represented by Corporation policy in Tamworth which in 1701 dismantled old and decayed timber-framed houses and re-erected them in the Gungate, well away from the prestigious Market Place in which they had stood.

The wider policy of the Common Hall, as the town's major property owner, was to make the town more attractive for investors, renters and visitors. This policy is reflected in a minute of 1701 … 'three new houses in Gunngate and one in Church Lane being designed to put such persons in as to the Towne pay the greatest Rent and that such shall be removed to those new houses and pay this sum & rent'.[909] The success of this policy in attracting the gentry was a matter of interest to the community. The steward to Viscount Townshend, for example, reported in an undated letter to his master 'that Mr Thurlow has purchased the large sashed house in Church St and intends making it the place of his residence in the Vacations'.[910]

The mechanism by which municipal landlords and charities, bodies usually with only limited amounts of capital, were able to persuade tenants to invest in improvements to rented property was the extended lease. In the years immediately following the Restoration most Tamworth leases were for either 21 or 31 years for houses and less for shops. But from the 1690s onwards there were a significant number of leases for 99 years, almost all of which were to tenants who had committed themselves to the rebuilding of the Common Hall's properties. A typical example was that of Thomas Pears who in 1727 was offered a lease of 99 years after 'having agreed to Build two Bayes with Brick and to tile the same'. Similarly, 99-year leases at initially

---

908   Jones, Porter and Turner, 62.
909   TBR, XII 1, 125.
910   LRO, D187/2/10.

low rents were offered to Thomas Underhill, John Wallis, Henry Sketchley, and Thomas Onyons, all improvers of their houses. The specific policy of the Common Hall is well described in the lease of a property in Market Street to John Wallis in 1708. It required Wallis to 'take down all the building & on sd premises within two years next … at his own expense and charge build, erect & set up a sufficient, hansome, uniforme, substantial building … with brick, stone, timber three stories high all the breadth & length of the building'. In return he was offered a 99-year lease at a rent of 35s per annum.[911] The overall success of this policy is reflected in the rent revenues obtained from improved housing. The Chamberlain Accounts are sporadic but in 1729-30 income was £99 2s 2½d and by 1758-59 had risen to £146 16s 1d. Disbursements rose from £96 19s 3d to £103 15s 4d allowing further investment in the town, for example in 1761 the main streets were paved.[912] The corporation's recognition of the commercial and financial benefits which arose from a deliberate policy of physical improvement helped to create a new and fashionable townscape of which the promotion and encouragement of brick was a significant feature.

In Birmingham the earliest reference to brick may be that of 'the brick barn' in Edgbaston Street in 1647-8 and a 'brick house' on Birmingham Heath leased in 1649, both were owned by the prosperous mercer Richard Smalbroke.[913] It was not until half a century later that brick was regularly supported by the King Edward VI Foundation, the major property owner in the centre of the town and which, as in Tamworth, employed a similar policy of extended leases in return for building. The leases of many tenants were extended from 21 years to 99 years on condition that they invested at least £100 in capital improvements and 'in consyderacon of building'.[914] Brick is not always mentioned but is implicit in many of the leases, for example in 1694 Elizabeth Holtham was granted a 99 year lease for 'seaven houses in Carrs Lane lately built', and in 1696 leases to Robert Rotten and Alice Baylis required the building of houses of 'three storeys'.[915]

Encouragement for brick building could be in the provision of brick clay – a lease of 1686 to George Fentham, a mercer, 'for the terme of 89 yeares

---

911 TBR, 10/23.
912 SRO, D4452/1/16/13/1.
913 BLAC, MS 1098/24, MS, 1098/25.
914 Dugdale Society, *The Records of King Edwards's School,* **II**, (1928), 140.
915 KES, 121, 129.

at the yearly rent of 32s-in consideracon of 100li pounds to be laid out in building … the sd george Fentham being at Liberty to dig clay therein for the making of Brickes to be used in the sd Buildings & not otherwise'.[916] Brick was obviously in demand on the Foundation lands and the Governors sought to control its manufacture to prevent environmental disruption. In 1696 the Governors decided that 'Richard Danks be forthwith forbidden to proceed to make Bricks on the School land at the Butts & that he pull down the hovel there built in order to make bricks'. In 1697 a lease to Thomas Ran included a covenant 'particularly not to make bricks & to level the ground where bricks have been already made', and in 1698 they met to consider the 'continuance' of a 'Brickekilne'.

The Governors also sought to control the appearance of the houses. In 1696 they met to discuss 'shopps in the Shambles … What money ought to be laid out in pulling down & rebuilding the same Shopps & in what manner'.[917] In 1694 a lease to Christopher Henman included a covenant 'to new build the sayd house … to lay out 100li … & to build all the front like & agreeable to the houses of the widow Jackson thereto next adjoining'.[918] The record of leases awarded is not available for all years but between 1686 and 1699 at least 52 leases were recorded. 18 of these were for 99 years and required the investment of usually £100 in 'new buylding'. A further 15 were also for 99 years of which some refer to houses 'lately built'. The remainder of the leases, often for shops, were for 21 years. As at Tamworth, the School governors adopted an identical policy of offering extended leases as an incentive for tenants to invest in the rebuilding in brick of the landlord's property.

A similar policy, although not so clearly presented, was executed in Nottingham. The loss of many municipal records in a fire in 1724 has destroyed much of the evidence but those building records that have survived show obvious similarities with those of Tamworth and Birmingham. There are frequent references to the paving of streets, municipal investment in the rebuilding of the Market Place, the sweeping of streets and the maintenance of the bridges and the water supply. There are many instructions on the building of uniform frontages and just one lease which required the investment of £100.[919]

---

916 KES, 110.
917 KES, 128.
918 KES, 124.
919 *RBN*, **VI**, 25, 61, 64, 99, 117, 123, 143, 161, 168, 180.

Specific references to the compulsory use of brick are rare, although in 1734 a room was to be built in the Shambles with walls of 'a Brick and a half'.[920]

In Newcastle-under-Lyme a unique response to the problem of providing brick was the attempt in 1709-1711 to establish a municipally financed brick works which was owned by the corporation, rented initially to corporation officials and whose product may have been a requirement for those building on corporation land.[921] The first documentary reference to the manufacture of brick in Newcastle was in 1665 when the corporation recorded that:

> *Andrew Beech have liberty to make brick in the lane over against Dean Croft provided he make it according to the statute, burn it well and furnish the town at the rate of 10s per thousand and to furnish them before the countery and is not to spoil or annoye the waye.*[922]

The restrictions imposed on Beech are significant. The relatively high price was controlled, the market was restricted to the town (at least before supplying the hinterland) and the brickmaker had to be aware of the environmental impact. Andrew Beech had been a capital burgess – a member of the Assembly. He had been removed from the Assembly in 1664 for abuse of other capital burgesses and for revealing private discussions. Noticeably after the municipal kiln was first built in 1709, all those who rented it were capital burgesses. In the summer of 1667, the Assembly withdrew their permission for Beech's kiln on the grounds of his failure to meet the requirements of the agreement:

> *It is also agreed that whereas Andrew Beech had liberty granted by the Towne to make bricks in the lane over against deane croft and was to make the same according to statute and to sell to the Townsmen at xs p(er) the mille and to townsmen before the Countrey, and for yt he hath abused yt liberty in not making it & following it accordingly That the said graint be made voide.*[923]

---

920   *RBN*, **VI**, 143.
921   Kingman, M., 'The Adoption of Brick in Urban Staffordshire: The Experience of Newcastle-under-Lyme, 1665-1760,' *Midland History,* **35**, **No. 1**, (Spring, 2010), 89-106.
922   *Newcastle-under-Lyme Corporation Order Book, 1590-1669*, 215.
923   COB, 1590-1669, 229.

Exactly why the enterprise had failed is uncertain. Beech almost certainly was not a brickmaker. Such an occupation would not have given him the status or income to be chosen as a capital burgess, but such relatively unskilled workers could have been easily hired. There was some building in Newcastle at this time and probably a reasonable market.

The Newcastle order books record permission for some very small cottages; presumably most of these and the barns were timber-framed. There is no specific reference in the order books to a 'brick house' until 1723, in what seems to be a case of municipal 'persuasion':

> *in case William Wakelin do sell to the Corporation that new brick built house adjoining to the Mill Pool in the possession of Roger Tittensor for £19 that he be admitted a burgess to follow the trade of baker.*[924]

There is however evidence from the 1660s of brick being used to add façades to timber-framed buildings and particularly to underpin jettied buildings. That such improvements were common is suggested by the surviving accounts of Ralph Keeling, a mercer and prominent citizen. Keeling owned about 20 properties 'in and about Newcastle under Lyme' and his accounts for 1704-1709 show consistent purchases of bricks. The first purchase noted is that of January 1704, 'pd for Jon Barnise for carriage of 1,000 brick for Jon Patesons House 2s 0d', his largest purchase was 2,250 bricks in 1707.[925] Such quantities were too small to be for new brick houses, but they do suggest that brick was regularly employed for repairs, 'nogging', alterations, the fashionable refronting and possibly for chimneys. One purchase is listed precisely as '300 brick for repair of a house'.

Newcastle's traditional function as a routeway town and as a regional marketing centre ensured a familiarity with fashionable ideas. The order books contain several references to increased rents for those citizens who wished to erect the stylish, large, semi-circular door-hood. Documentary evidence is scarce for brick houses not built on corporation land, the best source being John Fenton's 'Memorandum Book' of 1705 which includes, 'Charges of Building my house in New Castle, Nothing of any great Consequence (Save the shell over the Doore)'. Fenton, the rector of Stoke-upon-Trent, purchased an initial

---

924   COB, 1712-1769, 290.
925   SRO, D(W)1788p38B9.

107,500 bricks and a further 11,200 from Daniel Edwards at Burslem. He also recorded that he 'Pulled down 2 old Houses abt Lady Day 1702'.[926]

The removal of the town's timber-framed buildings was a slow process. A sketch of 1680 of property in the Ironmarket shows an unidentified house with the (presumably) medieval gatehouse removed and plots of land labelled as having had houses which stood there 'anciently'. But for the corporation small timber-framed cottages and houses were flexible, easily divided, relatively cheap, and could be let on short leases. In extremis the entire house could be removed and re-erected on a new site at almost no loss. In 1702 the Corporation discussed 'the house lately Mr Haddocks now leased to Mr Lawton the present mayor was to be viewed and reported on what charge there might be to pull it down and rebuild it', and decided 'Hugh Fosters house to be removed to a convenient place and a garden affixed'.[927]

In Birmingham and Tamworth, the willingness of private and municipal landlords to grant 99-year leases provided an obvious incentive for entrepreneurs to invest in brick houses. In Newcastle, corporation policy was to emphasise, where possible, the advantage of the 21-year lease in providing regular opportunities for increased rents. At times longer leases were granted, but in almost all cases these arose not from a policy of civic improvement but because of municipal debt. In 1685, for example, William Cotton, Thomas Hemings, John Burgesse Jun and Kilvard Oates or any three of them were encouraged to lease any parts of the town fields to raise money to pay the town debts and were permitted to make leases of up to 40 years for barns, houses and enclosed fields. There were also increased entry fines. The first references to 99-year leases occurred in 1712 and 1713. These were initially ground leases but the later one was qualified as 'being a building lease'.[928] In 1727 the corporation felt sufficiently strong to totally reject Mr Hordern's and Dr Harrison's proposals to have leases for 99 years. 'Such longe terme being hereby declared very prejudiciall and inconvenient and mainly dispensed with about 7 years ago when the corporation was much necessitated'.[929] There was one interesting exception to the refusal to grant long-term leases. In 1728 the order book recorded:

---

926   SRO, D(W)1788p251.
927   COB, 1669-1712, 33, 116.
928   COB, 1712-69, 4.
929   COB, 70.

in regards one part of the bay of barneng obstructs the prospect up the street from Mr Taylors new house. And as hee hath layd out a considerable of money in building thereof which is not only a service to the Corporation in general but alsoe an ornament to the town. THEREFORE It is hereby ordered that Mr Taylor have a lease for soe long a terme as ninety nine years of the said bay of barneng paying three shillings and four pence p(er) annum. And that he may take down same and rebuild soe much thereof as hee shall think convenient ...

Whereas it hath been found by experience that leases for above twenty one years have been very prejudiciall and inconvenient in many aspects to the Corporation And tho' some few leases for ninety nine years were made about seven yeares agoe for that payment of £3 10s a bay and a fine on purpose to supply the Corporation necessity wch at that time was very pressing. It is hereby ordered and declared that noo leases for the future exceed twenty one years except there bee some extraordinary reason for itt as in the case of Mr Taylors lease.[930]

This justification for short term leases is also the sole reference in Newcastle where the enhancement of the town is mentioned. There is no evidence of a deliberate policy of urban improvement to attract wealthy residents. The water supply was improved, street paving was laid, the Guildhall was erected and the stipends of the schoolteacher and minister were raised. Such investments were worthy but do not seem to have arisen from any vision of a more prosperous and enterprising Newcastle. The desire of tenants to make their property fashionable was seen more prosaically as a source of income for the corporation rather than a means of enhancing its public profile by creating an attractive town. The fundamental difference in approach between Tamworth and Newcastle was in the attitude of the respective town councils. Both towns were relatively modest examples of old corporate boroughs, but there was an energy and enthusiasm about the Common Hall at Tamworth which was not present at Newcastle.

The corporation policy in Tamworth was to grant 99-year leases for its properties as an incentive to build in brick and tile in a uniform style.

---

930 COB, 71.

MUNICIPAL SUPPORT FOR BRICKMAKING AND BRICK BUILDING

The aim was to obtain a brick house which would outlast the lease, for this outcome they were willing to accept initially reduced short-term financial returns. They worked in partnership with speculators, and willingly sacrificed 'old' buildings and materials to achieve a long-term goal of attracting visitors, wealthy residents and developing the civic economy. In Newcastle there is little evidence of any willingness to accept initially lower municipal revenues to support more intensive and fashionable development.

It was in this context of a continuity of timber-framed building, a limited amount of brick building and a failed local brick works that the decision to finance a municipal brick kiln was taken. In 1709 the Order Book recorded:

> *Ordered att this Assembly that Samuel Lowe acquaint Thomas Barker who hath lately erected a cotage and made an encroachment & inclosure in the lane leading betwixt this towne & Fowlea being the town land without consent of the Corporation that he will pay ten shillings per annum for the cotage and inclosure aforesaid the Corporation will take down for that William Lowe & Samuel Lowe do make brick & tyle in the said lande where they shall think most fitt for those of the Corporation.*[931]

In 1710 the assembly 'Ordered that the Mayor be desired to employ what fellows he findeth fitt to make brick in the farthest end of Kingsfield next to the same for the use and benefit of the Corporation'.[932] The mayor was William Lawton, a long-serving member of the Assembly. In the following year it was ordered that 'If any person commence any action or give any disturbance to the Overseer or workmen of the brickwork in the Kingsfield then they are to be taken care of and defended at the town charge'.[933] In 1711 the corporation:

> *Ordered & agreed at this Assembly that Mr Mayor shal have a lease for three yeares of the brick works in the Kingsfield for thirty six pounds to be paid downe in hand and that it be referred to Mr Latrell and Mr Procter to settle what farther is necessary refaring to the sd bargaine.*[934]

---

931 COB, 148.
932 COB, 156. The presence of an 'Overseer' would suggest that a skilled brickmaker was employed.
933 COB, 158. William Lowe whilst mayor also had a lease of the 'Watering Pits' which was a possible source of water for the bricks.
934 COB, 158.

One month later in December, the Mayor, William Lowe, informed the corporation 'that it was necessary to erect a hovel of thirty foot long for better carrying on the said work' and proposed that the town should bear two-thirds of the cost. This was accepted by the corporation.

The above statements are the only evidence which survives of this unusual decision to invest in a municipal brick kiln. It is difficult to tease out any explanation, but the following may be suggested. The most charitable justification for the investment of municipal funds would be that bricks were in short supply, prices were high and Newcastle, without a local kiln, faced high transport costs. Lacking a far-sighted entrepreneur, the Corporation took upon itself the responsibility of ensuring a consistent provision of bricks. The financial probity of the scheme was guaranteed by two disinterested members of the Assembly and it was as a measure of the importance of the decision that responsibility was carried respectively by the mayors of the town.

A more cynical interpretation would emphasise that although the agreement clearly states that the bricks were to be made 'for those of the Corporation', the lease of the kiln was for the personal profit of William Lowe. The only reward to the town was £36 rent for three years, and from that rent was deducted two-thirds of the cost of a large hovel and an indemnity against any legal action. No prices were given, but in 1665 Andrew Beech had been ordered to charge the high price of 10s per 1,000 bricks. If that price had been reconfirmed in 1710 as the basis for a near monopoly position in Newcastle then the consequent profits would have been considerable. Daniel Edwards of Burslem, for example, charged John Fenton only 8s 6d per 1,000 for bricks for his house in 1705. It is difficult at this distance to identify civic corruption and perhaps corruption is too strong a term but in 1708 the corporation issued a bond for £39 at 5% to William Lowe in recognition of a debt owed to him. Was the granting of the brick kiln some form of compensation? On the other hand, was it just coincidence that William Lowe was building a new house in 1710 and was given permission to build a new wall? Finally, there is the problem of the Guildhall. Shortly after the renting of the kiln the decision was taken to build the Guildhall. Did the investors anticipate its building in 1713 and the huge profits from this? (Or did they build the Guildhall because they had a surplus of bricks?)

The renting of the kiln by William Lowe was not a success. Compared with later payments the rent seems very high and it is doubtful whether the enterprise was profitable. In 1714, on the expiry of the lease, it was 'Agreed that some burgesses (unnamed) in trust for Daniel Edwards, have a lease of the Town brick kilns for 21 years on payment of £60 fine and £3 rent'. Although the lease was held by burgesses the inference of the decision is that only a skilled and experienced brickmaker could successfully manage the brick works. For how long Edwards, a Burslem brickmaker, sublet the brick works is not known, but John Fenton refers in his notebook in 1717 to the 'KilneField' and in 1720 to the 'Brickkilne Field'.[935] In 1723 it was 'Ordered that the Hovell next ye Highway in the Kingsfield bee sold to Daniel Edwards for what Mr Mayor Shall agree'.[936] There are no further references to the kilns until January 1736, when the receiver, William Terrick, was required 'to repair the hovel in the Kingsfield in order that brick might be made there next summer'.[937] Presumably there was not a consistent demand for brick in the early years of the eighteenth century and the brick works had fallen out of use. On 1st November 1737 Thomas Edwards, the son of Daniel, was offered a lease of the brick works in the Kingsfield for 13 years at £4 per year. If he refused the offer, it was to be made to John Harding, a burgess. The lease to Edwards was sealed in January 1738. On the 25th of March the lease was withdrawn, Edwards was compensated with £3 and Harding was awarded the lease.[938] The Order Book offers no explanation for the reversal. There is no evidence of a large building boom in Newcastle at this time but presumably profits were anticipated from some source. Harding certainly profited from the building of the Newcastle hospital in 1742-1744 and his bill for brick and tiles was its largest single cost at £94.[939]

Later evidence suggests that again the kilns fell into disuse, for in 1751 the mayor, the justices and William Terrick were ordered to enquire into the value of the Kingsfield brick works and make a report. Later that year Terrick was granted a lease of the brick works for ten years on payment of £4 per annum and the corporation allowed him £10 to erect hovels and ovens. Terrick was an experienced municipal bureaucrat who was frequently consulted on property matters and like other renters of the kilns had been mayor of the town. But even with his experience he was unable to make a profit from the brick kilns.

---

935   SRO, D(W)1788P25/1.
936   COB, 1712-69, 49.
937   COB, 116.
938   COB, 115-116.
939   SRO, D1798/HM/Bourne/29/2.

In 1759 the assembly 'Ordered that Mr Terrick be Discharged and Released from the Brickiln as no Benefit can be made thereof'.[940]

The history of the Newcastle brick kilns is insufficiently documented for a thorough analysis to be made, but the evidence of the decline in rent from £12 per year in the initial years to only £4 after 40 years, the constant need to subsidise the enterprise and the repeated need to survey what seems to have been often abandoned workings, all suggest that the enterprise was a financial failure. Such a lack of success presumably reflects an absence of consistent demand and an insufficient number of houses and industrial premises built in brick to justify large-scale investment in a brick works.

What is missing from the Newcastle order books is information on the potential monopoly position of the kilns. This is hinted at in the award made to Beech in 1665, but is only described as 'for the advantage of the Corporation' in 1711. The order was not explicit, but how far was assembly approval for building on corporation property conditional on using bricks made in Newcastle? Among those who rented the brick works were the most senior members of the municipal administration. Three ex-mayors, William Lawton, William Lowe and William Terrick were involved in renting the kilns and a fourth, John Hordern, also supplied bricks and tiles for the building of Newcastle hospital. On Horden's death the parish register noted that 'John Horden was mayor in 1721 when the New Church in the Town was rebuilt'. It would surely have been understandable if they had sought to use the authority of the corporation to support their investments.

The concentration on the municipal kilns may be part of the explanation for the absence of any references to independent brickmakers in Newcastle. Their absence is quite marked when compared with towns of comparable size. Some early brick houses were built in Newcastle, but their numbers seem low and much of the town's redevelopment can be dated only to the late eighteenth and early nineteenth centuries. In rapidly growing provincial towns, most houses were erected on new land and at Newcastle the draining of the Marsh and the development of Nelson Place at the east end of Ironmarket did not occur until after enclosure in 1782.

In Newcastle the deliberate policy of 21-year, short-term leases by the corporation, a major landholder, may have had the effect of preventing or

---

940   COB, 1712-69, 185.

hindering investment and there is little evidence of speculation by its prominent citizens. The largest private landowner in Newcastle was the Leveson-Gower family of nearby Trentham Hall. In the mid eighteenth century the power of the peerage was measured by its ability to control pocket boroughs and patronage networks. From 1720 to 1820 the Leveson-Gowers, despite two changes of party – from Tory to Whig and back again to Tory – continued to name 'by private nomination' one of the county members. They also controlled both seats at Newcastle and one of those at Lichfield. At Newcastle, they regulated voting in part by lavish hospitality at Trentham, dispensed at the right time, and in part by an ingenious device of owning the property in the town and letting the tenants' rents get 10 or 15 years in arrears. These were pressed for only on the evidence of unsatisfactory conduct on the hustings. Similarly at Tamworth Lord Townshend bought houses to secure votes – his steward reported in 1766 'Thos Barlow lives in a house of Mr Seals if I purchase it both will vote for us'.[941] The financial costs of such electioneering were considerable and 'all the property bought in the borough of Newcastle proved to be a very poor economic investment'. It has been estimated that the Newcastle and county elections, decided between 1742 and 1758, cost the Leveson-Gowers at least £4,000.[942] The potential rental income of properties in Newcastle was thus dissipated by the need to retain votes. This may well be the explanation for the limited redevelopment of the Leveson-Gower properties in Newcastle. 'The accounts show that cash grants for repairs in South Staffordshire were low and diminished steadily over the century'.[943] J.R. Wordie summarised the financial position of the Leveson-Gowers as one where the 5,000 tenanted acres were insufficient to support the expenses of Trentham Hall. At Trentham, the actual cash outlay of the landlord on tenanted property was so small as to be almost negligible, all cash surpluses from other estates being channelled into mansion building, fox hunting at Cottesmore, racing at Lichfield and Newmarket, or some similar aristocratic pursuit. The tenanted property was thus starved of liquid capital.

The exact size of the early-eighteenth-century Gower Estate in Newcastle is difficult to estimate, but a survey of 1797 showed a small area of 21a 1r 5½p

---

941 SRO, L, D187/2/8/131.
942 Wordie, J.R., *Estate Management in Eighteenth-Century England*, The Royal Historical Society, (1982), 242.
943 Wordie, 235.

strategically located in the centre of the town. It was occupied by 183 tenants. The voluminous Sutherland Papers appear not to contain any leases which refer, at least before 1760, to improvements or rebuilding of their Newcastle properties. In contrast, on their Wolverhampton Estate it was 'common practice for urban tenants to be given leases automatically. Very often they extensively renovated or completely rebuilt the tenements they were going to occupy and so were in a strong position to demand a lease as a guarantee of security of tenure'.

An indenture of 1719 between Lord Gower and Thomas Allen of Wolverhampton, carpenter, shows the process at work. Allen had 'erected and built at his own proper costs … a brick messuage' in 'place of an old & decayed messuage' previously leased (with 7 acres) for 16s 4d per annum. The rent was now £6 per annum with extra land for a garden. Gower was responsible for providing the 'Glass, Windows (Sashes or Casements), Shutters, Doors, Partitions, Wainscots, Chimney Pieces, Barrs, Staples, Colts, Hinges, Pumps, Pipes and other things' and reserved the rights for his workmen to annually inspect the house and its condition.[944]

A similar indenture with a Wolverhampton cordwainer, John Howlett, of 1723, required him to spend 'not less than fifty pounds in Erecting and Building a good and Substantial brick Messuage or Dwelling'. The lease was for 99 years at 5s per annum and 10s every fourth year for the first 50 years.

An indenture of 1733 between Samuel Leybridge and Lord Gower required Leybridge to 'build and Erect or arrange to be built & erected too new substantial houses with good brick & Timber scantlings & other materials & finished compleat the said houses in good plain & sufficient according to the best use and usage for building and finishing of Tradesmens houses'.[945]

An indenture of 1760 confirms the policy of demolishing timber buildings and replacing them with new brick buildings which could be leased at higher rents. The indenture describes 'four old decayed tenements' in Barn Street, rented at only £3 5s per annum, leased to Richard Fowler who had to spend £100 on a new house on the site of the four old tenements. The town experienced a flurry of building in the 1740-50s, in 15 years 130 new houses were advertised.[946]

---

944 SRO, D593/I/2/12, Gower leases 1671-1761.
945 SRO, D593/I/2/12, Gower leases 1671-1761.
946 Rowlands, M.B., 'Industry and Social Change in Staffordshire, 1660-1760,' *TSSAHS* **9**, (1967-8), 49.

The corporation order books and such documentary evidence as survives for Newcastle between 1660 and 1760 suggests that brick building was on a relatively limited scale. The use of brick was not discouraged but there were disincentives to its employment. The importance of the unique municipal brick kilns is by no means clear. In the agreement with Andrew Beech in 1665 the emphasis is very much on local production at the expense of the hinterland. This aspect is not stressed in the final agreement of 1711, but it would not be unreasonable to assume that the large initial rent paid reflects some sort of guarantee as to the size of the available market. The frequent need for restoration of the kilns suggests that the scheme was not successful and that there was not a consistent demand for bricks. How far the municipal kilns prevented competition is difficult to identify but there are no references to small scale brickmakers or brickmaker-builders in Newcastle before 1760. It may well be that the kiln represents the manipulation of public policy for the private interests of the town's ruling group. The policies of the two major landholders were generally prejudicial to large-scale development. The emphasis of the corporation on 21-year leases, although not totally consistent, was a disincentive to those who might have invested in the rebuilding or replacement of timber-framed houses.

The failure to release building land on the fringes of the town also restricted the growth of the town. As Hawke-Smith concluded, 'In Newcastle by contrast [with the Potteries] some of the burgesses fought to the last to resist sale for building and put a brake on development until the late nineteenth century'. The potential income of the Newcastle Estate of Lord Gower (and later Earl Gower) was sacrificed to control the parliamentary vote of the resident freemen. In 1716 the Trentham steward, William Paxton, wrote to Lord Gower about 'the absolute necessity of building some houses' to increase his lordship's rental income. There is no evidence that this strategy was attempted. The policies of the corporation and the Leveson-Gowers coincided to restrict fashionable brick buildings to a small minority of independent townsfolk.

The desire to invest in new or improved fashionable buildings relates to a complex mixture of factors such as social standing, personal disposable wealth and patterns of consumption. The study of Tamworth and Birmingham demonstrates in urban communities that equally important was the sense of economic security created by long-term tenure. Such tenure provided an incentive to build which in its turn promoted a market for building materials.

Chapter 12

BRICK BUILDING 1540-1660

PRIOR TO the Reformation the Church had been a major promoter of brick, but after 1540 there was a significant redistribution of ecclesiastical wealth and churchmen were less willing and less able to commission ostentatious buildings. In many counties the Dissolution of the Monasteries and the ability to purchase former monastic lands created families with pretensions of gentility, as well as allowing the older county families to establish their dominance. The acquisition of monastic estates provided new opportunities for the gentry and aristocracy to demonstrate their wealth by building in fashionable brick.

In Leicestershire there were 12 medieval abbeys or priories just under half of whose lands were allocated to the nobility and gentry. John Beaumont built at Grace Dieu, the site of Grace Dieu Priory, the Earl of Huntingdon built a house at Leicester Abbey and the Babingtons developed Rothley Temple. The brick 'Priory House' on the site of Hinckley Priory was partially excavated in 2004, it is poorly documented but may date from 1598.

In Staffordshire James Leveson, a wool merchant, built Trentham Hall in 1540 on the site of the priory. Gregory Stonynge, the High Bailiff of Lichfield built a house on the site of the Lichfield Friary in 1545. In 1562 Sir Thomas Paget planned an enormous house at Burton Abbey but finally built Beaudesert on the site of an episcopal manor house surrendered by the Bishop of Lichfield. Keele Hall was built by Ralph Sneyd in the 1580s on an estate previously held by the Knights Hospitaller. At Calwich Priory, Erdeswick stated that he had heard that the Fleetwoods had converted the priory church into a dwelling, 'making a parlour of the chancel, a hall of the church, and a kitchen of the steeple'.[947]

In Nottinghamshire parts of Felley Priory were rebuilt in brick in 1557 by the Strelley family and Wallingwells Priory was given a brick façade, probably by Sir Richard Pipe who bought the estate in 1578. Shelford Manor house was built of brick and ashlar in 1600 on the site of Shelford Priory. It was burnt down in 1645 and rebuilt in 1678, mainly in brick. Blyth Hall was built on the site of the priory also in 1678.

In Derbyshire the brick Repton Priory tower became the main residence of the Thacker family after 1538. The Elizabethan/Jacobean Stydd Hall was built on the site of the Knights Hospitaller preceptory at Yeaverley and a seventeenth/eighteenth century house stands on the site of Kings Mead Priory, Derby. Further south in Warwickshire, as early as 1545, Edward Boughton built Cawton Hall on the site of a monastic grange, Stoneleigh Abbey was built in the 1580s and incorporated the south transept and south aisle of the Cistercian abbey and at Wroxall Abbey, Robert Burgoyne built a brick house in the 1590s.

In Shropshire, the brick-built White Abbey Farm of 1578 stands on the site of Alberbury Priory. An example of the opportunities afforded by the Dissolution is that of Sir Rowland Hill, a wealthy merchant adventurer in London trading in wool. He lent money to Henry VIII and was deemed to be one of those who was 'contented to forebear to another day' so far as the King's debts were concerned. He was selected Lord Mayor of London in 1549 and appointed to the Council in the Marches in 1551. Between 1538 and 1555 he purchased around 17 manors mainly in the north of Shropshire and built Soulton Hall.

The period after 1540 was an era of prolific building with a dramatic expansion of permanent homes built more for pleasure, comfort and social status than for defence. In Warwickshire 20 large country houses were erected in the period from 1560 to 1630. Some were timber-framed as at the Old Castle, Studley, others were timber and brick hybrids like Netherstead Hall and Gorcott Hall where the centre was rebuilt in diapered blue/black brick in c.1540. Brick was employed at Charlecote House c.1558, at Diddington Hall, reputedly 1580, and at Aston Hall, 1618-1635.

In Nottinghamshire there are 75 listed buildings dated to the sixteenth century and 368 from the seventeenth century. Of these, early brick buildings

---

947   Erdeswick, 489-90.

include Staunton Hall, 1573, Thrumpton Hall, 1609-1616, and Ragnall Hall c.1626. In Shropshire brick was used at Acton Scott Hall, 1560-80, a wing at Albrighton Hussey Hall, 1560, at Alkington Hall, 1592 and at Crowleasowes, in the early seventeenth century.

In Derbyshire Longford Hall is late sixteenth century and the main phase of Bentley Hall was built in c.1630. The many grand houses in the county such as Chatsworth and Hardwick, and many impressive smaller houses such as at Barlborough and Snitterton, were almost all in stone.

In the predominantly stone area of the Peak District there survives a rare reference to the use of brick in an important civic building. In 1630 the lawyer Justinian Pagett included in his journal the 'remarkable things which I observed in my journey,' he noted, 'in the town of Buxtons we saw a pretty little brick house where in a lowe roome is a bath with 7 springs, 6 of them being hot, and the seventh cold'.[948] This may be the 'Great Bath' of c.1600, it being built in brick would be most unusual and may reflect an attempt to attract wealthy and fashionable visitors. In Staffordshire 24 brick buildings survive from the period 1550-1660 of which 10 are rural manor houses.[949]

Those early buildings, whose original appearance is often hidden behind later re-building, coupled with the scarcity of documentary records for the period, might suggest that brick was a relatively unimportant material prior to 1660 and that, at least in large quantities, came to the Midlands at a later date. Thus Alec Clifton-Taylor suggests that:

> *In both, (Staffordshire and Cheshire) until about the end of the C17, most of the churches and a few major houses were of sandstone; some Elizabethan and Stuart houses were of brick, but before 1700 most of these were half-timbered. From the early years of the C18 the usual material, in Staffordshire as in Cheshire, was brick.*[950]

Although Clifton-Taylor does acknowledge that 'several small brickfields were certainly in operation here during the reign of Elizabeth I', he suggested that

---

948 Pagett, J., 'A visit to Derbyshire, 1630', *DAJ*, **9**, (1887), 54. Presumably this was the 'Old Hall' built by Bess of Hardwick and the Earl of Shrewsbury in 1573. Frequently rebuilt in stone no evidence of brick survives.
949 Kingman, *Brickmaking and Brick Building* 31-35.
950 Clifton-Taylor, A., 'Building Materials', in Pevsner, *Staffordshire*, 44.

'It was not, however, until the Georgian period that local brick making really came into its own'.[951] In fact in Robert Plot's *Staffordshire* of 1686 10 of the 22 mansions illustrated were brick-built.[952]

The number of surviving brick buildings which can be dated to before 1660 is limited, but it may well be only a small proportion of those actually built. A significant number of large brick buildings were erected which have since been demolished. In Staffordshire at least 24 early brick buildings, one half of all those built, have been demolished, of which 12 were substantial manor houses and one, Beaudesert, assessed at 50 hearths in 1666, was a major aristocratic mansion.[953] In Nottinghamshire Aspley Hall, an undistinguished mansion, was found on demolition to contain a medieval brick tower, while Stapleford Hall, originally timber-framed, was refaced in brick in 1689 and demolished in 1970. Thurland Hall, a huge fifteenth century Nottingham mansion, refaced in brick in 1626 and taxed at 47 hearths in 1674, was demolished in 1831. In Shropshire the grand brick house of Sir Francis Newport at Eyton-on-Severn, built in 1607, has also been 'lost', save for a small 'summer house'. He also built High Ercall Hall in brick and sandstone at about the same time. It was partially ruined by Parliamentary attack in 1646.

In Warwickshire, Weston Hall built by Sir Edward Belknap, perhaps as early as the 1490s was demolished in 1730. Grendon Hall of 20 hearths was Sir John Repington's house at Atherstone where, in 1617, 'he built a fair house of Brick upon the ruins of [the] Friary'. Lower Skilts Hall built by William Sheldon (d.1570) of 32 hearths and Weddington Castle (Hall) built in 1566 by Humphrey Adderley, Groom and later Yeoman of the Wardrobe to four successive monarchs, are further examples of demolished brick houses in a county in which 43 large houses of different periods and materials have been 'lost'.

The period before the Civil War is marked by the building of many substantial brick mansions as some landowners moved from the traditional timber-framed hall-house to houses of brick and stone and stylistically from a vernacular tradition to buildings influenced by the Renaissance. Inspired by

---

951 Ibid., 46.
952 Elmhurst, Beaudesert, Enville (Enfield), Broseley, Blithfield, Fisherwick, Aqualate, Bentley, Okeover and Ingestre. A supporter of the publication, Sir Thomas Wilbraham refused to have his new brick house at Weston-under-Lizard engraved. Greenslade, M.W. The Staffordshire Historians', *SHC*, (1982), 61.
953 Kingman, 36-39.

the aristocracy many gentry sought to emulate their tastes, lifestyles and values in the building or rebuilding of their houses, thus Ingestre Hall in Staffordshire was clearly influenced by the frontage of Robert Cecil's Hatfield House. In Leicestershire a wave of building after the first decade of the seventeenth century saw the erection of a number of gentry houses; for example, Sutton Cheney Hall (1612-13), Shenton Hall (1629), Ragdale Old Hall (rebuilt 1629 and demolished 1958) and Desford Hall (c.1640). Quenby Hall is an outstanding brick building, built between 1620 and 1636 at a cost of approximately £12,000. A recent re-assessment suggests that its owner, George Ashby, had 'grander aspirations than straightforward country gentry'.[954] In Shropshire, Plaish Hall was built in the 1580s by William Leighton who was to be Chief Justice of Wales and a member of the Council of the Marches. Stanwardine Hall of 15 hearths was built by Richard Corbet in the 1580s and Albrighton Hall was built on earlier foundations in 1630. In Warwickshire the central part of Bilton Hall was built in brick and sandstone in 1623. It has been suggested that the award or purchase of peerages contributed to the crescendo of extravagant building as recipients sought to build houses appropriate to their new titles. Sir Thomas Holte bought his baronetcy for £1,095 and built the magnificent Aston Hall as an 'aggressive assertion … of his wealth and social success'.[955] The cost was over £6,000. At Trentham the cost was a similar sum of £6,165.[956]

That the house should represent wealth and an awareness of fashion is apparent in a letter from Thomas Wentworth, Earl of Strafford to Sir William Savile. In 1633 Savile inherited the Nottinghamshire Estate at Rufford Abbey. The imbalance between his increased wealth and status and the small scale and old-fashioned appearance of his principal house, was emphasized by Wentworth, 'Considering that your houses in my judgement are not suitable to your quality, nor yet your plate and furniture, I conceive your expense ought to be reduced to two thirds of your estate, the rest saved to accommodating of you in that kind'.[957]

---

954   Green, A., and Schadla-Hall, R.T., 'The Building of Quenby Hall – A Reassessment', *TLAHS*, **74**, (2000), 21-36.
955   Fairclough, O., *The Grand Old Mansion, the Holtes and their Successors at Aston Hall 1618-1864.* Birmingham, (1984) 57.
956   Fairclough, 65.
957   Smith, P., 'Rufford Abbey and its Gardens in the 17th and 18th Centuries,' *English Heritage Historical Review,* **4**, (2009), 125.

The Civil War provided a hiatus in the history of the use of brick, as for obvious reasons there was little building, although it is claimed that the Earl of Clare provided one million bricks for the Parliamentary defence of Nottingham Castle. The Earl was a major property developer and builder in West London.[958] The Plumptre Vault in the church of St Mary the Virgin, Nottingham, contains brick shafts and may be his burial chamber. The Midlands was an area of key significance during the Civil War. Over 200 houses were either attacked or destroyed by their owners to prevent them falling into enemy hands. Many towns were besieged and their suburbs often deliberately destroyed to preserve a line of sight.

The historian of the Civil War in Shropshire recognized that one of the consequences of the war was 'Ruined towns and villages, demolished churches, pillaged homes and crippled fortunes'.[959] Destruction was widespread and the scale of loss greater than any provincial fire. Tong Castle was burnt to prevent it falling into the hands of the Parliamentarians and Moreton Corbet Castle was damaged and subsequently set on fire by the Parliamentary forces. As at Tong, most of Wormleighton Hall in Warwickshire was also destroyed by its owner. Churches which stood close to such fortified houses, but were not incorporated in the defences, could also be demolished. The governor of Edgbaston House in Warwickshire caused the nearby church to be pulled down and used the stone and timber from it for the Hall's defence. High Ercall Church was similarly destroyed. Suburbs were cleared from many towns in the war zone and small country towns which were fortified, like Stafford, Ludlow and Wem, lost buildings in this way. At Oswestry the vicarage and several houses were burnt down in 1644, 'pulling down part of town' during a siege. At Bridgnorth the socially superior suburb of High Town was destroyed with the loss of 300 houses and total damage assessed at £60,000.[960] Larger towns and cities were also seriously affected – in Birmingham 80 houses were fired, at Coventry about one-tenth of its buildings were destroyed and Leicester claimed the loss of 120 houses.[961] Some towns and villages were not defensible

---

958 Barnes, T.G., 'The Prerogative and Environmental Control of London Building in the Early Seventeenth Century: The Lost Opportunity', *California Law Review,* **58**, (1970), 1339.

959 Farrow, W.J., *The Great Civil War in Shropshire, 1642-1649,* Wilding, (1926), 123.

960 When the Town Hall of Bridgnorth was taken down the shingles were saved. *HMC Bridgnorth,* 436. The Town council of Coventry also saved timber for re-erection.

961 Stocks, J.E., *Leicester,* 349.

in themselves, but contained a building or group of buildings which could be fortified as a citadel such as Lichfield Cathedral Close and Dudley Castle. The towns themselves were useful as garrisons and sources of taxation. Only as a last resort were they fired by their governors, as at Nottingham where St Nicholas's Church and at Dudley where St Edmund's Church were both deliberately destroyed. To prevent 'too many sad marks left of the calamity of war', the Committee of Both Kingdoms, set up during the Commonwealth, had the authority to advise local committees not to burn down certain houses, so as a result houses of national importance such as Chatsworth or Hardwick survived. In Shropshire High Ercall Hall was confined to 'slighting (removing outer walls) and draining the moat'.[962]

Several Royalist families never recovered from the penalties and losses suffered during the Interregnum. Newcomers took their place, such as James Winstanley, a Lancashire lawyer and the Recorder of Leicester in 1653, who bought Braunstone Hall from Ferdinando Hastings in 1650, and a London merchant, Christopher Packe, who was knighted by Cromwell and purchased Prestwold from the Skipwiths. In the 1650s estates had been sequestrated and were insecurely held and recovery continued to be sluggish until the 1670s. After the Civil Wars, with so many places adversely affected by the conflict, governmental assistance was both reduced in scale and more widely diffused. This was reflected in the much longer delays that characterised post-war rebuilding, compared with the time usually taken to replace property burned down in other fire disasters.

The significance of Civil War destruction was that brick was often the material employed in the rebuilding. Coughton Court in 1662-63 and St Nicholas Church in Nottingham in 1671 were both rebuilt in brick, while Ossington Hall, Notts, described by Thoroton as 'some part having been ruined in the late rebellious warr', was restored in the 1670s.[963] At Dudley the rebuilding of St Edmunds was not completed until 1722-4. In Shropshire, Cheney Longville Castle was rebuilt in 1682 and Moreton Corbet Castle was not completed until 1685. The potential for rebuilding was huge – William Sheldon, a Warwickshire catholic, described in 1649 the hardships he had had to endure during the civil war:

---
962 Porter, S., *Destruction in the English Civil Wars,* Sutton Publishing, (1994), 63.
963 Thoroton, 172-175.

In September, 1643, my house at Weston … was ransacked, and my cattle and goods taken by soldiers … In December following, my house at Beoley … was burned to the ground and all my goods and cattle plundered … Immediately after, all my flock of cattle for my provision of housekeeping was taken from us at Weston by a party of soldiers … [We] removed [later] to a small farm house in the parish of Clift on upon Tyme … where we remained about eight months, until all our goods and horses were also taken by soldiers and the house threatened to be burned.[964]

The period before 1640 had been one of continuous building of substantial houses. In the Civil War many were destroyed in conflict and families underwent considerable social and economic hardship. As Sir Robert Shirley wrote in the inscription over his new church at Staunton Harold of 1653 (and before his imprisonment and death in 1656), 'Founded this Church … to have done the best things in ye worst times'. In the 1650s in the richer parts of England important buildings such as Coleshill House, Wisbech 'castle' and Brasenose College Chapel and library were financed. In the Midlands there is limited evidence of substantial building save the unique Staunton Harold Church and the grand mansion of Edward Peyto at Chesterton in c.1657. Of the latter only the red brick gateway survives.[965]

After 1660 not all lands were restored, rents were low and the opportunities for immediate rebuilding were limited. Property destruction was widespread and visible and restoration was a slow process as over 200 country houses had been destroyed. Rebuilding was expensive and although indebtedness was not uniform it was common. Sequestration fines were often heavy, rents were more difficult to collect and between 1640 and 1660 eight 'deficient' harvests denied patrons the opportunities to save income.[966]

---

964 Mosler, D.F., 'Warwickshire Catholics in the Civil War', *Recusant History*, **15**, (1980).

965 The date of the Gateway is disputed. It is either a three-quarter scale copy of the Inigo Jones gateway at St Paul's Covent Garden of the 1630's or by John Stone in the 1650s. Stone was a pupil of Jones.

966 Hoskins, W.G., 'Harvest Fluctuation and English Economic History, 1620-1759', *Ag Hist Rev*, **16 pt1** (1968), 15-32.

Chapter 13

BRICK BUILDING 1660-1780

IN THE late seventeenth and eighteenth centuries hundreds of members of the affluent elite commissioned substantial brick houses. Brick made new building styles possible and particularly suited Georgian architecture with its flat surfaces, horizontals and verticals. In Nottinghamshire alone at least 30 substantial houses were built or rebuilt before 1780. Brick mansions were erected at Blyth, Clumber, Thoresby, Kelham, Ollerton, Shireoaks, Winkburn and Worksop Manor. In Shropshire houses included Longnor, Loton (when Robert Leighton of Wattlesborough, a brickmaker, moved there), Brand Hall, Cound, Condover, Hawkstone, Henley and Kinlet. L. Stone and J.C. Fawtier Stone in their study of *An Open Elite?*, have examined the traditional views about the ease with which businessmen and others were absorbed into the traditional landed elite and were able to grasp 'the glittering rewards of social prestige'.[967] They argue that 'land and a country seat … signified power and status'. That status might be founded on the possession of land, but it was most obviously observable in the quality of the house itself. The central assumption of the Stones' study 'is that … ownership of a country seat was an essential qualification for membership of the local elites, from whose ranks the ruling class was drawn'.[968] They emphasise the importance of brick as a material 'less strong but much cheaper than stone' in meeting the requirements for a fashionable, uniform and classical house.

---

967 Stone and Stone, 4.
968 Ibid., 199.

It was in this context that old and unfashionable houses were remodelled, or new buildings erected. In Leicestershire the magnificent Gopsall Park was built by Charles Jennens whose family's great wealth came initially from charcoal and iron production. The park included ornamental fountains with the water raised by a steam engine. This was housed in an engine house between 70 and 80 feet high, 'built of Brick and Rustick Coines'.[969] Belgrave Hall was built in brick in 1709 by Edmund Cradock, a hosiery merchant. Ambrose Phillipps, a London lawyer, bought Garendon Park in 1683 for £28,000, and later passed it to his son William, a 'Turkish merchant'. In 1770 at Hinckley another hosiery merchant, William Hurst, built the outstanding Castle Hill House, while in Nottinghamshire, Brunsell Hall was built in 1662 by Samuel Brunsell, Rector of Bingham and Screveton. In Shropshire in 1698 Richard Lyster, a merchant draper, bought Rowton Castle and instructed his executors to spend £1,000 on building a new mansion 'on the bank where the old castle stands'. In Warwickshire the red brick Honington Hall was built in 1682 by a wealthy Levant trader, Henry Parker, and sold in 1737 to Joseph Townsend, the son of a London brewer. In Staffordshire, the building of the superb Oakley Hall in 1710 reflects the status of Sir John Chetwode the first baronet in the family. Equally large was Hilton Hall, the home of the Vernon family and the administrative and social centre of a large estate. Okeover Hall of 1745-9 is an excellent example of the rebuilding of a Tudor or Jacobean house in the fashionable Palladian style as is Noseley Hall rebuilt in 1721 by Sir Robert Hazelrigg.

These new entrants to the landed elite built substantial brick houses to emphasise their arrival – Harracles Hall was built of brick in a traditional stone area by Josiah Wedgwood following his marriage to an heiress, Elizabeth Shaw of Blackwood. A good marriage to a wealthy heiress was often marked by a new building. Erdeswick's eighteenth century editor, Simon Degge, noted that in Alrewas is 'the seat of William Turton, a good freeholder, who married the daughter and heir of Thomas Holmes of Orgreave ... whose estate he possesses ... and built a pretty house. He hath lately ... built a second house for his son John'.[970] Erasmus Darwin built a magnificent home, which is now Darwin House, Lichfield, immediately following his marriage in 1757 to a rich heiress, Mary Howard. On the early death of Robert Hill his six daughters

---

969 Floud, R., *An Economic History of the English Garden,* London, (2019), 193.
970 Erdeswick, 315.

each received over £1,000 which, on their respective marriages, contributed to the rebuilding of five mansions.[971] Arthur Gregory of Stivichall Hall, in a letter to his son encouraging 'frugality and economy', explained that he inherited an estate with considerable debts, but his first wife's fortune was £3,000 and she lived for only four years. His second wife's estate, 'after the loss of the Jamaica Estate which cost me as much in defending a long Chancery suit as I ever received from it', was worth £6,000 of which £3,800 was in funds.[972] He restored the Hall at a cost of £5,961 8s 8d which was obviously excessive, for in 1761 he wrote to the Earl of Bute soliciting a post as Commissioner of Excise. He explained that 'I was tempted after some years, as my family was not large, to build a better house than I found upon the premises' but that, no sooner had he finished the building than his family 'began to increase and I have now eight children, my youngest not a year old, without the means of providing for more than a third of them'.[973]

The profits of office-holding frequently supported new houses. Hales Hall was built in 1712 by a granddaughter of the Chief Justice, Sir Mathew Hale. Sir Nathan Wrighte, a former Recorder of Leicester and Lord Keeper of the Great Seal from 1700-06, bought estates at Brooksby and Broughton Astley. In Shropshire, Sir Richard Hill was deputy paymaster to the Flanders army of William III and built the magnificent Hawkstone Hall. At Stafford, Richard Drakelow, a naval Prize and Pay Agent, financed his new town house on the prize money shared after the capture of the French trader *St Pierre* in the Caribbean in 1744.[974]

The willingness of patrons to incur extensive debts in the pursuit of social acceptance indicates the pressures exerted on them. Alterations and rebuilding could be halted if money ran out or was needed for other purposes, but for new buildings the threat of bankruptcy or debilitating debt was ever-present. Thomas Fuller warned prospective builders not to follow those who 'by overbuilding their houses have dilapidated their lands, and their states have

---

971 Williams, G., *The Country Houses of Shropshire,* Boydell, (2021), 67-68.
972 SBT, DR10/1978.
973 SBT, DR10/1974.
974 SRO, D1798 H.M. Drakelow/19. Richard Drakelow, fl. 1709-1757, was a Captain's Clerk and Ship's Purser and rose to be a Prize and Pay Agent. He owned several properties in Stafford including Forebridge Hall.

been press'd to death'.[975] Typical of such extravagance, Robert Taylor, the royal doctor, began in the 1750s to create a large estate at Winthorpe, Notts. His second wife brought a dowry of £5,000 and he in return had to settle all his Winthorpe property on her and her heirs. Using the dowry he began the huge Winthorpe Hall, but he died in 1762 and his wife was left practically penniless with the house unfinished. An expensive Act of Parliament was required to set aside the terms of the will and the estate and house were purchased after three years.[976] Stebbing Shaw noted how Michael Brandreth 'hurt himself by building Shenstone mansion' in the 1720s.[977] In 1720 Normanton Hall was sold by Sir Thomas Mackworth because of debts incurred in electioneering – it was bought and grandly restored by Sir Gilbert Heathcote, Lord Mayor of London.

The best example of an overambitious enterprise is the incomplete Clifton Campville Hall in Staffordshire. In the fields just outside the village stand two imposing early eighteenth-century pavilions. They were built as the wings of a great house whose builder, Sir Charles Pye, ran out of funds and was unable to finish the project. In Nottinghamshire, the Pigot family attempted a spectacular showpiece at Thrumpton Hall, but in 1685 the house was taken over by their lawyer, a Mr Emerton, to whom they had been unable to keep up mortgage payments. Similarly at Eastwood Hall, Derbyshire, Sir Thomas Reresby gained £2,000 by marriage to an heiress and overspent on rebuilding. He mortgaged the estate for £1,123 6s 8d to a London merchant who foreclosed in 1623.[978] On a much smaller scale was the pathetic letter from Ellis Farneworth of Mickleover in 1678 to Sir John Gell, 'I have made hitherto to carry on this building without entering into debt but costs have risen beyond my income', and asking for a loan of £10.[979] Eight years later, having been 'endamaged', he asked for a further loan of £20, he had 'built a barn and is finishing the house'.[980] Ironically at that time the Gell family were to all intents and purposes bankrupt.

---

975 Fuller T., *The Holy State,* Book 3, Chapter 7, Cambridge: Roger Daniel, (1642), 169.
976 'An Act for the sale of the copyhold estates late of Dr Robert Taylor …' 'The finishing of the Mansion and the building proper …, will require large sums of money … and will in a short time become ruinous and go to decay.' Private Acts, 5 Geo. III. c.96.
977 Shaw, *Staffordshire,* **II**, **Pt 1**, 42.
978 Glover, S., *The History and Gazetteer of the County of Derbyshire,* **2**, (1831), 60.
979 DRO, 258/10/35/4. Farnworth was a clergyman who had recently married, his wife's money was held by Gell.
980 DRO, 258/10/35/5.

Large-scale ventures imposed on a local and relatively unskilled workforce could also be delayed and expensive. The voluminous records of William Herrick for the rebuilding of Beaumanor include the contract, dated 15th February 1726 with John Westley, 'Joyner and Carpenter' … 'to Erect and build you a house' for £1,020.[981] Westley was paid in instalments and Herrick provided some of the materials including 60,000 bricks. In March 1727 Herrick authorized Westley to 'employ such men as he thinks fit in order to finish the house by the contract date'. In September 1727 Westley, having spent £930 8s, withdrew from the contract which was then completed later the next year.[982] Westley may well have been too busy to complete the contract, for in 1726 he was hired by the Leicester Common Hall to produce a plan for a new 'shambles' in the city and the following year he planned a new 'Gainsborough', an unusual combination of judicial courts, legal chambers and shops.[983]

An interfering and domineering landowner who allowed no freedom to the builder or estate steward could be another cause of delay. A wonderful series of letters from Simon File to Leeke Okeover concerning the building of Okeover Hall in the 1740s and 1750s, includes reports in the most intimate detail of Okeover's selection of glass, doors, locks and plaster walling 'common' and 'alabaster'. File reported in January 1748, 'they have hardly any thing got redy towards ye middle pediment so that the business is much neglected for want of some body to look after it better'. Okeover insisted on stone being cut to such dimensions that it was difficult to move and whose appearance was ruined by 'Brown Veins'. Typical was File's report, 'Sir I mentioned we should want 2 hundred foot (of mahogany) and you sent 180 foot … very wet and green'.[984]

Other patrons constantly changed their minds. At Hawkstone Hall John Hill reported to his brother, 25th June 1701, 'I … have told the carpenter Mr Broughton that he must go according to the first design, and he will observe your order in it. He says the first story now can be but 13 foot high by reason the stairs are already framed'. On 24th January, 1702, he reported, 'A plan of the house will be sent shortly' and on 17th February, 1702, 'I have received yours of the 7th and did acquaint the carpenter that you did dislike the plan of the house which I sent up by Mr Husbands, so he has drawn another which

---

981   ROLLR, DG9/2135.
982   ROLLR, DG9/2141.
983   Thompson, J., *Leicester in the Eighteenth Century*, (1871), 47, 76.
984   DRO, 231/M/E 99-123.

I now send, and he thinks you cannot but approve of it, there being no jetts out in it but very regular'.[985]

Artisan Mannerist Buildings

The Artisan Mannerist style was developed in the mid-seventeenth century by masons (rather than architects) using pattern books and is 'characterised by a rough classicism' which varied regionally.[986] In Leicestershire and particularly in the Soar and Wreake valleys this consisted of 'moulded bricks in raised courses at eaves and first-floor levels, swept into semicircular arches over windows and doors'.[987] Chequer board patterning of diaper work is often associated with this style. Examples of Artisan Mannerism survive at Queniborough Old Hall, the oldest to be dated (c.1670), Syston (1686), Anstey (Leics, 1690) and Barsby (1691). All are rectangular units built with their long axis parallel to the street. In Nottinghamshire aspects of the style are present at The School House, Tuxford (1669), the Manor House at Beeston (1675), the Old Manor House, South Leverton (1691), The Old Hall Farmhouse, East Leake and nos. 1 and 2 Church Street, Farndon. In Warwickshire Pevsner believed that the details of Anstey Hall of 1678 connect with Artisan Mannerism.

The Brick Threshold

When did the Midlands reach the 'Brick Threshold' when most buildings employed brick? It is difficult to calculate the speed with which brick was adopted in the period after 1660. A common assumption is that brick rapidly replaced timber and became the dominant building material. This exaggerates the speed of adoption, even in Norfolk, a county generally regarded as sympathetic to brick, only a third of all new buildings were built of brick as late as 1790.[988] In the towns and cities of the Midlands the evidence suggests that the process of replacement, simple refacing or complete rebuilding was a slow and hesitant process. As brick buildings were regarded as stylish, fashionable and a symbol of a prosperous society there was a tendency to exaggerate their numbers and their impact. In the rural Midlands at village and farm level brick was more slowly adopted. From the village of Yoxall there survives 323 inventories for

---

985 SA, 112/1/1866/17/32.
986 Society of Architectural Historians, *Archipedia*.
987 Smith, D., 63-64.
988 Lucas, R., 'When did Norfolk Cross the Brick Threshold?' *Vernacular Architecture,* **28**, (1997), 68-80.

the period 1533-1700 (although some are for the same properties). The first reference to brick is in 1648 with further mentions in 1666 and 1678, all of these are for small quantities with the first significant brick building being the 'Court House' of 1688-9. The earliest reference to the word 'chimney' is 1682 and a glazier is listed in 1684, the word 'coalhouse' first occurs in 1699. After 1720 references to brick are relatively common and occur in the Town Lands accounts in connection with the school and the bridge over the Trent.

Some villages contain a house or farm called 'The Red House', 'The Brick House' or something similar, such as Brick Wall Farm at Audlem, Brick Chimney House at Carlton-on-Trent or Red Gables at Uttoxeter. Typical names are the Brick House Farm, as at both Rowley Regis and Greete, the Red House Inn at Ollerton, the Red House at both Trysull, Market Drayton and Barford or a combination such as the Redbrick House at Edwinstowe. Such names suggest that in these villages these houses were unique, or at least unusual, and that their building material or colour made them prominent in an environment of mainly timber, mud or stone buildings. An obvious example is that of 1637 when 'Richard Heath … was presented for forestalling the king's highway in Libbers lane in Solyhull near the brickhouse'.[989] The 'brickhouse' was obviously a conspicuous feature in the village. Dating such buildings is often the only direct evidence for the introduction of brick. The name 'Red House' appears in a will of 1541 in Aldridge, a later important brick producing centre, and the phrase 'Brick House' appears in a mid-sixteenth century inventory at Winshill in Burton-on-Trent.[990] In 1615 the term 'brickhouse' was reported in Tanworth-in-Arden.[991] The visual impact of brick is apparent in 'The Red House' at Dronfield which David Hey describes as a 'sensation'. Built in 1731 for the Usher of the Grammar School, it was the first brick building in a town dominated by the substantial stone houses of wealthy lead smelters and merchants.[992] The list below is of those for which there is a precise or near approximate date.

---

989 Ratcliffe S.C. and Johnson, H.C., eds. *Warwick County Records,* **VI**, *Sessions Indictment Book, 1631-1674,* (1941), 51.

990 Gould, J.T., 'Settlement and Farming in the Parish of Aldridge', *TSSHAS,* **XX**, (1979-80), 51, LRO, B/C/11 William Hampe, 1556.

991 WRO, DR 37/2/Box 79/64, 15 Nov. 1615, 'Budfields Between the Lands of Richard Waring Called Brickhouse on south'.

992 Hey, D., 'The Houses of the Dronfield Lead Smelters and Merchants 1660-1730', in Dyer, C., Hopper, A., Lord, E., and Tringham, N., eds. *New Directions in Local History Since Hoskins,* University of Hertfordshire, (2011), 126.

Table 14: House Names Suggesting the Use of Brick

- Red House, Aldridge, 1541.
- The Reed Prebende, Southwell, 1553.[993]
- Brick House, Burton-on-Trent, 1556.
- Brickhouse, Tanworth-in-Arden, 1615.
- Brickhouse, Solihull, 1639.
- Red House, Lydbury, c1640. (a stone area)
- Bricke House, Leicester, near South Gate, 1642. Built by David Papillon.[994]
- Brickhouse, Barn Street, Wolverhampton, 1616-1647.[995]
- Brickhouse, Packington, 1635-1693.[996]
- Brick House Close, Welbeck Estate, 1652.[997]
- Brickhouse, Elford, before 1657.[998]
- Brick House, Burslem, 1656.[999]
- Brickhouse, Packwood, 1663.[1000] 'Now the glasshouse'.
- The Brickworke, Wilnecote, 1669.[1001]
- Brick House Farm, Highfield Hall, 1669-70.[1002]
- Brickhouse, Hartshorne, Derbyshire, 1673.
- Brick House, Wolverhampton, 1675.[1003]
- Brick Houses, Frankton, 1688.[1004]
- Red House, Etwall, C17th, refronted in the early C18th.

---

993 Pevsner, *Nottinghamshire*, 332, 'the earliest brick building in Southwell'.
994 Airs, M., 'David Papillon: Architect, Military Engineer, Developer, Author and Jeweller'. *The Georgian Group Journal*, **XXIV**, (2017), 5.
995 SRO, 3279/1/1.
996 SRO, 3005/35-45.
997 NA, **DD/P/6/1/18/22**.
998 BLAC, MS3878 /268A, the brick house was Elford Hall.
999 Adams, P.W.L., '*The Adams Family of North Staffordshire*', St. Catherine Press, (1915), 107, the author refers to John Adams of 'Brick House' and to the 'Brick House' Potteries in 1656. They were later rented to Josiah Wedgwood. E. Meteyard, '*Life of Wedgwood*', **1**, (1865), 329 claims it as the first pottery entirely built of brick in Burslem.
1000 SBT, 12/63/50, 'now the glasshouse'.
1001 WRO, HR109/4.
1002 WRO, **CR299/288/1-33**.
1003 Mander and Tildesley, 117.
1004 SA, 103/1/5/320-321, marriage settlement of Lloyd Estate, '2 (houses) called the brick houses'.

- Brick Houses, Hayfield? 1688.[1005]
- Brick House Farm, Craven Arms, was presumably called so with the tongue firmly in the cheek as the main axis is of timber-framing and only the stack is brick. Humour and sarcasm were often employed in the naming of houses as in Thimble Hall, a small cottage near the ironically named isolated settlement of Botany Bay by Whittington, Staffordshire and an identically named cottage at Lowesby, Leicestershire.
- Brickhouse, Nuneaton, 1691-2.[1006]
- Brick House, Asterley, 1693.
- Red House, Fenny Compton, 1707 (a stone area).
- Brickhouse, Malvern Hall Estate, 1717.[1007]
- Old Red House, Etwall, 3 storey, 5 bay frontage to timber-framed house, early C18th. Red House, Dronfield, 1731.[1008]
- Brickhouse, Stanton Lacy, 1741.
- Red House, Wellesbourne, 1745.
- Red Gables, Uttoxeter, 1747.
- Brickhouse Farm, Bickenhill, 1750-60.[1009]
- Brick Chimney House, Carlton-on-Trent, 1751.
- Brickhouse Farm, Chesterton (St), 1756-85.[1010]
- Red House, Brewood, 1758.[1011]
- Red House, Barford, 1760s (replaced the timber-framed Barford Hall).
- Red House, Tong, 1766.
- Redcourt House, Lichfield, 1766.[1012]
- Red House, Much Wenlock, 1770s.[1013]

16thc	1600-50	1651-1700	1701-1750	1751-1780
3	6	13	6	8

1005 DRO, D513/M/E/328.
1006 Chancery, C11/1568/10.
1007 WRO, CR1291/292.
1008 English Heritage Building, ID: 79509.
1009 WRO, **CR1291/70/31-33**.
1010 SRO, D1798/559/13.
1011 SRO, D590/17/9-22.
1012 Built by Dr Johnson's stepdaughter.
1013 English Heritage Building, ID: 254845.

Most of the names date from the mid-seventeenth or eighteenth centuries which suggests that even as late as the third quarter of the eighteenth century in many villages a brick building was a conspicuous feature. The concentration of names in the late seventeenth century brick suggests that it was in these years that brick made its most obvious visual impact. By the end of the eighteenth century it was more common and less distinctive. Similarly, the replacement of thatch by tiles could be uncommon in some communities, hence the Slated House, Middleton, Derbys, of 1698 and the Tiled House, Kingswinford, in existence in 1799.[1014]

The Redhouse/Brickhouse names are evidence of the visual impact of brick and of the colour which they added to the landscape. They reflect the status of the owner in possessing a house built of such relatively unusual material. An obvious example is the Brick House at Eyam, the only brick building in a village of stone, it stands arrogantly, almost offensively, directly opposite the Manor House. Similarly, Longstone Hall, brick-built in 1747 by Thomas Wright, in a stone-built village also stands opposite the Manor House. To see a brick house was to see a relatively unusual material. Even the Earl of Oxford, on a visit and personally conducted tour of the Welbeck Estate by its owner the Duke of Portland, noted in his diary that they had passed the brick kilns and included a rare mention of a house as 'a good brick house of Mellish esq.', at Blyth.[1015]

It is just possible that the term 'Red House' is an indication of a brick house which was painted red. In 1580 the Beaudesert accounts included the purchase of madder 'to paynte the chymneyes and the House' and show that here the natural colour of the brickwork was enhanced by artificial reddening or 'ruddle'.[1016] In 1568-9 the brick walls of Grafton Manor were enriched by 'oker' to make the colour more obvious.[1017] In the Charlecote Estate records there survives a document of 1763 in which is a set of instructions headed 'wash for colouring Brick fronts'.[1018] One interesting question raised by Jonathan Foyle is whether the painting of the house front in red limewash obscured

---

1014 Dudley Archives, DSCAM/5/9/1/1.
1015 'Journey of the Earl of Oxford from London to Scotland', 1726, recorded by Rev. Thomas, quoted in Welbeck Heritage Trail, 34.
1016 SRO, D(W)1734/3/4/119.
1017 Humphreys, J., ed. 'The accounts of Robert Caldewell Estate Agent to John Talbot of Grafton Manor, Worcestershire, for the years 1568-9', *TBAS*, **44**, (1918), 35.
1018 WRO, L6/1107.

the diaper work or encouraged their potash glaze to act as a repellent, like wax beneath watercolour paint, so that the glazed bricks would show through the red wash?[1019] There is little evidence of white colouring in the Midlands, although in 1557 the Venetian ambassador reported on the fashion for brick in Southern England, 'but at great cost, and it is very usual to whitewash the houses, from the abundance of chalk, of which here they have mountains'.[1020] White House Farm of 1711 at Great Wyrley, now demolished, would suggest the limewashing of this brick building.

Urban Brick

The statute book of 27th Henry VIII, 1535, contains an act passed for 're-edifying' several Midland towns. From the preamble it is possible to deduce the deplorable state of the towns, and the still more desperate condition of its inhabitants:

> *For so moche as dyverse and many houses, messuages and tenements of habitations, in the town of Nottingham, Shruysbury, Ludlow, Bridgeworth, Northampton and Gloucester, now are and long time have been in great ruyne, and decays, and especially in the pryncypal and chief stretes there beying, in the which chief stretes, in tymes passed, have byn bewtyful dwellyng-houses there, well inhabited, whiche at this day moche part thereof is desolate and voyde grounde, with pyttes, cellars, and vaultes lying open and unkovered, very perillous for people to go by in the nyghte, without jeopardy of lyf, whiche decayes are to the great impoveryshyng and hindrans of the same town; for the remedy whereof, it may please the kyng, our soveraigne lorde, by the assent of his lordes spiritualy and temporal and the commons in this present Parlyament assembled, and by the authorite of the same that may be enacted, &c.[1021]*

How accurate these comments were and what the reaction was is unclear. James Orange follows the above record in his *History and Antiquities of Nottingham* with a contemporary doggerel quoted by Deering: '*I cannot without lye and shame Commend the town of Nottingham The people and the fuel stink The place*

1019 Foyle, para. 10.
1020 *CSPD, 1557*, 1658-1673.
1021 Orange, 627.

as sordid as a sink'. As late as the end of the seventeenth century Leicester was described as 'An old stinking town situated by a dull river mainly occupied by tradesmen'.[1022]

The general assumption of architectural historians is that in the Midlands brick was rarely used for urban buildings before 1660. Many towns had one or two brick buildings, for example in Tamworth is the Moat House of 1572, in Derby the Corporation built the Moot Hall in 1610 and in the 1630s the first mayor of the city, Henry Mellor, built the huge St Peter's House of 18 hearths. Only ten years earlier in 1621 his older brother had built a substantial timber-framed house at South Sitch. In Coventry there are no records of early brick structures, the city was dominated by timber-framed buildings and later employed stone obtained from the dissolved religious houses and, after 1660, the demolished gatehouses and walls. That some brick was used in the city is suggested by an entry in the *Leet Book* in 1542 insisting that brick size should be 10 inches by 5 inches by 2 inches.[1023] In Stratford-upon-Avon, other than Hugh Clapton's house of brick of 1483, brick was not common until 'The Swan's Nest and No. 5 Church St of about 1673. In Birmingham the earliest reference to a brick house is 1649-50.[1024] According to Deering the first brick house in Nottingham was built in the year 1615. More specifically Thoroton recorded in 1627 that Samuel Staples 'hath rebuilt part of it of brick and stone, which before was but like the rest, of wood'.[1025] The earliest dated brick building in Stafford is *The Swan* of c.1667. In Wolverhampton John Leveson built 'The Great Hall' in the Elizabethan period but not until 1671 is there another clear reference to a brick building.[1026]

In Shrewsbury there were few early brick buildings until well after 1660. Nigel Baker has stated that, 'the earliest known brick house to survive is Rowley's Mansion of 1618 built by a prosperous brewer at one end of his substantial timber-framed commercial range. St Alkmund's Vicarage is probably of a similar date. A brick house adjacent to Rowleys Mansion may have been slightly earlier but was demolished as was Thorne's Hall of c.1630'.[1027] He concludes, 'brick

---

1022 Historical Mss. Commission, Portland Mss. II (1893), 308.
1023 Harris, M.D., ed. *The Coventry Leet Book,* Early English Text Society, (1907), 767.
1024 BLAC, MS1098/1/1/25.
1025 Thoroton **2**, 230-231.
1026 SRO, D593/f/1/6h is an undated building account of Richard Murchall who married in 1671.
1027 Baker, N., *Shrewsbury: An Archaeological Assessment of an English Border Town.* English Heritage, (2010), 71.

building became the norm for higher-status buildings around 1700, before that, as surviving examples and archaeological evidence show, most buildings were built of wood'.[1028] In Ludlow a town of stone and timber-framing, a 'Brick close' was recorded in 1596 but the next mention in the Corporation Minutes is in 1679.[1029]

Most towns and cities had a few examples of brick buildings but there were no large-scale developments. Leicester provides a good example of the hesitancy with which brick was adopted. It is recorded at the Greyfriars Church and precinct and later at the precinct wall at Leicester Abbey in c.1500. After this early evidence the first specific reference to brick is in 1587 but it was only used for a water conduit. In 1583 it had been agreed that 'no kilns be newe erected in the city' and in 1588 Valentine Wells was ordered to take down his kiln.[1030] There is reference to a 'Claypitt' in 1556 but no indication of its use.[1031]

The city was late in adopting brick, Evelyn called it the 'old and ragged city of Leicester, large and pleasantly seated but despicably built. The chimney flues like so many smiths' forges'.[1032] One exception was the 'bricke house' by the South Gate built in 1642 by the architect and property developer David Papillon.[1033] James Brome in 1694 described the city as 'Tis more venerable for its Antiquity than its comeliness, or present beauty'.[1034] Celia Fiennes in 1698, wrote that 'the town is old timber building except one or two of brick'. The first mention of brickmaking is in 1697 when land was leased for kilns and was significantly 'ground not fit for grazing'. Bricklaying first occurs in the in the Freemen's Register of 1696, when John Kirk was described as the son of Joshua Kirk, brickmaker. After Joshua Kirk, a few brickmakers appear in the Freemen's Register, for example Edward White who was registered in 1702. The scarcity of early references would suggest that brick building was not extensive before the end of the seventeenth century.

The earliest significant brick buildings were probably the newly refaced Castle and the 'Great Meeting', the joint chapel of the Presbyterians and

---

1028 Ibid., 68.
1029 Roberts, *Ludlow*.
1030 *RBL*, **III**, 241, 288, 318.
1031 *RBL*, **III**, 85.
1032 Evelyn, Vol. 1, 294.
1033 Airs, 5.
1034 Brome, J., *Travels over England, Scotland and Wales*, 2nd ed. (1707), 66.

Independents of 1708. As the population rose in the early eighteenth century, by 20% between 1670 and 1712 and by a further 2,000 to 8,000 by 1730, brick building became more extensive. Responding to population pressure in 1720, the Common Hall expressed a wish to build 'convenient small tenements'.[1035] A brickyard was recorded in 1715 and in 1741 a group of kilns is shown on Robert's map of the city.[1036]

There is little evidence of extensive improvement in the Midland towns until after 1660. Total urban populations grew absolutely and relatively between 1520 and 1700. E.A. Wrigley has calculated that 5.5% of the English population lived in towns c.1520 and 17% in 1700.[1037] Thus the town in the late seventeenth and early eighteenth centuries provided an expanding economic, social and cultural context for the diffusion of brick. Malcolm Wanklyn believes that, 'Historians are increasingly coming to see the period 1660-1800 as one of urban prosperity in which towns grew in size and number and in which the percentage of populations living in towns also increased'.[1038] The fortunes of individual towns varied a great deal and any generalisation is difficult, but there is agreement that many towns which were in the mainstream of Midland commercial, industrial and social development during this period experienced significant and visually obvious alterations to their townscapes. For McInnes, the period from 1660 to 1760 was marked by 'vitality and major movement'.[1039]

Measuring the degree to which such 'vitality' is reflected in the use of brick is a difficult task. Derby, for example, has about six or seven surviving brick houses of the seventeenth century. Does this reflect a city in which brick was popular or the survival of odd rarities? Celia Fiennes in 1698 described the city as 'built all of brick or for the most part'. Certainly, early brick-built buildings have been lost at 'The Manor House', Derby Gaol, Liversage Almshouses and Wilmot's Almshouses. George Bailey in 1879 recorded surviving seventeenth

---

1035 Thompson, 39.
1036 Simmons, J., *Leicester Past & Present,* **1**, *Ancient Borough,* Eyre Methuen, (1974), 100.
1037 Wrigley, E.A., 'Urban growth and Agricultural Change: England and the Continent in the Early Modern Period', in Rotberg. R.I., and Rabb, T.K., *Population and History,* Cambridge: CUP, (1986), 128.
1038 Wanklyn, M., 'Urban Revival in Early Modern England: Bridgnorth and the River Trade, 1660-1800', *Midland History,* **XVIII** (1993), 39.
1039 Borsay P., and McInnes, A., 'The Emergence of a Leisure Town: or an Urban Renaissance?' [Debate] *Past & Present,* **126** (1990), 202.

century brick houses in 'Tenant Street, Full Street, Bag Lane, Walker Lane, and St Peter's Churchyard'.[1040]

The Museum of Making in Derby holds a naïve and anonymous 'Prospect' of the town dated to 1725-45. Of significance is that, apart from a few stone buildings, all the other buildings shown are of brick making a brilliant red feature set in bright green fields. The painter ignored the reality of medieval timber and made the new silk mills the centre of the picture. Derby was unusual in publishing an early eighteenth-century newspaper whose advertisements may reflect the quality and materials of houses and other premises offered for sale. From the 1730s books which would enable the purchaser to calculate how many bricks were required for any size of building were regularly promoted, for example the Builders Guide of 1736 included, 'What Number of **Bricks** are required to **build** any Piece of Brickwork, from I to 14,000 Feet, and at any Thickneſs. What Number of **Bricks**, Lumps, or Clinkers laid flat or edgeways, or of paving Tiles …'

Most of the sales advertised in the *Derby Mercury* are for 'new brick-built' houses which suggests that these were the products of property developers, but their numbers suggests a relatively slow adoption rate. Between 1730-39 there were four advertisements of which only two were specific to Derby. In the next decade there were 46, of which 38 related to Derby, with others in Ashbourne, Repton and five in the new middle-class suburb of Chaddesden. An average of three brick houses were offered per year, except in 1745 when 16 were advertised. In that year the Jacobite army approached Derby, was this coincidence or panic?

Between 1750-59 there were 82 buildings advertised of which 64 were specific to Derby, although some are repetitions. They contain the first references to brick houses in Duffield Bank, another suburban middle-class area. Between 1712 and 1788 the population doubled to 8,563 with a consequent rise in the number of houses. In 1768 the Corporation promoted an Improvement Act which stipulated that purchasers were to, '… erect, build or cause to be erected … one or more dwelling houses handsome in front towards the publick street not less than three storeys high decently sasht'.[1041] Many of these were built along Friar Gate (then part of Nuns' Green). The

---

1040 Bailey, G., 'Notes on some old houses of Derby', 'Notes on some old houses in Derby' (continued) *DAJ*, **1** and **2**, (1879), (1880).
1041 House of Lords, HL/PO/PB/1/1768/8G3n98.

architect Joseph Pickford was involved in the purchase of at least five of these plots.

The high-quality eighteenth century town houses reflect Defoe's earlier view that the town was a 'Town of Gentry rather than Trade'. They display the typical features of Georgian architecture: sash windows, moulded stone cornices, classical doorcases with engaged columns, traceried fanlights and six-panelled doors. Stone was incorporated in plinths and quoins and curiously Nos. 59 and 60 Friar Gate have a stone course at eaves level forming a low parapet. At No. 93 stone was used to face the house although the side elevations are of red brick. The source of the brick was almost certainly from a brick kiln rented by the Rowe family from before 1725 and located on Nuns' Green. Richard Rowe the brickmaker was a man of some civic status being successively a freeman, one of the 'Brethren of the Corporation' and finally in 1742 a capital burgess. The area of his yard became Brick Street and the site of 'The Brick and Tile' public house. Between 1760-69 there were 72 advertisements of which only 19 refer to a 'brick house' in Derby but some are presumably brick such as 'well built Sashed House for Gentleman's family three stories high'. In the next decade there were 121 advertisements and increasingly the references are to a 'house' with the material unreported because brick was now implicit in the description of a new urban house.

One problem which arose from the brick terrace was that of the party wall – at least two agreements survive from Derby in which a house owner agreed to allow his neighbour the right to run his joists into the owner's wall. In 1715 Thomas Goodwin agreed to pay 1d p.a. for the right to place joists on the wall of Alexander Stanhope's mansion in Full Street.[1042] In other houses the fashionable and deeply overhanging hipped roof could irritate neighbours. In 1702 in Newport, it was agreed that 'Abraham Hadderton's eves next the said Richard Lowes are not to come over or hang above 4 ins from his wall perpendicular'.[1043]

In 1620 a royal proclamation declared that 'First floors not to be raised so as to need steps into the street'.[1044] By the eighteenth century this prohibition was ignored and the most fashionable urban brick houses were those set back from the road and raised above street level. Amongst many are Donegal (sic)

1042 DRO, D518/MT/545. See also D1955/2/133.
1043 SA, P207/V/6/1.
1044 Crawford, 6th July, 1620.

House, built by Francis Smith for the Lichfield merchant James Robinson, and later the town house of the Marquis of Donegall together with Beaumaris House, Newport (Salop) attributed to Smith on stylistic grounds and Vine House and Quarry House, both in Ashbourne. Many wealthy men 'of the middling sort' were willing to meet the demands of fashion by erecting large town houses incorporating fine details in essentially Palladian houses.

The well-established market town of Ashbourne provides a revealing example of the impact of fashion. It was sited in a traditional stone-building area, yet many of the domestic buildings of the town were rebuilt in the more expensive brick during the eighteenth century with Church Street and Market Place lined with large three storey Georgian houses. The rebuilding coincided with a period when Ashbourne became a fashionable social centre and achieved considerable repute as an adjunct to the Lichfield intellectual circle associated with Erasmus Darwin and Matthew Boulton. The turnpiking of the six main roads which served the town increased trade and two extensive and architecturally similar brick-built coaching inns, The Green Man and The Blackamoor's Head, were erected by rival competitors in c.1750.

An early significant brick building was the Mansion House of 1680. Its owner in 1763-5, the Rev. John Taylor, with an income of £7,000 p.a., employed the leading Derby architect, Joseph Pickford, to refront the house. He designed an octagonal drawing room to close the gap between the rear wings of the house and crowned it with an opulent copper dome.[1045] Immediately opposite, the owner of the stone-built Grey House, Brian Hodgson, also employed Pickford. The two houses are stylistically similar, but it may well be that the fashionable brick house was a competitive response to the Hodgson's apparently stone building.[1046] Recent observations by the author have revealed that the 'stone' house is in fact built of brick with a stone facing of approximately four to six inches (the house also has a very rare speaking tube built into the doorway).

High quality three-storey civic brick buildings were also erected at Smaldens Almshouses in 1723-4 and the wonderful Clergy Widows Almshouses of 1753 (although the rainwater hood is dated 1768) which were clearly influenced by the London Inns of Court. The popularity of brick was emphasised by a public

---

1045 Sadler, E.A., 'The Mansion', *DAJ*, **53**, (1932) 39-50. Sadler claims that the rebuilding was the work of Robert Adam. There is no evidence other than the coincidence that Adam was working at nearby Kedleston in 1761-63.

1046 Saunders, *Pickford*, 69.

house called 'The Sign of the Brick and Tile Mould', which was certainly in existence in 1760.[1047] Nearby Wirksworth lacked the social cachet of Ashbourne, but even here, in this stone-built village, there were occasional references to brick. In 1717 a mercer, John Alsop, left his wife 'the brick chamber' and in 1739 the King's Head was described as 'a good large brick house'.[1048]

A similar town to Ashbourne was Leek, the social and economic focal point of the Moorlands area. Here was a provincial centre of law, commerce and education where the pressures to conform to the social and cultural mores were felt equally strongly. Leek was a town of stone buildings and continued that tradition with important civic buildings, such as the Vicarage of 1714 and the Grammar School of 1723. Yet from the period 1700-1760 there have survived 13 brick buildings most of which were sited in the Market Place or in Derby Street, the two most socially prestigious streets.[1049] Stone continued to be used in the villages around Leek until well into the nineteenth century. The choice of brick in Leek was not therefore the result of a price advantage or the loss of masonry skills but was based mainly on social grounds, on the impression the owners wished to make. Similarly in Rutland, where almost all buildings were of stone, bricks were made in the two largest towns, Oakham and Uppingham at the end of the seventeenth century.

The most attractive and well-presented Midland town was Nottingham, in the 1530s Leland described it as, 'was both a large town welle builded for tymber and plaister'. By the end of the seventeenth century, it had developed into an elegant town filled with fine brick townhouses some with generous gardens. In 1690 Thomas Baskerville in his *Travels* described Nottingham as, 'Paradise restored, for here you find large streets, fair built houses, fine women, and many coaches rattling about, and their shops full of merchantable goods'. Celia Fiennes noted in her only reference to brick manufacture in England that 'They make brick and tile by the town'.[1050] Defoe, in the 1720s, wrote

---

1047 *Derby Mercury,* 20th June 1760.
1048 Dack, C.A., 'Urbanisation and the Middling Sorts in Derbyshire Market Towns: Ashbourne and Wirksworth, 1660-1830', PhD. University of Leicester, (2010). *Derby Mercury*, 16th August 1739.
1049 Staffordshire Moorlands District Council, *List of Buildings,* **1.** The most prestigious of the brick houses, 10, Derby Street, of 1760, 'displays a provincial uncertainty of brick in a stone area by having stone mullion and transom windows at the lowest level'. The brick may have been supplied from the kiln whose accounts describe it as standing at Meerbrook. The exact site of the kiln is unknown but there is a Red Earth Farm at SJ 972592.
1050 Fiennes, 88.

that 'Nottingham is one of the most pleasant and beautiful towns in England … I might enter into a long description of all the modern buildings lately erected in Nottingham'. Dr Pococke recorded in the 1750s that 'Nottingham begins to be much frequented by gentlemen, some who retire to it from their country houses, others who have left over trade, and many gentlemen of the neighbourhood have houses here for the winter'. To enhanced municipal buildings, such as the Exchange of 1723, the Town Hall rebuilt in 1744 and the Shire Hall rebuilt in the 1770s, new public buildings were also added, including the Assembly Rooms, the Racecourse Grandstand and a new Hospital built on Castle Hill, (1781-82).

Many high-quality brick townhouses added to the attractiveness of the town amongst which are Pierrepoint House, (1657, 23 hearths), Newdigate House, (1674, 12 hearths), County House, (1726), Abigail Gawthern's House, (1723), Willoughby House, (1738) and Morley House, (1750).[1051] As in Derby and Ashbourne, new or renamed public houses reflect the increase in workers in brick and building craftsmen. In Nottingham in 1761 amongst 137 separate licensed premises were the 'Plaisterers Arms' and the 'Trowell and Brush'.[1052]

The Brick Church

In many communities the dominant building both physically and spiritually was the parish church. To rebuild or encase the medieval church in brick was both a statement of the regard in which this material was held and a reflection of its cheapness relative to stone. In major towns such as Nottingham or Birmingham, centrally situated brick churches reflected a continuity of brick building within the town, but in some villages brick churches were often one of very few brick buildings and thus served as an encouragement for others who sought to improve or rebuild. Where influential landowners had built imposing brick mansions the estate was often completed with a brick-built church. At Castle Bromwich, the timber-framed church was encased in brick in 1726 to make it uniform with the Hall and its many outbuildings, similarly at Aston Hall (Salop) a brick chapel was built in 1742.[1053]

1051 Smith, P., Historic Buildings Report, *Sherwin House and the Townhouses of Nottingham in the Seventeenth and Eighteenth Centuries.* English Heritage, (rev. 2008), 6.
1052 *NBR,* **VII**, 17.
1053 Aston Hall, three miles S.E. of Oswestry.

The rapid rise in population placed great pressure on the original mother churches. As early as 1700 an elaborate brick chapel was built, probably to the designs of Sir William Wilson, in Hall Green, near Birmingham. Job Marston left £1,000 to build 'a handsome, convenient, firm and durable chappel for the cicumjacent inhabitants who live at a great distance from their parish church'.[1054] In the rapidly expanding Black Country there was even greater demand for new churches and chapels. In Wolverhampton there was considerable dispute between St Peter's Church and the demands of the outlying industrial settlements for freedom from marriage, funeral and other fees. Encouraged by Dean Penniston Booth, a brick chapel was erected in Wednesfield in 1746 through community subscription. The near-derelict, timber-framed St Giles at Willenhall was replaced in 1751 by a utilitarian brick chapel and in 1753 a chapel was built in Bilston.

By the eighteenth century many medieval churches were in a poor condition and required consequent rebuilding and repair, for example at Scalford the complete tower was rebuilt in 1639. At Hampton-in-Arden the church carried a tall spire, 'till by the extraordinary violence of Lightning and Thunder, hapning on St Andrew's day at night, in the year 1643, it was cloven, and fell to the ground, at which time the whole fabrick, with the tower, were torn in divers places'.[1055] The Quarter Sessions ordered that repairs 'shall not be done in winter nor shall the inhabitants be enforced to build a high steeple'.[1056]

Other major damage was recorded at East Retford, St Mary in Arden (Market Harborough), Edingley and Measham. The scale of such disasters is difficult to determine but the registers of Burton Fleming Church in Yorkshire contain an unusually detailed list of national appeals for donations for church repairs. Between 1711 and 1737, 295 'briefs' were received of which 130 were for churches, of these, 12 were in Staffordshire and ten in Derbyshire. In Leicestershire between 1660 and 1784, 32 Briefs were issued for 'Repair' of churches, all required more than £1,000.[1057] In most cases the cries of distress

---

1054 Whitehead, D., 'Job Marston's Chapel', *Georgian Group Journal*, **II**, (1992), 79.

1055 Dugdale W., *Antiquities of Warwickshire*, (1656), 700.

1056 Ratcliffe, S.C., and Johnson, R.C., eds. *Warwick County Records, Sessions Order Book, 1650-1657,* **III**, (1937), 134.

1057 Fletcher, W.D.G., 'Leicestershire Church Briefs', *Trans, Leicestershire Architectural and Archaeological Society,* (1896) 387-390.

fell upon deaf ears.[1058] Such briefs are further evidence of the poor state of so many churches and the consequent opportunities provided for repair in the much cheaper material of brick. In 1733 an appeal to the Staffordshire Quarter Sessions described Baswich parish church:

> … that the steeple thereof is a very high one too heavy for the foundations being in thickness but seven inches which has nothing to hold it together but some few cramps of iron which cannot possibly hold long, the cramps themselves being so loose that they may almost be plucked out with one finger, the walls of the body of the church are bulged of the foundation, the Timber of the roof so rotted at both ends … must be pulled down and rebuilt the Charge wherof will amount unto the sum of one thousand six hundred and ninety five pounds twelve shillings and one penny.[1059]

A 'brief' and probably a 'Pound Rate' on the parishioners provided the money for the rebuilding. The finances were supervised by Henry Dolphin 'cashier' who, in 1739, agreed with Richard Trubshaw and Richard Jackson 'Builders', 'to pull down and rebuild the church and steeple for £336' – considerably cheaper in brick than in stone![1060] The new contract was highly detailed in terms of dimensions, the quality of the lead used, stone ornaments and stage payments. Trubshaw and Jackson were contracted to finish by Christmas 1740 and '… they were to provide all Stone Brick & Tile Timber Iron Lead Lime Glass laths and nails'. How was this profitable for these builders? Almost certainly it was by possession of all the building materials of the old church. In 1808 when there was an unfulfilled plan to move the church, the estimate included 174 yards of brickwork at 340 bricks per yard, all the materials were valued at £277 6s 4d from a total estimate of £1,988 0s 9d. In 1753 Trubshaw had agreed to rebuild the church in the town of Stone, 'having ye old Materials & 20 Tun of Lead allowed me for £2,500', and where incidentally the foundations would require 111,000 bricks.[1061]

Where a church was apparently restored in stone, brick interior walls reduced the expense. In 1760-61 Okeover Church was, 'repair'd, rais'd and beautified' by

---

1058 Park, G.E., and Lumb, G.D., *The Registers of the Parish Church of Burton Fleming otherwise North Burton, 1538-1812*, (1899).
1059 SRO, D3361/5/3.
1060 SRO, D3361/2/1.
1061 SRO, MF115/1.

Leeke Okeover and his wife Mary. The detailed contract included 'to take the Old Battelments of and the Course which is beneath it … and to back the Stone with bricks as high as it will be wanted'.[1062] A particularly complete contract for the rebuilding of Sibson Church in 1723-4 emphasised the use of 'old stone' … 'but when the old stone is used up the inside … to be laid with brick'.[1063]

In some churches the tower or steeple, exposed to the weather, was the most eroded part and was reinforced with brick or totally rebuilt in brick. The earliest example may be Holy Rood Tower at Edwalton which Pevsner hesitantly ascribes to the mid-sixteenth century. Other examples are at Seighford (St) seventeenth century, Tythby, (N) Wychnor, (St), Bicton Chapel, (Sa) 1719, Chelmarsh, (Sa) 1720. At Barston, (W) the church was almost entirely rebuilt in brick in 1721 for £363 9s 2d and the Churchwardens' accounts contain the first reference to 'bricking up'.[1064] At Halston, (Sa) a red brick tower was added to a timber church in 1725 and brick additions or partial additions were added to towers at Cleobury North, (Sa), Great Bolas, (Sa) 1729, Gayton, (St) 1732 (of purple brick) and Walton-on-the-Wolds, (L) 1736-39.[1065]

Other churches completely or partially rebuilt in brick include Minsterley, (Sa) 1689, the north transept of Packwood, (W) 1704, the porch at Barrow, (Sa) 1705, Ryton, (Sa) 1710-20, Trusley, (D) 1713, Leighton, (Sa) 1714, Burslem, (St) 1717, Fitz, (Sa) 1722, Petton, (Sa) 1727, Twyford, (D) 1739, Stirchley, (Sa) 1740, Eyton-upon-the-Weald-Moors, (Sa) 1743, Farewell, (St) 1745, Marchington, (St) 1742, Longdon-upon-Tern, (Sa) 1742, Shareshill, (St) 1742, Eyton-upon-the-Weald-Moors, (Sa) 1743, Awsworth, (N) 1746, Whittington, (Sa) 1747, Snarestone, (L) 1752, the chancel at Worthen, (Sa) 1761 and Whittington (St) c.1761.[1066] At Moreton Say, (Sa) the medieval stone church was completely refaced in brick between 1769-1788 in exactly the same way as were many houses. At Eastwood, (N) the near derelict parish

---

1062 DRO, D231M/E177.

1063 Friedman, T., 'High and Bold Structures, A Georgian Steeple Sampler', *Georgian Group Journal*, **1**, (1991), 19.

1064 WRO, DR(B) 46/140.

1065 For the rebuilding of Great Bolas church there survives a wonderful collection of the most detailed accounts which reveal how the whole community participated in raising money, collecting materials and supporting the craftsmen. Fletcher, W.D.G., 'The Building of the Church of Great Bolas, 1726-1729, *TSalopAS*. **43 pt2**, (1926), 222-231.

1066 It has been suggested that the bells sound sweeter in brick towers, Blyth, R., *Akenfield*, Penguin, (1999), 75. Akenfield is based on the Suffolk village of Charsfield whose church has a brick tower.

church was rebuilt in brick in 1764, poorly financed and slightly built it collapsed in 1854. In West Stockwith, (N) an inland port and shipbuilding settlement, a retired shipbuilder, William Huntington, on his death left £740 to build a chapel (later the parish church) and ten almshouses. Built entirely in cheap brick in 1722 for less than £300, a simple and most attractive oblong forms both nave and chancel. At Saxby (L) the mortuary chapel was rebuilt in brick as the parish church in 1775 by the Earl of Scarborough.

One of the explanations for the relative cheapness of churches rebuilt in brick was the ability of the builders to use the original foundations. Where these were not available then the outlay was higher, at Wolverhampton the new and illegal Catholic chapel of Giffard House (later St Peter and St Paul) erected in 1728-29 in total cost £1,069 2s 2½d. This chapel which was hidden under a 'great new house' required 164,547 common bricks and over 8,000 front bricks.[1067] A similar brick Catholic church, unobtrusively presented as a house was built in Yoxall in 1794 following the Catholic Relief Act of 1791.

Nonconformist Chapels

Many nonconformist meetings were held in the houses of licensed preachers, in barns or in outbuildings built of cheap brick. In 1717 Edward Elwall wrote to Earl Gower about a barn built on the waste, 'I am the Presbyterian who built ye Barn near the Town which is now said to be my Lords land'.[1068] Gradually as congregations expanded small brick meeting-houses began to be built, adding not just to the religious landscape but also making a new physical feature in the town and village environment. Under the Toleration Act of 1689 all dissenting meeting houses had to be registered with the Quarter Sessions.

In Staffordshire a 'list of teachers and meeting houses in Staffordshire 1693' registered 58 buildings.[1069] Typical was a house occupied by Simon Jess in Burton-on-Trent, which was converted into a meetinghouse in 1699. Unfortunately, the list does not indicate which of the buildings were newly erected. In Warwickshire an incomplete list of meeting houses registered at the Warwickshire and Coventry Quarter sessions between 1689 and 1750

1067 SRO, DRO/634.
1068 SRO, D593/P/16/1/10.
1069 Atherton, I., 'The Early Registration of Dissenters' Meeting Houses in late Seventeenth-Century Staffordshire', *Staffordshire Studies* **11**, (1999), 51-68. The list is not complete at least 7 houses were omitted.

recorded 154 buildings, of these 13 were described as 'newly' or 'lately' built, and as 'houses', they were almost certainly of brick for most communities were poor.[1070] In Leicester the oldest complete surviving brick building is the Unitarian chapel of 1708. In the county the earliest chapel was probably Bardon Park registered in 1702 but listed by John Nichols in 1694.[1071] Early brick Baptist chapels were also built at Arnesby in 1702, Foxton in 1716 and Barton-in-the-Beans in 1745. Other Baptist chapels were opened in 1735 at Alcester and at Kirkby Woodhouse in 1754. In Rutland, a county of stone, the earliest purpose-built Presbyterian chapel in Oakham was built of brick in 1727. The first exclusive Quaker meeting house in Leicestershire was erected in Wigston Magna in 1677-8, other were at Mansfield in 1702 and at Wishaw in 1724. At Wigston the Presbyterian Chapel was built in 1732 at a cost of £234 7s 6d, a sum which suggests that it was not too restrained or austere.[1072] The Presbyterians were generally regarded as the most prosperous of the dissenting faiths and did not share the Quakers favouring of 'plainness'. Without Christian symbols or furnishings and requiring only a meeting room, simple Quaker buildings were often, before the 1689 Act, erected in a domestic idiom to hide their real purpose. An extensive Moravian Settlement was founded in Ockbrook, near Derby, in the years after 1751. All the buildings including the Chapel, the Brethren's House and the Sisters' House were built of locally produced brick. The Moravians were disliked intensely by some traditional villagers and their hostility was reflected in various attempts to sabotage and divert brick supplies intended for the Chapel.[1073] Following the Declaration of Indulgence of 1687, a Franciscan chapel and priest's house was erected in Masshouse Lane, Birmingham, from bricks costing £15. These were supplied by George Fentham a devout Protestant of whom it was said that his principles never got in the way of a good deal. The Chapel was burnt down in 1689.

1070 Johnson, H.C., ed. *Warwick County Records, Proceedings in Quarter Sessions, 1682-1690,* **VIII**, (1953), lxix-cxxxviii.

1071 Wykes, D.L., 'Bardon Park Meeting House; The Registration of Nonconformist places of worship under the Toleration Act (1689)'. *TLHAS,* **64**, (1990), 31.

1072 Royal Commission on the Historical Monuments of England, Nonconformist Chapels and Meeting-houses in Central England, London, (1986), 133.

1073 Martin R.H., 'John Ockershausen's Ockbrook Diary: the First Three Years of a Derbyshire Moravian Community 170-1753', *Transactions of the Moravian Historical Society,* **29**, (1996), 1-22.

The Parsonage

The Georgian brick parsonage is almost a landscape cliché as in many counties the parsonage was rebuilt, often in brick, as financial support became increasingly available. Queen Anne's Bounty was a scheme established in 1704 to augment the incomes of the poorer clergy of the Church of England. Eventually, Queen Anne's Bounty, along with a number of other forms of assistance to poor livings, provided an increased income that could be invested in improved accommodation. Rolleston Vicarage for example, in 1698, was described as 'ancient with kitchen adjoining' and of five bays, but by 1714 was 'handsome made of brick' with many outbuildings, a brick court, and a 'fine necessary house'. Madeley Vicarage had three bays in 1600, two bays in 1699 and was rebuilt in brick in 1716. It was described in 1781 as 'much better' than the average parsonage.[1074] At Church Eaton the rector was licensed to rebuild the parsonage in 1712, a single-storey hall only nine feet from the ground was reconstructed in brick as a two-storey symmetrical building.

Initially the livings to be augmented were selected by lot from those with an annual income of less than £10 or those where a donation by a third party was offered conditional upon augmentation by Bounty funds. There was enormous variety in the size and quality of parsonages. At Plumtree, for example, the rectory in 1674 was assessed at ten hearths, as large as many aristocratic or gentry houses. Kingswinford in 1638 was 'a large and ancient dwelling house with a barn and other necessary buildings' which in 1698 was described as '10 bays'. Others were small and squalid particularly if they were curacies. At Gayton in 1682 the churchwardens reported 'our old parsonage house is downe but there is a house in being which our Minster lives in'. At Whatton in 1743 the incumbent informed Archbishop Herring's Visitation that 'the reason for my Non-Residence is because the Vicarage is not fit for any Clergyman to live in'.[1075] At Warsop 'the Parsonage House is not yet thoroughly repaired',[1076] and in Staunton the rector admitted, 'I do reside personally in my Parsonage House. And my Annual Expences Therein only exceed by much my income as Rector'.[1077]

1074 *VCH, Salop*, **11**, (1985), 59.
1075 Ollard, S.L., and Walker, P.C., *Archbishop Herring's Visitation Returns, 1743*. Cambridge, (2013), 162.
1076 Ibid., 168.
1077 Ibid., 136.

The value of livings varied considerably. In Derbyshire in 1772 more than 70% of the livings were valued at less than £50. In Leicestershire parishes with glebe of less than 12 acres were also valued at £50, but here the average glebe was 40 acres.[1078] Rosemary Lucas in her study of the 'Parsonage Houses in the Derby Deanery' concluded that in the eighteenth century there was little change with only three houses completely rebuilt two of which were by incumbents with access to financial support and one by a patron for his own ends. Gilbert Mitchell of Breadsall married a member of the landholding Dixie family, Henry Cantrell of Derby St Alkmunds had a wealthy benefactor and Kedleston was replaced by the estate owner. Substantial improvements in brick were also made to Ockbrook and Spondon.[1079]

In other wealthier areas there was considerable rebuilding which was financed by personally prosperous incumbents, loans, support from the patrons and income from investments derived from Queen Anne's Bounty. Mortgages remained stable throughout the eighteenth century at about 4-5% and at that level were an incentive to borrow capital. At Wymeswold in 1737 the parish register recorded the purchase by the vicar, of 29 acres of land 'for the augmentation of the vicarage', the money advanced was £200 from Queen Anne's Bounty, £50 from a fund left by a previous vicar of Wilford, £20 from Trinity College and the rest from local clergy and gentry. In Hoby, Leics, in 1703 the Parsonage house was 'entirely new built in Brick with blew tiles at the sole expense of Richard Cox Master of Arts, the then rector'.[1080] At Southwell an extract from the glebe terrier of 1764 notes that, 'Our Church is at this time rebuilding by the charity of a Brief and the Chancel by our Rector, both with brick'.[1081] Richard Hill of Attingham, in his will of 1725, gave £200 to Eton College for 'augmentation of poorest vicarage or curacy'.[1082]

In terms of the adoption of brick the importance of the parsonages was that they served as exemplars, for men of substance, education and social standing had deliberately chosen to build in brick. The result was a general

---

1078 Jacob, W.M., *The Clerical Profession in the Long Eighteenth Century, 1680-1840*, Oxford, (2007), 122, 124.
1079 Lucas, R., 'Parsonage Houses in the Derby Deanery during the Seventeenth to Nineteenth Centuries: part 2', *Derbyshire Miscellany,* **12**, (1991), 133-138.
1080 Hoby Church glebe terrier, 1730, transcribed Ellis, C., *Hoby and District Local History Society,* (2014).
1081 Southwell and Nottingham Church History Project, Eastwood St Mary.
1082 SA, 112/1/1866.

improvement in their quality. James Bickham, the Archdeacon of Leicester, inspected 123 parsonage houses between 1773 and 1779, he found five houses in 'extremely good repair', two in 'excellent repair', 20 in 'good repair', 14 in need of repair or rebuilding, and two as 'ruinous'.[1083]

Almshouses

Poverty, infirmity and old age were major social problems in Tudor and Stuart society. The government attempted to deal with the problem of providing relief for the needy poor by various Acts which essentially made the parish responsible for outdoor relief and by outlining a range of punishments for those who did not genuinely need assistance. Many philanthropists appear to have recognized that the dissolution of monastic institutions had removed the long-established basis for the support of the needy. In many parishes additional support was offered through the building of almshouses and in the sixteenth and seventeenth centuries their number expanded considerably. In Warwickshire there were seven in 1550, 14 in 1600 and 21 by 1670 with a rise of 131% in the number of inhabitants.[1084] The pace of expansion slowed with Knatchbull's Act or The Workhouse Test Act of 1723 which allowed groups of parishes to set up workhouses and encouraged a degree of compulsion or incarceration for the needy.

Inspired by their monastic origins, many seventeenth century almshouses were often built as small individual buildings arranged in a terrace or courtyard. Because they were physically related to each other, perhaps by a common corridor, they were architecturally different from most other buildings in towns and villages.[1085] Built by men and women of substance, some were generously equipped, others were small and required considerable personal and communal discipline. Many foundations incorporated the name of the patron, a constant reminder to the inhabitants and the community of his or her generosity.

Typical of the well-supported almshouse was that of Nicholas Eyffler built in Warwick of brick and stone in 1597 at a cost of £72 5s 2d. Bess

---

1083 Jacobs, 155.

1084 Nicholls, A., *Almshouses in Early Modern England: Charitable Housing in the Mixed Economy*, Woodbridge (2017), 45.

1085 Hussey, D., and Ponsonby M., *The Single Homemaker and Material Culture in the Long Eighteenth Century*, Abingdon, (2016), 183-4.

of Hardwick, Countess of Shrewsbury, built a Derby almshouse in stone as befitted her rank but most Midland almshouses were brick-built, beginning with St John's, 1495 and Dr Milley's, 1503, in Lichfield. Others included Wilmot's 'Black Hospital' in Derby of 1638, in Nottingham a brickmaker, John Patten, founded a small almshouse in 1651,[1086] Sloswicke's Hospital, East Retford 1657, Sir Martin Noel's almshouse at Stafford, 1660, Dorrel's Hospital, West Retford, 1666, Thomas Guy's, almshouses, Tamworth 1678, Sir John Port's almshouses, Etwall, founded in 1557 and rebuilt in 1681-90 and George Willoughby's Hospital of 1685. These and many others brought brick into the community to be recognized as a socially acceptable material, for no benefactor would wish to be associated with poor quality buildings. Their cost was often high – at Abbots Bromley the initial accounts included 60,500 bricks for a total of £115 19s 11d.[1087] A later set of accounts personally maintained by Lambard Bagot for 1703-7 gives a total of £250 plus £70 for a replacement house for 'Widdow Wigon' whose original home had been demolished to provide a long and prominent High St. frontage.[1088] Amongst the grandest of these institutions was the Hospital at Preston-on-the-Weald-Moors, believed by Pevsner to be 'a most spectacular example of Georgian almshouse architecture'. Erected in 1725 for 20 women and 20 girls at a cost c.£7,000, it was built in brick in the style of Gibbs with elaborate giant pilasters, a huge doorway and sophisticated decorations around three sides of a huge quadrangle. Such almshouses brought colour and novelty, making a vivid contribution to the streetscape. Their costs proved a strong recommendation of purpose and material.

Residents, parishes and their charities frequently built cottages for the poor, a typical example is that in the will of Thomas Levinge of Parwich who in 1639 recorded that there are 'many poore Women in Parwich which lacke maintenance and neighbours are straite handed towards them and the rest of the poore there And that I have built two little houses in lencliffe Croft for two poore Women to dwell in'.[1089] Margaret Spufford has suggested that it was only in the late seventeenth century that permanent cottage accommodation

---

1086 Deering, 140.
1087 SRO, D4038/F/3.
1088 SRO, D4038/D/3.
1089 Cox, C.J., 'The Wolley Manuscripts No. 11, An Analysis of Volumes Six to Ten', *DAJ*, **34**, (1912), 94-97. See also SRO, D591/5/2.

was built that survived more than a couple of generations. She suggests that the increasing use of brick for cottages made structures more permanent.[1090]

For the poor who were maintained in their own cottages brick was often provided, usually in small quantities and probably for small-scale repairs. The Shifnal 'Town and Parish Book' maintained by the Churchwardens between 1672 and 1723, includes the purchase of 200 bricks in 1689 and 50 in 1704.[1091] The Gnosall 'Overseers of the Poor Account' of 1714 similarly includes the payment of 3s 'For carrying brick for mittens house'. At Hatton in 1736 the churchwardens built a house 'of 1 bay', at a price of £8 for Thomas Granger who had to pay twice yearly towards the cost.[1092]

The Toll House

The early eighteenth century saw the first major investment in the transport infrastructure as trusts enabled the first of a wave of turnpike roads and bridges to be built. A new and mainly brick building in the landscape was the toll house. Between 1750 and 1780 a particularly dense network of turnpike roads was established in the Midlands as this area began rapidly to industrialise. Before 1780 at least 206 trusts were established and, assuming a toll house at each 'bar', then at least 750 were built. Most were built outside urban areas and hundreds of them dotted the Midland countryside, bringing a splash of colour to the landscape. They were usually small, single-storeyed with a bay or octagonal end from which to aid the observation of travellers. Often isolated and prominently sited, most early houses were of brick and of a higher standard than local vernacular architecture. Their cost is suggested in the Nottingham-Newhaven accounts of 1759, 'house and Gate will cost £55 00'.[1093] The following table lists the number of trusts, their longest road and the total in each county.

1090 Spufford, M., *The Great Reclothing of Rural England: Petty Chapmen and Their Wares in the Seventeenth Century,* History Series, **33**, (1984), 1-3.
1091 SRO, 641/3/K/2/5.
1092 WRO, DR0123/2.
1093 Johnson, R., 'The Nottingham-Newhaven Turnpike Road', *Derbyshire Miscellany,* **5, pt 1**, (1969), 7.

Table 15: Midland Turnpike Trusts before 1780[1094]

County	Acts, before 1780	Longest Road	No. of 'bars' per county
Derbyshire	30	Chesterfield-Hernstone Lane, 1758, 58 miles, 11 'bars'	124
Leicestershire	27	Bridgeford Lane, Kettering, 1754, 47 miles, 3 'bars'	89
Nottinghamshire	20	Bawtry Bridge-Hainton, 1765, 41 miles, 6 'bars'	63
Shropshire	52	Ludlow and branches, 1756, 103 miles, 14 'bars'	220
Staffordshire	49	Lichfield, 1728, 50 miles, 'bars' not recorded Tamworth-Green Man, 1770, 40 miles, 10 'bars'	194
Warwickshire	28	Birmingham, Warwick, Warmington, 1725, 36 miles, 8 'bars'	98

In summary most brick buildings of the sixteenth and seventeenth centuries were rural high-quality houses and after 1660 substantial numbers of newcomers permeated landed society buying small or medium estates and often gracing their lands with brick halls and manor houses. The scale of change was slow but gradually brick became the material employed for new buildings or the refacing of older houses. One element of this expansion was in the range of buildings and its use in institutional buildings such as churches, chapels, almshouses and turnpike toll houses, all these collectively enhanced the visual impact of brick.

Capability Brown considered buildings to be the cornerstone that defined the character of the landscape. In this sense brick brought new elements to the scenery of town and countryside. It offered prominent features and variety, but above all it brought vivid colour to a drab landscape. Modest red brick

---

1094 Turnpike Roads in England and Wales, *www.turnpikes.org.com*

vernacular became part of the Midland landscape. The increase in hard and constructed elements contributed to a landscape which was perceived and valued not just for the comfort and convenience it brought but also for the social message it delivered. Brick provided a setting in which people could experience new relationships with place and community.

Chapter 14

THE INDUSTRIAL AND HORTICULTURAL USE OF BRICK

IN THE seventeenth and eighteenth centuries many industries expanded and modified their processes using specialist bricks. In the iron industry, for example, the increase in the number of forges, the advent of the blast furnace and the coke-consuming furnace all demanded larger and more secure buildings. Brick increasingly replaced timber in traditional industrial buildings such as the timber-framed water mills which gradually gave way to brick-built structures. In the Tame valley a lease of Old Forge Mill in 1714 from John Shelton, Lord of the Manor of West Bromwich, to Richard Geast included as an allowance for maintenance and repairs the 'liberty to get, dig, take or use stones, land or clay from the common of the said Manor of West Bromwich for the doing and making of bricks' and 'liberty to fetch pitcoles gratis at the colepits of the said John Shelton'.[1095] However, this was limited to the 'burning of four clamps of bricks', sufficient for the rebuilding of the Mill but too small for a commercial enterprise. At Wednesbury Forge the timber-framed wheel pits and tailrace were rebuilt in brick in 1678 by their new owners the Foley family.[1096]

The traditional image of the early Industrial Revolution is one of coal, steam and iron. It is a dramatic picture, but rarely does it include the crucial importance of the refractory brick. Many historians have emphasised the growth rates in the production of manufactured goods and natural materials, but few

---
1095 Dilworth, 40.
1096 Belford, P., 'Five Centuries of Iron-Working at Wednesbury Forge', *Post-Medieval Archaeology*, **44/1**, (2010), 12-13.

have even mentioned that such expansion was based on those ovens and kilns able to withstand the necessary high temperatures. It is not an exaggeration to suggest that there would not have been an 'industrial revolution' without the support of the brick industry. An obvious example is the production of iron. This view was forcibly expressed by three prominent ironmasters, John Wilkinson, William Reynolds and the Earl of Dudley who, in their opposition to the Brick Tax of 1784, claimed that 'Ironworks maintained a vast demand for bricks'. By that date the widespread use of coal in blast furnaces and slightly later the introduction of Cort's puddling process had led to the enormous expansion of iron production.

Philip Riden has identified in the Midland counties 38 charcoal-fired blast furnaces in use after 1660, with each one (although not all working at the same time) producing at the least 200 to 300 tons per year.[1097] Most of the furnaces were built of stone but some, including the famous Coalbrookdale furnace initially built in 1658, were of brick.[1098] Reinhold Angerstein noted in Shropshire that 'the construction of the blast furnaces is the same as other British furnaces and stone for the hearth is procured from the Forest of Dean … in other places where this stone is not available Stourbridge brick is used instead but it only lasts about 3 months whereas the stone stands up for 2 years or more'.[1099]

The chronology of the change from refractory stone to firebrick for the construction and lining of furnaces is uncertain. A very early reference is the purchase of 'one hors loade' of 'fier clay' in 1702 for the Stapenhill brick kilns of Lord Paget.[1100] In 1712 the Treasury accounts for the Mint refer to 'hardened bricks to line the furnace' for gold smelting.[1101] Midland references would suggest its increasing use after 1715-20. For most furnaces the temperatures achieved were too high for common brick and the specialist 'kiln bricks' and 'furnace bricks' began to be recorded, for example, in the Giffard building accounts of 1720.[1102] 'Sturbridge brick' was recorded at

---

1097 Riden, P., *A Gazetteer of Charcoal-fired Blast Furnaces in Great Britain in use since 1660*, Chesterfield, (1993).
1098 The furnace lintel is painted 1638, but photographic evidence suggests the later date.
1099 Angerstein, 340.
1100 SRO, D603/F/3/1/22.
1101 Shaw, W.A., ed. 'Declared Accounts: Mint', *Calendar of Treasury Books*, **26**, 1712, London: (1954), CDXI-CDXVIII.
1102 SRO, D593/663/3.

Coalbrookdale by 1718.[1103] It is specifically mentioned in a 1725 mining lease to Humphrey Batchelor, a Stourbridge glassmaker, but not in an earlier one of 1709. Batchelor is named in the ironwork's accounts as the vendor of five tons of Stourbridge clay in 1720.[1104] Precisely how the Coalbrookdale Company used this material is not wholly clear. It was not the main lining of the hearth and boshes (the hottest part of the kiln) as hearth stones were obtained from Highley. It did not begin to manufacture its own firebricks until the 1750s.

Firebrick was considerably more expensive than common brick – in 1733 a lease of coal and ironstone bearing land at Lightmoor included royalties of 1s per 1,000 for ordinary brick and 3d per dozen for firebrick (21s per 1,000). The recipients, the Ferriday family, were probably exploiting the white fireclays of the Middle Coal Measures.[1105] In 1739 the Old Side Works was opened in Amblecote by Harris and Pearson on land owned by the Earl of Stamford and Warrington, a member of the Grey family who had been builders of very early brick houses at Bradgate and Enville. This works appears to be the first recorded example of a large purpose-built firebrick workshop in the area.[1106]

Basic fireclay contains two mutually insoluble components, silica and alumina and the solidus (a curve in a graph of the temperature and composition of a mixture below which the substance is entirely solid) in natural fireclay is 1,587+/-10°C which is only just above the melting point of iron at 1,538°C.[1107] Firebrick which contain both silica and significantly more than 25% alumina can withstand blast furnace temperatures up to 1,775°C. Stourbridge fireclay at the 'Old Mine' had between 25-40% alumina content. In the Severn valley at Broseley the red clay was analysed at 61.1% silica and 21.7% alumina and it too produced an extremely hard brick. Records show its employment at the Horsehay blast furnace between 1754 and 1756.[1108] In 1782 Samuel Butler reported that they also make there a kind of bricks which, 'when once sufficiently hardened by the fire will endure the most intense heat'.[1109] These were fortunate discoveries, for other local fireclays for example

---

1103 SA, 6001/17/329.
1104 King, P., *The Iron Trade in England and Wales 1500-1815: the charcoal iron industry and its transition to coke:* Ph.D. Thesis, Wolverhampton University (2003), 56-57.
1105 SA, 1681/183/2.
1106 Harris and Pearson Company History.
1107 Claughton, P., 'Clay Mining Framework', **pt 2 v2**, (2012), 129.
1108 Randall, J., *The Clay Industries,* Madeley, (1877), 9. *VCH, Salop* **10**, 257-293.
1109 Quoted in Hudson, *Broseley,* 41.

at Nuneaton, Tamworth, Swadlincote and east of the Erewash valley are not highly refractory.[1110] At Newhaven in the Peak District, where fireclay was quarried for the lead smelters at Whiston, it was presumably of poor quality for 'the mine was a prodigious consumer of them' (bricks).[1111] The hardness of fireclay-produced brick and its potential for the export trade was suggested in a letter of June, 1764 from Johan Cahman, of Stockholm, to Mr Francis Floyde, care of Mr Downing, Little Dawley, Shropshire, which engaged Floyde to go to Gothenburg to erect an air-furnace, 'He must bring all the necessary utensils, and the Windsor bricks (high quality facing bricks) and mortar. He must also know how to prepare the mortar, as there are no ingenious workmen in Sweden, and no brick or stone that will stand the heat'.[1112]

Firebricks were obviously important in the production of iron because several days later the Government banned the export of both bricks and iron technology. The author has been unable to find examples of firebrick used for domestic building in the eighteenth century but a century later this yellow and golden brick was commonly employed.

The earliest furnaces in England to produce steel by the cementation process were built at Coalbrookdale c.1645 with the kilns built of stone and perhaps with brick linings.[1113] Only 40 years later, Plot in 1684, described a steel producing furnace at Bromley, near Kingswinford, as 'a round *Oven* built of brick, not unlike those used by *Bakers*'.[1114] The cementation process, based on brick furnaces, became increasingly popular. A further two furnaces operated in Birmingham by John Kettle were established at the end of the seventeenth century, a 'furnace for converting of Iron into Steel' was built at Tern in Shropshire in 1712-13, while Westley's 1731 *Plan of Birmingham* shows a third furnace on the north side of the town, just a short distance from Kettle's works. By the 1730s there were at least five or six furnaces in the West Midlands.

Brick also contributed to the production of glass – glass kilns were built at Wollaton in 1615, Woore Hall Farm (Salop) and Bagot Park (Staffs), where

---

1110 Oldendorf, W., *Basics of Magnetic Resonance Imaging*, Springer US, (1988), 70-71.
1111 Porter, 43.
1112 *Calendar of Home Office Papers (George III) 1760-1765*, HMSO, (1878), 2 June, 1764, pcl 76, No. 43.
1113 Belford, P., and Ross, R.A., '17th Century Steelmaking in Coalbrookdale', *Historical Metallurgy*, **41 (2)**, (2007), 111.
1114 Plot, 374.

15 excavated glass-house sites, most dated to the sixteenth century, were built. They were mainly of stone but at all sites bricks were recorded. These bricks probably were used to build extensions to the furnace or walls which could be removed to withdraw the crucibles and may well date to the time when Flemish glassmakers were recruited.[1115] Not all glass kilns were specialist structures – a Nottingham deed of 1759, reciting deeds of 1683, describes a messuage in Carter Gate as 'formerly brick, pot and glass works'.[1116] (Defoe mentioned the glass houses of Nottingham 'of late rather decayed', this he attributed to the rise in tea drinking and the demand for tea pots and cups.)[1117]

After 1660 nationally there was an unprecedented demand for better quality flat glass for a variety of fashionable purposes, especially mirrors, coaches and sash-windows. According to Neve, by 1726 there were 13 different types of window glass regularly available in the market.[1118] The glass varied in quality, the most important centres of production being Newcastle and London. 'Staffordshire Glass' was of inferior quality, which Neve described as 'a sort of Glas but seldom used in these parts of the Kingdom'. To save wood supplies, an Act of 1615 required the glass industry to use mineral fuel, this resulted in rapid technological innovations.

By 1700 the coal-fired reverberatory furnace, where separate chambers separated the fuel and metal, had been perfected as a manufacturing process unique to this country. In the Midlands, as firing moved from wood-ash to the use of coal, the cone shaped glasshouse built of brick became an outstanding feature of the local industrial environment. The earliest Stourbridge cones have been dated to 1691 and 1692. A Glasshouse Lane was recorded in Nottingham in 1689 and Nathaniel and Samuel Buck's engraving of the city in 1743 shows one (possibly two) smoking cones in the east of the city.[1119]

The refractory quality of the brick was a key feature in the expansion of the pottery industry – during the late seventeenth and early eighteenth centuries the fundamental ideas of bottle kiln design were developed, and the basic

---

1115 Crossley, D.W., 'Glassmaking in Bagot's Park, Staffordshire in the sixteenth century', *Post-Medieval Archaeology,* **1**, (1967), 67-72. Linford P., and Welch C., 'Bagot's Park, Abbots Bromley Staffordshire 111', *Archaeomagnetic Dating Report,* (2002).

1116 NA, M/20789.

1117 Defoe, II, 145.

1118 Neve, 149-154.

1119 *NBR,* **V**, 356.

updraught and the 'hovel' were well established. In the hovel type kiln, the outer shell, a device for inducing natural updraught, was not subject to intense heat and therefore could be made of ordinary bricks. In 1755 Angerstein described such kilns at Hanley and Derby. Archaeologists have excavated an example at Albion Square, Hanley of 1690-1714, with an internal diameter of seven feet and an external diameter of 13 feet. Others have been revealed at the Pomona Pottery at Newcastle-under-Lyme of the 1720s and at Longton Hall of the 1750s. By the 1750s they were a familiar part of the Potteries' landscape. Dr Pococke noted, 'they bake 'em (earthenware pots) in kilns built in the shape of a cone … there being great numbers of them in all the county beyond Newcastle'.[1120] The bricks for the kilns may have been fired in Tunstall where Pococke recorded, 'they are famous for the best bricks and tiles.'[1121]

In the early eighteenth century, the process of conversion of kilns from wood burning to coal fired produced higher temperatures and demanded harder bricks for the linings. At temperatures not much higher than 1,000°C ordinary bricks become distressed and start to melt. Wedgwood was faced with this problem and his accounts and correspondence chart the debate over the practicalities of conversion. The demand for firebricks increased throughout the region and Angerstein noted that a brick even harder than that of Stourbridge and made from a very hard clay was used for 'furnace bricks' and came from just west of Crich in the Wirksworth area. This was particularly valuable in Derbyshire with its prolific iron works, lead smelting and potteries and where brick was replacing sandstone as furnace lining. In 1772 the Wirksworth China Works was re-established and amongst its few surviving records are six tickets, dated between September and October, for the combined purchase of 1546 'common Square fire Brick', 390 'keyed fire Brick' and 31 lbs of clay and slip clay which was probably used to seal the brick joints of a new kiln.[1122]

Brick formed the basis of several other types of kilns and as early as 1718 coal-fired kilns, commonly called 'hot houses', were erected in the Potteries to dry ball clay prior to its moulding and firing. They were eventually replaced by machines which used pressure to extract water. Brick was also used for the

---

1120 Pococke, 7.
1121 Ibid., 8, 257-293.
1122 DRO, D258/35/51/5.

small furnaces, typically 6 feet by 7 feet, used for the manufacture of red and white lead. Other furnaces included the muffle furnace, a modification of the updraught kiln, in which the wares were totally separated from the flame. One dating from 1660-90, used for clay pipe manufacture, has been excavated at Benthall, Salop.[1123] The reverberatory furnace, where again the product was isolated from the heat source, was traditionally employed in the lead and copper industries, but Joseph Moxon, in the 1703 edition of his *Mechanick Exercises*, includes its use in producing lime from flint in the context of house building.[1124]

In 1764, at the Ecton copper works of the Duke of Devonshire, £20 18s 6d was spent on bricks for a calcining furnace based on a Potteries style bottle oven.[1125] Between the years 1760 and 1790, bricks were required at the highly profitable copper works at Ecton, Wetton and Whiston in the Staffordshire Moorlands. Prior to 1786 common bricks were imported from local coal mines or fired at Whiston itself. One technique was to build the kiln in unburnt bricks and let them harden in the smelter. In 1779-80 the works were redeveloped; this involved the delivery of 126,500 bricks of which 12,000 were unburnt. The difficult terrain of North Staffordshire added to the delivery costs – in 1779 the carrier, Thomas Allcock, transported 27,500 bricks from Kingsley to Whiston (3-4 miles) at 7s per 1,000. Bricks continued to be measured in both volume and weight and in 1786 8½ tons of brick were sent from Whiston to the mine. In 1783 the building of a lead cupola furnace gives clear evidence of the sophistication of local brick production; the invoice was for 3,054 Circular bricks, 646 Narrow square, 412 Large square, 509 Arch bricks, 1,563 Furnace roofs, 213 Large flues and 639 Large keys.[1126]

Confusingly it has been claimed that the inventor of the firebrick was William Weston Young (1776-1847) who in 1822, working in South Wales, devised a method of 'building the whole furnace from a "silica firebrick," made with a 1% addition of lime, to bind the blue-grey "clay" of the Dinas rock. The idea being that the interior of the blast furnace would vitrify and be vastly more durable and ultimately economical than a mere veneer of silica within a comparatively fragile ceramic shell'. This was an exceptionally successful

---

1123 HER PRN 17219. There were probably many such furnaces all over the country.
1124 Moxon, J., *Mechanick Exercises, or, the Doctrine of Handy-Works applied to the ART of Bricklayers-works*, 3rd ed., London, (1703), 241.
1125 Porter, 108.
1126 Ibid., 43, 108, 131, 138-40, 146.

method of lining a furnace for which the company eventually became world-famous, but the term 'firebrick' suggesting a hardened brick was in use in the Midlands, Newcastle and South Lancashire for nearly a century earlier.[1127]

Before 1780 there were few large-scale industrial premises – the earliest brick-built factory was probably Cotchett's Silk Mill built by the engineer George Socorold in Derby in 1702, this measured 62 feet by 28 feet. Lombe's Silk Mill which replaced it in 1722 was more ambitious and of three storeys. The main requirement of the silk doublers and throwers was light, and the advantage of a brick walling was the ability of the builders to pierce the wall with windows, 'each storey had 51 windows to the East and the same to the West … these are but small sash windows, being only 3 feet 1 inches high and 20 inches broad, but being set regular cause the East and Wiest fronts to look beautiful. In total there were 468 windows'. William Hutton estimated the total cost at £30,000.[1128] In Shrewsbury in 1757 a lease at Cann Hall, Mill St., for 'two pieces of building for manufacture' gave their sizes as 77 feet by 16½ feet and 62 feet by 14 feet with 'good stone and brick'.[1129] The Derby mills had important consequences, for it was on Lombe's Silk Mill that later factory owners based their designs. It became the model for the factories erected by Arkwright and Strutt, and these were copied in all essential points, sometimes illegally ignoring patents, by other cotton manufacturers. Nationally by 1788 there were at least 340 mills built on the Arkwright pattern many of which were in Derbyshire and Nottinghamshire and based on the rivers Derwent, Amber, Wye and Noe.[1130] Their financial success encouraged other entrepreneurs and in 1786-7 the steward of the Shifnal Estate of Sir Edward Jeringham proposed converting the Shifnal Corn Mill into a 'manufactory' making 'Manchester' fustians', which would employ 1,000 people including children aged 4. The estimated cost was £3,160 which included £600 for wood.[1131]

The first cotton mill in England was built in Nottingham by Richard Arkwright in 1768 and powered by horses. At the end of the period under

---

1127 Scotland's Tile and Brick Industry, 'Early References to Firebrick Manufacture', www.scottishbrickhistory.co.uk
1128 Hutton, W., *The History of Derby*, (1791), 163.
1129 SA, 796/36.
1130 Chapman, S., 'Peter Nightingale, Richard Arkwright and the Derwent Valley Cotton Mills 1771-1818', *DAJ*, **133**, (2013), 166.
1131 SRO, D641/3/E/6/15/34.

review Arkwright's Haarlem Cotton Mill at Wirksworth (1777-81), was the first to be powered by a steam engine, although this did not power the machinery but actually pumped water to a water wheel. It had a stone ground floor but much lighter brick allowed for six further floors. The diarist Lord Torrington described it in 1791 as 'seven storeys high and filled with inhabitants … and when they are lighted up, look luminously beautiful'.[1132] Seven years earlier it had been painted by Joseph Wright, its windows all aglow, which was a sight never previously seen in rural England. Torrington decried the environmental impact of industrialisation but emphasised the impact of the mills in the colour they added to the new landscapes, 'these vales have lost all their beauties; and filled with inhabitants the rural cot has given way to the lofty red mills and the grand houses of the overseers; the streams perverted from its courses by sluices and aqueducts will no longer ripple and cascade'.[1133]

Of equal importance to the Cromford mills was Matthew Boulton's 'Manufactory' of 1762, 'a prime example of the factory as a country house' with a formal drive and the initial appearance of a landed estate, it had housing for 500 workers.[1134] Similarly Josiah Wedgwood built an industrial village all in brick at Etruria in 1768-1771, initially with workshops and forty-two workers' cottages. The cost of these houses averaged £45 with rents of between £2 and £3 per annum.[1135] Torrington again emphasised colour when he described Wedgwood's own Palladian mansion as 'staring red brick; as are many in the vicinage belonging to the principal traders'.[1136] The bricks for the enterprise were all locally made, presumably in the adjacent enclosure called 'Brick Kiln Field'. A small number of brick-built houses which combined domestic and workshop functions began to be erected from the mid-eighteenth century, such as the ribbon weavers' cottages at Longford near Coventry and the chainmakers' settlement at Mushroom Green.

Windmills in the form of the post mill were usually made of wood and their erection continued well into the late eighteenth century, for example at Cubbington c.1780, Fenny Compton in 1789 and at Claverdon as late as 1803.

1132 *Torrington Diaries*, **2**, 196.
1133 *Torrington*, **2**, 195.
1134 Tann, J., and Burton, A., *Mathew Boulton: Industry's Great Innovator,* History Press, (2013), 16.
1135 Wedgwood Archive, WMSS 28693-43, 'Expences of Building Dwelling Houses for Work Men'.
1136 *Torrington*, **3**, 111.

Their great advantage (like timber-framed houses) was that they could easily be dismantled and re-erected as at the Cat and Fiddle Mill at Dale Abbey in 1788 and at Sneinton in 1807. All the late post mills stood on brick piers while tower mills, based on a brick body, were more commonly early nineteenth century, although a very early example is mentioned in a Cheshire lease of 1677.[1137] A brick tower mill is shown on the Atherstone town map of 1716.[1138] Early brick examples were also erected at Albrighton in 1768, at East Bridgford in 1769, at Castle Donington in 1773, and at Leamington and Kenilworth in 1778.[1139]

Derbyshire, Nottinghamshire and Leicestershire were regarded as the premier 'malting counties' – in 1693 in the city of Derby alone there were 76 malthouses. Woolley wrote in 1712, 'the principal trade is that of malting, with which many good estates have been raised'.[1140] In 1673 Samuel Burrow sold a messuage in Friar Gate, Derby, 'with malt-houses, kiln-houses and other buildings belonging' for £275.[1141] As late as 1789, before Burton-on-Trent became pre-eminent, there were still 42 maltings in the city. In the county there were maltings at Ashbourne, Dale Abbey, Ilkeston, Long Eaton, Stoney Middleton, Matlock, Bull Bridge and Shardlow.[1142]

There was a close relationship between brickmaking and malting; beer brewing and brickmaking were complimentary trades for beer cannot be produced in the summer months and it was illegal to fire bricks in the winter. The kiln therefore could be employed throughout the year. Both trades require kiln management skills and an awareness of critical temperatures. This dual economy is reflected in a Chesterfield mortgage of 1724 which describes a property as 'Malthouse Close or the Old Brick Yard, a malthouse now used as a pothouse'.[1143] Two eighteenth century Nottingham burgesses were described as 'maltsters and brickmakers'.[1144] Early malthouses and kilns were frequently built of stone although evidence is scarce because of their propensity to catch fire. Church Farm, Edgton is a rare

---

1137 WRO, CA, CR34/11.
1138 WRO, PH1035/F3992.
1139 Baker, P.H.J., and Wailes, R., 'The Windmills of Derbyshire, Leicestershire and Nottinghamshire', *Trans. of the Newcomen Soc.*, **33**, (1960-1961), 113-128; 34 (1961-1962), 89-104. Angerstein noted a brick-built windmill for grinding calamine near Bristol in 1753-4, 145.
1140 Woolley, 23.
1141 DRO, D37/MT/16.
1142 English Heritage, *Maltings in England*, (2004), 27.
1143 DRO, D1290/T/28.
1144 *NBR,* **VI**, 342, 353.

survival with a stone house, timber-framed malthouse and eighteenth-century brick kiln. 'The Stew', a maltings and mansion house at Frankwell Quay, Shrewsbury, was mainly timber-framed but does contain some earlier brick of c.1660. At Alton, Staffs, the 'Malthouse' uniquely includes an underground brick kiln and associated cellars. Maltsters faced the same problems as iron founders and potters and it was only in the eighteenth century that larger and more commercial kilns could be built from harder bricks. Angerstein describes a malt mill in Gloucestershire where 'These bricks were made in Stourbridge'.[1145]

The conversion from wood to coal also created problems when smoke affected the taste of the barley. Nathan Bailey in his *Dictionarium Domesticum* of 1736, recommended the use of coke to produce finer ales and the storage of malt on bricks or stone to reduce the fieriness of the malt.[1146] Houghton in 1693 attributed the success of the Derby malting industry to its early use of coke rather than the usual straw.[1147]

Although not strictly industrial, one unusual use of brick was in the form of brickdust, a new element in the domestic life of the eighteenth century. Its main use was as an abrasive to remove corrosion and it was particularly recommended for the polishing of muskets.[1148] In conjunction with oil it was used as a high polish for Honduras mahogany,[1149] mixed with lime or gypsum it was used to polish floors and added to menthol or oil of cloves it made toothpaste. It was also used to adulterate chocolate and paint. There is little evidence for its sale in the provinces, but in London street sellers were sufficiently prominent to be the subject of prints by James Watson and Thomas Rowlandson. As early as 1709 Swift satirized the cries of 'Brickdust Moll' in his poem, *A Description of the Morning*. In 1772 a popular opera, 'The Brickdust Man', was written by a well-known dramatist Charles Dibdin. Brickdust was a practical product, but it was also a modish colour. In 1775 the Ambassador to Spain, Thomas Robinson, ordered a 'Chaise for Spain, it is to be painted light green' despite 'brick dust being the fashionable colour'.[1150]

1145 Angerstein, 170.
1146 Bailey, N., *Dictionarium Domesticum*, (1736) 402, 406.
1147 Walton, W.H., 'The Early Use of Coke in Derby', *DAJ*, **54**, (1933), 16-18. (Houghton, June 16th, 1693).
1148 *Standing Orders and Instructions to the Nottinghamshire Regiment of Marksmen*, established by Lord George Sutton, (1778), Section XI, 7.
1149 Houghton suggests the use of brickdust to thicken turpentine, **3**, 36.
1150 Bedfordshire and Luton RO, L30/14/408.

The Relationship between the Lime and Brick Industries

For lime burning a kiln was a prerequisite and most were built of brick or stone. Usually, the lime kiln was quite distinct from the brick kiln, Neve described the difference as, 'But they (lime kilns) have no Arches in them only a sort of Bench … on which they lay the biggest stones'. As early as 1581 an indenture at Warwick Priory made a clear distinction between the structures.[1151] Recent research into lime burning in the chalk areas of England has revealed a few rare examples of lime produced alongside bricks in the same kiln with the bricks fired above the lime.[1152] There are no Midland references to this unusual practice where the kiln was built roughly two-thirds below ground level and in which the two materials required different temperatures. All the Midland examples clearly distinguish between lime and brick kilns.

As bricks were of little value without mortar, lime was a crucial material in brick building. It was available from the Silurian Limestones at Much Wenlock, at Dudley and particularly at Walsall where there were three productive beds. It was also extracted from the thin limestones within the Carboniferous Halesowen Group, in the Blue Lias of South Warwickshire, in the Carboniferous Limestone of North Derbyshire and in the Lower Lias horizons around Barrow-on Soar in Leicestershire. At Barrow more than a hundred brick-built lime kilns have been excavated.[1153] In other areas there were smaller deposits, for example at Ticknall in Derbyshire where the Harpur-Crewe family had several kilns and at Breedon where as early as 1654 the Curzon family had three 'limeworks'.[1154] A small inlier in the industrially important area around Crich was described by Angerstein.[1155] An inlier of Carboniferous Limestone within unconformable Triassic pebble beds at Turnditch in South Derbyshire supported a compact lime industry for many years.[1156]

Christopher Chalklin has estimated that c.1790 in a medium sized terraced house (ground floor area – 442 square feet, including a small single storey rear extension), the requirement of lime was 179.6 bushels or 5 tons 12 cwts

---

1151 WRO, CR0026/1/2/5.
1152 Murless, B.J., 'Eighteenth Century Accounts of Firing Bricks and Burning Lime in the Same Kiln,' *BBSI,* **147**, (2021), 35-37.
1153 Barrow on Soar Heritage Group. All the kilns have been lost under modern buildings.
1154 ROLLR, 26D53/2330.
1155 Angerstein, 204.
1156 Woore, S., 'An Account of the Lime Kilns and Associated Quarries at Turnditch, Derbyshire'. *Derbyshire Miscellany,* **18**, **pt 1**, (2007), 5.

per building.[1157] Lime was not only required for pointing but also for wall plastering which could be decorated with the newly fashionable wallpaper. Increased housing demand coupled with the need for lime for such industries as soap boiling, glassmaking, papermaking and iron production led to an enormous demand for kiln bricks.

Lime was expensive – at Barrow the churchwardens of St Martins revealed how the composition of mortar 'for pargeting and floors' was bulked out by lime, sand, pieces of calves leather, glovers' offcuts and 'Smythie coine' (furnace ashes).[1158] As lime was naturally rarer than brick clay, it was carried for greater distances and therefore added to overall building costs. For limited purchases in communities without a kiln, transport costs could be relatively high. At Hanbury the churchwardens' accounts include the purchase of small quantities of lime from the Harpur-Crewe family at Ticknall and from Tutbury. The cost of its carriage as a percentage of the cost of the lime varied from 35% in 1663 to 21% in 1699 and 75% in 1708.[1159] The Welbeck Abbey Estate in 1726 paid £1 1s 0d for 3 loads of lime and 12s for carrying it.[1160] An estimate of 1729 for building a house on the Ingestre Estate suggested that 10.5% of the total cost would be for lime and its carriage. For the building of Newcastle Hospital, the cost of the lime was £59 3s 2d (6.5%) plus the additional costs of 'coal to burn plaster' and transport costs. In 1753-54 in building Hatton vicarage, 15 different providers or carriers were employed.[1161]

On the much larger estates, where there was extensive building and rebuilding, enormous quantities of lime were purchased and transported for considerable distances. For the elaborate Meriden Hall the initial purchases of lime in 1720 cost £40 6s from a total of £1,101 8s 3d (3.6%). In 1728 on the Jervis Estate at Darlaston Hall the accounts include payment for 453 horse loads of lime at a cost of £19 19s 9d, plus many other bills for smaller quantities which together totalled £39 19s 6d.[1162] At Meerbrook in 1749, 639 loads of lime were carried into Birchwood Park, and between 1752 and 1754 a further

---

1157 Chalklin, C., *The Provincial Towns of Georgian England*, McGill-Queens UP, (1974), Appendix IV.
1158 North, *Accounts,* 149.
1159 SRO, D1528/4/1.
1160 NA, DDP5/1/1.
1161 WRO, CR3124/17/56.
1162 WSL, 49/44/36/10.

1,822 loads were received in a trade confined to the summer months. For Lord Chetwynd's new house at Talke-on-the-Hill, 19 tons 2 cwt of lime was delivered between April and October, 1736, at a cost of £9 3s. In the following year a further 31 tons was carried to the site in 65 separate journeys with the cost of carriage being 5s per ton in the summer months and 5s 9d in winter.[1163] For his new house at Betley, lime was brought from Newbold Astbury, one mile south-west of Congleton, a distance of at least 12 miles.[1164] These payments are included in an area of the accounts concerned with building materials.

In other accounts some of the lime purchased may have been for agricultural purposes such as the 'sweetening' of acidic soils. The farm accounts of George Parker of Caverswall, for example, reveal that between 1700 and 1705 he purchased bricks, chimney pieces and lime for the improvement of his house. The accounts also suggest that much of the lime was used on his farm, for example in April 1701 he paid Rich(ard) Beech 'for mixing lime and marl' presumably for spreading on the land.[1165]

Many standard husbandry covenants required the liming of fields, for example a Fairfield, Derbyshire, lease of 1766 required the leasee 'to apply 200 horse loads of lime to the land'.[1166] Not all sources of lime were appropriate for the sweetening of the soil and the difficulties in obtaining lime were also heightened by the quality of the various limestone deposits. The anonymous author of a travel journal of 1766-67 noted on a visit to Earl Gower's lime pits at Lilleshall, that the 'snuff coloured lime is not rich enough for Land … the white which is best for the land but little work for buildings'.[1167] John Phillips in his *Inland Navigation* of 1793 refers to the huge lime works of Earl Gower at Linsel, near Newport, producing 35,000 tons p.a. and of Brook Forester at Steeraway producing 20,000 tons.[1168]

The Perry Hall Estate of the Gough family stood on the Triassic deposits which provided excellent brick clays but no exploitable limestone. Their extensive building works between 1745 and 1760 required a considerable amount of lime and its carriage to a variety of building sites mainly in the

---

1163 SRO, D1798/HM/Chetwynd105.
1164 SRO, D1798/HM/Chetwynd105.
1165 SRO, D3806.
1166 DRO, D239 M/E 5462.
1167 SRO, mf 31, p. 116.
1168 Philips, 143.

Black Country. The provision of this was costly, for example, in six days in the late August and early September of 1749, £9 2s was spent on the carriage of stone, timber, brick and lime to these sites.[1169] Lime, which was carried long distances, was the most expensive material. Their main supplier, William Forester from Walsall, even had commercially printed receipts for his trade and on 26th January 1748 he was paid 'for 3 loads of lime delivered at the Lymeworks'.[1170] The term 'Lymeworks' and references in 1733 to 'one waggon of Lime … & Lime Kiln' would suggest that on this wealthy estate the owners were buying limestone, buying local coal to burn it and using the resultant lime powder for building purposes.[1171] In 1734 for William Clempson's house, Gough paid 8s 6d for lime and 6s for carriage to the building site (70%).[1172] In 1758 for 'Repairs at Duggens Inn', 6 loads of lime cost £3 19s 2d with the cost of carriage £3 (75%). The cost of carrying bricks, made at Perry Hall, to the site was 3s per 1,000 (33%).[1173] On Lord Gower's estate at Trentham there is similar evidence for a kiln burning limestone and using imported coal. In 1741 Thos. Wood was paid 8s 4d for 'Building a Kiln to Burn Lime' and in 1744 Jn. Bagnall received 19s 1d 'for building a lime kiln'.[1174]

Subsequent accounts contain many references to the burning of lime and the production of many tons of burnt lime. Altogether 37,500 bricks were sent to the 'limestone pitts' presumably to build or rebuild the kilns.[1175] At Aston Hall in 1754-7 the materials for the park wall and their transport cost over £2,600 of which regular deliveries of lime contributed £409 4s 4d (15.7%). In just one month between 20th December and 22nd January, 1769-70, for the building of 'the Workmens Houses' at Etruria, Josiah Wedgwood spent in total £72 11s 4¼d on lime and processing.[1176]

In some areas of the Midlands there was an alternative to lime for floors – a recent scientific investigation of the floors of Pear Tree Farm, Yoxall, revealed that the sixteenth/seventeenth-century floors were composed of a mixture of gypsum

---

1169 BLAC, Gough Mss. 3145/334/13a.
1170 Gough Mss. 3145/334/10.
1171 Gough Mss. 3145/262/2.
1172 Gough Mss. 3145/262/4.
1173 Gough Mss. 3145/334/41g.
1174 SRO, D593/F/3/2/15-18.
1175 SRO, D593/F/3/2/18-19.
1176 Wedgwood Archive, WMSS 28693-43.

and furnace ash. Gypsum was readily available at Fauld at a distance of 5-6 miles but again required carriage.[1177] Around Nottingham it is plentiful in the form of alabaster, to which William Harrison referred later in the sixteenth century when describing how 'such as are of abilitie doo oft make their floores and parget of fine alabaster burned, which they call plaster of Paris, whereof in some places we have great plentie'.[1178] Alabaster was also present at Burton-on-Trent and in smaller deposits at Humberstone, east of Leicester. The arrival of the canals encouraged the diffusion of gypsum. The first year's accounts of the Staffordshire and Worcestershire canal in 1773 included the carriage of 20 tons of 'plaister' from Burton-on-Trent to Heywood Wharf.[1179] Later the canals were also important in the siting of lime works, as at Walker's Lime Works established in 1776 on the Blue Lias at Bilton, near Rugby. In all cases brick-built kilns were required.

One problem for local historians has been to explain the presence of lime kilns in areas where deposits of limestones were not present. This may represent evidence of the extensive carriage of unburnt limestone.[1180] Quicklime was dangerous to transport, and it made more sense to refine it locally. Richard Wilkes recorded in his diary for 1738 that 'Mr Altree of Weston had his Barns, Stables Ricks of Hay & Corn all burnt by a load of Lime wch was sleeked by throwing Water upon it'.[1181]

1177 Information from the owners. The garden soil of this farm also contains chert, a siliceous deposit found within the Carboniferous Limestone and analogous to flint in chalk. In this case the chert probably represents a deposit from within the Carboniferous Limestone east of the Ashbourne-Buxton Road. It most probably is the result of a fluvio-glacial deposit but it might just possibly be evidence of limestone being brought into South Staffordshire to be burnt. There is evidence of burnt limestone amongst the garden stones. An undated document from the Antrobus Estate in North Staffordshire and headed 'Annual Profit arising from the manor of Horton and payable to the Lord of the Manor', includes 'Compensation for getting Brick Clay at 1s per thousand' and also compensation for stone, sand and 'Chirt stone'. SRO, D(W)1909K/2/6/12. Derbyshire chert was also transported by canal for use in the manufacture of glass. Marshall, *The Review and Abstract*, 157.

1178 *Of the Manner of Building and Furniture of Our Houses. Chapter VIII*. [1577, Book II., Chapter 10; 1587, Book II., Chapter 12]. *A Description of Elizabethan England. The Harvard Classics* (1909-14). See also, Allen, P., and Cooper A., 'The Use of Gypsum Plaster and Lime-Ash for Flooring in the Medieval East Midlands: Evidence from Bingham, Nottinghamshire', *TTS*, **120**, (2016), 55-71.

1179 SRO, 3186/1/8/1/22.

1180 In other areas of the country crushed chalk was transported, but this is unlikely in the Midlands where the nearest chalk deposits were in Lincolnshire, the East Riding of Yorkshire or the Marlborough Downs.

1181 SRO, 5350.

In many parishes there were surface outcrops of coal which were described in the eighteenth century as either 'housecoal' or 'kilncoal'. The latter was probably used for burning lime particularly for agricultural improvement. Norden noted that in Shropshire industrious farmers 'do buy dig and fetch limestones two three and four miles off and in their fields do build lime-kilns, burn it and cast it on their fields'.[1182] The remains of kilns and the survival of lime kiln related place-names in some north Staffordshire parishes 'attest to the economy of carrying limestone on to the sandstone terrain to be burned with local coal'.[1183] The context for lime manufacture was the burning of large quantities of brick. The paradox was that to lay bricks, lime was required and to burn lime, bricks were required.

The Horticultural Use of Brick
In a recent study Roderick Floud has argued that 'spending money on gardens has been one of the greatest forms … of spending on luxury in England'.[1184] The obsession of royalty, aristocracy and gentry, gardens were planned and re-planned to demonstrate that the elite were men and women of taste, fashion and wealth. Maintaining fashionable houses and gardens could be very expensive. In 1731 for Congreve Hall, Edward Byrke, 'an able and experienced workman' estimated that 'Wm. Congreve must have expended on the Seat at least between eight and nine thousand pounds' and judged 'it would cost sixty pounds a year to keep all buildings and repairs'. The 'Gardiner', Wm. Cooper, calculated that, 'By Computation to keep ye gardens in order at Stretton Seat would cost 50li a year'.[1185]

Gardens proved a huge market for bricks. They were used for the construction of large-scale landscape alterations such as the base of the embankments of Capability Brown's lakes – for example the one at Croome Park is 20 feet high and over half a mile long. Bricks were also employed for walls, paths, ornaments, follies, wells and grottoes and added significantly to the potential of the garden for both ornament and the production of fruit, vegetables and flowers by providing

---

1182 Metzloff, M., ed. *John Norden's The Surveyors Dialogue*, (1618), Burlington, (2010), 180.
1183 Leach, J.T., 'Coal Mining around Quarnford', *Staffordshire Studies*, **8**, (1996), 82, 88.
1184 Floud, 4.
1185 SRO, D1057/J/2/13.

shelter from frost and protection for bees.[1186] Recent archaeological investigation of the Tudor Greenwich Palace has revealed brick cellars which it is believed were for housing bee skeps during the winter. In 1686 Plot recorded a visit to a 'most intelligent Bee-Master' who of his 'hives he preferred before all the rest, he made of brick'. At Packwood House in the famous Yew Garden the heated wall includes small alcoves which housed bee skeps. Heated brick garden walls were common and one still survives at Flintham Hall, Notts. Other domestic examples of early brick-built 'bee boles' survive at Pipe Ridware Hall and West Bromwich Manor House.[1187] In 1771 the Gell accounts recorded, 'paid for Brick Beehouse 7s 6d' and later that year, 'paid Joseph Spencer for Beeouses £4 1s 0d'.[1188] Specialist bricklaying skills were also required at considerable cost for the building of the domed icehouse. On the Gell Estate in 1774, for 'sinking Ten feet Deep in the Icehouse', Thomas Steeple was paid £6 8s.[1189] On aristocratic estates the brick garden wall usually enclosed about two or three acres, Plot described one of '23 acres' at Packington but this was more properly an orchard rather than formal garden.[1190] An exception was perhaps the walled garden at Gopsall, described by many reputable commentators as of 20 acres. Reputedly the largest walled kitchen garden in England was at Croome Court which was serviced by five furnaces. More typical is the contract at Sugnall in 1738 where Viscount Glenorchy agreed with the brickmaker Richard Hammersley for 200,000 bricks for a garden wall enclosing two acres. The patron was to provide the kiln, coal and the moulds and the brickmaker was paid 5s per 1,000 for the bricks. By 1739 he had delivered 244,600 bricks at a cost of £61 3s.[1191] Used only for walling the bricks were often of poorer quality, at Stanton By Bridge a walled garden was established by the rector 'at a time when bricks cost 6d a load'![1192]

Appearance was crucial, at Stydd the garden wall was built of stone on the east side and brick on the fashionable west side. Many walls were over 12 feet

---

1186 Floud, Brown's account book shows employment by 1 king, 7 dukes, 26 earls and 20 other peers, 63.
1187 There is a national register of about 1590 'bee boles' at the International Bee Research Association, (IBRA).
1188 DRO, D258/4/5.
1189 DRO, D258/4/5.
1190 Plot, 227.
1191 Jacques D., *Walled Kitchen Gardens*, Staffordshire Gardens and Parks Trust (2003), 26.
1192 Baker, J., 'The Rev. George Greaves (1746-1828) and Stanton By Bridge During his Incumbency', *Derbyshire Miscellany*, **17, pt 1**, (2004), 12.

high, provided shelter and warmth for semi-tropical plants and extended the growing season for fruit and vegetables by two or three weeks. Their considerable value in supporting plants is suggested in an agreement of 1674 by Nicholas Harvey to lay a lead pipe in Whittington, near Lichfield, 'in return for liberty to plant, tie and nail fruit trees to his side of Babington's brick garden wall'.[1193] In a memorandum of 1743 Alice Barker suggested:

> … whereas the gable end of the barn next to Mr Parker's garden was in great decay and repair and would cost more than she could afford … that Parker … if he were to pay for the bricks … 'should have liberty to fix his trees to the -- wall'.[1194]

Of value was the 'crinkle-crankle' wall in which waving ribbons of brick in curving lines provided alcoves. These were cheaply built for despite its sinuous configuration it was made just one brick thick and did not require buttresses. Many crinkle-crankle walls have survived, including those at Hopton Hall, Sudbury, behind St Wilfrids church Eggington, at Kedleston Hall and Burley-on-the-Hill. Not all gardeners preferred such walls, Phillip Miller in his celebrated *A Gardeners and Florists Dictionary* of 1724 advised that, 'In some places the bricks are not substantial enough of themselves for walls … Walls made of earth and straw' ('Mud Walls') are preferred, 'tho they are not very handsome'.[1195]

Brick brought colour to the garden not only as walls and features but also as brick dust in the winter months where it, as well as crushed clay tiles, was also used to provide colour in the formal the *parterres de broderie* of the knot garden. This preoccupation with colour was extreme; the Marquis of Rockingham even purchased 'Blue John' for his gravel paths.[1196]

On some estate gardens fired tiles were used to provide edging for flower or plant beds. As early as 1629 John Parkinson, in his *Paradisi in Sole Paradisus Terrestris,* wrote that 'Tyles are also made by some … many are pleased

---

1193 WSL, S.D. Pearson/1483.
1194 DRO, D754/E/10.
1195 Miller. P., *A Gardeners and Florists Dictionary*, **2**, (1724), np, see under 'Walls'.
1196 Steer, J., 'The Rise & Progress of the Spar Manufactory of Derbyshire', *Derbyshire Miscellany*, **17 part 2**, (2004), 51.

with them … and keepe up the edge of the beds'.[1197] Plot, writing in 1686, described the manufacture by Thomas Wood in Newcastle-under-Lyme of a particular weather resistant tile which was fired in a pottery kiln. The tiles were apparently used as dividers in knot gardens.[1198] Unfortunately there are relatively few references to their use, for example at the archaeologically researched high-class garden at Castle Bromwich only evidence of wooden edges was found.[1199] However an anonymous estate brickmaker, possibly in Derbyshire, recorded a 'Garden Edge Tile Mould' in his list of 'Brickmaking Toles' of c.1800.[1200] Wedgwood also employed his pottery kilns to manufacture plant pots, these apparently were of such quality that they were used as table decorations! In a letter to Mr Bentley Wedgwood wrote, 'you both want Vases you both want flowerpots … we have but two turners and a half … Abram is turning flowerplots at Etruria'.[1201]

The dovecote is traditionally associated with the medieval landscape, but the greatest number were built probably between 1650 and the late eighteenth century, when corn was relatively cheap and abundant and an Act of 1761-2 permitted any tenant to build their own dovecote with the landlord's permission. It was only the effect of the French Revolutionary Wars of the 1790s and the consequent dramatic rise in corn prices which led to their decline. The later brick dovecote was only incidentally a source of food, its main function was as an 'eyecatcher', a dramatic feature of the landscape as for example at Staunton, Notts, where there is an unusually tall seventeenth-century dovecote with 1,100 nesting boxes.

Brick was in some cases used to disguise earlier dovecotes as at Haselour where a timber-framed dovecote of c1600 was given a brick façade. In 1668 the Jervis accounts recorded, 'For bricking the walls and tyling the dovehouse amending pigeon holes £1 14'.[1202] The convenience of brick for regular nesting holes was recognised in the sixteenth century and is demonstrated in many estates including Wollaton Old Hall, Pipe Ridware Hall and Croxall Hall. At

---

1197 Parkinson, J., *Paradisi in Sole Paradisus Terrestris*, (The Ordering of the Garden of Pleasure) (1629), 7.
1198 Plot, 336.
1199 Currie, C.K., *Gardens Archaeology Project*, (2001). Trial excavations in the North Garden, Castle Bromwich Hall, West Midlands, (1991).
1200 DRO, D5336/2/24/26.
1201 Wedgwood Archive, E25-18247.
1202 WSL, 49/44/38.

Frodesley, Shropshire, a barn was converted into a dovecote by removing bricks to make nesting boxes.[1203] The more flamboyant styles usually date from the seventeenth to nineteenth centuries and the most unusual are associated with large houses or estates. The simplest square form is for example that standing at Dunton Hall, Curdworth and the Old Manor House, Thrussington which is dated 1716, although this has detailed moulded brick eaves work.

More elaborate forms of dovecotes were built in the upper floors of three-storied towers containing summer houses and prospect rooms in the lower stories. An upper storey dovecote was recorded in the Hoby Parsonage Terrier of 1703, pigeon houses still survive at Woodborough (Notts) and in The Manor Cottage, Marston Montgomery. Octagonal brick dovecotes were erected at Moseley Hall, Banhurst Farm (Wolverhampton) and Offchurch Bury, Warks. Circular brick dovecotes survive at Whitton Court of c.1720 and at Barnby in the Willows, one of three of that shape in Nottinghamshire.

Several dovecotes in Nottinghamshire are remarkable for the use of nest boxes of brick/tile which were plastered to add to their architectural quality. William Sacharvell's design for an octagonal dovecote of 1677 at Barton in Fabis has his arms on the interior. Robert Lowe remarked in 1798 that there were more pigeons (and therefore more dovecotes) in Nottinghamshire than any other county, particularly in the north.[1204] At Clifton there was built an enormous dovecote, 38 feet by 18 feet, with 2,300 nesting boxes.

Not all dovecotes were detached buildings some were integrated within the house. In At Old Hazelwood Farm, Preston Bagot the dovecote was integrated into the brick chimney stack. Gresley Old Hall has a pigeon loft dated by dendrochronology to about 1709.[1205] At 65 Church Street, Melbourne, brick-built nesting boxes still exist in the eastern wall of the attic. The Melbourne Estate accounts include a pigeon loft in Shaw House of 1717.

Floud has argued that gardening influenced a range of technologies that have been crucial to the growth of the British economy. The canal network was anticipated in the ornamental 'canals' and lakes of the seventeenth and eighteenth centuries and steam engines were used for water displays long before their use in the manufacturing industries. Gardening played a crucial,

---

1203 Historic England, 1390533.
1204 Lowe, R., *A General View of the Agriculture of Nottinghamshire*, (1789), 132.
1205 English Heritage Legacy ID: 82575.

and underestimated, part in the growth of the economy and Floud has suggested that gardens were one of the greatest and most conspicuous forms of expenditure on luxury and that they were as important as the calicoes, silks, furniture and porcelains on which so much emphasis has been placed. Within the massive investment in gardening was the crucial role of brick in providing both the physical structure and its ornamental features.[1206]

1206 Floud, 4.

Chapter 15

CONCLUSION

DR JOHNSON described brick as 'A mass of burnt clay, squared for the use of builders' – this study demonstrates that brick was much more than this prosaic definition. The circumstance of its adoption and diffusion was not a spontaneous event but a long-term development, inspired by its practical advantages, its role in fashion and its connection to a wider cultural context in which the house reflected the personality of its creator. Above all bricks were an external and therefore immediately obvious, visible expression of wealth, prestige and status.

Only in early Stuart London was there a legal obligation, enforced by the Star Chamber, for new buildings to be of either stone or brick. James I issued 12 proclamations on building, most of which include regulations of the size, quality and use of brick.[1207] In 1667, following the Great Fire, Charles II issued a declaration, 'And we do therefore hereby Our express Will and Pleasure, that no man whatsoever shall presume to erect any House or Building, great or small but of Brick or Stone'.[1208] These requirements were aspirations rather than legal obligations and, in the Midlands, where there was large scale redevelopment brick was only rarely a statutory requirement. In Warwick, after the Great Fire of 1694, the Fire Act made the use of brick or stone mandatory. In other developments, as in the leases of the King Edward VI's Foundation in Birmingham, brick is understood but not specifically

---

1207 Crawford, 148, 152.
1208 Parliamentary Archives, HL/PO/PU/1/1666/18&19C2n14, *An Act for the Rebuilding of the City of London*.

mentioned. In Derby the Improvement Act of 1768 only tacitly required brick by demanding houses to be of three storeys.

The material of choice by royalty, aristocracy and high churchmen was slowly adopted by different levels of society, until, by 1780, it had reached cottage level and was increasingly the substantial support for furnace, factory, church, chapel and the new civic suburbs. Brickmaking was still small-scale and had yet to be transformed from a manual to a mechanised process, but improved by blended clay, better moulding and more even firing, brick became a more standardised and consistent product. It was produced in a wide variety of shapes, sizes and density as brickmakers responded to an increasing range of social and industrial demands.

Brick was not familiar in some areas of the Midlands where the name 'Red House' publicly advertised its rarity. As late as 1780 it was still not the dominant building material, for many rural buildings were constructed of mud and timber-framing, but it was the material of choice of those who sought a durable and socially impressive building. A heightened public acceptance resulted in new suburbs and new townscapes employing bricks fired from the mellow Triassic red clays. Brick became a new medium whose uniformity allowed an innovative and exciting evolution of design and embellishment. This simple building material offered strength and economy which encouraged discipline in appearance and a vocabulary of proportion and volume. As early as 1622 the Commissioners of Buildings in London insisted that 'Brick is a much better material, (than timber) and reflects great credit on the city that builds with it'.[1209] In the countryside it contributed to new landscapes and brought utility, beauty and an eruption of new colour into a world of rural tones.

1209 Crawford, 158.

SELECT BIBLIOGRAPHY

Primary Sources:

Adams, D.P., ed. et al., *Probate Inventories of Cannock, 1562-1791*, Adams, (1976).

Angerstein, R.R., ed. Borg, T., *Illustrated Travel Diary*, 1753-1755. Science Museum, (2001).

Broadway, J., 'The Probate Inventory of Philip Greene: A Restoration Brickmaker in Gloucester, 1685'. *Transactions of the Bristol, Gloucestershire Archaeological Society*, **121**, (2003).

Byng, Sir J., *Torrington Diaries*, ed. Bruyn Andrews, C., London, Methuen, (1970).

Carter, W., ed., *The Records of King Edward's School Birmingham*, Vol. II, London, Dugdale Society, (1928).

Crawford, J., '*Biblotheca Lindesiana*', *Bibliography of Royal Proclamations* of *the Tudor and Stuart Sovereigns*, Oxford, Clarendon Press, (1910).

Defoe, D., *A Tour through England & Wales*, (1724-27) Vols. I & II, ed. Cole, G.D.H., London, Dent, (1927).

Downing, T., *Records of Knowle*, Privately Printed, (1914).

Dudley, D., *Metallum Martis*, (1665) ed. Bagnall, J.N., London, (1854).

Erdeswick, S., *A Survey of Staffordshire*, 5th edition, ed. Harwood, T., London, Nichols, (1844) Fiennes Celia, *The Illustrated Journeys of Celia Fiennes c.1682-c.1712*, ed. Morris, C., Exeter, Macdonald, (1984).

Garbett, S., *The History of Wem and other Townships*, Franklin, (1818) Garbett died in 1751.

Gerbier, B., *Council and Advise to all Builders*, London, Thomas Mabb, (1663).

Glover, S., *History of the County of Derby*, (1829).

Gough, R., *The History of Myddle*, ed. Razzell, P., London, Macdonald, (1984).

Historical Manuscripts Commission; 'The Corporation of Shrewsbury: Municipal Register' in *The Manuscripts of Shrewsbury and Coventry Corporations [Etc.] Fourth Report, Appendix: Part X*, London, (1899).

Houghton, J., *Periodic Letters on Husbandry and Trade*, London, (1696).

Jones, J., '*Stratford-upon-Avon Inventories 1538-1699*', Vol. II *1626-1699*, Dugdale Society, (2003).

Leland, J., *Itinerary of John Leland in or about the years 1535-1543*, ed. Toulmin Smith, L., London, Centaur Press, (1964).

Leybourne, W., *The Builders Guide*, London, (1684).

Moxon, J., *Mechanick Exercises or the Doctrine of Handy-Works*, London, (1703).

Neve, R., *The City and County Purchaser's and Builder's Dictionary*, 2nd ed. London, (1726).

Newcastle-under-Lyme Corporation Order Books, 1590-1669, 1669-1712, 1712-1769 (These are held in Newcastle Museum).

North, T., ed. *The Accounts of the Churchwardens of S. Martin's Leicester 1489-1844*, (1884).

Phillips, J., *A General History of Inland Navigation*, 4th ed. London, (1803).

Plot, R., *The Natural History of Staffordshire*, (1686), republished Manchester, E.J. Morten, (1973).

Primatt, S., *The City and Country Purchaser and Builder*, London, (1667).

Richardson, C., ed. *Minutes of the Chesterfield Canal Company, 1771-80*, Derbyshire Record Society, (1996).

Savage, R., and Fripp, E., eds. *Minutes and Accounts of the Corporation of Stratford-upon-Avon and other Records, 1553-1620, Vol. II, 1566-1577*. Dugdale Society, London, (1924), Vol. III, 1577-1586, (1926).

Shaw, S., *The History and Antiquities of Staffordshire*, Vol. I, (1798), Reprinted with an introduction by Greenslade, M.W. and Baugh, G.C., Wakefield, E.P. Publishing, (1976).

Svedenstierna, E.T., trans. Dallow, E.L., *Svedenstierna's Tour of Great Britain, 1802-3*, Newton Abbot, David and Charles, (1973).

Vaisey, D.G., ed., *Probate Inventories of Lichfield and District, 1560-1680*, S.H.C., 4th series, Vol. 5, (1969).

Ward, J., *History of the Borough of Stoke-Upon-Trent*, (London, 1843, reprinted Wakefield, S.R. Publishing, (1969).

Woolley, W., ed. Glover, C., and Riden, P., *History of Derbyshire*, (c.1712). Derbyshire Record Society, Vol. VI, (1981).

Secondary Sources:

Airs, M., *The Tudor & Jacobean Country House, A Building History*, Stroud, Bramley, (1998).

Airs, M., 'David Papillon: Architect, Military Engineer, Developer, Author, Jeweller'. *The Georgian Group Journal*, **XXV** (2017).

Alcock, N.W., 'Innovation and Conservatism: the Development of Warwickshire Houses in the late 17th and 18th centuries', *TBWAS*, **100** (1981), 133-154.

Alcock, N.W., 'After the Stamp Collecting, the Context of Vernacular Architecture', *Transactions of the Ancient Monuments Society*, **46** (2002), 9-17.

Alvey, R.C., 'A Post-Medieval Brick Kiln at Flintham Hall, Nottinghamshire', *TTS*, **86** (1982), 118-123.

Appleby, J., 'Lord Harrowby's Home Farm at Sandon', unpublished D.Phil. thesis, University of Nottingham, (1997).

Arnold, D., 'Defining Femininity: Women and the Country House', in Arnold, D., ed. *The Georgian Country House Architecture, Landscape and Society*, Stroud, Sutton, (2003).

Baggs, A.P., 'Pattern Books and Vernacular Architecture', *Vernacular Architecture*, **3** (1972), 22-23.

Baker, D., 'Swannington Coal-Master Seeks Capital: Gabriel Holland in 1760', *The Leicestershire Historian*, **3**, No. 1 (1982-3).

Baker, N., *Shrewsbury: An Archaeological Assessment of an English Border Town*. English Heritage, (2010).

Baker, P.H.J., and Wailes, R., 'The Windmills of Derbyshire, Leicestershire and Nottinghamshire', *Transactions. of the Newcomen Society*, **33** (1960-1961).

Barker, T., and Gerhold, D., *The Rise and Rise of Road Transport, 1700-1900* Cambridge, Cambridge University Press, (1993).

Barley, Maurice, W., *The English Farmhouse and Cottage*, London, Routledge, (1961).

Barley, Maurice, W., 'Rural Building in England', in Thirsk, Joan, ed. *The Agrarian History of England and Wales, V, 1640-1750*, Cambridge, Cambridge University Press, (1985).

Barnes, F.A., 'Lenton Priory after the Dissolution, Its Buildings and Fair Grounds', *TTS*, **91** (1987).

Barre, D., and Chaplin, R.A., eds, *William Winde: Advice on Fashionable Interior Decoration … transcriptions of Winde's correspondence with Lady Bridgeman … 1685-1703*, Birmingham, (1983).

Bayliss, A., *The Life and Works of James Trubshaw (1777-1853)*, Bayliss, (1978).

Beresford, M.W., 'Prometheus Insured: The Sun Fire Agency in Leeds during Urbanisation', *Econ. Hist. Rev.*, 2nd series, **XXXV** (August, 1982), 373-389.

Berg, M., *Luxury and Pleasure in Eighteenth-Century Britain*, Oxford, Oxford University Press, (2005).

Bishop, M., Badderley, V., and Mordan, J., *An Archaeological Resource Assessment of Post-Medieval Nottinghamshire 1500-1750*, (Nottinghamshire County Council, n.d.).

Borsay P., *The English Urban Renaissance, Culture and Society in the Provincial Town, 1660-1760*, Oxford, Clarendon Press, (1989).

Borsay, P., and McInnes, A., 'The Emergence of a Leisure Town: or an Urban Renaissance?', [Debate] *Past & Present*, **126** (1990), 189-202.

Bourdieu, P., *Distinction: A Social Critique of the Judgement of Taste*, Cambridge, Harvard University Press, (1984).

Bowden, P.J., 'Statistical Appendix', in Thirsk, Joan, ed., *The Agrarian History of England and Wales, Vol. IV, 1500-1640*, Cambridge, Cambridge University Press, (1966) 814-870.

Bowden, P.J., 'Agricultural Prices, Wages, Farm Profits and Rents', in Thirsk, Joan, ed. *The Agrarian History of England and Wales, Vol. V, Part II, Agrarian Change, 1640-1750*, Cambridge, Cambridge University (1984), 1-118, 827-902.

Brian, A., 'The distribution of brick bonds in England up to 1800', *Vernacular Architecture*, **11** (1980), 3-10.

Bridgeman, E.R.O., and Bridgeman, C.G.O., 'History of the Manor of Weston-under-Lizard in the County of Stafford', *S.H.C.*, **XX**, Vol. II new series, (1899).

Brown, R.J., *English Farmhouses*, London, Hamlyn, (1985).

Brunskill, R.W., and Clifton-Taylor, A., *English Brickwork*, London, Ward Lock, (1977).

Brunskill, R.W., *Houses*, London, Harper Collins, (1982).

Brunskill, R.W., *Brick Building in Britain*, London, Gollanz, (1997).

Campbell, J.W.P., 'The Myth of the Seventeenth Century Pug Mill', *BBSI*, **86** (December, 2001), 7-8.

Campbell, J.W.P., and Sant, A., 'A Bibliography of Works on Brick published in England before 1750', *Construction History*, **17** (2001), 17-29.

Campbell, J.W.P., and Sant, A., 'The Manufacture and Dating of English Brickwork 1600-1720', *Archaeological Journal*, **159** (2002), 170-193.

Campbell, J.W.P., 'Seventeenth-Century Bricklayers' Contracts: Wren's City Churches', *Construction History Society Newsletter*, **64** (October, 2002), 7-12.

Campbell, J.W.P., 'The Study of Bricks and Brickwork in England since Nathaniel Lloyd', *Construction History Society Newsletter*, **66** (June, 2003), 31-38.

Chalklin, C.W., *The Provincial Towns of Georgian England, a Study of the Building Process 1740-1820*, London, Edward Arnold, (1974).

Chalklin, C.W., 'Estate Development in Bristol, Birmingham, and Liverpool, 1660-1720', in Chalklin, C.W. and Wordie, J.R., eds. *Town and Countryside, The English Landowner in the National Economy, 1660-1860.* London, Unwin Hyman, (1989) 102-115.

Chapman, S., 'Peter Nightingale, Richard Arkwright and the Derwent Valley Cotton Mills 1771-1818', *DAJ*, **133** (2013).

Charles, F.W.B., *Swan Hotel, Greengate St. Stafford,* (1966).

Chester, H.A., *The History of the Cheadle Coalfield, Staffordshire*, Ashbourne, Landmark, (2002).

Clark-Maxwell, W.G., 'The Chantries of St Leonards Church Bridgnorth, *TSalop AHS*, **41 pt2** (1922).

Clark, P., ed. *The Transformation of English Provincial Towns, 1600-1800*, London, Hutchinson, (1984)

Clark, P., 'Small towns in England 1550-1850', in Clark, Peter, ed. *Small Towns in Early Modern Europe*, Cambridge, Cambridge University Press, (1995).

Clarke, L., *Building Capitalism*, London, Routledge, (1992).

Clayton, T., 'Publishing Houses: Prints of Country Seats', in. Arnold, Dana, ed. The *Georgian Country House Architecture, Landscape and Society*, Stroud, Sutton, (2003).

Clifton-Taylor, A., *The Pattern of English Building*, London, Batsford, (1962).

Cochrane, D., *A Brief History of Lye & Wollescote*, Halesowen, Cochrane, (2005).

Colvin, H., *A Biographical Dictionary of British Architects 1600-1840*, 3rd ed. New Haven and London, Yale University Press, (1995).

Cooper, N., *Houses of the Gentry, 1480-1680*, New Haven, Yale University Press, (1999).

Cooper, N., 'Display, Status and the Vernacular Tradition', *Vernacular Architecture*, **33** (2002), 28-33.

Cooper, W., *Wootton Wawen, its History and Records*, Whitehead, J., (1936).

Corfield, P., *The Impact of English Towns, 1700-1800*, Oxford, Oxford University Press, (1982).

Court, W.H.B., *The Rise of the Midland Industries, 1600-1838*, Oxford, Oxford University Press, (1953).

Cranfield, I., *Georgian House Style*, Newton Abbot, David & Charles, (2003).

Craven, M., and Stanley, M., *The Lost Houses of Derbyshire*, Ashbourne, Landmark, (2002).

Craven M., and Stanley, M., *The Derbyshire Country House*, Ashbourne, Landmark, (1991).

Currie, C.R.J., 'Time and Chance: Modelling the Attrition of Old Houses', *Vernacular.*

Dean, J. and Hill, N., 'Burn marks on Buildings, Deliberate or Accidental? *Vernacular Architecture*, **45** (2014) 1-15.

Deering, C., *History of Nottingham*, Ayscough and Willington, (1751).

Denholm, A.F., 'The Impact of the Canal System on Three Staffordshire Market Towns 1760-1850', *Midland History*, **XIII** (1988), 59-77.

Dilworth, D., *The Tame Mills of Staffordshire*, Chichester, Phillimore, (1976).

Dobson, E., *A Rudimentary Treatise on the Manufacture of Bricks and Tiles*, London, John Weale, (1850). Facsimile of the 1850 edition edited by Celoria, F., *Journal of Ceramic History*, No. 5, Stafford, (1971).

Dyer, A., 'Small Market Towns, 1540-1700', in Clark Peter, ed. *The Cambridge Urban History of Britain, II 1540-1840*, Cambridge, Cambridge University Press, (2000), 425-452.

Earle, P., *The Making of the English Middle Class*, London, Methuen, (1989).

Ebdon, H., 'Michael Biddulph of Lichfield and Elmhurst', *Transactions of the Lichfield and South Staffordshire Archaeological and Historical Society*, **IV** (1962-3), 23-26.

Ede, J., *History of Wednesbury*, Birmingham, Wednesbury Corporation, (1962).

Edwards, P., 'The Horse Trade in Tudor and Stuart Staffordshire', *Staffordshire Studies*, **13** (2001), 31-54.

Ekwall, E., *The Concise Oxford Dictionary of English Place-Names*, 4th ed. Oxford, (1960).

English Heritage, *A Building Stone Atlas of Warwickshire*, (2011).

Ferris, I.M., 'A Survey of Hamstall Hall, Staffordshire', *TSSAHS*, **XXVI** (1984-5), 44-82.

Field, J., *English Field Names*, Newton Abbot, David and Charles, (1972).

Firman, R.J., and Firman, P.E., 'A Geological Approach to the Study of Medieval Bricks', *Mercian Geologist*, **2** (1967), 299-318.

Firman, R.J., and Firman, P.E., 'Loessic Brickearth and the Location of Early Pre-Reformation Brick buildings in England – An Alternative Interpretation', *BBSI*, **47** (February, 1989), 4-14.

Floud, R., *An Economic History of the English Garden*, London, Penguin, (2019).

Foster, C., *Seven Households: Life in Cheshire and Lancashire 1582 to 1774*, Arley Hall Press, (2002).

Foyle, J., 'Some examples of external colouration on English brick buildings, c.1500-1650', *Bulletin du Centre de recherche du château de Versailles*, (2007).

Fraser, W., *Field Names in South Derbyshire*, Norman Alderd, (1947).

Girouard, M., *Life in the English Country House*, Harmondsworth, Penguin, (1980).

Girouard, M., *The English Town*, New Haven, London, Yale University Press, (1990).

Glass, D.V., 'Two papers on Gregory King', in Glass, D.V. and Eversley, D.E.C., eds. *Population in History: Essays in Historical Demography*, London, (1965).

Gomme, A., *Smith of Warwick, Francis Smith, Architect and Master-Builder*, Stamford, Shaun Tyas, (2000).

Gould, J.T., 'Settlement and Farming in the parish of Aldridge', *TSSAHS*, **XX** (1979-80), 41-56.

Green, A., and Schadla-Hall, R.T., 'The Building of Quenby Hall – a Reassessment', *TLAHS*, **74** (2000), 21-36.

Greenslade, M.W., 'The Staffordshire Historians', *S.H.C.* 4th series, **11** (1982).

Guillery, P., *The Small House in Eighteenth-Century London*, New Haven and London, Yale University Press, (2004).

Habakkuk, Sir J., 'Daniel Finch, 2nd Earl of Nottingham: His House and Estate', *Rutland Record*, **10** (1990).

Hadfield, C., *The Canals of the West Midlands*, Newton Abbot, David and Charles, (1966).

Hamel, E.B., *Illustrations of Old Tamworth*, 1st edition 1829, reprinted Tamworth, Tamworth Borough Council, (1980).

Hammersley, G., 'The Charcoal Industry and its Fuel, 1540-1750', *Econ. Hist. Rev.*, 2nd series, **XXVI**, No. 4 (November, 1973), 593-613.

Hammond, M.D.P., 'Brick Kilns: An Illustrated Survey', *Industrial Archaeology Review*, **1**, No. 2 (1977) 171-192.

Harley, L.S., 'A Typology of Brick with Numerical Coding of Brick Characteristics', *Journal of the British Archaeological Association*, **38** (1974), 63-87.

Harrison, C.J., *The Great Fire of Nantwich*, Keele Adult Education Department, (1985).

Hartley, R., 'The Tudor Miners of Coleorton, Leicestershire', *Bulletin of the Peak District Mines Historical Society*, **12**, No.3 (Summer, 1994).

Hatcher, J., *The History of the British Coal Industry, Vol. 1, Before 1700: Towards the Age of Coal*, Oxford, Clarendon Press, (1993).

Heathcote, C., 'Coal Mine Soughs Draining into the Rivers Goyt and Sett in North-West Derbyshire,' *Mining History, Bulletin of Peak District Mines Historical Society*, **16**, No. 4, (Winter, 2006).

Hewlings, R., 'The Architect of Weston Park', *Georgian Group Journal*, **XX** (2012).

Hey, D., *Packmen, Carriers and Packhorse Roads; Trade and Communication in North Derbyshire and South Yorkshire*, Leicester, Leicester University Press, (1980).

Hunneyball, P.M., *Architecture and Image-Building in Seventeenth-Century Hertfordshire*, Oxford, Clarendon Press, (2004).

Hurst, L., 'The Rise and Fall of the Use of Bond Timbers in Brick Buildings in England', *Proceedings of The Second International Congress on Construction History*, **2** (2006).

Hutchinson, R.A., 'Occupations in Middle England in the Second Half of the Seventeenth Century', *Staffordshire History*, **33** (2001), 3-5.

Hutton, B., *Historic Farmhouses around Derby*, Cromford, Scarthin Books, (1991).

Hutton, W., *An History of Birmingham*, 2nd ed. (1784).

Hutton, W., *The History of Derby*, (1791).

Janssen, J., 'The Transformation of Brick making in 17th Century London', *Construction History Society Newsletter*, **71** (May, 2005), 1-9.

Johnson, M., *Housing Culture, Traditional Architecture in an English Landscape*, London, UCL Press, (1993).

Johnson, M., 'Vernacular Architecture: The Loss of Innocence', *Vernacular Architecture*, **28** (1997) 13-19.

Jones, E.L., Porter, S., and Turner, M., 'A Gazetteer of English Urban Fire Disasters 1500-1900', *Historical Geography Research Series*, **13**, Norwich, (1984).

Jones, E.L., and Falkus, M.E., 'Urban Improvement and the English Economy in the Seventeenth and Eighteenth Centuries', in Borsay, Peter, ed. *The Eighteenth Century Town, A Reader in English Urban History*, London, Longman, (1990).

Jones, R.J.A., 'Soils in Staffordshire III', *Soil Survey Record No. 80*, Harpenden, (1983).

Kennell, R., 'The Riddle of the Skewbacks', *BBS Information*, **90** (February, 2003), 27-28.

Kennett, D.H., 'Structural Brick', *BBS Information*, **34** (November, 1984), 13-14.

Kennett, D.H., 'Early Brick Houses in England: Patrons and Incomes', *BBS Information*, **98** (November, 2005), 11-12.

Kennett, D.H., 'Caister Castle, Norfolk and the Transport of Brick and Other Building Materials in the Middle Ages', in Bork, R., and Kann, A., eds. *The Art, Science and Technology of Medieval Travel*, London, Routledge, (2008).

Kennett, D.H., 'Thomas Rotherham, a Fifteenth-Century Bishop and Builder in Brick: A Preliminary Note', *BBSI*, **112** (2010) 6-17.

Kent, H.S.K., 'The Anglo-Norwegian Timber Trade in the Eighteenth Century', *Econ. Hist. Rev.*, 2nd series, **VIII** No. 1 (August, 1955), 62-74.

Kiln, *BBSI*, **147** (March, 2021), 35-37.

Kingman, M., 'Brickmaking and Brick Building in Staffordshire, 1500-1760', unpublished Ph.D., Keele, (2006).

Kingman, M., 'How large was a load of bricks? Some Staffordshire evidence and its implications', *BBSI*, **106** (February, 2008), 4-12.

Kingman, M., 'Civic Improvement and the use of Brick: A Case Study of Tamworth, 1572-1760', *TSSAHS*, **42** (2008), 68-80.

Kingman, M., 'The Building Notebook of Charles Trubshaw of Colwich, Staffordshire, 1753-56', *BBSI*, **111** (November, 2009).

Kingman, M., 'The Adoption of Brick in Urban Staffordshire: The Experience of Newcastle-under-Lyme, 1665-1760', *Midland History*, **35** No. 1 (Spring, 2010), 89-106.

Kingman, M., 'An Unusual Collection of Leicestershire Brickmaking Accounts, 1776-1809', *BBSI*, **131** (2015), 6-17.

Kingman, M., 'A Mid-Eighteenth-Century Brick Clay Mill?', *BBSI*, **124** (June, 2013).

Kingman, M., 'The Long Brick', *BBSI*, **129** (February, 2015).

Klemperer, D., and Boothroyd, N., Excavations at Hulton Abbey, Staffordshire, 1987-1994, *Society of Medieval Archaeology Monographs*, **21** (2004).

Lane, J., *Apprenticeship in England, 1600-1914*, London, UCL Press, (1996)

Langton, J., 'Town Growth and Urbanisation in the Midlands from the 1660s to 1841', in Stobart J., and Lane P., eds. *Urban and Industrial Change in the Midlands 1700-1840: Trades, Towns and Regions*, Centre for Urban History, University of Leicester, (2000) 7-27.

Laithwaite, P., 'An Account of Briefs Collected in Bilston Chapel 1685', *S.H.C.*, (1938) 203-263.

Large, P., 'Urban Growth and Agricultural Change in the West Midlands During the Seventeenth and Eighteenth Centuries', in Clark, P., ed. *The Transformation of English Provincial Towns 1600-1800*, London, Hutchinson, (1984).

Leach, J.T., 'Coal Mining around Quarnford', *Staffordshire Studies*, **8** (1996), 66-95.

Lemmen, H., *Delftware Tiles*, Haverfordwest, Shire Publications, (1998).

Lewis, Parry, J., *Building Cycles and Britain's Growth*, London, Macmillan, (1965).

Lindert, P.H., 'English Population, Wages and Prices, 1541-1913', in Rotberg, Robert, I., and Rabb, Theodore, K., *Population and History*, Cambridge, Cambridge University Press, (1986).

Little, B., *Birmingham Buildings, The Architectural Story of a Midland City*, Newton Abbot, David and Charles, (1971).

Lloyd, N., *A History of English Brickwork*, 1st ed. 1925. (Republished Antique Collectors Club 2003).

Locock, M., 'The Development of the Building Trades in the West Midlands', *Construction History* **8** (1992), 3-19.

Locock, M., 'The Eighteenth-Century Brickmaking Industry in the Forest of Arden', *Warwickshire History*, **8** (1990), 3-20.

Locock, M., '18th Century Brickmakers' Tally Marks from Castle Bromwich Hall, West Midlands', *TBWAS*, **95** (1987-8) 95-97.

Lucas, R., 'Parsonage Houses in the Derby Deanery during the Seventeenth to Nineteenth Centuries: Part 2', *Derbyshire Miscellany*, **12** (1991), 133-138.

Lucas, R., 'When Did Norfolk Cross The Brick Threshold?', *Vernacular Architecture*, **28** (1997), 68-79.

Lynch, G., *Brickwork, Vol.1: History, Technology and Practice*, Shaftsbury, Donhead, (1994).

Lynch, G., *Brickwork, Vol. 2: History, Technology and Practice*, Shaftsbury, Donhead, (1994).

Lynch, G., and Pavia, S., 'The Characteristics and Properties of Rubbing Bricks used for Gauged Brickwork – Part One', *Journal of Architectural Conservation*, **9** (March, 2003), 7-22.

Machin, R., 'The Mechanism of the Pre-industrial Building Cycle', *Vernacular Architecture*, **8** (1977), 815-819.

Machin, R., *Rural Housing, An Historical Approach*, The Historical Association, (1994).

Mander, G.P., *History of Wolverhampton to the Early Nineteenth Century*, ed. Tildesley, N., Wolverhampton, Wolverhampton Corporation, (1960).

Manley, G., 'Central England Temperatures, Monthly Means 1659 to 1973'. *Quarterly Journal of the Meteorological Society*, (1974).

Martin R.H., 'John Ockershausen's Ockbrook Diary: the First Three Years of a Derbyshire Moravian Community 1750-1753', *Transactions of the Moravian Historical Society*, **29** (1996), 1-22.

Marshall, P., *Wollaton Hall, An Archaeological Survey*, Nottingham, Nottingham Civic Society, (1996).

Mason, R.T., *Framed Buildings of England*, Horsham, Coach Publishing, (1972).

Mayes, P., 'A Medieval Tile Kiln at Boston, Lincolnshire', *Journal of the British Archaeological Association*, 3rd series, **28** (1985) 86-106.

McCann, J., 'Brick Nogging in the Fifteenth and Sixteenth Centuries with Exam Drawn Mainly from Essex', *Transactions of the Ancient Monuments Society*, **31** (1987) 106-133.

McKendrick, N., 'The Consumer Revolution', in McKendrick, N. Brewer J. and Plumb, J.H., eds. *The Birth of a Consumer Society, the Commercialisation of Eighteenth-Century England*, London, Hutchinson, (1982).

McKendrick, N., 'Josiah Wedgwood and the Commercialisation of the Potteries', in McKendrick, N., Brewer, J. and Plumb, J.H., eds. *The Birth of a Consumer Society: The Commercialisation of Eighteenth Century England*, London, Hutchinson, (1982).

McInnes, A., 'The Golden Age of Uttoxeter', in, Morgan, P., ed. *Staffordshire Studies, Essays Presented to Denis Stuart*, Keele University, (1987), 113-128.

McInnes, A. 'The Emergence of a Leisure Town: Shrewsbury, 1660-1760', *Past & Present*, **120** (1988), 53-85.

McWhirr, A., 'Brick Making in Leicestershire before 1710', *TLAHS* 71 (1997), 37-59.

Meeson, R., and Sheridan, K., 'Eighth Report of Excavations at Tamworth, Staffs, 1971 – A Timber-Framed Building in Market Street', *TSSAH* **XV** (1974), 5-12.

Meeson, R., and Kirkham, A., '6 Market Street, Tamworth: A Timber-Framed Building of 1695 and Its Context', *TSSAHS*, **XXXIII** (1991-1992), 42-48.

Mercer, E., *English Vernacular Houses*, London, Royal Commission for Historic Monuments of England, (1975).

Mercer, E., 'The Unfulfilled Wider Implications of Vernacular Architecture Studies', *Vernacular Architecture*, **28** (1997), 9-12.

Mitchell, R.B., *British Historical Statistics*, Cambridge, Cambridge Archive, (1988).

Moore, N.J., 'Bricks', in Blair, J., and Ramsay, N., eds. *English Medieval Industries, Craftsmen, Techniques, Products*, London, Hambledon Press, (1981).

Moore, N.J., 'The Supply of Bricks to Coughton Court, Warwickshire, in 1663-66', *BBSI*, **69** (October, 1996), 12-14.

Moran, M., *Vernacular Buildings of the Whitchurch Area and their Occupants*, Frome, Logaston Press, (1999).

Moran, M., *Vernacular Buildings of Shropshire*, Frome, Logaston Press, (2003).

Morrice, R., 'The Payment Book of William Baker of Audlem', in Bold, J., and Chaney, E., eds. *English Architecture Public and Private: Essays for Kerry Downes,* London, Hambledon Press, (1993), 231-246.

Moseley, O., *History of The Castle, Priory and Town of Tutbury*, London, (1832).

Mowl, T., *To Build the Second City*, Bristol, Redcliffe Press, (1991).

Mugridge, T., 'Broseley Clay Weekend, June 2001, Results of Clamp Firing' *BBSI*, **86** (December, 2001), 4-6, *Architecture*, 19 (1988), 1-9.

Murless, B.J., 'Eighteenth century Accounts of Firing Bricks and Burning Lime in the Same'.

Myers, J., 'Staffordshire', part 61 of *The Land of Britain, The Report of The Land Utilisation Survey of Britain*, ed. Stamp, L.D., London, (1945).

Nef, J.U., *The Conquest of the Material World*, London, (1964).

Newman, J., 'A "Polite" View of Vernacular Architecture', *Vernacular Architecture*, **15** (1984), 10-11.

Oakden, J.P., *The Place-names of Staffordshire, Part One, Cuttlestone Hundred*, LV, English Place-Name Society, (1984).

Oates, W.E., and Schwab, R.M., 'The Window Tax: A Case Study in Excess Burden', *Journal of Economic Perspectives*, **29**, **1** (2015), 163-180.

Orange, J., *History and Antiquities of Nottingham*, Hamilton, Adams & Co. (1840).

Oswald, A., 'William Baker of Audlem, Architect', *S.H.C.*, (1950-51), 109-135.

Owen, C., *Anslow, The History of a Staffordshire Village*, Anslow, (1995).

Palliser, D.M., *The Staffordshire Landscape*, London, Hodder & Stoughton, (1976).

Pape, T., *Newcastle-Under-Lyme from the Restoration to 1760*, Keele, (1973).

Peacock, R., *The Seventeenth Century Foleys, Iron, Wealth and Vision, 1580-1716*, The Black Country Society, (2011).

Peters, J.E.C., *The Development of Farm Buildings in Western Lowland Staffordshire up to 1880*, Manchester, Manchester University Press, (1969).

Pevsner, N., *The Buildings of England, Cornwall*, Rev. Radcliffe E. Harmondsworth, Penguin, (1990).

Pevsner, N., *The Buildings of England, Derbyshire*, Rev. Williamson, E., Yale University Press, (1986).

Pevsner, N., *The Buildings of England, Leicestershire and Rutland*, 2nd ed. Rev. Williamson, E., Yale University Press, (1984).

Pevsner, N., *The Buildings of England, Shropshire*, Yale University Press, (2002).

Pevsner, N., *The Buildings of England, Staffordshire*, Harmondsworth, Penguin, 1974, reprinted 1996).

Pevsner N. and Pickford C., *The Buildings of England, Warwickshire*, Yale University Press, (2016).

Phelps Brown, H., and Hopkins S.V., *A Perspective on Wages and Prices*, London, Methuen, (1981).

Platt, C., *The Great Rebuilding of Tudor and Stuart England. A Revolution in Architectural Taste*, London, Routledge, (1994).

Porter, L., *Ecton Copper Mines under the Dukes of Devonshire 1760-1790*. Ashbourne, Landmark Publishing, (2004)

Porter, S., *Destruction in the English Civil Wars*, Stroud, Sutton, (1997).

Porter, S., *The Great Fire of London*, Stroud, Sutton, (1996).

Porter, S., Fires in Sixteenth Century Stratford-on-Avon, *Warwickshire History*, **3** (1976) 97-105.

Quiney, A., *Period Houses*, London, George Philip, (1989).

Quiney, A., *The Traditional Buildings of England*, London, Thames and Hudson, (1990).

Rackham O., 'Grundle House: on the Quantities of Timber in certain East Anglian Buildings in relation to Local Supplies', *Vernacular Architecture*, **3** (1972) 3-8.

Rackham, O., *The History of the Countryside*, London, Dent, (1989).

Reed, M., 'The Urban Landscape, 1540-1700', in Clark, P., ed. *The Cambridge Urban History of Britain, II*, Cambridge, Cambridge University Press, (2000), 289-314.

Rice, M.A., *Abbots Bromley*, Shrewsbury, (1939).

Riden, P., 'The Charcoal Iron Industry in the East Midlands, 1580-1780', *Derbyshire Archaeological Society*, **111** (1991).

Riden, P., *A Gazetteer of Charcoal-fired Blast Furnaces in Great Britain in use since 1660*, Merton Priory, (1993).

Roberts, J., 'Well Temper'd Clay: Constructing Water Features in the Landscaped Park', *Garden History*, **29**, No 1, (2001).

Roper, J.S., *History of Coseley*, Coseley, Coseley U.D.C., (1952).

Roper, J.S., *Dudley: The Seventeenth Century Town. It History to 1660*, Dudley, (1965).

Roper, J.S., *Dudley: The Town in the Eighteenth Century*, Dudley, (1968)

Rowlands, M.B., 'Industry and Social Change in Staffordshire, 1660-1760. A Study of Probate and Other Records of Tradesmen', *TSSAHS* **IX** (1967-68), 37-58.

Rowlands, M.B., 'Houses and People in Stafford at the end of the Seventeenth Century', *The Stafford Historical and Civic Society*, (1965-67) 46-67.

Rowney, I., 'Change and Decay: The Bishopric of Lichfield and Coventry, 1350-1550', *Staffordshire Studies, essays presented to Denis Stuart*, ed. Morgan, P., Keele UP, (1987) 40.

Saunders, E., *Joseph Pickford of Derby, A Georgian Architect*, Stroud, Sutton, (1993).

Scott, K., and Mory, A., 'Brickmaking in North Warwickshire', *TBWAS*, 89 (1979), 138-143.

Searle, A.B., *Modern Brickmaking*, 4th edition, London, Ernest Benn, (1956).

Selby, R., *A History of Sandon*, printed privately, (1996).

Shaw, M., 'The Great Hall: An Elizabethan Mansion in Wolverhampton', *West Midlands Archaeology*, **45** (2002) 11-13.

Sherlock, R., *The Industrial Archaeology of Staffordshire*, Newton Abbot, David and Charles, (1976).

Shryane, J., *Buildings of Staffordshire, Timber-Framed Buildings of Stafford District*, (Staffordshire County Planning and Development Department, n.d., 1985?).

Simmons, J., *Leicester Past and Present*, **1**, London, Eyre Methuen, (1974).

Slack, P., *The Impact of Plague in Tudor and Stuart England*, London, RKP (1985).

Smalley, I., 'The Nature of "Brickearth" and the Location of Early Brick Buildings in Britain', *BBSI*, **41** (February, 1987) 4-11.

Smith, D.T., 'Industrial Architecture in the Potteries', *North Staffordshire Journal of Field Studies*, **5** (1965), 81-94.

Smith, J.T., *English Houses 1200-1800, The Hertfordshire Evidence*, London, Royal Commission on the Historic Monuments, (1992).

Smith, P., Historic Buildings Report: *Sherwin House and the Townhouses of Nottingham in the Seventeenth and Eighteenth Centuries,* English Heritage, (2005) rev. (2008).

Smith, T.P., 'A Note on Samel Bricks', *BBSI,* **31** (November, 1983), 5-7.

Smith, T.P., 'Brick Prices and the Cost of Living', *BBSI,* **32** (February, 1984) 2-3.

Smith, T.P., 'The Medieval Brickmaking Industry in England, 1400-1450', *British Archaeological Reports,* British Series, **138**, Oxford, (1985).

Smith, T.P., 'Bricks, Tiles and Ballast: A Sceptical View', *BBSI,* **85** (October, 2001), 5-9.

Smith, T.P., 'Introit: The Noble Art of Bricklaying', *BBSI,* **90** (February, 2003), 5-9.

Spufford, M., 'Poverty Portrayed: Gregory King and the Parish of Eccleshall', *Staffordshire Studies,* 7 (1995).

Stobart, J. and Lane P., eds. *Urban and Industrial Change in the Midlands 1700-1840: Trades Towns and Regions,* Centre for Urban History, Leicester, (2000).

Stone, L., and Stone, J.C.F., *An Open Elite? England 1540-1880,* Oxford, Clarendon Press, (1984).

Stuart, D., ed., *A Social History of Yoxall in the Sixteenth and Seventeenth Centuries,* Keele University, (1990).

Taylor, R., 'Population Explosions and Housing, 1550-1850', *Vernacular Architecture,* **23** (1972), 24-28.

Thirsk, J., 'Agricultural Policy: Public Debate and Legislation', in Thirsk, J., ed., *The Agrarian History of England and Wales,* V, 1640-1750, Cambridge, Cambridge University Press, (1984), 298-388.

Thompson, A.H., 'The Building Accounts of Kirby Muxloe Castle, 1480-1484', *TLAHS,* **11** (1915-16), 193-292.

Thompson, J., *Leicester in the Eighteenth Century,* Leicester, Crossley and Clarke, (1871).

Thompson, W.J., *The Industrial Archaeology of North Staffordshire,* Stafford, Moorland, (1975).

Thorold Rogers, J.E., *A History of Agriculture and Prices, IV,* Oxford, Clarendon Press, (1891).

Thoroton, R., *Thoroton's History of Nottinghamshire: Republished With Large Additions By John Throsby,* ed. John Throsby, Nottingham, (1790), *2 Volumes.*

Tildesley, N.W., 'Dr. Richard Wilkes of Willenhall, Staffs, An Eighteenth-Century County Doctor', *Transactions of the Lichfield and South Staffordshire Archaeological and Historical Society*, **VII** (1965-66) 1-10.

Trinder, B., *The Industrial Revolution in Shropshire*, Chichester, Phillimore, (1973).

Veblen, T.B., *The Theory of the Leisure Class*, (1899), reprinted New York, Prometheus Books, (1998).

Vickery, A., 'Women and the World of Goods: A Lancashire Consumer and her Possessions, 1751-81', in Brewer, J., and Porter, R., eds. *Consumption and the World of Goods*, London, Routledge, (1993), 274-301.

Walker, B., 'Some Eighteenth-century Birmingham Houses and the Men Who Lived in Them', *Transactions of the Birmingham Archaeological Society*, **LVI** (1934), 1-36.

Wanklyn, M., 'Urban Revival in Early Modern England: Bridgnorth and the River Trade, 1660-1800', *Midland History*, **XVIII** (1993) 37-65.

Weatherill, L., *The Pottery Trade and North Staffordshire, 1660-1760*, Manchester, Manchester University Press, (1971).

Weatherill, L., *Consumer Behaviour and Material Culture in Britain, 1660-1760*, 2nd ed. London, Routledge, (1996).

Welch, C., 'Elizabethan Ironmaking and the Woodlands of Cannock Chase and the Churnet Valley, Staffordshire', *Staffordshire Studies*, **12** (2000) 17-74.

Whitehead, D., 'Brick and Tile Making in the Woodlands of the West Midlands in the 16th and 17th Centuries', *Vernacular Architecture*, **12** (1981), 42-47.

Wight, J., *Brick Building in England from the Middle Ages to 1550*, London, John Baker, (1972).

Williams, M.W. and Herbert, D.T., 'The Social Geography of Newcastle-under-Lyme', *North Staffordshire Journal of Field Studies*, **2** (1962), 108-126.

Williamson, T., *Polite Landscapes: Gardens and Society in Eighteenth Century England*, Stroud, Sutton, (1995).

Wilson, R., and Mackley, A., *Creating Paradise, The Building of the English Country House 1660-1880*, Hambledon Continuum, (2000).

Woodward, D., *Men at Work. Labourers and building craftsmen in the towns of northern England, 1450-1750*, Cambridge, Cambridge University Press, (1995).

Woolley, P., and Ellwood, J., *The History of Marchington*, Marchington, n.d., (1990?).

Woolley, P., *Seven Studies in the Economic and Social History of Uttoxeter and its Adjacent Rural Parishes 1530-1830*, Woolley, (1995).

Wordie, J.R., 'Estate Management in Eighteenth-Century England', Studies in History Series, *The Royal Historical Society*, London, (1982).

Wrightson, K., *English Society, 1580-1680*, London, Hutchinson, (1989).

Wrightson, K., *Earthly Necessities, Economic Lives in Early Modern Britain, 1470-1750*, Harmondsworth, Penguin, (2002).

Wrigley, E.A., and Schofield, R.S., *The Population History of England 1541-1871*, London, Edward Arnold, (1981).

Websites

Clark, G., and Jacks, D., 'Coal and the Industrial Revolution', *www.econ.ucdavis.edu/faculty/gclark/papers/Coal2006*.

Of particular value is the website of the Ludlow Historical Research Group of which Kate Roberts has transcribed the Ludlow Corporation Minutes 1590-1889.

Hoffman, T., *The Rise and Decline of Guilds with particular reference to the Guilds of Tylers and Bricklayers in Great Britain and Ireland*, (2007).